Teaching Students in Inclusive Settings

From Theory to Practice

Dianne F. Bradley

Johns Hopkins University
Montgomery County Public Schools

Margaret E. King-Sears

Johns Hopkins University

Diane M. Tessier-Switlick

Montgomery County Public Schools

Allyn and Bacon
Boston • London • Toronto • Sydney • Tokyo • Singapore

Executive Editor: Ray Short
Editorial Assistant: Christine Svitila
Editorial-Production Administrator: Joe Sweeney
Editorial-Production Service: Walsh & Associates, Inc.
Composition Buyer: Linda Cox
Manufacturing Buyer: Megan Cochran
Cover Administrator: Suzanne Lareau

Copyright © 1997 by Allyn & Bacon
A Viacom Company
160 Gould Street
Needham Heights, MA 02194

Internet: www.abacon.com
America Online: keyword: College Online

Library of Congress Cataloging-in-Publication Data

Bradley, Dianne F.
    Teaching students in inclusive settings : from theory to practice
/ Dianne F. Bradley, Margaret E. King-Sears, Diane M. Tessier
-Switlick.
      p. cm.
    Includes bibliographical references and index.
    ISBN 0-205-16703-9
    1. Mainstreaming in education—United States. 2. Handicapped
children—Education—United States. 3. Lesson planning—United
States. 4. Classroom management—United States. 5. School
management and organization—United States. I. King-Sears,
Margaret E. II. Tessier-Switlick, Diane M. III. Title.
LC4031.B685 1996
371.9'046'0973—dc20   96-29157
                                              CIP

Printed in the United States of America

10 9 8 7 6   05 04 03 02

DEDICATION

To our families
Maurice Zeeman
Michael Sears
Mike Switlick
Jena Switlick
Michelle Switlick

for their patience and support

Contents

Foreword

Discussions of how best to provide special education services has been going on for some time, with terms such as "mainstreaming," "regular education initiative," and "inclusion" arising to describe conceptualizations and reconceptualizations of what represents "the right thing to do" for children with (and without) disabilities. These discussions have highlighted some of the perceived requirements for a new service delivery model to be successful, including overall school restructuring, the merging of general and special education, and the formulation of a unified educational system.

Rhetoric, and even name calling, at times, detracted from the search for improved education. Yet, the 1980s witnessed progress toward inclusion first with mainstreaming (i.e., participation of students with disabilities in general education when deemed academically, socially, or emotionally *ready*) and then the regular education initiative (REI) (i.e., education of students with *mild* disabilities within general education through shared responsibility among general and special educators).

By the 1990s, advocacy efforts had extended the REI notion to students with moderate and severe disabilities. The concept grew to one in which the focus was on "heterogeneous" or "inclusionary" schools, where *all* children are educated with necessary supports in general education environments of their local neighborhood schools and communities. In such schools, the traditional *continuum of placement* special education paradigm that removed some children to other places to receive curriculum and instruction was replaced by the *inclusion* paradigm, in which curriculum and instruction could be modified for any student.

Until recently, most of the debate about inclusion was fueled by research based on opinion rather than data, which *speculated* on what would be required of the new approaches. In the late 1980s, attitudinal studies yielded results that educators were comfortable with maintaining the status quo of pullout special education services.

More recently, perceptions of elementary and secondary general and special education teachers and administrators *with experience* working in inclusion-oriented schools in six states and two Canadian provinces were examined. Results indicated that school personnel with actual experience with inclusive education favored the education of children with disabilities in general education through a shared, collaborative relationship among general and special education. Teacher commitment was found to be critical to implementation of innovations. However, teacher commitment often emerges at the end of an implementation cycle, *after* they gained mastery of the expertise needed to implement the new innovation. This would help to explain the positive attitudes of the educators with inclusion experiences versus the less favorable views of those without.

The inclusion debate is not likely to end tomorrow. There will remain educators and community members who doubt inclusion's feasibility and actively strive to stand in its way. But, despite doubts and expected resistance, inclusive schooling is spreading and moving forward as a natural extension of civil and human rights and multicultural education movements. Reports like *Winners All: A Call for Inclusive Schools* by the National Association of State Boards of Education (1992) and resolutions passed by major educational organizations (e.g., Association of Supervision and Curriculum Development, 1992) strongly support inclusive schooling, noting the need to eliminate tracking and segregation. Further, as chapters throughout this book indicate, data-based evidence of the positive effects of inclusive schooling is mounting.

Teaching Students in Inclusive Settings: From Theory to Practice is a text that is exactly right for this moment in time in North American education. The title, as well as the content of the book, illustrates what can be done when a body of people care about, advocate for, experiment with, and tell stories about something that really matters to them. The authors, through their clear writing and use of accompanying vignettes and rich examples, demonstrate what teachers, administrators, families, and children have learned from the journey from exclusion to inclusion.

This book is composed of fourteen chapters, all introduced by a helpful Advance Organizer and illustrative vignettes. Chapter 1 introduces the reader to the rationale for and history of inclusive schooling trends. Chapter 2 describes the thirteen disability categories identified in federal law and, through a presentation of current court cases and issues about the labeling of people, provides a thoughtful introduction to the disability field. Chapter 3 offers a comprehensive review of personal and organizational change through a review of the literature as well as the actual words of educators who have experienced the transformations of going through a change process.

Both Chapters 4 and 5 recognize the importance of collaboration and teaming in the success of educational reform and inclusion. Chapter 4 offers tools for assessing team effectiveness, provides instruction in interpersonal communication skills, and highlights the role of parents and students in effective decision making. Chapter 5 describes various ways special and general educators can collaborate to support one another to respond to student diversity.

Chapter 6 examines assessment strategies for including students with disabilities in general education settings. Margaret King-Sears describes and provides examples of the application of a useful five-step framework for developing curriculum-based assessments for students with disabilities. Chapter 7 follows with descriptions of both general and specific processes for teams to employ in planning for student programs.

Chapter 8 examines the relationship of related services—specifically, speech and language, occupational, and physical therapy services—to inclusive schooling. The authors describe how therapists and educators can work effectively together to support students through a *transdisciplinary* team approach and spark creative ideas for linking therapies to the curriculum. Chapter 9 continues by helping readers clarify ways in which educators can modify instruction for students with widely differing characteristics. As in other chapters, Chapter 9 provides useful conceptual frameworks, checklists, and questions for planning for change.

Chapter 10 provides actual examples of activities that successfully integrate life skills and social-emotional curriculum within the school and classroom. Chapter 11 details two models for teaching students learning strategies and describes a framework for students to develop their own learning strategy systems, thus enhancing their independence and self-determination in learning.

Chapter 12 includes a comprehensive examination of the elements of a proactive behavior management program and features of a schoolwide discipline policy intended to result in faculty and students working cooperatively as a learning community as well as strategies for empowering students to develop skills in self-regulation and self-control.

The last two chapters of the book focus upon the classroom and students as communities of support. Chapter 13 describes specific methods to help students to get to know one another, develop caring relationships, and practice select social skills with a special emphasis on cooperative learning. Chapter 14 highlights a variety of approaches for building student relationships, including cooperative games, peer tutoring programs, and peer advocacy and support networks.

As you read this book, and the last two chapters in particular, it will become evident that there is a heavy focus upon helping and support. As leaders in the inclusive schooling movement have discovered and pointed out, a number of principles must be observed when applying the action planning and support networking strategies presented in this book. Specifically, remember:

- Trust and confidentiality are two basic issues that always must be addressed.
- None of the suggested strategies and approaches are tricks, gimmicks, or quick fixes. They are all intended to bring people together to create or support common inclusionary visions for a person, family, or organization.
- Change (and the suggested processes for change and peer support) is always a very personal experience, sometimes takes time, and always takes commitment.
- Educators remain the most powerful model in the classroom. If our interactions with one another and children are respectful, children will take their cues accordingly.
- All people have strengths and talents, including children identified as having a disability, that they can use to support and benefit others.
- Help and support must be a two-way street for mutual valuing to be developed and maintained. Both adult and student support relationships must be reciprocal. There should never be a standard group of "helpers" or "helpees."
- Change processes and supports should be driven by those directly affected by and involved in the schools and classroom community (i.e., students, teachers, parents, secretaries and other school personnel, support personnel, community volunteers, administrators).

Teaching Students in Inclusive Settings: From Theory to Practice offers conceptual and technical tools to enable its readers to expand their own capacity to create results and guide their schools to be learning organizations in a rapidly changing, pluralistic world, where disability is but one of many human differences brought to the school by our increasingly diverse student body. This comprehensive book offers a lens for viewing student differences as strengths and a broad range of specific strategies for capitalizing upon these differences to enrich the curriculum, individualize for any student, and expand all educators' instructional repertoires through teaching and problem-solving partnerships.

Jacqueline S. Thousand
California State University, San Marcos

Preface

I have been in many different schools. Some of them were far away from my house, and I had to ride the school bus for more than one hour each way. Three years ago I was not able to read, write, or do math, and my scores on I.Q. tests they gave me were dropping. My mom and dad decided my school was not helping me reach my vision. They asked to have me included in the eighth grade, and I was partly included in regular academic classes for the first time. I am now 18 years old and have been fully included in regular classes in the high school in my community for four years. The resource teachers and my peer buddies support me. I ride the bus to school each day with my friends.

Information on my I.Q. seems to be important to some educators, but it is not important to me because I know that if I am given a chance I can do a lot of things. Two years ago my I.Q. was 43. Now it is 65. I think many things are more important than an I.Q. score. There are many kinds of intelligence. For example, I would rate very high on people-skills intelligence.

Because of inclusion my future is bright. My school and my buddies are helping me reach my goals. They help me a lot, but I help them too. They all tell me how much they have learned from me. Two of my friends wrote term papers about inclusion because they saw how much I have learned. They concluded everyone with a disability should be included in their home schools. On my 17th birthday one of my friends gave me a birthday card that he and 58 other friends signed and wrote messages on. He said, "Cecelia, thanks for being such a great friend. You always know how to cheer everyone up. Keep on smiling." After I graduate from school, I want to have a job, get married, have kids, have a house of my own, take trips, and go to college.

Cecelia Pauley, High School Student, Potomac, MD

As a growing number of schools and classrooms are developing a focus on providing appropriate education to all students in their community, supports and services for students with disabilities must be reconfigured, and new skills must be acquired. Appreciation of what each student, educator, and parent has to offer helps to reestablish the school as a community of learners, a place where people regard each other as members who belong. When all members of this educational community are empowered through appropriate acquisition of knowledge and skills, they can join together to reclaim responsibility for educating all their students regardless of these students' learning challenges or the type and severity of their disabilities.

Hard work is involved in building this type of comprehensive cohesiveness within any community. Inclusive schooling practices rely on maximum utilization of all the resources available. Collaboration that extends in all directions and includes educators, families, and students, is essential.

The focus of this book is to provide not only an informational background and philosophical base for inclusion, but more importantly, to provide practical and educationally sound ideas for teachers and others who educate students with disabilities in inclusive settings. Rationale, methods, and effects of inclusive practices are examined. Practical approaches that facilitate inclusion are described and are highlighted by the real stories of educators, parents, and students who have made the journey from exclusionary to inclusive practices.

This text could not have been completed without the contributions of many people. The authors would like to take this opportunity to thank the outstanding contributions of each of the co-authors: Stephanie L. Carpenter, Donna K. Graves, Teri Musy, Thomas J. O'Toole, and Julie Stone. In addition, we are deeply indebted to the teachers, parents, and students who inspired us and who contributed their stories and experiences, and to the following reviewers for their input: Kim Stoddard, University of South Florida; and Fred West, Institute for Education Development and Training. Finally, we would like to thank our friends, families, and colleagues who have encouraged us to pursue our ideas and to create a book that we sincerely hope is genuinely practical and useful to educators involved in inclusive practices.

About the Chapter Authors

Dianne F. Bradley, Ph.D., is a least restrictive environment support teacher in Montgomery County Public Schools in Maryland. She has worked extensively in school settings as a general educator, special educator, and guidance counselor as well as a practicum supervisor and special education learning center coordinator. Her research and teaching interests are in inclusive and collaborative practices for educators who work with diverse groups of students. She is also a faculty associate at Johns Hopkins University.

Stephanie L. Carpenter, Ph.D., is an assistant professor in special education and practicum coordinator for the Mild/Moderate Disabilities and Inclusion graduate programs at Johns Hopkins University. Her research interests are in self-determination and self-advocacy skills for students with disabilities, as well as in strategy instruction to facilitate students' independent use of these skills. She has taught students in elementary and secondary settings with a range of disabilities.

Donna K. Graves, M.Ed., is an instructional specialist in the Department of Academic Programs, Montgomery County Public Schools, Maryland. She has been a general education classroom teacher, a special educator, and a reading specialist. She has taught graduate courses in special education, reading methodology, and cooperative learning. She has conducted extensive staff development programs on a broad range of topics including teaching thinking skills and classroom accommodations for student with special needs. She is currently teaching courses on multicultural education and teacher leadership.

Margaret E. King-Sears, Ph.D., is an associate professor at Johns Hopkins University and Program Coordinator for the Mild/Moderate Disabilities and Inclusion graduate programs. She has taught students with a range of disabilities in elementary and secondary grades in Georgia, Florida, Japan, and Germany. Her research interests are in data-based methods that support teaching methods for students with disabilities, and students' use of self-management techniques that promote their independence in school, work, and leisure activities.

Teri L. Musy, M.Ed., is a special education teacher in Montgomery County Public Schools, Maryland. She has taught students with a range of disabilities in elementary and secondary settings. Her areas of expertise include behavior management methods and data collection techniques that support effective academic and social gains for her students. She is also a faculty associate in the Mild/Moderate Disabilities Graduate Program at Johns Hopkins University, teaching classroom management and applied behavioral programming courses.

Thomas J. O'Toole, Ed.D., has worked in Montgomery County Public Schools in Maryland as director of Special Education and Related Services, director of Pupil Services, and supervisor of Speech and Hearing Services. He has served as a consultant to the U.S. Office of Education and several state departments of education. At present, he is a faculty associate at Johns Hopkins University and a consultant to several educational programs.

Diane M. Switlick, M.A., has held a variety of positions in teaching and administration in Montgomery County Public Schools, Maryland, where she is currently an assistant principal at Gaithersburg Middle School. She teaches inservice and university courses on collaboration and has developed and taught coursework on inclusive curriculum at Johns Hopkins University. She has co-authored a book on accommodations for students with learning disabilities. Her research and teaching interests are in the development of inclusive practices and teacher training at the school-based level.

Julie Stone, M.S., is currently a middle school special education teacher in Las Vegas, Nevada. She has held a variety of positions as a special educator working with students with mild to severe disabilities in inclusive settings. She has taught graduate level courses at Johns Hopkins University in inclusive practices.

The Past and the Future of Special Education

DIANNE F. BRADLEY AND DIANE M. SWITLICK

◆ ADVANCE ORGANIZER ◆

The inclusion of students with moderate and severe disabilities as well as the movement to keep students with mild disabilities in general education environments present educators with new challenges. The resulting changes have a significant effect on all students in both special education and general education. This chapter explores the background and reasons for these new directions in education. It discusses what needs to be done in order for these changes in education to be effective. The concepts of inclusion, regular education initiative, and mainstreaming are clarified. The characteristics of successful inclusive schools are explored, and the pros and cons of inclusive education are presented.

A young mother, Lisa Grant, approached New Castle School. She had been very pleased with her daughter's program and progress here and came to inquire about registering her son for kindergarten. After explaining to the secretary why she had come, she was given a packet of papers to complete. When she had been working for several minutes, the principal, Mrs. Waters, came in and introduced herself. "You are Amanda's mother, aren't you?" "Yes, I've come to enroll my son Jeremy for kindergarten." Mrs. Waters suggested that she bring Jeremy to kindergarten orientation next month.

Lisa took a deep breath and decided this was the time to inform the principal that Jeremy had Downs syndrome. Mrs. Waters listened intently while she spoke. After hearing about some of Jeremy's needs, Mrs. Waters told her that there was an excellent program for children with Downs syndrome at Evans Elementary. Mrs. Grant admitted that she knew of the program, but didn't feel she wanted Jeremy to attend that program. The principal seemed surprised and asked her why.

Lisa slowly began to enumerate her reasons. She didn't want her son to go to Evans because it was twelve miles away. He wouldn't know anyone there. He wouldn't meet anyone from his neighborhood, and he may not get the same program opportunities that her daughter had gotten in school. She told Mrs. Waters how Jeremy had been in preschool for three years with the other children from the neighborhood. They all knew him and he knew them. He knew where his sister went to school and that his friends would be going to school here. She understood that there would have to be accommodations and program adaptations for Jeremy.

After a thoughtful few moments, the principal suggested that they set up an appointment to talk further and that the kindergarten teacher and some other staff should be present at the meeting. Mrs. Grant agreed to this meeting with strong fears that she would be told by an imposing group of professionals that what she asked for would simply be impossible. As she said good-bye to the principal and headed out the door, she felt a sense of relief that the process was begun, and she was more convinced than ever that she was doing the right thing for Jeremy. But she also had a sense of overwhelming anxiety. This was only the first step, and the road ahead seemed long and rocky.

How will the teachers react?

Will the school create a successful program for Jeremy?

Will the school personnel and parents have a working relationship or an adversarial one?

What has brought us to these questions?

We also must expand educational opportunities by developing programs that involve inclusion, not exclusion. All people can lead fulfilling and rewarding lives if they are given the chance to contribute.

William J. (Bill) Clinton, 1993

Changing Paradigms of Special Education

- Inclusion
- Integration
- Mainstreaming
- Regular education initiative
- Heterogeneous school
- Full participation
- Collaborative teacher
- Disjointed incrementalism
- Zero reject philosophy

A unique set of terminology has been emerging in the educational arena. Some of these terms have been a part of the educational jargon for years. Others have infiltrated the educational scene more recently. Why this sudden need for new descriptors in the field of education? And what do all these terms have in common?

In 1986, Madeleine C. Will, the former assistant secretary for the U.S. Office of Special Education and Rehabilitation Services, called for a partnership between special and general educators. This propelled the movement toward two major complementary reforms in education. One is the integration or inclusion of students who have severe disabilities into regular classes in their neighborhood schools, and the other is the movement to keep students with mild disabilities in regular classroom settings, moving away from services that pull students out of class for instruction and isolate them from their peers in self-contained classes. In the subsequent sections, terminology related to these two reforms will be defined and the reasons for their emergence will be explained.

What Have We Learned from the Past?

Historical Perspective

Historically, the education of students with disabilities has progressed from neglect, to institutions, to residential schooling and other isolated schools and classes, to pullout programs and mainstreaming and is continuing in the direction of full inclusion for all students with disabilities.

Reynolds and Birch write that "The [early] history of education for exceptional children is mainly a simple story of massive neglect, denial, and rejection" (1982, p. 18). Before the nineteenth century it was believed that children with disabilities could not be taught.

In the early 1800s, such pioneers as Thomas H. Gallaudet (1787–1851) and Louis Braille (1809–1852) established special schools and systems of communication that assisted children who were blind or hearing impaired to learn. However, the first organized arrangements in the United States for the education of students with disabilities were copied from European asylums, which were established for the purpose of providing custodial care and "protecting persons with disabilities from the outside world" (Halvorsen & Sailor, 1990, p. 114). After these institutions proved that students with various disabilities were educable, residential schools were established.

By the late nineteenth century most states were demonstrating a public acceptance for the education of people with disabilities. Residential institutions even began to train specialized teachers for special programs in some local schools. However, it was not until the middle of the twentieth century that parents of children with disabilities organized for political action and that state and federal governments began to demonstrate support for special education programs in the form of research, training, and legislation (Reynolds & Birch, 1982; Turnbull, 1990).

Recent History

The past two decades have contributed dramatic changes in legal, social, and economic forces that have affected both general and special education. The environments in which students with disabilities receive educational services continue to be the focus of some of these changes. Concurrently, educational practices have been continually refined to reflect changes that benefit a wide variety of learners.

In 1975, Public Law 94-142, The Education of All Handicapped Children Act, was passed by Congress. Among the requirements of this law are that children and youth with disabilities are guaranteed a free appropriate public education. It also stipulated that these students be educated in the least restrictive environment, that is, to the maximum extent possible along with their peers without disabilities in the school that they would attend if they did not have a disability. To meet the intent of this law, many school systems nationwide responded by creating segregated programs rather than by providing services to students in general education schools and classrooms. Today, many of these segregated programs continue to maintain service delivery models that remove students from the mainstream to other classrooms, to separate wings of a school, or to specialized schools that have been established to deal with specific types of disabilities.

> *In the process of implementing the letter of the law (that students are entitled to education), the spirit of the law (that children have the right to learn together) was virtually lost.*
>
> Schaffner & Buswell, 1991

The resulting fragmentation promoted the development of separate training, administration, names, and buildings that increasingly isolate special education from general education. Many separate categories of children with special needs have been created to form what Thousand (1991) calls "Disjointed Incrementalism," that is, the creation of so many categorical programs (Chapter I programs, bilingual education programs, programs for students with mental retardation, programs for students with severe emotional disturbance, etc.) encourages competition between special needs groups for resources such as money, materials, and personnel.

> ***Mainstreaming:*** *Participation in the general education environment when deemed academically/emotionally ready.*

Dominique is ready to be mainstreamed. She has improved her reading and math skills. She can handle the assignments currently being completed by the other eighth graders. She should only require a minimum of classroom support, such as extra time to complete her assignments.

Mainstreaming

The 1980s witnessed an increase in the move toward the progressive inclusion of students with challenging learning needs and behaviors in the general education environment. Additional federal legislation such as Public Law 99-457, passed in 1986, and Public Law 101-476, passed in 1990, has required that students with disabilities be educated in general education classes and other integrated environments to the maximum extent appropriate. One of the responses of the educational community to these laws was to make substantial efforts to mainstream students. The mainstreaming effort encouraged the exit of students with disabilities from self-contained programs as soon as they demonstrated the academic and/or social skills deemed necessary to function in the general education environment (Rogers, 1993; Van Dover, 1995).

The concept of mainstreaming is focused on fitting students who have previously been separated back into general education environments. This differs from inclusive schooling, which focuses on developing school communities that nurture and support all students from the onset.

> **Regular Education Initiative:** *Shared responsibility and joint ownership between special and general educators for the education of students with mild disabilities within general education classrooms in which instruction is differentiated.*

Sandra and Lamar are in Mr. Jones' ninth grade American history class. Both students have learning disabilities and have testing accommodations on their Individualized Education Plans (IEPs). Sandra has difficulty comprehending questions she reads, and Lamar needs assistance in retrieving information he knows. Before tests, Mr. Jones provides all students with a study guide. The resource teacher works in conjunction with Mr. Jones to change short essay questions into multiple choice questions for Lamar to be given to him in the classroom. She meets with Sandra during the test to read it out loud to her.

The Regular Education Initiative

The regular education initiative (REI) is based on the premise that children with mild disabilities should be viewed as the shared responsibility of all educators rather than as sole responsibility of special educators (Will, 1986). Rather than creating programs in which students with mild disabilities are removed from their general education classroom environment for specialized instruction, general education classes are adapted to meet the needs of a variety of individual learners (Semmel, Abernathy, Butera, & Lesar, 1991).

REI encompasses a philosophy that considers all students as capable of learning in most environments even though they may differ in intellectual, behavioral, and/or physical characteristics. As Sailor (1991) describes it:

> *In one sense, REI is to children with moderate and mild disabilities as the integration imperative is to children with low-incidence and severe disabilities. The common denominator is the principle of the least restrictive educational environment which, in turn, is born of the recognition that social and communicative development in children with disabilities is predicated upon opportunities for mainstream socialization as well as academic experiences, and constitutional guarantee of freedom of association. (p. 11)*

Thus REI is one step closer to inclusive schooling than mainstreaming because the focus is on adapting the general education setting to nurture and support students with mild disabilities. However, it is not as comprehensive as inclusive schooling because it fails to address the needs of the student with more significant disabilities and more intensive needs.

> ***Inclusion:*** *Participation by all in a supportive general education environment that includes appropriate educational and social supports and services.*

James is in a regular sixth grade classroom. He has significant learning needs that require adjusted expectations for his academic performance. The special educator plans with the classroom teacher to develop functional activities that parallel the instructional content provided for his peers. He works on social skills during his interactions with peers in cooperative groups. Life skills of dressing, fine motor activities, and other organizational objectives are integrated at unobtrusive and logical points. An instructional assistant and parent volunteer are available to work with James and other students as necessary. The presence of James in the classroom provides a multitude of new learning experiences for the students in the classroom just as these students provide James with support and new opportunities.

Inclusion

Educators, parents, and legislators continue to question the existing separateness between general and special education. There is increasing legal and community support for more inclusive and less categorical groupings of all special education students with their peers without disabilities (Halvorsen & Sailor, 1990; Stainback & Stainback, 1992a; Tessier-Switlick, 1991). There continues to be a growing trend to join together these once separated educational systems as an emerging philosophy of the least restrictive environment evolves.

The terms "inclusion," "inclusive school," and "integration" have appeared in the literature to describe the instruction of students with disabilities within the general education program. Integrated or inclusive schools do not require that students be ready to fit into the established educational programs as mainstreaming does, but instead develop classroom communities that support the educational and social needs of all students with or without disabilities.

Those involved in developing and supporting inclusive programming offer a variety of perspectives:

- "Everyone is welcome, valued, and supported and everyone contributes" (Stainback & Stainback, 1992b, p. vii).
- "Having each student participate as a valued member of a sustained social network within his or her home community" (Halvorsen & Sailor, 1990, pp. 112–113).
- "Inviting those who have been left out (in any way) to come in, and asking them to help design new systems that encourage every person to participate to the fullness of their capacity—as partners and as members" (Forest & Pearpoint, 1992, p. 1).

- "Heterogeneous Schooling" (Villa, Thousand, Stainback, & Stainback, 1992).
- "The responsibility for all students is shared" (Working Forum on Inclusive Schools, 1994, p. vii).
- "Full Participation" (Ayres, 1988).
- "A movement to merge special and regular education" (Yell, 1995).

An inclusive school has what is known as a "zero reject philosophy", that is, no one is turned away because of the presence of a disability (Lilly, 1971; Thousand & Villa, 1989). Inclusion, unlike mainstreaming, maintains an open door policy to all students regardless of abilities and disabilities, resulting in schools that reflect the heterogeneous makeup of society. Instruction is designed around individual strengths and needs rather than the placement of students in already existing programs where instruction is based on the type and severity of the students' disabilities. Inclusion assumes an attitude of acceptance of all students as members of the school and classroom environment.

For example, Melissa, a student with severe, multiple disabilities was included in a regular second grade class for most of the day. One of the dilemmas facing the students and teacher in making Melissa a true part of the class was to have her participate in the class jobs. The students examined the various classroom jobs for which they were responsible and identified those which Melissa would be able to do. One they selected was to take the attendance to the office. This would mean that another student would push Melissa's wheelchair for her. The students and teacher wanted to make sure that the school secretary knew that Melissa, as the one doing the job, would be addressed, thanked, and acknowledged rather than the student who was pushing the wheelchair. The students designed a holder that was attached to the wheelchair and also talked with the school secretary about the arrangement. The students became very invested in making Melissa a part of the class rather than seeing her as so disabled that she could not participate in normal classroom activities.

Ben is a student with moderate developmental disabilities who is attending a high school in his neighborhood. He spends part of his school day in a community-based education program learning critical travel training and life skills that are necessary for him to live relatively independently as an adult. He spends the other half of his school day in the general education program. In addition to participating in physical education and art class with peer support, he attends a tenth grade biology class where he works on vocational goals. He counts and distributes materials and follows oral directions for setting up equipment. His classmates request materials, give him clues and reminders, and provide general social support. Ben participates actively in the classroom with the students studying biology, but focuses on very different learning objectives.

Reasons for Developing Inclusive Schools

Much of society's support of the concept of inclusive education is based on the ethical, legal, and educational benefits to its members. Recently many parents, educators, and legislators have questioned the efficacy of separate educational programs for students with disabilities (Sailor, 1991; Stainback & Stainback 1992a; Villa, Thousand, Stainback, & Stainback, 1992; Willis, 1994).

Ethical Considerations

Ethical considerations of equity and individual rights justify removing students from categorical programs and providing support for neighborhood schools and their communities to welcome these students. Not doing so may deny them access to quality education and the same quality of life as others in their community. These students need to make the linkages that they will need after they leave the school setting to live, work, and play near their homes. It also eliminates the segregation of a child from siblings and peers, which can be traumatic for most students. Being transported to a different school on a special education bus is a clear indication that one doesn't measure up to expectations, with resulting loss of self-esteem. The effects of not belonging can hinder achievement. When students attend schools within their neighborhoods, a natural proportion of students with disabilities usually exists within each school. Each school staff becomes responsible for all students residing in their community.

The recent emphasis on the importance of success for all students, which has grown out of parental and professional concerns, focuses on the individual educational needs of *all* students regardless of learning differences. Most schools seem willing to make minor accommodations to the instructional program to accommodate the range of student performance and diversity evident in their communities. However, when a student does not fit into any of these programs, that student can be excluded and placed in a different program (e.g., special education, English for Speakers of Other Languages [ESL], or alternative education). As long as these avenues exist to exclude students that do not fit, there is no strong incentive to significantly adapt a program to the individual needs of the student, and the resources necessary to facilitate more significant program adaptations are drained from the school into the specialized program.

In addition, present and projected budget shortfalls demand that resources be allocated as efficiently as possible with optimal outcomes for students. A shift in spending from instructionally irrelevant uses (i.e., lengthy transportation to specialized programs, separate administrators for special education programs) to instructionally relevant classroom supports (i.e., specialized materials and staff, staff training) is a much more productive use of funds.

Legal Issues

The term "integration" refers to the removal of barriers that impose segregation on identified groups of people. In the 1950s, integration referred to the desegregation of schools that previously had separated a race of students by maintaining separate educational facilities. Miller (1990) contends that "special education has become a 'second system' in education" (p. 7). In fact, the move to integrate students with disabilities is rooted in the "separate is not equal" clause of *Brown v. The Board of Education* and is viewed by many as a civil rights issue (Block & Haring, 1992).

Public Law 94-142 and IDEA (Individuals with Disabilities Education Act of 1990) require that students with disabilities receive their education in the least restrictive environment. These laws also stipulate that supports and services accompany the student in this environment. The range of services within the local school can take many forms. Students may spend the entire day in general education classrooms or participate in a "school within a school" organization. The specific needs of individual students determine the organization and delivery system in each school. Thus, general education, special education, and related services can be available based on student-specific goals and needs. *The services are made available where the students are instead of moving the students to where the services are provided.*

Placement issues are further clarified by the case of *Pennsylvania Association for Retarded Citizens (PARC) v. Commonwealth of Pennsylvania* (1982). "Placement in regular public school class is preferable to placement in a special public school . . ." (p. 2). For students with severe disabilities, programs must provide "age-appropriate schools attended also by nonhandicapped students in natural proportions" (p. 2). Further discussion of classroom logistics and integrated services are offered in Chapters 8, 9, and 10.

Educational Value

In addition to ethical and legal considerations for integrating students with disabilities, educational reasons exist as well. The *Disability Rights, Education, and Defense Fund* (1982) states, "regardless of race, class, gender, type of disability, or its onset, the more time spent in integrated public school classes as children, the more people achieved educationally and occupationally as adults" (Ferguson & Asch, 1989, p. 124). Research shows that students with moderate and severe disabilities can achieve comparable and improved educational outcomes in a general education setting (Halvorsen & Sailor, 1990; Mercer & Denti, 1989; Stainback & Stainback, 1990; Villa et al, 1992; Willis, 1994).

Educational systems that maintain a narrow view of the mainstream emphasize sorting students rather than educating them in the least restrictive environment. In addition, many general educators no longer feel empowered to teach children who have disabilities (Bradley & West, 1994). Moreover, studies have shown that once students are placed in special education programs, it is rare that they ever leave (Gersten & Woodward, 1990). In addition, there are continuing questions being raised about the misidentification of students for all specialized programs.

An inclusive vision is not compatible with a "separate but equal" dual system. The vision implies a commitment to educate all students in their community schools. The most important reason for students with disabilities to become a part of their neighborhood schools is preparation for the future. If the education of all students closely reflects the norms and cultural patterns of society, they will be better prepared to function in the complex and heterogeneous world anticipated when they are adults.

> *America must fulfill the potential of all its citizens, including all students with disabilities, if it hopes to maintain world-class economic status in the next century.*
>
> National Council on Disability, 1993

Preparing for Inclusive Schools

The philosophy that embraces the inclusion of students into the general education setting is one that is based on welcoming all neighborhood students into the community school and meeting their needs in that educational system. There are several critical factors to consider when making the transition to an inclusive or heterogeneous school:

1. To create an atmosphere and a school philosophy based on egalitarianism and democracy
2. To get the support and ideas of all who will be involved
3. To integrate students as well as personnel and resources so that general and special educators can work together
4. To utilize "Best Practices" of education throughout the school

Several Best Practices of education have been identified that must be incorporated for inclusion to operate at its best (Bradley, 1993; Fox, 1987; Halvorsen and Sailor, 1990; Thousand, 1991; Tessier-Switlick, 1991). These practices benefit not only students with special needs, but the general education population as well. They include the following:

- The inclusion of each child in the regular program with peers who do not have disabilities for at least part of the day
- Heterogeneous grouping whenever possible
- Technical expertise and equipment
- Curriculum adaptations when necessary
- Assessments that are curriculum-based and give information about how students learn instead of what is wrong with them
- Behavior management techniques
- Social skills curriculum
- Data-based instructional practices
- Empowerment of students through the use of such techniques as peer teaching, cooperative learning, and self-developed rules
- Ongoing staff development

System Preparation

Current directions in school system reform and preparation for the twenty-first century emphasize demonstrated improvements not only in the general education population, but improved performance of more challenging populations as well in order to address the changing demography of U.S. schools (Sailor, 1991). Sailor suggests that we use the opportunities that now exist for school reform and educational reorganization to merge the new goals of general and special education and work toward a "shared educational agenda" (p. 8).

To accomplish this, support networks for all who will be involved in and expected to implement changes in the school program must be a part of the planning (Fox, 1987; Peterson, 1989; Thousand, 1991). Students, school personnel, and families must be willing to support and commit to inclusionary education. A crucial factor is gaining administrative support. Superintendents as well as building principals must understand, support, and be able to explain the reasons for establishing inclusive schools. The ideas and concerns of families of students with and without disabilities must be taken into consideration. Support teams and networks must be set up for teachers so that the concerns of regular and special educators can be addressed on a continuous basis. Students will also need to be prepared. The students who are moving from a self-contained environment must receive instruction and support to make the transition. The receiving students must also be educated and sensitized to accept and appreciate individual differences. This will require that educational planning and instruction be a shared responsibility among general educators, special educators, administrators, families, students, and peers.

Preparing Educators

> *General educators cannot educate students with disabilities alone, but research has shown that special educators cannot do it alone either.*
>
> Stainback & Stainback, 1990

In schools in which the special education population is included in general education, teachers are being asked to provide an appropriate education to students with increasingly diverse educational needs. As the mainstream widens, a paradigm shift is occurring. Educators operating out of the old paradigm saw students who were not successful in the mainstream as needing special education programs. The problem was attributed to the student. In an inclusion approach, this same problem is attributed to the methods of instruction or materials used. The new paradigm emphasizes that all students can learn if instruction and materials meet their needs (Bradley & Fisher, 1995). This shift in thinking requires that general and special educators work together for every student. As general educators become increasingly sensitive to individual differences, they will need to support students with specialized materials and staff. The teaming of general and special educators has become essential.

Special and general educators must work together to gain knowledge about how the best teaching and learning occurs. Teacher expertise as well as materials need to be shared. Restructuring the delivery of services can free personnel and resources to be available to all students. For example, special educators can serve as co-instructors and consultants and also be available to make instructional adaptations (see Chapter 5 for more specific information on cooperation in teaching). Miller (1990) suggests a merger of the following to provide all educators with more specific skills and training and to help them address the challenges of their students who require specialized instruction:

- Materials
- Knowledge
- Skills
- Personnel
- Resources
- Categorical programs (Chapter I, Bilingual, Headstart)

Preparing Families

It is crucial to involve families in creating an inclusive school philosophy as well as to include them in all decisions that affect the instructional program of their children. Families of students with disabilities are being asked to make adjustments in their thinking about the education of their children. These families were once told that a self-contained classroom was the best setting for quality instruction. Now they are being asked to consider that the best place for their child's education is in the general education classroom with modifications and services (Bradley & Fisher, 1995). Offering families information about inclusion and the ways in which it will be implemented in their child's educational environment can help make a smooth transition to inclusive practices.

Preparing Students

If major changes are taking place within the school, the students need to have a clear understanding of the processes and purposes for these changes. Students exhibit various reactions to changes going on around them, especially when groups of new students, teachers, and assistants are placed in their classes. It is best to explain the inclusion process before these changes take place and to solicit ideas and suggestions from the students. When students feel that their input is valued, they make more of an investment to support the program (Bradley & Fisher, 1995) (see Chapter 14 for further information on student supports).

For students in general education, the delivery of specific lessons that explain the inclusion process is often a successful approach. Students should have the opportunity to discuss their questions, fears, and concerns. They need to know how, when, and why to help students with disabilities.

Students with disabilities need to be informed about the changes and new responsibilities that come with inclusion. Students who receive special education must have time to adjust to the changes. They may need more instruction to prepare them for the physical move to the general education setting such as using lockers, following schedules, and finding locations in the school. Establishing networks of peer support can address many of these changes and help make a smooth transition to the general education setting.

Outcomes of Inclusive Schooling

Academic Advantages

The world of academics is designed to prepare students for the world of work. Reports of follow-up studies of special education students show that graduates of self-contained programs are employed less and often have lower self-esteem than those who received their education in the mainstream (Brown et al., 1987; Lipsky & Gartner, 1989; Thousand, 1991; Wagner, 1989). However, when appropriate programs and services are provided in inclusive settings, students tend to develop into more viable adults with fewer needs for costly taxpayer-supported adult services (Brinker & Thorpe, 1984; Madden & Slavin, 1983; Piuma, 1985; York & Vandercook, 1989).

> *Students with disabilities in integrated settings achieved statistically significant academic gains in writing, language comprehension, and receptive language.*
>
> Marwell, 1990

Halvorsen and Sailor (1990) point out that in inclusive programs there is an increase in the number of IEP objectives that are accomplished. Peterson's studies (1989) highlight students placed in heterogeneously grouped programs who showed significantly more improvement than students grouped by ability levels. He found that students with special education needs who were placed in mixed ability groups participated more in class activities and presented fewer discipline problems.

Some of the results that occur when the focus of special education moves away from labeling and moves toward instruction are the following:

- More of the special education teacher's time can be spent in direct service to students rather than in attending meetings and conducting testing.
- Continuity with grade level academic programs is more likely to occur.
- Students make better use of instructional time because they are not moving from one class to another to receive their special services.

Moreover, general education teachers who have accepted students with disabilities into their classes report that they have become more proficient in a variety of teaching styles, which benefits all their students (Marwell, 1990).

Socialization Gains

The inclusion of students with disabilities into their community school environments provides them with two major opportunities: normalization and ultimate functioning. The condition of normalization merely means that the qualities and conditions of the life of a person with disabilities reflect the norms and cultural patterns of the society in general (Halvorsen & Sailor, 1990). People with disabilities should also be provided with opportunities for ultimate functioning, which means participation in programs that facilitate the acquisition of skills that will enhance their functioning in the general environment (Brown et al., 1987; Halvorsen & Sailor, 1990). When planned programs of interaction are instituted, students with and without disabilities can learn to interact, communicate, develop friendships, work together, and assist one another. This helps them develop understanding, respect, sensitivity, and comfort with individual differences and similarities

Inclusive education offers students with disabilities access to a range of learning opportunities and social models. More appropriate social development occurs, and the stigma and isolation that come with segregated programs are minimized.

Inclusion of all students in the general learning environment enables students with disabilities to generalize their skills to the nondisabled environment and provides these students with opportunities to make the connections that they will need to live as well as to participate in meaningful work and recreational activities in their communities. It also encourages the person who has been educated in the mainstream to seek more normalized living arrangements.

Benefits to the General Education Population

General education teachers worry that having students with disabilities in their classes, especially those with severe disabilities, will have detrimental effects on their other students. Thus, several researchers set out to measure these effects. Their studies have indicated that the presence of students with disabilities in general education classes *does not* negatively affect the performance of typical students. Hollowood, Salisbury, Rainforth, and Palombaro (1995) studied the use of instructional time in classrooms in which students with severe disabilities were included. When compared to classes without these students, it was found that "students with severe disabilities had no effect on losses of instructional time" (p. 242). Sharpe, York, and Knight (1994) used test scores and report card grades to measure academic achievement and conduct of general education students in classes in which students with severe disabilities were included and compared them to classes that had no included students. Results revealed that no significant difference exists for the two groups in either academic or behavioral performance.

In addition to having no significant effect on behavior, academic achievement, or loss of classroom time, it has been found that students participating in general education programs alongside their peers with disabilities actually gain skills and insights that are of benefit to them such as developing tolerance and appreciating human differences (Willis, 1994). All students have the opportunity to acquire valuable life skills when there is concentration on ways to develop supporting and caring attitudes.

Having students with severe disabilities in my class brought out the best in my first graders. They learned life lessons they would not have learned otherwise. They learned not to pity people and that we all have something to offer. They learned mutuality.

At first, we assigned the brighter students to assist the students with disabilities. But we found that some other children, those who were shy or had milder disabilities, turned out to be the best helpers. They demonstrated leadership skills and dependability that we might not have seen.

Sharon Thorne, first grade teacher, Germantown, Maryland

Kids in my second grade class became very creative problem solvers because they wanted to make sure the students with significant challenges were included in all the activities in a meaningful way. They worked very hard at including all students in games and activities including all field day activities. Their level of awareness of the needs of all people was heightened. An issue with my students was dignity—the value and respect that each person deserves regardless of their abilities. This transferred over into their actions with each other.

Bonni Rubin-Sugarman, second grade teacher, Mt. Laurel, New Jersey

Stainback and Stainback (1990) and Marwell (1990) found that students become more comfortable with individual differences and focus on similarities in their peers when they are educated together. Halvorsen and Sailor (1990) and Peterson (1989) have observed that the presence of students with disabilities in the classroom can foster understanding and respect about individual differences among all members of the class.

All students can benefit from the varied approaches used by teachers who successfully work with students with disabilities in general education classrooms (Marwell, 1990; Willis, 1994). Where peer tutoring is used as a strategy, improved learning for both the tutor and tutee as well as increased self-esteem has resulted (Franca, Kerr, Reitz, & Lambert, 1990). Integrated classrooms also produce future employers who are more likely to have positive attitudes toward persons with disabilities (Stainback & Stainback, 1990).

> *The greatest gain for students without disabilities who are educated with peers who have disabilities is that they develop values that enable them to support the inclusion of all citizens in the various aspects of community life.*

Barriers to the Development of an Inclusive School

Role Changes for Educators

Although inclusive schools tend to be beneficial for those involved, the system has obstacles to surmount as well. Kauffman, Gerber, and Semmel (1988) and Bradley and West (1994) contend that data that reflect the attitudes of general education teachers and other school-based educators is not well documented in the literature on inclusive schools. Bradley states: "For twenty years we've told general education teachers, 'You don't know how to do this. It's all magic.' Now we've done an about-face and told them that good teaching is good teaching. They're skeptical and they're scared" (in Miller, 1993, p. 32). Classroom teachers fear being put in the position of being caught between inclusion and test score accountability. The range of students' abilities in a single classroom often spans the continuum from gifted students to those with limited ability and/or severe physical, academic, and emotional challenges. Changes in instructional preparation, delivery, and assessment are often required to meet the needs of such a diverse group. In addition, general educators often feel uncomfortable as they move into new roles that include providing meaningful educational and social experiences for students with disabilities, dealing with special education jargon and paperwork, and working with more comprehensive record keeping systems. General educators sometimes anticipate that inclusion as a mandate will require them to do more with less. Some general educators fear a lack of support from special educators and some have expressed fear that these supports will be eliminated altogether. With time and resources already at a premium, a designated partnership with special educators is essential for the general educator to effectively teach all students in the mainstream.

The REI and inclusion models also present some disadvantages for the special educator. Some even go so far as to view it as an attack on special education. Because significant role changes are required, there may be some confusion as to who is responsible for the implementation of IEP goals as well as the behavior and general achievement of the students with disabilities (Bradley & Fisher, 1995; Sailor, 1991). Some special educators have a highly structured classroom with a strong behavior management system in place for their students and fear that the mainstream environment can not maintain the required intensity of such a system. Planning with the general educator is often time-consuming, and the logistics of high structure can be difficult to weave into a larger classroom setting (see Chapter 3 for more information on role changes for educators).

Logistical difficulties can arise as well. Funding formulas, as they presently exist, encourage restrictive placements and "reward" systems for labeling and placing students in special education (Bergan, 1995; Katsiyannis, Conderman, & Franks, 1995). Space and accessibility limitations in schools housing students with disabilities for the first time may exist, and service delivery in sparsely populated regions can be very difficult and may require cooperative agreements between school systems.

Possible Adverse Effects on Students

Sailor (1991) points out that given the negative attitudes toward individual differences that exist in many of our schools, social discrimination could occur. Moreover, some parents who have become accustomed to their children receiving their education in small groups with much individual attention are wondering if programming in general education settings is adequate to meet the needs of their children with disabilities.

There are other possible disadvantages for the students as well. Reviews by Kauffman and colleagues (1988) cited studies that refute the notion that self-concept improves for children with mild disabilities when they are educated in regular classes. They found that students with disabilities exhibited lower self-esteem, when educated together in a regular classroom, than did children without disabilities. Students with disabilities were also teased more. Obviously, much preparation and thought must go into the conversion of a segregated service delivery model to an inclusive one.

Characteristics of an Inclusive School

If a school were to take the steps required to make the transition to become an inclusive school, what evidence would there be to show that this had occurred? What would one observe in an inclusive school? How could these characteristics be measured?

✓ All students attend their home school.
✓ There is a philosophy of "zero reject."
✓ Students with disabilities in the school are proportionate to those in the general community.
✓ There is one building administrator who is responsible for all programs in that school.
✓ Students with and without disabilities have frequent contact with each other.
✓ Students are placed in age-appropriate classes.
✓ All students receive the benefit of the grade level curriculum.

✓ Grouping is heterogeneous.

✓ Individualized instruction, cooperative learning, and peer tutoring are evident.

✓ Related services are provided in the natural instructional environment.

✓ Expertise and materials are shared.

✓ Collaboration among the school staff is evident.

✓ Natural support systems are used.

✓ Teachers and students are encouraged to develop an appreciation for diversity.

✓ The rules reflect fairness and equality, and the acquisition of social skills are valued as much as acquisition of academic skills.

One important component of the inclusion model is that all students would attend their neighborhood school. They would be placed in age-appropriate classes, and students with and without disabilities would have much contact with each other (Hallahan, Kauffman, Lloyd, & McKinney, 1988; Halvorsen & Sailor 1990; Tessier-Switlick 1991; Kirner, Gerber, & Krafcik, 1991). Students with disabilities in the school would be proportionate to those in the general community. There would be a philosophy of acceptance assuring that no student would be turned away because of a disability.

Peterson's (1989) studies show that the success of inclusion can be measured by the rate of interaction between students with and without disabilities. He believes that to calculate the extent of inclusion, one need merely observe the extent of integrated social interaction among students.

In addition to seeing much physical integration with peers, related services such as speech and physical therapy should be provided in the natural instructional environment whenever possible, whether it be the classroom, playground, lunch room or on field trips. All students would receive the benefit of the grade level curriculum adjusted to individual needs. There would be ownership by building administrators for all students and programs within that school instead of separate administrators for special education programs.

In an inclusive school, instruction would be fluid, and students would be heterogeneously grouped whenever possible. When grouped for instruction, students would be able to move easily from one group to another depending on skills acquisition. Individualized instruction for all students would be a natural occurrence.

The students in an inclusive classroom would be empowered by frequent participation in cooperative learning, peer tutoring, and decision making. They would be encouraged to utilize natural support networks, including all teachers, instructional assistants, and each other. Each student's talents would be valued and their limitations accepted.

Teachers in inclusive schools would work together by engaging in co-teaching, peer coaching, or collaborative problem solving. Time would be provided for special educators, general educators, instructional assistants, administrators, parents, and students to plan curriculum and discuss strategies. Expertise and materials would be shared. In an inclusive classroom, it would be difficult to differentiate between the general educator and the special educator, and the skills of all the teachers would be available to all the students.

Teachers might find themselves with new titles such as "Integration Teacher" or "Collaborative Teacher." Thousand (1991) advocates dropping all the specialist titles and just calling everyone "Teacher."

Conclusions

To accomplish the educational goals inherent in providing inclusive education for all students, it will be necessary for the educational system to undergo some major changes in philosophy, funding and personnel allocations, teaching methods, and distribution of resources. Some states, school districts, and individual schools have already reorganized in order to provide appropriate educational programs for all students in their neighborhood schools. Others are experimenting by creating some integrated schools with the anticipation of including more each year.

Marion Wright Edelman, president and founder of the Children's Defense Fund, reminds us: "We do not have a child to waste. We will not be a strong country unless we invest in every one of our children" (in Terry, 1993, p. 5). Including all our students in the general education environment is one way to offer our future citizens an opportunity to use their strengths and talents for the good of the community. Therefore, to ensure that our nation continues to maintain international excellence, it is essential that students with disabilities, who offer a wealth of human potential and resources, be included in all efforts to reform and improve our education system (National Council on Disability, 1993).

As educators respond to the legal, ethical, and educational challenges of ensuring that all students have the right to learn together, they continue to seek ways in which students with disabilities can be included to the greatest extent possible in general education schools and classrooms. When students with and without disabilities are given opportunities to learn alongside each other and experience each others' gifts and talents, they become better prepared to function meaningfully in a diverse society that includes all its citizens.

References

Ayres, C. B. (1988). Integration: A parent's perspective. *Exceptional Parent, 18*(6), 22–25.

Bergan, J. R. (1995). Evolution of a problem-solving model of consultation. *Journal of Educational and Psychological Consultation, 6,* 125–144.

Block, J. H., & Haring, T. G. (1992). On swamps, bogs, alligators, and special educational reform. In R. A. Villa, J. S. Thousand, W. Stainback, & S. Stainback (Eds.), *Restructuring for caring and effective education: An administrative guide to creating heterogeneous schools* (pp. 7–24). Baltimore: Paul H. Brookes Publishing Co.

Bradley, D. F. (1993). *Staff training for the inclusion of students with disabilities: Visions from educators.* Unpublished doctoral dissertation. Walden University, Minneapolis.

Bradley, D. F., & Fisher, J. F. (1995). The inclusion process: Role changes at the middle level. *The Middle School Journal, 26*(3), 13–19.

Bradley, D. F., & West, J. F. (1994). Staff training for the inclusion of students with disabilities: Visions from school-based educators. *Teacher Education and Special Education, 17,* 112–128.

Brinker, R. P., & Thorpe, N. E. (1984). Integration of severely handicapped students and the proportion of IEP objectives achieved. *Exceptional Children, 51,* 168–175.

Brown, L., Rogan, P., Shiraga, B., Zanella, A. K., Kessler, K., Bryson, F., VanDeventer, P., & Loomis, R. (1987). *A vocational follow-up evaluation of the 1984–86 Madison Metropolitan School District graduates with severe intellectual disabilities.* Madison: University of Wisconsin and Madison Metropolitan School District.

Clinton, W. J. (1993). Personal communication. (Available from Dianne F. Bradley, 13900 Broomall La., Silver Spring, MD 20906).

Ferguson, P., & Asch, A. (1989). Lessons from life: Personal and parental perspectives on school, childhood, and disability. In D. Biklen, A. Ford, & D. Ferguson (Eds.), *Disability and society*. Chicago: National Society for the Study of Education.

Forest, M., & Pearpoint, J. (1992). Inclusion! The bigger picture. In J. Pearpoint, M. Forest, & J. Snow (Eds.), *The inclusion papers: Strategies to make inclusion work* (pp. 1–7). Toronto: Inclusion Press.

Fox, T. 1987. *Best practice guidelines*. Burlington, VT: Center for Developmental Disabilities.

Franca, V. M., Kerr, M. M., Reitz, A. L., & Lambert, D. (1990). Peer tutoring among behaviorally disordered students: Academic and social benefits to tutor and tutee. *Education and Treatment of Children, 13*, 109–128.

Gersten, R., & Woodward, J. (1990). Rethinking the regular education initiative: Focus on the classroom teacher. *Remedial and Special Education, 11*(3), 7–16.

Hallahan, D. P., Kauffman, J. M., Lloyd, J. W., & McKinney, J. D. (1988). Questions about the Regular Education Initiative. *Journal of Learning Disabilities, 21*(1), 3–5.

Halvorsen, A. T., & Sailor, W. (1990). Integration of students with severe and profound disabilities: A review of research. In R. Gaylord-Ross (Ed.), *Issues and research in special education* (pp. 110–172). New York: Teachers College Press.

Hollowood, T. M., Salisbury, C. L., Rainforth, B., & Palombaro, M. M. (1995). Use of instructional time in classrooms serving students with and without severe disabilities. *Exceptional Children, 61*, 242–253.

Katsiyannis, A., Conderman, G., Franks, D. J. (1995). State practices on inclusion: A national review. *RASE, 16*, 279–287.

Kauffman, J. M., Gerber, M. M., & Semmel, M. I. (1988). Arguable assumptions underlying the regular education initiative. *Journal of Learning Disabilities, 21*(1), 6–11.

Kirner, M., Gerber, S., & Krafcik, N. (1991). *Connecticut's early intervention project: Alternatives to referral*. Middletown, CT: Special Education Resource Center.

Lilly, M. S. (1971). A training based model for special education. *Exceptional Children, 37*, 745–749.

Lipsky, D., & Gartner, A. (Eds.). (1989). *Beyond separate education: Quality education for all*. Baltimore: Paul H. Brookes Publishing Co.

Madden, N. A., & Slavin, R. L. (1983). Mainstreaming students with mild handicaps: Academic achievement and social outcomes. *Review of Educational Research, 53*, 519–569.

Marwell, B. W. (1990). *Summary evaluation report: Integration of students with mental retardation*. Madison, WI: Madison Metropolitan School District.

Mercer, J. R., & Denti., L. (1989). Obstacles to integrating disabled students in a "two roof" elementary school. *Exceptional Children, 56*, 30–39.

Miller, L. (1990). The regular education initiative and school reform: Lessons from the mainstream. *Remedial and Special Education, 11*(3), 17–22.

Miller, D. (1993, November 18). Members of the family. *The Howard County Times: The Columbia Flyer*, p. 22.

National Council on Disability. (1993). *Progress and prospects: A report to the President and the Congress of the United States*. Washington, DC: National Council on Disability.

Pennsylvania Association for Retarded Citizens (PARC) v. Commonwealth of Pennsylvania, Consent Decree on Enforcement Petition in Fialkowski et al. v. School District of Philadelphia et al., entered June, 1982.

Peterson, J. M. (1989). Remediation is no remedy. *Educational Leadership, 6*(6), 24–25.

Piuma, C., (1985). *A case study: Cost analysis study of selected integrated and segregated classrooms serving severely disabled students in San Mateo County*. Unpublished manuscript, San Francisco University, California Research Institute.

Reynolds, M. C., & Birch, J. (1982). *Teaching exceptional children in all America's schools* (rev. ed.). Reston, VA: Council for Exceptional Children.

Rogers, J. (1993). The inclusion revolution. *Research Bulletin: Phi Delta Kappa, 11*, 19–26.

Sailor, W. (1991). Special education in the restructured school. *Remedial and Special Education, 12*(6), 8–22.

Schaffner, C. B., & Buswell, B. E. (1991). *Opening doors: Strategies for including all students in regular education*. Colorado Spring, CO: Peak Parent Center.

Semmel, M. I., Abernathy, T. V., Butera, G., & Lesar, S. (1991). Teacher perceptions of the regular education initiative. *Exceptional Children, 58*(1), 9–24.

Sharpe, M. N., York, J. L, & Knight, J. (1994). Effects of inclusion on the academic performance of classmates without disabilities. *Remedial and Special Education, 15,* 281–287.

Stainback, S., & Stainback, W. (1992a). *Curriculum considerations in inclusive classrooms: Facilitating learning for all students.* Baltimore: Paul H. Brookes Publishing Co.

Stainback, S., & Stainback, W. (1992b). Introduction. In J. Pearpoint, M. Forest, & J. Snow (Eds.), *The Inclusion papers: Strategies to make inclusion work.* Toronto: Inclusion Press.

Stainback, W., & Stainback, S. (1990). *Support networks for inclusive schooling: Interdependent integrated education.* Baltimore: Paul H. Brookes Publishing Co.

Terry, W. (1993, February 14). Making things better for somebody. *The Washington Post, PARADE,* pp. 4–5.

Tessier-Switlick, D. (1991). *Concept paper: The delivery of special education services in the least restrictive environment.* Unpublished manuscript. Montgomery County Public Schools, MD.

Thousand, J. (1991, November). Organizational and structural change strategies for inclusive schools. Lecture given at Johns Hopkins University, Rockville, MD.

Thousand, J. S., & Villa, R. A. (1989). Enhancing success in heterogeneous schools. In S. Stainback, W. Stainback, & M. Forest (Eds.), *Educating all students in the mainstream of regular education* (pp. 89–103). Baltimore: Paul H. Brookes Publishing Co.

Turnbull, H. R. (1990). *Free appropriate public education: The law and children with disabilities.* Denver: Love Publishing Co.

Van Dover, T. (1995). *A principal's guide to creating a building climate for inclusion.* Manhattan, KS: The Master Teacher.

Villa, R. A., Thousand, J. S., Stainback, W., & Stainback, S. (1992). *Restructuring for caring and effective education: An administrative guide to creating heterogeneous schools.* Baltimore: Paul H. Brookes Publishing Co.

Wagner, M. (1989). Youth with disabilities during transition: An overview and description of findings from the national longitudinal transition study. In J. Chadsey-Rusch (Ed.), *Transition Institute at Illinois: Project Directors 4th annual meeting* (pp. 24–52). Champaign: University of Illinois.

Will, M. (1986). *Educating children with learning problems: A shared responsibility.* Washington, DC: Office of Special Education and Rehabilitative Services, U.S. Department of Education.

Willis, S. (1994, October). Making schools more inclusive. *Curriculum Update,* Association for Supervision and Curriculum Development (ASCD), 1–8.

Working Forum on Inclusive Schools. (1994). *Creating schools for all our students.* Reston, VA: The Council for Exceptional Children.

Yell, M. S. (1995). Least restrictive environment, inclusion, and students with disabilities. *Journal of Special Education, 28,* 389–404.

York, J., & Vandercook, T. (1989). *Strategies for achieving an integrated education for middle school aged learners with severe disabilities.* Minneapolis: Institute on Community Integration.

C h a p t e r 2

Disability: Legalities and Labels

MARGARET E. KING-SEARS

◆ ADVANCE ORGANIZER ◆

This chapter describes the thirteen disability categories specified in federal legislation along with significant legal mandates. Litigation related to least restrictive environment issues that may influence current special education delivery systems are highlighted. A discussion of the use of the terms mainstreaming and inclusion is presented and are distinguished from the legislative mandate of least restrictive environment. The special education process is reported, and the changing nature of effective practices for students with disabilities is briefly characterized. Finally, the use of labels is depicted as they relate to positive images and meaningful outcomes for individuals who "have" those labels.

Memories of Susan Vaughan King

November 25, 1964 to October 28, 1971

What can I say about Susan? My heart is full of many poignant and wonderful memories of her short lifetime. What a wonderful thing God did when he gave Susan to us. As is often the case, sometimes we don't realize that we have been given a very special gift.

Author's note. Appreciation and acknowledgment is extended to the educators and parents who provided descriptions of youngsters with disabilities in this chapter: Janie Atkinson, Monica Folkins, Ann Ingram Gold, Mary King, Alison Levy, Melissa Reda Hamilton, and Debbie Stine.

At first I was sad because she had Downs syndrome. Our other children were great though and wiser than I. They accepted Susan as a precious little baby sister who was perfect in their eyes. Of course, they were right, and I soon learned from my children. Joseph was just as supportive as the children. Any worries we might have had about what the future would bring just seemed to fade away as we all loved and enjoyed our baby girl.

I shall always remember and appreciate what our pediatrician told me when I had some "what if..." questions about something in the future. He said, "By that time, you won't even think of her as retarded—she will just be Susan," and he was so right.

From Remembering *by Mary S. King, May 1993*

When disability areas first began receiving recognition in the United States during the late nineteenth and early twentieth century, the focus was on maintaining people who exhibited severe—and usually physical—disabilities and on protecting them from people and situations in the outside world (Halvorsen & Sailor, 1990). Institutionalization in large, depersonalized buildings was popular, and little regard was given to educating, either the people with disabilities or the outside world. Wolfensberger (1991) recalls that people with retardation were "despised" as late as the 1960s, and it was thought that mental retardation was "hopeless" and that institutionalization was the only rational "solution" for them.

The purpose of this chapter is to familiarize the reader with disability areas as found in the federal legislation and to discuss how legislation and litigation continue to shape the federal agenda for services for children and youth with disabilities. First, federal laws that have been influential are described. (The reader should note that the ways in which states and school districts have implemented those laws can vary.) Next, the disability areas that are specified in federal legislation are identified, and characteristics of students labeled with disabilities are presented. Litigation related to least restrictive environment issues is described to highlight how practices and guidelines are shaped by legal interpretations. The special education process used to determine eligibility for special education is described. Finally, the effects of labeling students with disabilities is discussed as well as the changing nature of "best practices" for instructing students with diverse learning needs.

Legal Precedents

Since 1975, federal legislation has required that students with disabilities receive a free and appropriate public education and be educated to the maximum extent appropriate with their nondisabled peers. Almost 5 million students with disabilities were served in U.S. schools during the 1992–1993 school year (United States Department of Education [USDOE], 1994). According to these data, the number of students being classified as having disabilities is increasing. Of these students, almost 24 percent are served in separate classes and over 5 percent are served in separate facilities (see Figure 2-1). Widespread implementation of inclusion programs will affect 3.2 million students with disabilities who are assigned to segregated special education classrooms (United States General Accounting Office [USGAO], April 1994b).

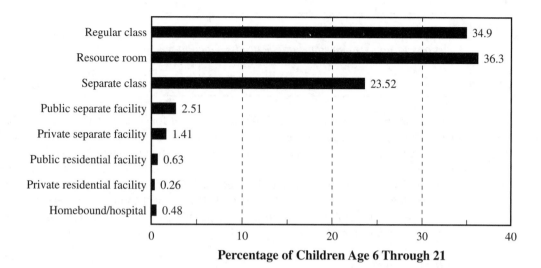

Source: *U.S. Dept. of Education, 16th Annual*
Rpt. on Disabilities Ed. Act, 1994

FIGURE 2-1 **Different educational environments for all disabilities during the 1991–1992 school year.**

Furthermore, the characteristics of school-aged students today are such that many students now qualify for some sort of specialized program, such as Chapter I, English as a Second Language, and Gifted and Talented. Even with a broad spectrum of specialized programs, some students who appear in need of supportive services are not eligible for these programs. Some of these students are the products of a multitude of societal and familial challenges: insufficient prenatal care, dysfunctional family environment, poverty, children arriving in the United States from countries where civil war has been occurring, gangs, and inner city violence (Children's Defense Fund, 1995; USGAO, April 1994a). Although the focus in this chapter is on disability, one underlying premise for inclusion is that students other than those with identified disabilities could benefit by specialized instruction (within general and special education), resources (e.g., counseling, therapy), and access to typical education environments that inclusive classes offer. The following section describes legislation that has guaranteed access to students with disabilities.

Legislation

Because federal legislation frequently guides the types of specialized programs found in public schools, examination of the federal requirements is a starting point for determining who is eligible for special education services and what procedures must be followed both in determining eligibility and in delivering services.

> *The term "special education" means specially designed instruction, at no cost to parents or guardians, to meet the unique needs of a child with a disability.*
>
> IDEA, 20 U.S.C., section 1401 (16)

The legislation that requires special education services for students who are eligible for those services had its beginnings before 1975, but the law that was signed in 1975 was the first to have substantial impact on education because of its requirements. This law is commonly referred to as Public Law 94-142, and it is considered landmark special education legislation. Two other legislations are described: PL 99-457 extended the age range to include children younger than 5 years old, and PL 101-476 is the most recent reauthorization of PL 94-142. The following describes each legislation individually, and then discusses the mandates within all of the laws.

Public Law 94-142

Signed by former President Gerald Ford, this law is titled the "The Education for All Handicapped Children Act of 1975." The law's influence is of significance because, although prior legislation had occurred, this law carried with it some requirements and guidelines that compelled states to provide education for *all* students with disabilities. Underwood and Mead (1995) note that only ten states mandated education for students with disabilities in 1970—3 million children with disabilities were *not* receiving an education. Cohen (1995) notes that 80 percent of all deaf children were educated in residential programs prior to PL 94-142. The requirements of PL 94-142 were more extensive than previous legislation had dictated. The following are some of the requirements:

- Procedures for referring children suspected of having a disability
- A team comprised of personnel from varied disciplines to determine eligibility
- Team development of an Individualized Education Program (IEP) transpires
- Specialized instruction and placement in an educational setting appropriate to the child's needs
- Procedures for parental notification and participation
- Time limits on how rapidly the eligibility/referral process happens
- Periodic reassessment of the student's eligibility
- Procedures for resolving disagreements/disputes

Public Law 99-457

Public Law 99-457 was signed in 1986 by former President Ronald Reagan, and its passage stressed the importance of early intervention with very young children. The age group of PL 94-142 was 5 to 21 years old, and this law extended the age group to include children from birth to age 5. Part B of IDEA provides children from ages 3 to 21 with a right to a free and appropriate education, while Part H provides incentives for working with infants and toddlers with disabilities (birth through age 2). An Individualized Family Service Plan, required in the legislation, emphasizes the critical nature and involvement of the family as well as the need for several agencies (typically referred to as "multidisciplinary interagency cooperation") to coordinate services to young children with disabilities. An Individualized Family Service Plan must contain:

> *(1) a statement of the infant's or toddler's present levels of physical development, cognitive development, language and speech development, psychosocial develop-ment, and self-help skills, based on acceptable objective criteria, (2) a statement of the family's strengths and needs relating to enhancing the development of the family's infant or toddler with a disability, (3) a statement of the major outcomes expected to be achieved for the infant or toddler and the family, and the criteria, procedures, and timelines used to determine the degree to which progress toward achieving the outcomes is being made and whether modifications or revisions of the outcomes or services are necessary, (4) a statement of specific early interven-tion services necessary to meet the unique needs of the infant or toddler and the family, including the frequency, intensity, and the method of delivering services, (5) the projected dates for initiation of services and the anticipated duration of such services, (6) the name of the case manager from the profession most immedi-ately relevant to the infant's or toddler's or family's needs who will be responsible for the implementation of the plan and coordination with other agencies and per-sons, and (7) the steps to be taken supporting the transition of the toddler with a disability to services provided under subchapter II of this chapter to the extent such services are considered appropriate (U.S.C., section 1477(d)(1–7)).*

Developmental delays can qualify a child for early intervention services without hav-ing to label a child with a particular disability. The amount of developmental delay is deter-mined by the multidisciplinary team (this is also influenced by how the particular state defines and describes developmental delay), and the idea of providing services without hav-ing to label a student is especially helpful for young children who appear in need of services and early intervention but in whom it may not be evident that the delay is due to a specific disability, such as learning disabilities. More severe disabilities, however, can be apparent early on (e.g., a child who has congenital physical disabilities).

Public Law 101-476

Signed by former President George Bush in 1990, this law is the most recent reauthoriza-tion of PL 94-142. The title of the law changed to "Individuals with Disabilities Education Act" and added two disability areas (autism and traumatic brain injury). One of the trade-marks of the reauthorized legislation is its reemphasis on least restrictive environment. Another emphasis in this law is transition services:

> *A coordinated set of activities for a student, designed within an outcome-oriented process, which promotes movement from school to post-school activities, including*

post-secondary education, vocational training, integrated employment (including supported employment), continuing education, adult services, independent living, or community participation (20 U.S.C., section 1401 (19)).

The reason for including an explicit statement about transition services was due to the dismal outcomes experienced by students with disabilities after they exited public schooling (Carson, Sitlington, & Frank, 1995; Sitlington & Frank, 1993). By explicitly including transition in the law, educators now must plan with students no later than when they are 16 years old about their future after public schooling. In many instances, this has resulted in schools working in partnership with future employers during the school years (e.g., determining natural supports in the work place, community-based work experiences).

Concepts taken directly from the law have become common language among educators, although their interpretation and operationalization in different schools and school systems can vary. The following section describes the primary concepts, using the language taken directly from the law and then elaborates on some aspects of each concept's meaning.

Free and Appropriate Public Education

It is interesting to note that the right to a free and appropriate public education for students with disabilities was not guaranteed until the mid-1970s. Prior to 1975, public schools in some locations educated students with some disabilities, but all students with disabilities were not provided education in public schools.

The term "free appropriate public education" means special education and related services that (A) have been provided at public expense, under public supervision and direction, and without charge, (B) meet the standards of the State educational agency, (C) include preschool, elementary, or secondary school education in the State involved, and (D) are provided in conformity with an individualized education program required under section 614(a)(5) (20 U.S.C., section 1401 (a)(18)).

The term that receives the most scrutiny in this concept is "appropriate." Osborne (1992) states that earlier court decisions on what "appropriate" meant were interpreted as "some" educational benefit for the student. However, more recently this has been clarified so that "some" is not synonymous with "trivial," and court decisions have been made in light of "meaningful" benefit. Osborne notes, again, the many possible interpretations of "meaningful" and that decisions continue to be made on a case-by-case basis.

Several states (e.g., North Carolina, Massachusetts, Michigan, and New Jersey) use language in their state statutes (that were designed to operationalize how the state would implement the federal legislation) that actually go beyond the intent of IDEA. Phrases such as "maximize the potential" (Massachusetts), "develop the maximum potential of the child" (Michigan), and "how the student can best achieve success in learning" (New Jersey) in state statutes have resulted in a higher standard for "appropriate" than required by federal legislation. Subsequently, court decisions are made in light of not only individual circumstances and characteristics of the student but also in light of current state guidelines.

Least Restrictive Environment

Fuchs and Fuchs (1994) state that least restrictive environment (LRE) must satisfy two criteria: (1) to provide students with disabilities an education appropriate to their unique learning needs and (2) do so in as close proximity as possible to normally developing, age-appropriate peers. There are multiple interpretations of what types of services and aids (e.g., instructional techniques, assistive technology, personnel support) need to be in place for a student to successfully function within a general education classroom. The LRE clause in the federal law states:

> *(1) That to the maximum extent appropriate, children with disabilities, including children in public or private institutions or other care facilities, are educated with children who are nondisabled; and*

> *(2) That special classes, separate schooling or other removal of children with disabilities from the regular educational environment occurs only when the nature or severity of the disability is such that education in regular classes with the use of supplementary aids and services cannot be achieved satisfactorily (20 U.S.C., section 300.550(b)(1)(2)).*

Underwood and Mead (1995) describe the LRE process as (1) developing an appropriate program as outlined in the IEP, (2) determining in which settings that program can be implemented, and (3) choosing the placement option that maximizes interaction with non-disabled peers. Yell (1995b) notes that school districts are increasingly being required to provide data to support their recommendation to move a student to a more restrictive environment. Statements that a general education classroom placement is inappropriate now need to be accompanied by proof that the school district has adequately explored that option for an individual student.

In previous years school districts may have contended that placement, for example, for a student with severe disabilities should be a special education classroom or school. That option was the only one considered available from the continuum of services at that time, in part because that option was the traditional, available choice for school districts and parents. Now, however, more options are available because advances in educational techniques have occurred (e.g., Forest & Lusthaus, 1989; Giangreco, Cloninger, & Iverson, 1993). These educational advances have, in reality, expanded the previously available continuum so that more of a student's education possibly can occur within a general education environment—the decisions and recommendations always are made in light of the individual student's characteristics. The types of supplementary aids and services used to promote and facilitate education in general education classrooms for students with a variety of disabilities remain pivotal and critical factors.

Maroney (1993), in describing ways to return students with emotional or behavioral disorders to the LRE, comments on the potential that the inclusion movement can have on expanding the placement options: "Whether each and every professional in special education adopts the philosophy of inclusion is not important. What is important is the fact that the inclusion movement will serve to open up many new doors within the LRE for all students with disabilities" (p. 30).

Individualized Education Program

The IEP is the written document that synthesizes the educational program necessary for the student to benefit from education. The intent of the IEP is to ensure suitable service by mandating individualized program planning and parental involvement. This is accomplished via the IEP conference among school personnel, the parents, and sometimes the student:

> *The term "individualized education program" means a written statement for each child with a disability developed in any meeting by a representative of the local education agency or an intermediate educational unit who shall be qualified to provide, or supervise the provision of, specially designed instruction to meet the unique needs of children with disabilities, the teacher, the parents or guardian of such child, and whenever appropriate, such child, which statement shall include: (A) a statement of the present levels of educational performance of such child, (B) a statement of annual goals, including short-term instructional objectives, (C) a statement of the specific educational services to be provided to such child, and the extent to which such child will be able to participate in regular educational programs, (D) a statement of the needed transition services for students beginning no later than age 16 and annually thereafter (and, when determined appropriate for the individual, beginning at age 14 or younger), including, when appropriate, a statement of the interagency responsibilities or linkages (or both) before the student leaves the school setting, (E) the projected date for initiation and anticipated duration of such services, (F) appropriate objective criteria and evaluation procedures and schedules for determining, on at least an annual basis, whether instructional objectives are being achieved (20 U.S.C., section 1401 (20)).*

Individuals who must be in attendance at an IEP meeting include a representative of the public agency (e.g., the school), the student's teacher, one or both of the student's parents, the student (when appropriate, especially at age 16 when transition plans are being developed), and other individuals at the discretion of the parent or agency (e.g., parents may bring a friend, the agency may invite other people who have evaluated the student). Parent involvement and participation includes sufficient notice about when and where the meeting will be held. Some school systems have developed procedures to more actively involve parents prior to the IEP meeting by discussing possible IEP content via telephone conversations or written information sent home. In the event parents are not present at the IEP meeting, schools must have detailed documentation that sufficient and multiple efforts were made to involve the parents.

The IEP represents a time-consuming process for school personnel, and the merits of the process often are not perceived as outweighing the amount of time and effort used each year to develop an IEP. Some educators state that a less bureaucratic process would allow them to spend more quality time on implementing interventions with students. The required components of an IEP include the following:

- Present level of performance
- Long-term goals and short-term objectives
- Amount of time (typically written as a percentage) in general education

- Initiation date and duration of services
- Evaluation procedures
- Transition services (for students age 16 and older)

Students are required to participate in their IEP when transition services are addressed (by age 16), and if they do not participate then the school needs to document how the student's needs and preferences are addressed in the IEP. Frequently, however, students will need preparation in order to meaningfully contribute information to their IEP. For example, Van Reusen, Deshler, and Schumaker (1989) taught secondary students with learning disabilities a strategy to promote their participation in their IEP conference. Students were taught to identify and inventory their individual learning strengths and weaknesses, advocate for their perceived needs, ask relevant questions, provide appropriate responses to questions, and verbally summarize their understanding of the IEP goals during the IEP conference (refer to Chapter 11 for more information on teaching this strategy). Students who were taught how to accomplish these behaviors contributed significantly more relevant and positive statements during their IEP conference. The voices of many people should be heard on the IEP document, and when that happens, a more useful and meaningful implementation of the student's instructional program can result.

The IEP document is a more useful tool when the following events occur:

- Students are involved in the development and implementation of the goals and objectives (refer to Chapter 6 for ways to involve students in monitoring their performance)
- Peers of students who have severe disabilities take part and contribute information about how to include their peer in class situations, age-appropriate social circumstances, etc.
- Families are actively involved in the IEP formation and enactment
- General educators participate in determining the IEP content

Due Process

Parents and school system personnel need to be able to resolve issues when disagreements occur. The due process requirements of IDEA provide avenues for either party to appeal the decision(s) made at meetings. Goldberg and Kuriloff (1991) note that these requirements provide parents a means for objecting to the educational classification, program, or placement that schools offer their children. Among the information available are the right to (1) receive adequate notice of meetings, (2) examine school records about their child, (3) representation, (4) call and cross examine witnesses, (5) be heard by an impartial hearing officer, and (6) appeal adverse decisions. The primary reasons that due process disputes are instigated relate to identification, evaluation, placement, the components of a free and appropriate public education, and related services (Underwood & Mead, 1995).

Because the due process time frame is lengthy and can evoke considerable emotion among the parties who eventually must work together in some capacity, most school systems and families make significant efforts to resolve differences prior to due process procedures. When those differences cannot be resolved, then due process procedures can be instigated by either party. In the next section, distinctions are made for the terms used to describe the least restrictive environment.

Mainstreaming and Inclusion

In spite of the absence of the terms "mainstreaming" and "inclusion" in IDEA, these words have become the educational jargon for interpreting what's meant by the phrase that is in the laws—"least restrictive environment." Yell (1995a) notes that the terms "mainstreaming" and "inclusion" and "LRE" are often inaccurately used interchangeably. He distinguishes the three by reminding that LRE references the legislative IDEA mandate to educate students with disabilities to the maximum extent appropriate with students who do not have disabilities, while mainstreaming and inclusion are the educational terms that refer to placement of students with disabilities in the general education classroom.

Taylor (1988) refers to the principle of LRE as a policy that actually legitimates the existence of segregated environments for students, especially those with severe developmental disabilities. He recounts several "pitfalls" in the LRE principle—among the pitfalls is that LRE is based on a readiness model. "Implicit in LRE is the assumption that people with developmental disabilities must earn the right to move to the least restrictive environment. In other words, the person must 'get ready' or 'be prepared' to live, work, or go to school in integrated settings...." (p. 46). Taylor maintains that a commitment to inclusion requires movement in a direction that focuses on services, not placements. Table 2-1 displays traditional versus futuristic thinking about inclusion.

TABLE 2-1   From the past toward the future of inclusive communities.

From	To
developing facilities and programs into which people must fit...	providing services and supports necessary for people to participate fully in community life.
professional judgment as a basis for determining community involvement...	personal choice.
a presumption in favor of inclusion...	a mandate to provide opportunities for inclusion.
a conditional ("to the extent necessary, appropriate, feasible")...	an unconditional commitment to inclusion.
requiring individuals to change in order to participate in the community...	requiring service systems to change.
disability labels as a factor in determining community participation...	a recognition of common human needs.
placing people in the community...	helping people become part of the community.

Source: Constructed from information in Taylor, S. J. (1988). Caught in the continuum: A critical analysis of the principle of the least restrictive environment. *Journal of the Association for Persons with Severe Handicaps, 13,* p. 51.

Mainstreaming was the educational terminology used when PL 94-142 was first passed in 1975, and so it is an older educational term than inclusion. Mainstreaming has traditionally been interpreted as meaning that students with disabilities are returned to general education classrooms when they are ready to do the same work as the rest of the students in the classroom. Several terms and definitions from the professional literature that describe and interpret LRE are shown in Table 2-2. Note that some authors reference particular disability areas, but that commonalities exist among all of the definitions (e.g., explicit references to the amount of collaboration needed among educators and families).

The "readiness" viewpoint traditionally associated with mainstreaming is the perspective that is most deemphasized when inclusion (the more recent term, and one that asserts the difference from mainstreaming) becomes the terminology. Always, adaptations and accommodations have been incorporated into the mainstreaming effort, but typically with the expectation that when students could not accomplish general education curriculum then

TABLE 2-2   Definitions and interpretations of least restrictive environment.

Integration for students with severe disabilities:
. . . programs which provide all needed special education and related services (as outlined in each student's IEP), while educating students with severe disabilities within "regular" school buildings. Integration implies more than just physical presence within regular schools and includes (a) active participation with chronologically age-appropriate regular education classes and (b) the systematic use of any adaptive or support strategies needed to achieve mutually satisfying and ongoing relationships with nondisabled peers. . . . Successful integration requires the use of team approaches which include regular and special educators, parents, relevant therapists or other specialists, and important community contacts (McDonnell & Hardman, 1989, p. 68).

Inclusive education for students with emotional or behavioral disorders:
The provision of free services, with nondisabled age-mates, in neighborhood schools, in general education classes, under the guidance of general education teachers, with the assistance of special education staff and resources, to the full extent possible, as determined appropriate by an individualized education planning committee (Price, 1993, p. 25).

Mainstreaming:
. . . the carefully planned and monitored placement of students with disabilities into regular education classrooms for the majority of their academic and social educational program. The academic program within the regular education classroom should be adapted to address the instructional needs of the mainstreamed student, and the social program should be designed so that the mainstreamed student is assimilated into the social climate of the class and accepted by nonhandicapped peers. While the primary responsibility for the mainstreamed student's academic and social program lies with the regular classroom teacher, mainstreaming is a dynamic, on-going process that requires communication and sharing information between regular and special educators, ancillary support personnel and parents (Salend, 1990, p. 10).

Mainstreaming:
. . . the temporal, instructional, and social integration of eligible exceptional children with normal peers based on an ongoing, individually determined, educational planning process, and requires clarification of responsibility among regular and special education administrative, instructional and support personnel (Kaufman, Gottlieb, Agard, & Kukic, 1975, p. 35).

more specialized services, usually in another classroom, would become the appropriate service delivery option. For example, adaptations that might enable a person with learning disabilities to do the same work as the other students are (1) to work on the identical math concepts, but to work a fewer number of problems, (2) to listen to a tape recording of a text instead of reading the text, (3) to take a test that is read to them versus having to read it and respond to the questions, or (4) teach the student a test-taking strategy.

These adaptations are also appropriate for inclusive classrooms, but one extension for inclusive classrooms is that all students in the general education classroom may not be working on the same content or curriculum. In this way, students with a range of disabilities (e.g., a student with the label of moderate mental retardation may be working on functional life skills such as interacting appropriately with peers) are included in general education classrooms, and the work within general education classrooms is developed around student needs. That is, the overriding philosophy is that every student, regardless of diverse abilities, belongs to that community of third graders, or seventh graders, or English class students.

Another important distinction between mainstreaming and inclusion is the question of which educator—general or special—has the primary responsibility for a student's educational programming and progress. With mainstreaming, a student might receive his or her entire academic instruction in a separate special education classroom, but participate in some specific activities within the general education classroom. Primary responsibility rests with the special education teacher who is designated by disability certification (e.g., learning disability teacher). However, inclusive programming places the primary responsibility with the general education teacher who is accountable for the education of all of his or her students. An important condition exists: This teacher needs adequate support to make education work for *everyone* in the class (USGAO, April 1994b).

An inclusive philosophy is one that supports all students belonging to their grade level community and celebrates the differences that make up that community. Instruction is tailored to students' individual needs. Educators work in tandem to meet those needs, and students (both those with and without disabilities) are active participants in the learning and teaching.

Disability Labels

Thirteen disability areas are authorized to receive services under IDEA. These categories are the following:

- Autism (added in 1990)
- Deaf-blindness
- Deafness
- Hearing impairment
- Mental retardation
- Multiple disabilities
- Orthopedic impairment

- Other health impairment
- Serious emotional disturbance
- Specific learning disability
- Speech or language impairment
- Traumatic brain injury (added in 1990)
- Visual impairment (including blindness)

The following sections identify each disability individually by quoting the definitions from IDEA. Descriptions of students labeled in some disability areas are provided; however, due to the heterogeneity of student characteristics within each disability area, the reader is reminded that descriptions portrayed here do not necessarily represent all students of that respective disability category. Each state decides its labels based on the definitions and guidelines provided in IDEA (that is, labels, terminology, and descriptors can vary from state to state *and* within a state). Figure 2-2 displays a numerical account of students served in each disability area.

Autism

"Autism" means a developmental disability significantly affecting verbal and nonverbal communication and social interaction, generally evident before age 3, that adversely affects a child's educational performance. Other characteristics

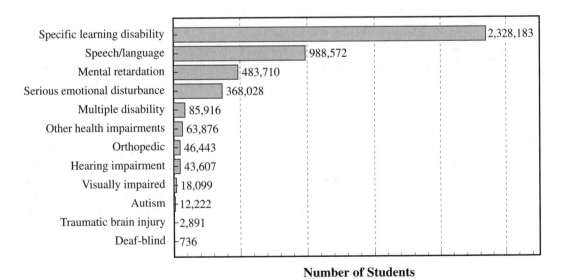

Number of Students

FIGURE 2-2 **Numbers of students (age 6–21) with disabilities served in each disability area.**

Source: U.S. Department of Education, *16th Annual Report on Disabilities Education Act,* 1994.

often associated with autism are engagement in repetitive activities and stereo-typed movements, resistance to environmental change or change in daily routines, and unusual responses to sensory experiences. The term does not apply if a child's educational performance is adversely affected primarily because the child has a serious emotional disturbance (20 U.S.C., section 300.7(b)(1)).

Characteristics of students with autism include difficulty responding to complex stimuli, behavioral responses (such as repetitive hand motions) that appear to be the result of sensory deprivation, inconsistent responses to previously mastered information, and poor interaction skills (Burke, 1991). Myles, Simpson, and Becker (1994) note that although there is agreement that autism is characterized by learning problems, social interactional deficits, language impairment, and response pattern aberrations, there is emerging within autism a higher-functioning autistic disorder that may be considered more of a mild disability (versus a severe disability characterized by extreme behaviors).

Individuals with autism can display unique strengths and weaknesses, as in the case of Andrew. Andrew, 12 years old, can make change from a $20 bill within a few seconds, and he can repeat almost any commercial he hears verbatim and with appropriate intonations. His interaction with other people is limited to inconsistency following directions and few, if any, initiations to socialize. The enigma is how he learns some information at such high (although not always functional) levels—information that has not been taught—and then he has difficulty remembering or using functional academic and social skills that are taught.

Deaf-Blindness

"Deaf-blindness" means concomitant hearing and visual impairments, the combination of which causes severe communication and other developmental and educational problems that they cannot be accommodated in special education programs solely for children with deafness or children with blindness (20 U.S.C., section 300.7(b)(2)).

Students with deaf-blindness comprise a small portion of the population, but they have a large number of needs related to their disabilities. Everson and McNulty (1995) note the difficulty in determining an exact number of students with deaf-blindness because some students may be categorized under a different label such as multiple disabilities, or students may be categorized under their primary sensory deficit (e.g., deafness). Educational programs emphasize orientation and mobility training, sign language for communication, and other nonvisual communication skills.

Deafness

"Deafness" means a hearing impairment that is so severe that the child is impaired in processing linguistic information through hearing, with or without amplification, that adversely affects a child's educational performance (20 U.S.C., section 300.7(b)(3)).

People who are deaf have a hearing disability that is so severe that, even with hearing aids, little useful hearing is available. Although sounds can be heard, hearing cannot be used as a primary way to gain information. The major method of communication is visual and includes lip reading as well as varied forms of sign(ed) language (e.g., finger-spelling, American Sign Language). Although medical science has designed powerful instruments for bringing sounds of the outside world to people who are hard of hearing or profoundly deaf, some individuals who are deaf feel they have established their identity as a deaf person (and *not* as a person who is in any way disabled by being deaf) and are most comfortable interacting within the deaf community.

Charles, who is now in middle school, spent his first several grades in a special school for the deaf. Unfortunately, the methods used at this school were not working well because Charles also had learning disabilities and he was not progressing in a first grade curriculum *and* classroom. Although many schools for the deaf do provide quality education for students, this was not one of them. Charles' mother, discouraged by his frustration and lack of progress, removed Charles from the deaf school and enrolled him in a public school. In the public school he was placed in an age-appropriate fifth grade classroom with assistance from a special education teacher. He also had a full-time sign language interpreter.

His homeroom teacher and his peers learned sign language so that they could communicate with him. Initially his peers felt awkward when talking through the interpreter (they looked and talked to her instead of Charles), but they soon felt comfortable enough to look and talk directly to Charles. He also spent some time with first graders teaching them sign language, too—it was a rewarding year for everyone. At the end of the year, his elementary school teachers did their best to prepare him and his sixth grade teachers for the transition to middle school. However, things did not go well; his mother transferred him back to the school for the deaf during sixth grade.

Another student who is deaf is six-year-old Daniel, who lost his hearing when he was about 15 months old due to a virus. Prior to the virus he was developing normally and using emerging language skills. His mother was not aware that Daniel was not hearing until he turned up the television volume extremely loud one day. Once he was diagnosed as deaf, his parents read much literature about deafness and decided to immerse themselves into the deaf culture. Daniel began learning sign language right away and attended a school for the deaf. Today he is an intelligent first grade student who has an incredible vocabulary and can read above grade level.

Hearing Impairment

"Hearing impairment" means an impairment in hearing, whether permanent or fluctuating, that adversely affects a child's educational performance but that is not included under the definition of deafness in this section (20 U.S.C. 300.7(b)(4)).

People who have hearing impairments typically can process information from sound, usually with the help of a hearing aid. Most students with hearing impairments have mild to moderate hearing loss. The National Institute on Deafness and Other Communication Disorders reports that 28 million Americans have some difficulty hearing. Estimates are that 80 percent of the difficulties cannot be corrected, though they can be improved.

Students who are hard of hearing may not hear certain ranges of sounds. For example, Ally is a seven-year-old student who does not hear lower tones well so that hearing male voice ranges is more difficult for her. Although she is progressing well in school, her parents are concerned that she is missing some of the conversation in classes and that her grades of B and C could improve if she had all of her hearing. Moreover, Ally has become a passive student who admittedly needs assistance with study skills and strategies. She is reluctant to ask questions in class because she does not know if she is repeating a question that has already been asked. Classwide discussions are also difficult for her because she's not sure she's hearing all of the discussion. When listening to class presentations, a "mental rewind" occurs for Ally that involves silently repeating the verbalizations while trying to "fill-in-the-blanks" with what terms or vocabulary might fit for what has not been heard, or understood. Teachers who pause occasionally, repeat major points, or reexplain (or rephrase) information are helpful. Using a semicircle or circle seating arrangement during discussions also is helpful as are outlines to help structure the presentation of information heard.

Mental Retardation

> *"Mental retardation" means significantly subaverage general intellectual functioning existing concurrently with deficits in adaptive behavior and manifested during the developmental period that adversely affects a child's educational performance (20 U.S.C., section 300.7(b)(5)).*

The American Association of Mental Deficiency criteria used to classify students with mental retardation states that IQ (intelligence quotient) levels of 55 to 69 constitute mild retardation and IQ levels of 40 to 54, moderate mental retardation. Individuals are typically characterized by their consistent low scores across achievement areas, which appear to be commensurate with their IQ. Another measure used in the diagnosis of mental retardation is adaptive behavior measures. The proficiency with which an individual responds to his or her environment appropriately and is able to take care of self are indicators of the level of developmental delay.

Severe or profound mental retardation typically exists as a combination of cognitive low functioning and physical impairments. For example, it is not unusual for a child with severe mental retardation to have a "tested IQ" of 24 (quotes used because assessment may not be valid) and several physical problems such as cerebral palsy and/or paralysis.

Although the IQ is universally used and referred to as a means of gauging, or predicting, one's potential, it must be noted that a student's performance on an IQ test is simply a numerical indicator of his or her performance on that test on that day. That is not to say that a child may test with a 25 IQ one day and may test with a 117 the next day; it is to say that people may have more potential, or in different areas, than might be tested on any given IQ test. For example, Susan is a six-year-old who has Downs syndrome and has a tested IQ of 54, placing her in the moderate mental retardation range. She is learning sight word vocabulary and learning to perform basic math computations. In a first grade classroom, she is able to keep up with the range of her peer's functioning in many, although not all, academic areas. Her potential, according to the IQ test results, would not indicate the performance that she is exhibiting in her classroom, which is due to the collaboration among her special education teacher, speech/language pathologist, general education teacher, and family. Nor do those results include her friendly nature, sensitivity toward her classmates, and willingness to please her teacher. Although written reports on students can provide much information, educators must also be prepared to look beyond the percentiles and stanines and standard scores to find the person they will teach.

Multiple Disabilities

"Multiple disabilities" means concomitant impairments (such as mental retardation-blindness, mental retardation-orthopedic impairment, etc.), the combination of which causes such severe educational problems that they cannot be accommodated in special education programs solely for one of the impairments. The term does not include deaf-blindness (20 U.S.C., section 300.7(b)(6)).

Individuals who have multiple disabilities make up almost 2 percent of the total special education population. Etiologies for these individuals can range from birth trauma to unknown causes. Medical technology that exists today can contribute to the numbers of people with severe or profound disabilities who attend school because those infants in the past who did not live now have more opportunity to survive.

Kirk is a seven-year-old who has spastic cerebral palsy and severe mental retardation. He uses eye gaze to communicate and is learning to use a "spinner" with pictures on it that he can control with head movements. In this way he is able to communicate his choices (e.g., what he wants to do for play, what he wants to eat) and responses (to academic questions such as what the weather is like). His attention span is unusually long as indicated by his interest in watching movies and television programs for a sustained amount of time. Kirk enjoys a range of music, from the Dave Clark Five to Tom Petty! His teachers and family continue trying different methods of communicating with him and facilitating his communication; due to his physical abilities, it is difficult to say with certainty how much he knows and feels that he cannot yet express.

Orthopedic Impairment

"Orthopedic impairment" means a severe orthopedic impairment that adversely affects a child's educational performance. The term includes impairments caused by congenital anomaly (e.g., clubfoot, absence of some member, etc.), impairments caused by disease (e.g., poliomyelitis, bone tuberculosis, etc.), and impairments from other causes (e.g., cerebral palsy, amputations, and fractures or burns that cause contractures) (20 U.S.C., section 300.7(b)(7)).

Multiple aspects of students with orthopedic impairments link directly to medical conditions. Although students may possess an orthopedic disability, it does not always result in a handicapping condition except when the educational performance of the student is affected adversely.

Other Health Impairment

> *"Other health impairment" means having limited strength, vitality, or alertness, due to chronic or acute health problems such as a heart condition, tuberculosis, rheumatic fever, nephritis, asthma, sickle cell anemia, hemophilia, epilepsy, lead poisoning, leukemia, or diabetes that adversely affects a child's educational performance (20 U.S.C., section 300.7(b)(8)).*

Note that unless a student's education performance is impacted in a negative way due to the health problem, a student may not be eligible for special education services. In actuality, a number of students have health problems that do not adversely affect their educational performance. Those students who do have their performance negatively affected typically have the ability to achieve as much as their peers. Their difficulties may be the amount of school they miss (due to hospitalization, illness) and how they feel when they are in school.

Lynch, Lewis, and Murphy (1993) report that educational services for students with chronic illnesses are now being delivered to students whose conditions, prior to advances in medical technology, were terminal ones. For example, transplant organs and advanced treatments now provide life for children with severe heart, liver, and kidney problems. As many as 100,000 infants and children now rely on technology, as well, to moderate their health problems, resulting in students who are "medically fragile" or "technology dependent."

Serious Emotional Disturbance

> *"Serious emotional disturbance" is defined as follows:*
>
> (i) *The term means a condition exhibiting one or more of the following characteristics over a long period of time and to a marked degree that adversely affects a child's educational performance—*
>
> A. *An inability to learn that cannot be explained by intellectual, sensory, or health factors;*
>
> B. *An inability to build or maintain satisfactory interpersonal relationships with peers and teachers;*
>
> C. *Inappropriate types of behavior or feelings under normal circumstances;*
>
> D. *A general pervasive mood of unhappiness or depression; or*
>
> E. *A tendency to develop physical symptoms or fears associated with personal or school problems.*
>
> (ii) *The term includes schizophrenia. The terms does not apply to children who are socially maladjusted, unless it is determined that they have a serious emotional disturbance (20 U.S.C., section 300.7(b)(9)).*

Schools respond to a wide variety of individual needs for students with serious emotional disturbance (SED), and the range of responses needs to encompass more than what schools typically offer or have available. Individuals with serious emotional disturbance require complex patterns of service delivery that frequently involve, or needs to involve, services from other disciplines and agencies (e.g., social services, mental health care). Outcomes to date for these students are more dismal than those reported for other students with disabilities. More students with severe emotional disturbance, than for any other disability area, are likely to (USDOE, 1994)

- have lower grades
- fail more courses
- dropout
- be educated outside of their local schools
- be from lower socioeconomic backgrounds
- encounter activity with the juvenile justice system

> *School districts frequently have SED classrooms where only students labeled seriously emotionally disturbed are placed.*
>
> Lewis, Chard, & Scott, 1994

Successful interventions for students with serious emotional disturbance include interpersonal problem-solving skills, social skills training, and structured behavior management programs. One student, Jason, is fifteen-years-old and has been raised for the past seven years by a variety of foster families. Some of his behaviors include becoming extremely upset when the order of the day is changed, or when expected, anticipated events do not occur. For example, when a scheduled field trip is missed because of a school cancellation due to weather conditions (snow day), Jason reacted the following school day with extreme disappointment and anger at missing the anticipated field trip. How to appropriately deal with frustration is one of the IEP goals for him, and the goals include explicit instruction in alternative and appropriate ways to express anger.

Specific Learning Disability

"Specific learning disability" means a disorder in one or more of the basic psychological processes involved in understanding or in using language, spoken or written, that may manifest itself in an imperfect ability to listen, think, speak, read, write, spell, or to do mathematical calculations. The term includes such conditions as perceptual disabilities, brain injury, minimal brain dysfunction, dyslexia, and developmental aphasia. The term does not apply to children who have learning problems that are primarily the result of visual, hearing, or motor disabilities, of mental retardation, or emotional disturbance, or of environmental, cultural, or economic disadvantage (20 U.S.C., section 300.7(b)(10)).

Specific learning disabilities as an educational term was first used in 1963. Prior to this time, individuals with learning disabilities posed a paradox for educators and parents because their primary characteristic was their ability to appear capable of accomplishing school tasks. Learning disability is the largest—and the largest growing—of all disability areas, with almost 52 percent of students who receive special education services falling into this category.

Characteristics include average to above average cognitive potential, yet a discrepancy between what an individual is deemed capable of doing and his or her actual achievement. People with learning disabilities represent a wide range of abilities. For example, Bobby is a seventh grader and the star of the school's track team, and he reads at a second grade reading level. He is a popular student who works very hard in his academic classes to keep up with the content, even when reading is so difficult for him. Most students with learning disabilities do have problems with reading, with reversals in letters while reading being a common error pattern. Benji, however, is another middle school student who reads and comprehends above his grade level. His learning disability is in math computations, and so his educational program focuses on techniques and strategies to develop proficiency in this area.

Speech or Language Impairment

> *"Speech or language impairment" means a communication disorder such as stuttering, impaired articulation, a language impairment, or a voice impairment that adversely affects a child's educational performance (20 U.S.C., section 300.7(b)(11)).*

Most students eligible for speech/language services also have another disability as their "primary handicapping condition." Almost 23 percent of the special education population receive some type of speech/language therapy. Speech impairments typically include mechanical areas such as voice (vocal quality, pitch, loudness, resonance, or duration), fluency (flow, rate, or rhythm of verbal expression), and articulation (atypical production of sounds). Language impairments include problems in the use of language (social contexts), content (understand or express words, sentences), and form of language use (rules for word sounds, meanings, sequence).

Rob is a twelve-year-old student who is now progressing very well in school, but his preschool years were quite distressing for him and his family. He did not talk by the time he was four years old, except words like "no," "Mom," and "come on." When initially examined by a multidisciplinary team, the prognosis was not optimistic: his mother was told he was moderately mentally retarded. However, when examined by a second multidisciplinary (e.g., speech/language, educational diagnostician, pediatric-neurologist) team one year later in a different location, the consensus was that intensive speech/language therapy was warranted. The therapy, along with attendance at a typical preschool where he was exposed to peers who provided age-appropriate language models for him, resulted in the boost he needed to continue with more "normal" language and cognitive development patterns. Although some academic areas (e.g., math) continue to be challenging for Rob, his development and academic accomplishments are well within normal ranges today. In fact, his family sometimes jokes that his pre-adolescent behavior makes them long for the days when he did not talk!

Traumatic Brain Injury

"Traumatic brain injury" means an acquired injury to the brain caused by an external physical force, resulting in total or partial functional disability or psychosocial impairment, or both, that adversely affects a child's educational performance. The term applies to open or closed head injuries resulting in impairments in one or more areas, such as cognition, language, memory, attention, reasoning, abstract thinking, judgment, problem solving, sensory, perceptual, and motor abilities, psychosocial behavior, physical functions, information processing, and speech. The term does not apply to brain injuries that are congenital or degenerative, or brain injuries induced by birth trauma (20 U.S.C., section 300.7(b)(12)).

Traumatic brain injury is severe trauma to the head that results in persistent physical and cognitive impairments. The National Head Injury Foundation reports that nearly 100,000 people are disabled permanently due to brain injury; 30,000 of them are children, yet according to IDEA data less than 10 percent of that number (2,891) qualify for special education services (refer to Figure 2-2). The most frequent causes of traumatic brain injury are motor vehicle accidents and abuse. Other causes include falling down stairs or out of windows, or off horses, bicycles, or chairs.

One fifth grade student lost her short-term memory after being involved in a traffic accident. She was at a special education school for a year, and then she went to a general education school with special education resource within the classroom. Her teacher at the special school comments that traumatic brain injury primarily affects boys, aged 8 to 15, and the primary causes are when children are on bicycles or they are pedestrians hit by a car. Emerging causes include gunshot wounds.

Another student was intellectually gifted and quite athletic prior to an accident in which he was hit by a truck. He was in a coma for two months, and his left arm was severely contracted. He "dragged" the left side of his body while working, which made him appear clumsy. Luckily he retained a great sense of humor. His brain injury resulted in poor organizational skills, and he would forget directions that he had just heard. For example, he would receive directions and walk to the other side of the classroom to carry them out, and in that amount of time he had forgotten what the directions were. Helpful accommodations for him were charts with steps to carry out (such as self-monitoring, described in Chapter 12) and cues for directions he needed to follow.

Visual Impairment (Including Blindness)

"Visual impairment including blindness" means an impairment in vision that, even with correction, adversely affects a child's educational performance. The term includes both partial sight and blindness (20 U.S.C., section 300.7(b)(13)).

Individuals with visual disabilities usually have some sight, although the amount is not typically functional without some type of assistive-correction. Students who are blind usually have little to no usable vision but can frequently communicate well when given accommodations and technology.

Eligibility for Special Education Services

The definitions of the disability areas are especially important because a student must be considered "eligible" according to each state's criteria and definition for receiving special education services. Additionally, although the federal definitions guide states in their definitions, each state may determine its own definition and must decide what types of procedures, assessments, and characteristics students exhibit to meet that state's guidelines. For example, students who meet the criteria for specific learning disabilities in one state may not meet the criteria in another state (Mercer, King-Sears, & Mercer, 1990). In addition to the variation of definitions across states, there is also variation both within a state and within school systems in a state. There is considerable subjective judgment involved in determining a student's eligibility for special education services: teacher input and tolerance, types of tests used, interpretation of guidelines, the quality of interventions used prior to referral to alleviate the areas of concern, and consensus of each of these areas according to the school team's decision. Furthermore, although the types of services and programs available are not legally nor technically supposed to enter into the eligibility decisions, the fact is that the free and appropriate education guaranteed by the law does not require that the best education and the most resources are available. A few states, however, do use language in their state legislations that require "best" or "to the maximum extent possible" progress for student with disabilities.

This section describes the general procedures used by schools to determine if a student is eligible for special education services (see Table 2-3 for a sequence of events). When an educator first realizes that a student is experiencing difficulties achieving and/or behaving like the "typical" student in their classroom, then those concerns can be addressed in several ways. Note that some students may enter public schools already identified as having a disability (i.e., via early intervention programs).

Prior to referring a child to the school team that meets regularly to discuss students who may be eligible for special education, teachers may try interventions on their own. Teacher Assistance Teams often assist in this process (Chalfant & Pysh, 1989; Fuchs et al., 1990). These teams provide teachers with an "in-school assistance" network, and sometimes problems can be resolved at this level. If, however, the problem is not resolved then a formal referral to the school team is appropriate. Reasons for referral can include concerns about academic progress, behavior, or physical limitations.

First, a teacher or parent notes that something is amiss for a child's achievement in the general education classroom. After efforts have been made to resolve area(s) of concern in the classroom (efforts vary), then a teacher who suspects a disability may refer the child to the school's assessment team. At a team meeting, the teacher presents information about the problem area, intervention methods tried thus far and the results of those efforts, and parent communication. Further questioning and discussion occur so that the problem is accurately—or more fully—identified, and if the team suspects that the student may have a disability then parent permission is secured so that a formal assessment may occur. (Some school teams may decide to first conduct a screening assessment to assist them in getting a more global picture of the student's overall functioning. Also, school teams require that a student's hearing and vision is screened to eliminate concerns that could be

TABLE 2-3   Sequence of events when a student becomes eligible for special education.

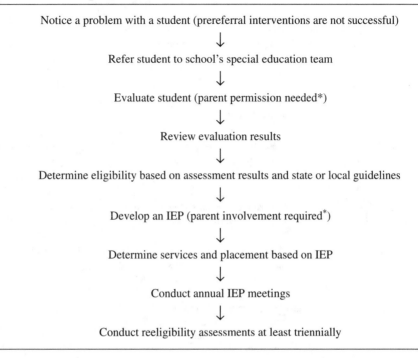

Notice a problem with a student (prereferral interventions are not successful)

↓

Refer student to school's special education team

↓

Evaluate student (parent permission needed*)

↓

Review evaluation results

↓

Determine eligibility based on assessment results and state or local guidelines

↓

Develop an IEP (parent involvement required*)

↓

Determine services and placement based on IEP

↓

Conduct annual IEP meetings

↓

Conduct reeligibility assessments at least triennially

*Parent involvement and permission can, and should, occur throughout this process.

ameliorated with glasses, health issues, etc.) The assessment tests given are dependent on the identified problem (see Table 2-4 for examples of assessments). For example, if speech/language development is the issue then these types of assessments are given. A student suspected of having a learning disability will receive an intelligence test and achievement tests. A student suspected of having serious emotional disturbance would receive assessments that focused on interpersonal skill functioning. Typically, the use of teacher and parent rating scales, observational techniques, and interviews with a variety of people who know the child well are used to corroborate or complement more formal assessments.

Assessment results are matched to the eligibility criteria for that disability area. Other factors such as parent and teacher interviews and behavioral observations of the student, in addition to assessment results, are also considered. Ultimately, the school team (typically composed of a psychologist, administrator, parents, special educator from the suspected disability area, and general educator) makes a decision about the student's eligibility. Once a student is determined eligible for special education services, an IEP is developed.

The IEP is a written document that states the student's need areas by designating annual goals and short-term objectives that enhance a student's performance in these areas.

TABLE 2-4   **Assessments that may be used during the special education eligibility process.**

Type	Use	Examples
Intelligence	To determine overall cognitive functioning	Wechsler Intelligence Scale for Children—Third Edition. Stanford-Binet Intelligence Scale, Fourth Edition.
Achievement	To determine present levels of achievement in varied academic areas	Woodcock-Johnson Psycho-Educational Battery–Revised.
Adaptive behavior	To determine self-help and independent social skills	Vineland Adaptive Behavior Scales.
Social	To determine interpersonal skills	Walker Problem Behavior Identification Checklist.
Language	To determine how language is used in communication	Peabody Picture Vocabulary Test–Revised. Test of Written Language 2.
Parent interview	To elicit information from the family perspective on the child's functioning at home and in other environments	May be an informal interview.
Student interview	To gather information from the student about perception of academic, behavior, and functional skills	May be an informal interview.
Behavioral observations	To observe a student's behaviors in a variety of environments and/or situations	Functional assessments or antecedent-behavior-consequence data; ecological assessments.

Goals and objectives are based on the assessments given during the assessment process (stated earlier). The student's present level of performance is noted, as well as personnel who will be providing the educational services noted on the IEP. *After* the IEP is developed, the student's placement is determined based on the goals and objectives written into the IEP. Although only briefly portrayed here, the significance of the IEP meeting, the dynamics among the participants, the decisions being made at this time, and the never-enough-time for discussion—these interactions and decisions are not without significant emotional and intellectual power.

The decisions on IEP goals and objectives, and subsequently on placement issues, can be sensitive areas for all involved. As much as possible, those decisions should be made with the consensus of all people, with parents having significant input, with justifiable and rational reasons given. At least annually, the IEP team (again, including parents and sometimes the student) is reviewed to note progress and to develop new goals and objectives. At least every three years, a student must undergo a comprehensive reevaluation to determine whether he or she is still eligible for special education services.

Litigation and Least Restrictive Environment

Because varied interpretations of the principles mandated in IDEA are available, the intent of the LRE principle is sometimes resolved through litigation when an interpretation is in dispute. (Readers may use the quiz in Table 2-5 to test their knowledge on current interpretations of LRE.) Osborne and DiMattia (1994) note that the majority of litigation about LRE prior to 1989 indicated that mainstreaming was not appropriate for some students with disabilities, provision of mainstreaming to the maximum extent feasible should occur when appropriate, and the courts in general seemed to favor specialized services (typically delivered in more segregated settings). However, more recent court decisions seem to favor inclusive programming for students with disabilities (Lewis et al., 1994; Osborne & DiMattia, 1995; Yell, 1995a). Underwood and Mead (1995) describe the range of school programs from those that are minimally appropriate to superb placements; the IEP team does not have to select the best option, nor do they have to select only from options that maximize the student's potential.

Each educator's expertise, experience, and familiarity with inclusive methodologies influences the extent to which these methods are used. Clearly there are a number of factors subject to interpretation (and expertise) that have the potential to positively impact a student's benefit from educational experiences. The following court cases represent five of the

TABLE 2-5   Quiz on least restrictive environment issues as decided in case law.

Statement	True?	False?
1. LRE does not require school districts to place students in neighborhood schools in all situations.		
2. All schools must be modified to be accessible for students with physical disabilities who use wheelchairs.		
3. Students with disabilities may be excluded from a general education setting when it is easier to educate them in a segregated or separate setting.		
4. Students who require a different curriculum or may not easily keep up with their typical peers cannot be educated in general education classrooms.		
5. Nonacademic and academic benefits must be considered when making decisions about including students with disabilities in general education classrooms.		
6. LRE does not mandate that all students with disabilities must be educated in general education classrooms.		
7. The effect from the presence of a student with disabilities on peers in the general education classroom cannot be considered in making LRE decisions.		

Answers: 1 is T; 2 is F; 3 is F; 4 is F; 5 is T; 6 is T; 7 is F

recent leading cases influencing the interpretation of LRE. The *Daniel R. R.* (1989) and *Clyde K.* (1994) cases found that more separate programs were appropriate, and the other three cases found in favor of more inclusive environments.

Daniel R. R. v. State Board of Education *(1989)*

A two-prong test was developed in this case that has been used extensively since 1989 to help determine LRE. The school district responsible for educating Daniel, a student with Downs syndrome, was found to have successfully passed both parts of the test so that placing Daniel in a self-contained classroom was an appropriate educational decision for him. The first prong of the test has to do with determining whether education in the general education classroom, with the use of supplementary aids and services, can be satisfactorily achieved. Schools must have taken steps to accommodate the child in order to "pass" this test; if sufficient efforts ("token" gestures do not suffice) have not been taken to accommodate the child, then the test stops there and no further action can be taken until it is known how the student progresses in a general education environment when supplementary aids and services (including modifying the curriculum) are provided. If sufficient efforts have been taken, and the answer to the first prong of the test is that education in the general education classroom cannot be satisfactorily achieved, then the second prong of the test is used. The second prong of the test requires school districts to determine if they have mainstreamed the student to the maximum extent appropriate. Factors that can be considered in responding to either prong of these tests include (1) how well the student can progress within the general education curriculum, (2) the nature and severity of the disability, (3) how the student's presence affects the general education classroom, (4) the benefits for the student when accommodated in general education, and (5) how much time is spent in general education (Osborne & DiMattia, 1994).

Greer v. Rome City School District *(1991)*

The Greers were seeking placement for their ten-year-old child (who had Downs syndrome, moderate mental retardation, and speech/language disabilities) in a general education classroom. Several years earlier they had resisted even enrolling their child in public schools because they felt she would automatically be placed in a self-contained special education classroom. When they finally did pursue public education, their initial fears were confirmed: the recommended placement was a self-contained program. The determination of LRE by the school system was not sufficient to represent a continuum of services because only three options—general education with no supplemental aids or services, the general education classroom with speech therapy, or the self-contained special education class—were considered. In other words, there are options within a continuum of services that should be available that fit in between the general education classroom with speech therapy and the self-contained class (e.g., general education classroom with resource special education, consultation special education, collaboration with speech therapist and special educator, resource in general education with speech therapy). This court also identified three factors to consider for determining LRE in that an individualized examination of the nature and severity of the child's disability and of his or her needs and abilities must occur:

1. The school may compare the educational benefits the child with disabilities would receive in the general education classroom, with the help of supplementary aids and services, to the benefits he or she would receive in a more restrictive environment. Among the areas of benefits can be academics, the availability of role modeling and language modeling, and social benefits.
2. The effect of the presence of the student with disabilities on other students in the class can be considered.
3. The cost of supplementary aids and services necessary to achieve a satisfactory education can be considered. The needs of the child with disabilities must be balanced against the needs of other children in the district, and if that cost is so great to impact the education of other children in the district then education in the general education setting may not be appropriate.

Bartlett (1992) notes that the *Greer* decision severely restricts school placement teams that had previously gone directly from determining that a student had a disability to a special education placement; a strong consideration for general education classroom placement *with supplementary aids and services* is required. When there is a likelihood that a student with disabilities will cause disruption in a general education classroom, then the IEP team is compelled to examine factors (e.g., behavior management systems) that may need to be in place to alleviate the student's potential for disruption.

> *Courts today require uncontroverted proof that inclusion is not feasible. In the past, courts were willing to accept the* judgment of school officials *at face value, with little evidence to support their position.*
>
> Osborne & DiMattia, 1995

Oberti v. Board of Education of Clementon School District *(1993)*

Rafael Oberti was a kindergarten student with Downs syndrome who attended his neighborhood kindergarten program during the morning for socialization and a special education class in another district in the afternoon. When he began exhibiting behavior problems in the kindergarten class, the teacher consulted with a psychologist, attempted varied interventions, but did not request an IEP team to convene to (1) add goals and objectives related to behavior issues or (2) request special education consultation/additional services to assist her with behavior management issues. The next year the school and parents finally agreed to a special program close to the neighborhood school (the school had originally proposed an out-of-district self-contained special education class for Rafael), with the condition that mainstreaming possibilities would be explored at that school. Rafael progressed in his new program, but his parents became discouraged that minimal mainstreaming was occurring (Rafael and his classmates with disabilities went to the lunchroom and assemblies with typical students) and requested that Rafael be allowed to attend a general education class in his neighborhood school.

A federal court upheld the right of Rafael to be educated in a general education classroom despite the previous issues about behavior difficulties. The court felt that the school district had not complied with the first prong of the two-prong test from *Daniel R. R.*—that the school had made only "negligible" efforts to include Rafael in a general education environment. Although Rafael had initially been placed in a general education kindergarten class for half of the school day, this placement had occurred without sufficient *supplementary aids and services*—"without a curriculum plan, without a behavior management plan, and without providing adequate special education support to the teacher" (p. 1220). Specifically, the court noted that when behavior was an issue in kindergarten the IEP was not reviewed or revised to include goals and objectives related to behavior. The burden of proof is on school districts, when they remove students with disabilities from general education classes, to demonstrate that a segregated special education placement is the best educational approach for the individual student when making placement decisions.

Sacramento City Unified School District v. Rachel H. *(1994)*

Rachel was an eleven-year-old student with moderate mental retardation whose parents wanted her placed in a general education classroom for all of the school day. The Sacramento school district proposed a special education classroom for academic instruction and general education for nonacademic subjects. The two-prong test from *Daniel R. R.* was elaborated on with a four-part test that found in favor of Rachel being placed in general education because the school district had not made sufficient effort to try that placement. A four-part balancing test was used to determine if a placement met the LRE standards of IDEA. The court's responses to each part found in favor of placing Rachel in a general education classroom with supplemental services. The parts are the following:

1. The educational benefit of full-time placement in a general education class.
2. The nonacademic benefits of such a placement.
3. The effect of the student on the teacher and other children in the class (two aspects could be explored: detriment to other students due to Rachel's disruptive behavior and Rachel's need for teacher's time that could result in other students not receiving teacher attention).
4. The cost of a general education placement with appropriate supplementary aids and services.

Clyde K. and Sheila K. v. Puyallup School District *(1994)*

Ryan K. was a fifteen-year-old student with attention deficit hyperactivity disorder and Tourette's syndrome who was receiving special education in a general education classroom with special education resource room assistance. His behavior, increasing over time, consisted of using obscenities, noncompliance, physical assaults, and harassing female students. After two incidents of assaultive behavior, he was suspended. Upon return to school, the IEP team and his parents agreed to his placement in a separate school facility with a plan for reintegrating him into general education. Later, the parents reconsidered their consent and requested a new IEP and a due process hearing. The four-part test from *Rachel H.* was applied in this case to determine this ruling. Notably, the school district was making sufficient attempts to maintain Ryan in general education. There was ample evidence of the harmful effect his presence could have on the classroom, so the courts found in favor of the school district's recommendation for a more separate placement.

Yell (1995a) synthesized the existing case law regarding LRE issues into seven principles (refer to Table 2-6 for a listing of the principles). Among the principles are the necessity of school districts making sufficient efforts to accommodate students with disabilities in general education classrooms, the consideration of peers that can impact on decisions made about LRE, and the individualized nature of decisions made. The disability label means different things to different people, contributing to both negative and positive connotations that can be resolved only when the label leads to services that enrich the quality of the individual's life. The next section describes some issues to consider (and some to avoid) when labeling students.

Labels and Disability

As early as a century ago, "disability" as a common term did not exist. At that time, those labeled "disabled" or "handicapped" typically had disabilities that could be seen, such as cerebral palsy or severe mental retardation (see Table 2-7 for distinctions between the terms "handicap" and "disability"). The labels tended to be negative and portrayed human beings who could never learn to be self-sufficient or benefit society. Some of the labels routinely used to describe people with disabilities were idiots, cripples, imbeciles, morons, and feebleminded. Even today, it is not unusual to hear solicitous and sympathetic pleas for "normal" people to feel sorry for the "less fortunate" or "handicapped."

Miringoff (1994) states that federal legislation ensured universal access to a free and appropriate public education for students with disabilities, but the legislation has been pri-

TABLE 2-6   Principles of case law on least restrictive environment.

Principles That Guide Least Restrictive Environment Decisions

1. Students with disabilities have a presumptive right to be educated in integrative settings.
2. The key to ensuring good faith efforts to maintain a child with disabilities in the general education settings lie in the provision of supplementary aids and services.
3. The proper forum for placement decision making is the IEP team.
4. Schools must consider the needs of classroom peers in LRE decisions.
5. A complete continuum of alternative placements must be available.
6. Students must benefit educationally from their placement.
7. Schools will bear the burden of proof in defending LRE decisions.

Source: Constructed from information in Yell, M. L. (1995). *Clyde K. and Sheila K. v. Puyallup School District: The courts, inclusion, and students with behavioral disorders. Behavioral Disorders, 20,* pp. 186, 187.

TABLE 2-7 Distinguishing "handicap" from "disability" as terms.

Handicap

Not a synonym for disability. Describes a condition or barrier imposed by society, the environment, or one's own self. *Handicap* can be used when citing laws and situations, but it should not be used to describe a disability. Say, "The stairs are a *handicap* for her," or "He is *handicapped* by the inaccessible bus."

Disability

A general term used for a functional limitation that interferes with a person's ability, for example, to walk, hear, learn, or lift. It may refer to a physical, mental, or sensory condition. Use it as a descriptive noun or adjective, for example, "persons who are mentally and physically disabled," "man with a disability."

Source: The Resource and Training Center on Independent Living (1987). *Guidelines for reporting and writing about people with disabilities.* Reston, VA: ERIC Clearinghouse on Handicapped and Gifted Children.

marily process-oriented rather than outcome-oriented in its approach to change. She states that special education is still more interested in labeling and placement rather than outcomes. Emphasis has been on identification, labeling, and special class placement rather than on what happens with the student as a result of using effective teaching strategies. The placement has been the end product of the labeling process instead of the means to achieve a desired outcome.

Similarly, Gallagher (1976) noted early on that labeling children can be used constructively or destructively. The cautions he gave over two decades ago about labeling students remain true today. Gallagher describes "sacred" uses of labeling as a positive practice when the label leads to differentiated treatment, assists in obtaining additional resources, and provides information that contributes to an ever expanding research base (e.g., etiology, prevention, treatment indications). "Profane" uses of labeling are those which lead to either negative consequences, or do not lead to consequences at all. Examples include preservation of social hierarchies, or when the individual is labeled and the "problem" is perceived to be entirely with the individual yet not at all with the surrounding environment. Gallagher describes labels as "tranquilizers" when the identity of the condition now has a name, but how to deal with the condition is not addressed.

> *Labels, in and of themselves, are not evil. How they are interpreted by others and by the labeled person determines whether they are harmful or ameliorative.*
>
> Hallahan & Kauffman, 1994

Disability areas specified in federal legislation are categorical (thirteen disability areas are identified), and the law is integral to how services in states and local school systems are supported and funded (Miringoff, 1994). Consequently, the impetus for schools to "decategorize" to serve students in inclusive settings may be negatively reinforced when funds are distributed based on program enrollment. The challenge is to move beyond the process of labeling and identifying while preserving the rights of students with disabilities and promoting educational environments that focus on meaningful outcomes for all students. Furthermore, school personnel involved in *successful* inclusion programs repeatedly note that a student's placement in an inclusive setting is dependent on the student's individual needs and *not* on the severity or type of disability (USGAO, April 1994b). Underwood and Mead (1995) emphasize the individualized nature of placement decisions in that a student is not placed in a program based on label, preconceived notions, or simply because a program exists; what must be considered are the student's emotional, social, physical, and academic needs. Alternatives to serving students by labeling are discussed next not as solutions, necessarily, but as points for school system personnel to consider.

Determine Benefits of Labels

Labels and definitions can serve several purposes, and it is important that educators distinguish the process of labeling from the process of determining—and using—appropriate interventions. If the labeling process and use of definitions are used primarily or solely for placement purposes, then the benefit for the student may not be realized.

Rather than focusing on the label, Gillet (1994) suggests that labels be deemphasized by developing eligibility criteria that (1) require the use of authentic assessment techniques, (2) document interventions that have been used, and (3) indicate the results of the interventions. Student characteristics and learning needs should be highlighted rather than the disability.

It is not that labeling is used that appears to be the dilemma, but rather to what end labeling is useful. Wang, Reynolds, and Walberg (1994) suggest that programs be labeled instead of students. For example, students who need to learn more about getting along with others might take courses from a "Community and Interpersonal Relationships" curriculum (i.e., Social Skills Program). The students would not need to be labeled "serious emotionally disturbed" in order to receive this instruction, and students who need social skills and interpersonal skills interventions also can qualify themselves for these classes based on their need and not their label.

Focus on Effective Interventions

There is an enormous amount of knowledge available about effective teaching, especially as compared to what was known two decades ago. In light of this extensive data base about what works, the challenge for researchers and practitioners alike is to figure out how to get methods into the classrooms where they belong. Although at first glance the idea of better methods may seem to be a desirable destination, the reality is that getting teachers to change their way of teaching (see Chapter 3 about change in schools and individuals) is a complex process that requires much effort and hard work, sustained energy and dedication, persistence toward improvements, and resiliency when problem solving. Change is hard work that takes a long time.

Additionally, techniques useful for students who do not have disabilities are useful for students with disabilities. (Conversely, techniques useful for students with disabilities also benefit students who do not have disabilities.) For example, Sapon-Shevin (1994) notes that strategies used for gifted education, such as curriculum compacting, independent study, and thematic instruction, can and should be a part of all classrooms. Creating more and more specialized and separate services to address students' increasing diversity of needs will only continue to fragment education; the result is that a relatively small percentage of students will qualify for "typical" education only. To counter this, specialized instruction could occur within all classrooms for all students—inclusion.

Assume Best Practices Will Change

A static perspective on effective teaching assumes that what is known today will be what is practiced today *and* tomorrow. However, a dynamic approach realizes that the context of schools and classrooms requires (1) adaptation of known methods to work in individual schools and classrooms, (2) an ongoing monitoring of how effective methods are for individual students within heterogeneous classrooms, and (3) consistent flexibility that focuses on constant improvement.

When "least restrictive environment" was first interpreted by the courts in the late 1970s, it was interpreted based on what was known then about how students with disabilities could be integrated into general education classrooms. Although the wording of the law has not changed, interpretations of LRE have evolved over the years in light of what is known about effective teaching. Osborne (1992) notes that the courts frequently defer to expert testimony when confronted with decisions about individuals with disabilities. Experts rely on research and data-based instruction to substantiate their information. What professionals know today is different from what was known in the 1980s, and today's best practice is also different from what will be known in the 2000s. For example, in the early 1980s it was best practice to build schools for students with moderate to severe disabilities and to educate them completely separate from their typical peers. It was also best practice to devote entire buildings, or wings in buildings, to programs for students with emotional or behavioral disorders, or students with physical disabilities, and so on. At that time, more attention was given to specialized methods delivered in, oftentimes, a fragmented manner, than to the wholeness of postschool outcomes for students.

For example, specialized techniques for a student with moderate mental retardation may have focused on speech/language therapy for language and articulation delivered several times a week in the therapy room. Little focus may have been on educating other teachers or school staff on the goals of the language lessons so that others could help reinforce and teach those skills. Today, a transdisciplinary approach is preferred that involves educators and parents collaboratively developing and implementing IEP goals (refer to Chapter 8 on Integrated Therapies). Similarly, a decade ago the methods used to teach work-related skills for that student were typically simulated work environments with few meaningful tasks used that generalized to future work environments. Today community-based training is best practice so that students are learning about work in real-world environments with real-world tasks.

Conclusions

Miringoff (1994) states that the restructuring of special education that is intended to move from full exclusion to full inclusion must first redefine how people—both professionals and students—and their roles are classified (refer to Chapter 3 for more information on role changes). Skrtic (1992) contends that one cannot modify practice without evaluating and reappraising underlying assumptions, and Miringoff states that revising assumptions means changing how we categorize and define those we serve. She cautions that "as we re-define where children should be educated by asserting that all children belong together, we cannot continue to label some. Progress in special education will only occur if the right to an education is preserved alongside the right to be integrated and to be treated equally and without discrimination" (p. 100). Where does "de-labeling" leave special education services in the future? Perhaps serving all students, regardless of label, with what they need via inclusive services is a step toward a future of no labels. How can educators balance labeling some students and delivering specialized services to all? Certainly this is a logistical and moral dilemma that the prospect of inclusive services raises. Furthermore, the major strides that researchers make toward specialized instruction is clearly dependent on labels and descriptions of student characteristics.

Wolfensberger (1991) notes that "the overwhelming bulk of the improvements [for educating individuals with mental retardation] all derived from two states of mind that are available anytime anywhere to anybody: imagination and a humane attitude" (p. 9). The combination of proven effective techniques in the hands of creative and compassionate educators dedicated toward improvements is a powerful outlook for the future.

References

Bartlett, L. D. (1992). Mainstreaming: On the road to clarification. *Education Law Reporter, 76,* 17–25.

Burke, J. C. (1991). Some developmental implications of a disturbance in responding to complex environmental stimuli. *American Journal on Mental Retardation, 96,* 37–52.

Carson, R. R., Sitlington, P. L., & Frank, A. R. (1995). Young adulthood for individuals with behavioral disorders: What does it hold? *Behavioral Disorders, 20,* 127–135.

Chalfant, J. C., & Pysh, M. V. D. (1989). Teacher assistance teams: Five descriptive studies on 96 teams. *Remedial and Special Education, 10*(6), 49–58.

Children's Defense Fund. (1995). *The state of America's children yearbook.* Washington, DC.

Clyde K. and Sheila K. v. Puyallup School District. 35 F.3d 1396 (9th Cir. 1994).

Cohen, O. P. (1995). Perspectives on the full inclusion movement in the education of deaf children. *Inclu-sion? Defining quality education for deaf and hard of hearing students* (pp. 1–13). Washington, DC: Gallaudet University.

Daniel R. R. v. State Board of Education, 874 F.2d 1036 (5th Cir. 1989).

Everson, J. M., & McNulty, J. J. (1995). What happens when children who are deaf-blind grow up?: An overview of transition services. In *Supporting young adults who are deaf-blind in their communities* (pp. 5–20). Baltimore: Paul H. Brookes Publishing Co.

Forest, M., & Lusthaus, E. (1989). Promoting educational quality for all students: Circles and maps. In S. Stainback, W. Stainback, & M. Forest (Eds.), *Educating all students in the mainstream of regular education* (pp. 430–457). Baltimore: Paul H. Brookes Publishing Co.

Fuchs, D., & Fuchs, L. S. (1994). Sometimes separate is better. *Educational Leadership, 52*(4), 22–26.

Fuchs, D., Fuchs, L., Gilman, S., Reeder, P., Bahr, M., Fernstrom, P., & Roberts, H. (1990). Prereferral intervention through teacher consultation: Mainstream assistance teams. *Academic Therapy, 25,* 263–276.

Gallagher, J. J. (1976). The sacred and profane use of labeling. In E. L. Meyen (Ed.), *Basic readings in the study of exceptional children and youth* (pp. 121–129). Denver: Love Publishing Co.

Giangreco, M. F., Cloninger, C. J., & Iverson, V. S. (1993). *Choosing options and accommodations for children.* Baltimore: Paul H. Brookes Publishing Co.

Gillet, P. (1994). Special education restructuring: A view from the Intermediate Unit. *The Special Education Leadership REVIEW, 2*(1), 25–32.

Goldberg, S. S., & Kuriloff, P. J. (1991). Evaluating the fairness of special education hearings. *Exceptional Children, 57,* 546–555.

Greer v. Rome City School District, 950 F.2d 688 (11th Cir. 1991).

Hallahan, D. P., & Kauffman, J. M. (1994). Toward a culture of disability in the aftermath of Deno and Dunn. *The Journal of Special Education, 27,* 496–508.

Halvorsen, A. T., & Sailor, W. (1990). Integration of students with severe and profound disabilities: A review of research. In R. Gaylord-Ross (Ed.), *Issues and research in special education* (pp. 110–172). New York: Teachers College Press.

Individuals with Disabilities Education Act of 1990 (IDEA), 20 U.S.C., Section 1402.

Kaufman, M., Gottlieb, J., Agard, J., & Kukic, M. (1975). Mainstreaming: Toward an explanation of the concept. In E. Meyen, G. Vergason, & R. Whelan (Eds.), *Alternatives for teaching exceptional children* (pp. 35–54). Denver: Love Publishing Co.

King, M. S. (1993). *Remembering.* Valdosta, GA: Author.

Lewis, T. J., Chard, D., & Scott, T. M. (1994). Full inclusion and the education of children and youth with emotional and behavioral disorders. *Behavioral Disorders, 19,* 277–293.

Lynch, E. W., Lewis, R. B., & Murphy, D. S. (1993). Educational services for children with chronic illnesses: Perspectives of educators and families. *Exceptional Children, 59,* 210–220.

Maroney, S. A. (1993). Welcoming back students with emotional/behavioral disorders into the least restrictive environments. In L. M. Bullock & R. A. Gable (Eds.), *Monograph on inclusion: Ensuring appropriate services to children and youth with emotional/behavioral disorders* (pp. 29–32). Reston, VA: Council for Exceptional Children.

McDonnell, A. P., & Hardman, M. L. (1989). The desegregation of America's special schools: Strategies for change. *Journal of the Association for Persons with Severe Handicaps, 14,* 68–74.

Mercer, C. D., King-Sears, P., & Mercer, A. (1990). Learning disabilities definitions used by state education departments. *Learning Disabilities Quarterly, 13,* 141–152.

Miringoff, N. M. (1994). Classification practices and their impact on special education. *The Special Education Leadership REVIEW,* 93–101.

Myles, B. S., Simpson, R. L., & Becker, J. (1994). An analysis of characteristics of students with higher-functioning autistic disorder. *Exceptionality, 5,* 19–30.

Oberti v. Board of Education of Clementon School District. 995 F2d 1204 (3rd Cir. 1993).

Osborne, A. G. (1992). Legal standards for an appropriate education in the post-Rowley era. *Exceptional Children, 58,* 488–494.

Osborne, A. G., & DiMattia, P. (1994). The IDEA's least restrictive environment mandate: Legal implications. *Exceptional Children, 61,* 6–14.

Osborne, A. G., & DiMattia, P. (1995). Counterpoint: IDEA's LRE mandate: Another look. *Exceptional Children, 61,* 582–584.

Price, J. P. (1993). Promoting inclusive education for students with emotional/behavioral disorders. *Monograph on inclusion: Ensuring appropriate services to children and youth with emotional/ behavioral disorders* (pp. 25–28). Reston, VA: Council for Exceptional Children.

Sacramento City Unified School District v. Rachel H. 14 F.3d 1398 (9th Cir. 1994).

Salend, S. J. (1990). *Effective mainstreaming.* New York: Macmillan.

Sapon-Shevin, M. (1994). Why gifted students belong in inclusive schools. *Educational Leadership, 52*(4), 64–70.

Sitlington, P. L., & Frank, A. R. (1993). Dropouts with learning disabilities: What happens to them as young adults? *Learning Disabilities Research & Practice, 8,* 244–252.

Skrtic, T. M. (1992). The special education paradox: Equity as the way to excellence. In T. Hehir, &

T. Latus (Eds.), *Special education at the century's end* (pp. 203–274). Cambridge, MA: Harvard Educational Review.

Taylor, S. J. (1988). Caught in the continuum: A critical analysis of the principle of the least restrictive environment. *Journal of the Association for Persons with Severe Handicaps, 13,* 41–53.

Underwood, J. K., & Mead, J. F. (1995). *Legal aspects of special education and pupil services.* Boston: Allyn and Bacon.

U.S. Department of Education. (1994). *Sixteenth annual report to Congress on the implementation of the Individuals with Disabilities Education Act.* Washington, DC: Author.

U.S. General Accounting Office. (April 1994a). *School-age children: Poverty and diversity challenge schools nationwide.* Testimony from Linda Morra before the Committee on Labor and Human Resources, United States Senate, Washington, DC.

U.S. General Accounting Office. (April 1994b). *Special education reform: Districts grapple with inclusion programs.* Testimony from Linda Morra before the Subcommittee on Select Education and Civil Rights, Committee on Education and Labor, House of Representatives, # 94-132, Washington, DC.

Van Reusen, A. K., Deshler, D. D., & Schumaker, J. B. (1989). Effects of a student participation strategy in facilitating the involvement of adolescents with learning disabilities in the individualized educational program planning process. *Learning Disabilities: A Multidisciplinary Journal, 1*(2), 23–34.

Wang, M. C., Reynolds, M. C., & Walberg, H. J. (1994). Serving students at the margins. *Educational Leadership, 52*(4), 12–17.

Wolfensberger, W. (1991). Reflections on a lifetime in human services and mental retardation. *Mental Retardation, 29*(1), 1–15.

Yell, M. L. (1995a). *Clyde K. and Sheila K. v. Puyallup School District:* The courts, inclusion, and students with behavioral disorders. *Behavioral Disorders, 20,* 179–189.

Yell, M. L. (1995b). Least restrictive environment, inclusion, and students with disabilities: A legal analysis. *The Journal of Special Education, 28,* 389–404.

Chapter 3

The Change Process: Change for People and Schools

DIANNE F. BRADLEY AND MARGARET E. KING-SEARS

◆ ADVANCE ORGANIZER ◆

Successfully including students with a range of disabilities in general education schools and classrooms means **changes** for all members of the educational community—changes in the characteristics of students in their classrooms, changes in the way curriculum is designed and delivered, and changes in professional and personal relationships. Transitions can be a difficult and emotional time for educators as they dismantle the existing system (which they know so well) and replace it with one whose purposes, process, and outcomes are questionable and unsure. These transformations do not come easily, and their genesis is each individual's fundamental philosophy and attitude about the education of individuals with diverse learning needs.

This chapter describes critical aspects of change from both a personal and organization perspective. The impact of the change process on educators' thoughts and actions when including students with disabilities is discussed, and the skills and expertise that are essential to empower educators to successfully make these changes are examined.

Author's Note: Many of the personal statements in this chapter were contributed by teachers in the state of Maryland who are taking special education graduate courses in inclusion. Thanks are extended to Kathleen Benedick, Jill Broer, Whitney Dorsey-Cooper, Cherry G.H. Edgerton-Bird, Janice Jacksits, Catherine Jones, Bambi Lowry, Michelle Wanner, and Jackie Willig for their contributions and insights as they have made the journey to inclusive teaching.

About midway through my first year of teaching, I was approached by our special class teacher who taught students with severe multiple disabilities. She was looking for a regular educator to accept one of her children into a class for short period of time each day. My first reaction was very negative. I had purposely not chosen to go into special education because I did not feel comfortable working with children who had intense special needs. I told her that I would not be able to take the child and was relieved when I heard that another teacher accepted this child into her room.

After this incident I started to evaluate my feelings on the subject of inclusion. As a child, I had never had the experience of sharing a classroom with any special needs children, and maybe that was why I felt so uncomfortable with the whole idea. Perhaps if I had, I would not be so hesitant now as a teacher to accept these children into my room.

I shared my feelings and concerns with the special class teacher. She was very sensitive to my feelings and said that she would do everything that she could to create an atmosphere that would be comfortable for the children and myself. I decided that I did not want to be the teacher who closes the door on these children, denying them the opportunity to feel a sense of belonging which is critical in their academic and social success. So I hesitantly decided that I would volunteer my classroom for any of her children who needed a placement. I am admittedly still a little fearful of the experience, and I feel that the fear stems from the experience being unknown to me. Therefore, I am willing to explore my feelings and to try new experiences. I am able to see that not only will this experience help the child with special needs, but it will greatly impact other children as well as myself. I feel that it is my responsibility as an educator to open my door to all children. After all, in the end, they are all just children.

Whitney Dorsey-Cooper, fifth grade teacher, Baltimore, Maryland

---

It must be considered that there is nothing more difficult to carry out, nor more doubtful of success, nor more dangerous to handle, than to initiate a new order of things.

Machiavelli, 1509

Past and Current Roles

Traditionally, education has been an isolated activity. Elementary teachers have seen their role as the center of a particular group of students while secondary teachers have focused on subject matter and graduation requirements. Consequently, students who were not successful in meeting traditional demands in these environments were viewed as having something "wrong" with them; there was a strong likelihood that those students would receive some type of label. Subsequently, the role of the special education teacher has been to gather these students and take them to a separate place to teach them. What has emerged is a separate sense of ownership of students, programs, and methods.

In addition to separation by disability, traditional schools have been organized in homogeneous groups. However, this separation of students by ability and achievement levels is no longer meeting the needs of our diverse educational society. Many schools are facing changes as their communities expand to include students with culturally diverse backgrounds, students whose families are economically impacted, those from various family styles, and students with a variety of academic and emotional challenges. Simultaneous with a more varied student population, curriculum demands are increasing, and laws requiring that students with disabilities be educated with their typical peers are being implemented. Problems that used to be viewed as solely student characteristics are now being examined within the context of methods, instruction, and materials used. "Changes in student demographics, increased demands on teachers and students, and the reduction of resources create instability and compel us to recognize that we cannot continue to 'do business as usual'" (Villa & Thousand, 1992, p. 110).

However, there is no recipe for inclusion; no one type of teaching, no one type of curriculum, and no one type of grouping arrangement will work perfectly for every student. Roles, responsibilities, relationships, and rules often change, and new skills and thinking patterns are required. What, then, is likely to happen as the educational system undergoes changes to better accommodate *all* its learners?

Personal Change

> *Change is primarily about individuals and their beliefs and actions rather than about programs, materials, technology, or equipment.*
>
> Villa & Thousand, 1992

One definition of change particularly pertinent for inclusion is "to undergo transformation, transition, or substitution" (Webster's, 1993, p. 190). Educators as well as their schools and school systems experience each of these when the education of student with disabilities becomes more inclusive, and traditionally accepted ways of educating students, defining teacher roles, and determining student outcomes are challenged.

When educators hear that it is time to change, this message is usually communicated through words such as "reform," "restructuring schools," "new initiatives," and "school improvement efforts." A change to inclusive schooling can disrupt traditional education practices; people react to those types of messages in very personal ways.

Members of any organization (i.e., schools) bring concerns and values based on their own personal experiences as well as those they have encountered in the workplace. When considering the transition from a school that educates its students with disabilities in separate programs to one that welcomes and includes all students, hopes are raised and fears are generated as evidenced in the following statements from teachers:

- *It's scary not only in that inclusion would be difficult to do, but how can I do another thing when I've got all these millions of demands being made on me already?*
- *I was afraid of the unknown, afraid to fail.*

It is not unusual for educators to "worry about their competence and their ability to meet the needs of a child with disabilities. Many feel overwhelmed by sympathy and sadness for the child. Some resent the fact that they must work with a child with disabilities on top of all their other tasks" (Volk & Stahlman, 1994, p. 13). Educators react with conflicting feelings: challenged, hopeful, excited, and motivated—and—frustrated, burdened, fearful, and inadequate (Bradley & West, 1994; Loucks-Horsley & Roody, 1990; Villa & Thousand, 1992). According to Hord, Rutherford, Huling-Austin, and Hall (1987), these reactions are strongly influenced by the following:

- Educators' beliefs about the innovation
- Perception of their ability to use it
- The setting in which the change occurs
- The number of other changes in which they are involved
- The kind of support and assistance they receive as they attempt to implement the change

Response to Change

Individuals and groups respond to change in varied ways, from positive to negative and from short-lived resistance to long-term rigidity. In a study conducted by Giangreco, Dennis, Clonninger, Edelman, and Schattman (1993) in which schools made a transition to include students with severe disabilities in general education classes, teachers expressed initial feelings of reluctance, fear, nervousness, apprehension, anger, and worry about anticipated role changes. Their attitudes about their changing roles were reflected in their comments:

- *My reaction was, I don't feel like she belongs in a public school. (p. 364)*
- *We are going to see how it works. The aide is going to take care of him. (p. 364)*
- *I have [my] students plus Michele. (p. 364)*

Initially in the experimental program, there was minimal involvement by the classroom teacher. Some teachers expressed greater confidence in the paraprofessionals assigned to work with the students than they did in their abilities as trained teachers. There was an expectation that someone else, such as the special educator or teacher aide, would be responsible for educating the student.

People need to be supported by one another and by their organization (i.e., their school system) as they undergo valid, necessary, and uncomfortable reactions to change. Although education is an ever-evolving science about human learning, only recently have teacher preparation programs begun to explicitly teach educators about the concept of change in education (e.g., Thousand & Villa, 1990). Hall and Loucks (1978) describe an educational change model that emphasizes how individuals relate to implied or explicit changes during implementation of a new practice or innovation. Figure 3-1 shows the stages of concern developed by Hord and her colleagues using the Concerns Based Adoption Model (CBAM). The numerical indicators accompany each of seven levels to show relative expertise, comfort, or experience with the innovation. That is, educators at level "0" are at an awareness level where they are minimally concerned or involved with the innovation. Con-

Focus	Stage	Typical Statements
Self	0—Awareness	• "I've heard about inclusion, but I'm not concerned because it won't affect me." • "What is inclusion, anyway?"
	1—Informational	• "I would like to know more about inclusion." • "How does inclusion differ from the mainstreaming that I'm already doing?"
	2—Personal	• "How will inclusive practices affect me in my classroom?" • "Who will be responsible for grading the students with disabilities?"
Task	3—Management	• "We need to plan different levels of outcomes for social studies." • "How can we differentiate grading for the students?"
Impact	4—Consequences	• "How do students' scores on class assignments differ from before we used lesson organizers?" • "Students seem to be more sensitive of each other since Staci entered our classroom."
	5—Collaboration	• "We need to meet regularly to compare notes and share ideas."
	6—Refocusing	• "This method works real well when we combine it with Dimensions of Learning."

FIGURE 3-1   Stages of concerns for individuals undergoing change.

Source: Adapted from Hord, S. M., Rutherford, W. L., Huling-Austin, L., & Hall, G. E. (1987). *Taking charge of change.* Alexandria, VA: Association for Supervision and Curriculum Development.

versely, educators who are at level "6" are highly involved in the innovation and are at a place where they are refining it and integrating its use with other methods.

If the implementation of inclusive practices is considered the innovation, educators who did not have, nor expect to have, students with disabilities in their classrooms might be only at the *awareness* stage because they feel that inclusion will not affect them. Hord and colleagues (1987) suggest providing material that provokes interest at this stage.

The next two stages are considered to be at the personal level because they indicate concern about how the innovation will improve or inconvenience their daily lives. In the second stage, *informational,* educators may already have an awareness of inclusion and are now interested in learning about the concept. At this stage, clear and accurate information about the innovation can be helpful. Wisniewski and Alper (1994) recommend the use of demonstrations, site visits, testimonials, and technical information to help explain the use of alternative and inclusive instructional arrangements.

The next stage that educators undergo deals with *personal* concerns such as the role changes involved when implementing inclusive practices, that is, techniques new to the individual educator that impact on the traditional instructional delivery patterns or arrangements. Contact with teachers who have already used the new techniques is beneficial at this point (Wisniewski & Alper, 1994). Encouragement for small steps taken toward implementation of inclusive methods is desirable.

After educators have information on what to use and how to use it and have gotten past personal concerns about how it affects them, they're ready to use it in their classroom and see how it goes. Thus, their next area of concern relates to the *management* of the tasks that promote inclusion. Technical assistance and support are critical at this stage if teachers are expected to maintain the use of sound inclusive practices. Most teachers (especially very effective teachers) are extremely uncomfortable using new methods because they are accustomed to the exemplary and organized way in which they already manage instruction in their classrooms (Joyce & Weil, 1986). Often knowing how hard it is to get new practices "up and running" prevents educators from trying them. Support and encouragement during this stage can "make or break" continued use of the new practice.

The next stage begins to deal with the impact of the innovation, that is, the *consequences* of the new practice. The ways in which it affects student growth in academic, behavioral, and social areas become the focus. When educators discuss how implementation of new practices affects students and no longer talk about their personal reactions, then a milestone has been reached. This leads to the next-to-last stage, which is *collaboration.* At this stage educators can be found trying new practices; meeting together to compare techniques, organization, and results; and pooling resources and expertise among themselves.

The final stage, *refocusing,* is achieved when educators are comfortable with their implementation of the innovation and are ready to evaluate its use, combine it with other methods, and develop more of a personalized perspective in their continued implementation efforts. Providing continued access to resources and promoting use of the innovation should continue. Often innovations are refined and/or modified at this point.

Individuals at any of these stages experience developmental and interactional concerns that are valid, and they need to receive the right kind of support (Hord et al., 1987). For example, educators may be focused on their self-concerns (e.g., information, personal). Training in how to use the innovation in combination with other techniques may not "take" because the educators are not ready to hear and use the information.

Becoming informed about the change process itself can often reassure teachers that their reactions are normal. When they understand the process, they can often identify their own stages as they move along the continuum of change.

Furthermore, movement through the stages is fluid, flexible, and occurs at different rates for different people. Assessing where an individual is by (1) listening carefully to comments and concerns, (2) acknowledging the individual's feelings and providing further information and support, and (3) promoting growth and movement of the individual and the vision are key elements for sustaining the innovation.

Perceptions of Change

The thought of including students with disabilities in classes in which this has never been done before can create a great amount of anxiety in teachers. Both special and general educators may find themselves going through a range of emotions from grieving for lost practices and programs, to discomfort or ambivalence. One teacher described it this way:

- *I enjoyed having* my *own classroom,* my *own lessons,* my *own worries, cares, etc.*

A center-based special education teacher relates:

- *I was grieving the loss of a close-knit, caring staff and was being forced into the real world [of inclusion] that we feared for our students.*

Teachers who bring personal concerns of this nature related to the change often have little receptivity to assist in the more advanced stages of the change process, such as the management phase, unless it responds to their personal concerns. In fact, they may bring a great deal of resistance and/or passivity.

One of the reasons for resistance to change is that it challenges competence and power (Evans, 1993; Volk & Stahlman, 1994). An imbedded message may be that educators have been teaching the wrong way, and that they now need to learn the right way to teach. Teachers worry about making mistakes, looking foolish, and feeling an initial awkwardness when implementing new programs and procedures. One of the adjectives used by teachers preparing for inclusion to describe themselves was "unqualified" (Giangreco et al., 1993). Most resistance comes from lack of information and fear that the change will require that teachers give up "tried and true" practices. Providing concrete information about successful programs already in place can lessen these fears. Articles and personal testimonies from teachers who have "been there" can be very reassuring. In addition, linking the change with other areas of concern for teachers such as instructional techniques that benefit *all* students helps them see how inclusive practices interface with existing best educational practices.

Positively Perceived Change
Even people who are initially accepting of an innovation are just as likely to resist the innovation somewhere along the way as the people who are originally, consistently, and steadfastly resistant to the innovation (Conner, 1992). A person who wants to change is typically thought to be one who will consistently deal well with the implementation. Yet that may not be true for people who want inclusion but have not yet actually implemented the education for youngsters with a wide range of disabilities in their schools or classrooms. Consider Ms. Atkinson, a seventh grade social studies teacher who readily embraces inclusion for students with mild disabilities but has difficulty conceptualizing inclusion for students with more moderate or severe disabilities. She considers herself to be an open-minded and well-informed educator who easily accommodates students with disabilities—when they are mild.

When Ms. Atkinson initially hears about the philosophy of inclusion, her first response may be that it will work (after all, she's already doing well with some groups of students with disabilities). Conner (1992) characterized this response as *uninformed optimism.* The concept of inclusion sounds good, the philosophy is a sound one, and Ms. Atkinson is optimistic that it can work as smoothly for students with severe disabilities in her classroom as it has for students with more mild disabilities.

Yet when Ms. Atkinson actually includes a student with moderate to severe disabilities and finds herself needing more information, resources, and support, her response pattern shifts in light of the new personal demands. This response is characterized as *informed pessimism.* Ms. Atkinson needs support at this point. If she does get support, then *hopeful real-*

ism occurs. If she does not get support, then she stagnates. How a person confronts their pessimism can be key in shifting from informed pessimism to hopeful realism.

Next comes *informed optimism.* Ms. Atkinson and the other educators are collaborating, and things are going well in the classroom. Concurrently, she reflects that she had no idea what she was getting into when volunteering to be an inclusion teacher, but she can see it all pays off when educators and students work together! Finally, the response is *completion* of the implementation venture. Ms. Atkinson, her colleagues, and their students are convinced that inclusion can work because they've done it and seen the results.

Negatively Perceived Change

Conner (1992) describes a person's reaction to perceived negative change by adapting the model for grieving developed by Elizabeth Kubler-Ross. First, a person knows *stability,* which is before a change is implemented. For example, students with severe disabilities attend a separate school, or maybe they receive services from a teacher in a comprehensive school but are housed in their own classroom away from the students' same-age peers. Educators are quite comfortable with the stability of providing services in a way that they believe is the most effective way to educate their students.

Then Ms. Huston, the administrator, decides to redesign the delivery service system and train the staff so that they can become more of a neighborhood school. Mr. Solomon is vehemently opposed to this, especially because he knows that one of the students will be in his fifth grade classroom next year. *Immobilization* occurs, and thoughts of not knowing what to do, who to access for more information or training, or how to effect a parallel curriculum prevents implementation efforts. Even if each of these areas are addressed, Mr. Solomon will next feel *denial* and then *anger* at having to change his typical way of teaching fifth grade. Before Mr. Solomon can successfully collaborate with other educators and effectively implement new programs, he will need to reconcile his feelings of resistance. However, this does not mean that no changes occur in Mr. Solomon's class until he is completely and positively ready to change; sometimes change doesn't happen until after the action or implementation has occurred.

When considering changing from segregated to inclusive programming, it would be wise to remember that "people will not change unless they believe that they are going to have their emotional needs met" (Villa & Thousand, 1992, p. 111). Each participant must work through a different set of personal and professional concerns and be given the opportunity to work out their own meaning to the change (Fullan with Stiegelbauer, 1991). Educators need support and empathy as they go through this process (Gersten & Woodward, 1990).

Change in the Schools

Change is highly personal while at the same time deeply embedded in the systemic structure of the organization.

Loucks-Horsley & Roody, 1990

When dealing with the changes of an organization such as a school, differing viewpoints, goals, levels of commitment, and emotional reactions must be considered. Many differences must be reconciled as educators work together to provide positive learning experiences for heterogeneous groups of students. For example, teaching to the class average (i.e., the typical student) does not address the variety of learners found in classrooms of today. More and more learners in general education classrooms do not qualify for special education services but still need some type of differentiated instruction such as students who are highly gifted, students who use English as a second language, and students who have learning problems but are not "labeled." Schedules, use of space and materials, classroom routines, and teaching techniques are often altered to facilitate the most appropriate learning for these heterogeneous groups of students.

Evans (1993) describes educational change as "a vast process of adaptation that must be accomplished teacher by teacher, school by school" (p. 19). Transformations that are "gradual and progressive rather than discrete and abrupt" (Giangreco et al., 1993, p. 365) are more likely to be successful. Differences in organizational structures, curricula demands, and range of skill levels that exist at the elementary and secondary schools result in inclusion issues that must be examined from these particular perspectives.

Elementary Schools

Because teachers at the elementary level usually see the same twenty to thirty students all day (as opposed to secondary teachers who usually see over a hundred students a day), they tend to take the successes and failures of their students more personally. This can cause apprehension to escalate when a student significantly deviates socially or academically from grade level parameters.

Bradley (1993) found that teachers in several elementary schools revealed confusion and anxiety about their roles in educating students with disabilities in general education classrooms. These teachers indicated such feelings as fear, panic, frustration, sadness, and being overwhelmed. In addition, their concerns included the loss of former roles and programs and confusion about the responsibilities of special and general educators as evidenced in this comment:

- *If you get the child in your classroom next year that doesn't mean anyone expects that child to do grade level work, does it?*

Other general educators at the elementary level have stated their concerns:

- *My first reaction was very negative. I had chosen education because of my love to work with children. I had not chosen special education because I did not feel comfortable working with children who had intense special needs.*
- *Students with special needs are better served by the small class sizes, special instruction, and individualized attention provided by the special education system.*

Moreover, special educators expressed their reactions to inclusion in the following statements:

- *I saw a great need for self-contained. I feared my students would be chewed up and spit out by those other children.*
- *I felt as if I had been to court and they took away my kids and gave me visitation rights.*

Obviously, for the general educator to take the primary responsibility for all of the students in the elementary classroom, including those with IEPs, a major shift will need to occur. However, when elementary teachers see the social and academic gains students with disabilities make when included in general education classes, they often become the strongest advocates for inclusion.

Secondary Schools

Special considerations must be observed when working with students in middle and high school. Factors such as the widening gap of skill levels among the students as they get older, as well as the lack of proficiency in the use of higher order thinking skills and strategies required at this age, affects the progress of secondary school students with disabilities (Schumaker, Deshler, & Ellis, 1986). MacKinnon and Brown (1994) found that the "historical-structural" make-up of secondary schools focuses on curriculum and homogeneity of students. "Emotional lows were evident when the teachers spoke of their shock and frustration when first confronted with the need to teach students with complex problems" (p. 143). One secondary school teacher's reaction was:

- *How am I supposed to be a preschool teacher or a primary teacher when I have always been a junior high school teacher? I felt almost like a first-year teacher all over again (p. 142).*

Another secondary teacher expressed her anxiety at including students with disabilities in this way:

- *I did have grave concerns about them being able to function successfully. I felt they would get lost in the shuffle and pull everyone else down as I dealt with lower skills and bad behaviors.*

Special education teachers in secondary schools often get asked, "Is he one of yours?" The expectation is that although the student may be spending time in the general education classroom, the special education teacher is the one *really* responsible for the student's academic and social program.

Sharing and clarifying roles is often a new experience for secondary teachers who traditionally concentrate in one subject area. In an inclusive setting, special education teachers may provide direct instruction in the general education setting, and an increasing number of special education assistants may work with general education teachers in the classroom. However, as the special education teacher's role evolves from an independent entity within the school to a resource consultant, co-teacher, and team member, the general education teacher takes on the primary responsibility for educating students with disabilities. Working as an interdependent team takes a great deal of planning, flexibility, and openness to new ways of doing things. "Teaching widely diverse groups of students is shared work. Because it is shared work, the structural configuration of the school must change to accommodate the common time for the necessary planning, problem solving, and creating new knowledge that is essential for successful inclusive educational practice" (MacKinnon & Brown, 1994, p. 149).

Middle School

Because middle school students are by nature diverse physically, emotionally, intellectually, and socially, it is at this level that the inclusion process can be very successful. The strengths and needs of students of this age are varied and change over time. Middle school educators know that their students are unique and that their programs must reflect the diverse needs and characteristics of this age group. When the needs of students with disabilities are viewed as another form of this diversity, the prospect of successful inclusion at the middle school level is promising (Bradley & Fisher, 1995).

High School

In high school inclusive environments, unique and significant challenges arise. The established roles of teachers are very specific because their focus is on subject matter and graduation requirements. It is easy for special education teachers to be identified and to identify themselves as educators who only work with students who have disabilities. Often teachers who are focused in a certain discipline (i.e., math) are perceived as very bright. Conversely, many believe that you do not have to be smart to teach special education. The suggestion of co-teaching, then, is often initially out of the question. The transition to maintaining ownership of *all* students with differing abilities is a paradigm shift that often requires a great deal of diligence and support for the high school teacher.

A Changing System

> *Organizing and implementing an organizational change program in an educational setting is a complex endeavor...*
>
> Illback & Zins, 1995

As educators and school systems develop inclusive schools, they are finding that change in one piece of the system affects the whole system (O'Neil, 1993). Improvement in existing practices (i.e., parts within the system) without attention to the entire system only addresses the symptoms. *Systemic change* must affect the core of the system so that sustained change can occur. As schools and classrooms change from segregated to inclusive educational practices, issues that affect the entire school system, such as grouping practices, instructional techniques, and teacher education, must be considered.

Frequently, two parts of the system, teacher collaboration and instructional modifications, are given the most attention as schools and schools systems change to an inclusive model. However, other components of the system must be addressed as well. The entire organization of special education, including eligibility for services, must be addressed. Moreover, the ways in which students with disabilities are included—or not—in testing and accountability systems (e.g., statewide tests given at certain grade levels) are also affected when a school system changes to a more inclusive philosophy. When students with disabilities are included in more substantial parts of the general education classroom, all parts (including assessment systems) of the existing educational system are affected.

Although it is most productive when individuals are committed to the proposed innovation before it is forced on them at an institutional level, mandates accompanied by appropriate and adequate assistance can help facilitate success in the change process (Loucks-Horsley & Roody, 1990). Fullan (1991) reminds us that people often need pressure to change even if they support the innovation. Systemwide or whole-school mandates can "grease the wheels" for the development of inclusionary practices. Evidence has shown that if implementation is successful and improved student performance is observed, favorable attitudes often result. Many teachers are no longer waiting for their schools systems to be ready to change, but instead are attempting individual and small-group change in order to ease the way for systemic change. "Most successful change is simultaneously top-down and bottom-up" (Loucks-Horsley & Roody, 1990, p. 53) and requires both collaborative and individual initiatives.

For example, educators who develop inclusive classrooms may have done so without overt administrative support and without an explicit district policy that supports inclusion. Although it is frequently noted that administrative support is critical for developing inclusive schools (e.g., Schattman, 1992), we have found a surprising and encouraging number of general and special educators who have developed outstanding programs in their classrooms.

Supporting the Change Process

Systematic Change

In order to accomplish systemic change (i.e., change in the system), a systematic way to address the components of the change is developed. Systematic change involves exploring the variables that impact on the change itself. With those variables in mind, the following questions are asked:

- Where do we want to go?
- How do we want to get there?
- What do we need?
- Who do we need?
- How can we make sure we'll all be all right along the way?
- Why should we do this?

Systematic change realizes that all of these questions need to have flexibly planned answers, resources, and pathways. Systematic change means that adequate attention is given to two primary factors: The *system* itself and the *people* associated with that system.

Because change is a process and not an event, increasing the likelihood that a change, reform, or innovation will actually occur involves balancing several elements. As illustrated in Figure 3-2, there are several key pieces to the change process; when one piece is missing, the end result is affected in a dramatic way.

Furthermore, there are over thirty steps to promote and produce change listed in business and education literature. A synthesis of this literature reveals that there are two predominant elements consistently found in steps for change: the identification of a *vision* and the development of a *plan* (see Figure 3-3).

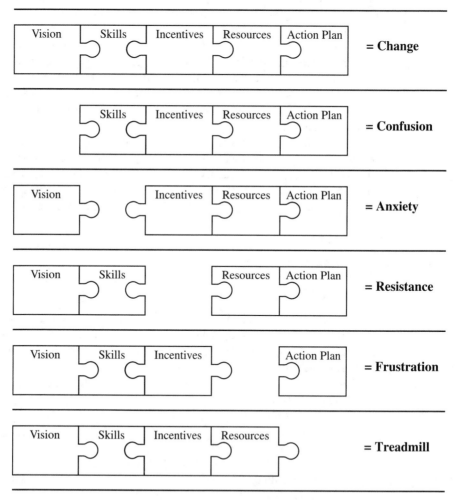

FIGURE 3-2   Interlocking components of complex change.

Source: Villa, R. A., & J. S. Thousand (Eds.). (1995). *Creating an Inclusive School.* Alexandria, VA: Association for Supervision and Curriculum Development. Copyright 1995. ASCD. Used by permission.

FIGURE 3-3 Ten plans for change.

Plan	Step 1	Step 2	Step 3	Step 4	Step 5	Step 6	Step 7	Step 8
Managing Complex Change (Knoster)	Identify the vision	Identify resources	Provide for skill development	Develop the PLAN for change	Provide incentives			
Process Steps to Achieve School Effectiveness (Rhode Island)	Form teams	Assess needs	Prioritize	Develop the action PLAN	Implement plan	Monitor progress	Evaluate impact	
Management of Change in Schools (Schlechty)	Define the problem	Create role structures to sustain change	Plan for institution-alization	Manage change via high authority	Involve affected people in change	Develop the PLAN for change	Identify the vision	Implement the plan
Process Improvement (Cyr)	Educate & involve senior management	Develop a PLAN for change	Provide training & skill development	Build in early wins to raise credibility & momentum	Recognize & celebrate success			
Reengineering as a Cooperative Process (Smith)	Prepare for change	Identify the process for change	Identify the vision	Identify the solution: technical and social design	PLAN the transformation			
Methods to Support Change (Harrison)	Set Direction	Develop a measurement system	Identify the vision	Develop problem-solving projects	Design improvements	Implement change	Imbed continuous improvement	
Elements of Complex Change (Gutleridge)	Need and want to change	Identify the vision	Develop the action PLAN	Identify how to maintain the change				
Six Conditions to Shift (Battaglia)	Need and want to change	Identify the vision	Communicate benefits & difficulties	Develop the implementation PLAN	Develop the measurement system	Reinforce change		
Strategic Management Process (Buhler)	Identify the vision	Move toward vision	Justify why vision important	Develop the PLAN for change				
Elements of Change (Anderson)	Identify the vision	Garner public & political support	Network	PLAN for teaching & learning changes	Identify administrator roles and responsibilities	Ensure policy alignment		

69

Identifying a Vision

With any change, the first step is the creation of a goal or a vision (Rigazio-DiGilio & Beninghof, 1994; Sparks, 1992/93; Villa & Thousand, 1992). Stump (1994) defines vision as a clear and straightforward statement of how an organization will look in the future. Articulating a vision assumes that the organization's members are capable of self-management and self-direction when they clearly understand where they are headed. Using the vision, decisions about the organization's operations, policies, and procedures are made in light of how well they support the vision.

Short-term, strategic planning that only reacts to problems is not sufficient to sustain a change process (Senge, 1990). Several definitions about vision note both the futuristic and personal value elements involved:

- Contains a clear, positive, forceful statement of what the organization wants to be in five or ten years (Hunt, 1992)
- Comes from personal desires and values (Stoner, 1990)
- Emerges when individual's visions can be unified into a shared vision (Senge, 1990)
- Inspires, empowers, and challenges while encouraging people to take risks to advance the vision (Peters, 1987)

Creating a vision statement begins with a close examination of "the values, ideals, hopes and beliefs that motivate program change" (Rigazio-DiGilio & Beninghof, 1994, p. 82). Input and active participation should be sought from as diverse a group as possible as the vision is developed (Zins & Illback, 1995). For example, one school's vision statement reflected the school's commitment to ownership for educating all students in the general education setting as a school priority. Accompanying the vision was a commitment by educators to provide the best and most inclusive program for every student while also meeting their needs for differentiated instruction and curriculum. Goals to support this school's vision were delineated.

Involving school-based educators in the development of the vision statement and plans for change can lower anxieties and give educators both motivation and a sense of empowerment (Bradley & West, 1994; Giles, 1992; Villa & Thousand, 1992). In this way their values, opinions, attitudes, and contributions become part of defining and implementing the new system.

Developing a Plan

Once the vision is established and the change is a reality, then the *plan* is developed. Those who will be responsible for implementing the plan need to have input into the plan itself. It is difficult to describe a plan that works well for every school; considerable attention must be given to the individual characteristics of the school as well as the elements of the plan and how they are to be accomplished. Although a variety of steps can be used and the sequence can vary, the following guidelines apply to most successful plans:

- Assess needs, and involve the people who will carry out the plan in its development.
- Develop a measurement system that lets you know when you get closer to where you want to go.

- Don't expect that the plan will maintain itself without careful preplanning, attention, and support—make institutionalization of the innovation a part of your plan.
- Celebrate movement toward the vision—reinforce people frequently.
- Make steps in the plan clear and practical so that they will be useful and measurable, yet leave room for creativity and originality.

Introducing the Change

Villa and Thousand (1992) remind us that through observation and imitation, people can be convinced of the feasibility of new practices. Therefore, successful examples of the vision need to be available. Experimental, model, and demonstration projects can provide educators with opportunities for study and replication as well as a format to ask questions and obtain first-hand experience from the people involved. Innovations are more likely to succeed if they are well defined and have been tried before with successful results (Loucks-Horsley & Roody, 1990). An action plan needs to be developed so that participants have a clear picture of the direction of the innovation. Delineating anticipated outcomes as well as the identification of objectives, timelines, and people responsible provides a helpful structure (Rigazio-DiGilio & Beninghof, 1994).

When the idea of inclusion is introduced, resistance can be expected. It is often a good idea to maintain some stability and familiarity with old paradigms while slowly implementing various facets of the change to inclusion as staff members build their commitment. People need opportunities to grieve old practices and program structures (Evans, 1993; Williamson & Johnston, 1991). They need a chance to discuss and develop an understanding of the change. At some point people need to believe in the inevitability of change; that it is really going to happen!

Expanding the Innovation

As a new order (e.g., the plan) is determined to fit the structure of the new paradigm, there are several methods that the school system can employ to help educators move from an awkward to a more automatic use of new skills and practices. Loucks-Horsley and Roody (1990) suggest three important methods for helping people move through the stages of change in a positive manner: (1) information, (2) inservice training, and (3) technical assistance. Rigazio-DiGilio and Beninghof (1994) offer a four-step process to operationalize an action plan:

1. Share the vision.
2. Amass a cadre of interested staff members.
3. Address program needs through a professional development plan.
4. Reallocate resources (physical, financial, human).

Villa and Thousand (1992) suggest several ways to empower educators as they move through the change process:

1. Create a format so educators can share their expertise, materials, and successes.
2. Ensure that everyone is represented on the decision-making team.
3. Provide a format so people can express and advocate for their concerns.
4. Build in rewards for incremental progress.

Common elements from the above methods are the sharing of information, ideas, and talents to support educators and establish an ongoing process for including all stakeholders in the process. Professional development in the form of in-service training, conferences, and collaboration is essential.

Concerns of teachers during the change process are influenced not only by the type of change they are being required to make, but especially by the amount of assistance that accompanies the change (Hord et al., 1987). Breaking down the planned change process into manageable parts helps to set reasonable expectations. Introducing and then implementing the change in stages facilitates appropriate assignment of responsibilities and prevents staff members from feeling overwhelmed. During this transition phase, the most important type of support is technical—training and materials (Bradley, 1993; Evans, 1993). As educators move toward building an inclusive school model, the expertise of those in the school building needs to be recognized. Successes need to be shared and celebrated to encourage people to move even further ahead and to take new risks. Pointing out to teachers that they already attend to individual differences in their classrooms can help to lower their anxiety (Giles, 1992). As people begin to make changes, Villa and Thousand (1992) advocate rewarding anything that is consistent with the vision even if it does not contain all the components of the planned change.

Maintaining the Change

Completion does not involve simply getting to the change, but also developing ways to continue being there. Ways to sustain and maintain change are necessary pieces of change plans.

Educators often undergo positive transformations as they become comfortable with an innovation. Seventeen out of the nineteen teachers taking part in a program in which they had a student with severe disabilities in their general education classes underwent attitudinal changes from negative reactions to positive support. They described the ways in which they had changed over the year (Giangreco at al., 1993):

- Learned new skills
- Became willing to interact with the student with disabilities
- Changed their attitudes toward the student
- Changed their attitudes about themselves (from fighting against having the child in the general education classroom to advocating for the student to be included the following year)
- Felt more pride in themselves
- Increased their confidence levels
- Acquired better planning skills
- Became more aware of individual needs of all students
- Gained an ability to recognize and build on *similarities* among students rather than differences

They expressed feelings such as "positive, good, successful, interesting, amazed, pleased, great, wonderful, and enjoyment" (p. 364).

In addition, the benefits to the students with disabilities that were observed included:

- More awareness of their environment
- Increase in skill levels

- More participation in school and community life
- Better availability of role models and other types of stimulation

Some of the most important benefits that occurred were to those students without disabilities. These students not only served as role models for the teachers as they accepted and demonstrated a comfort level with the students with disabilities, but they also showed increases in the following:

- Awareness of people with disabilities
- Appropriate social relationships
- Levels of social development and empathy

As both teachers and students began to view the students as people instead of as disabilities, they gained valuable life skills and increased confidence (refer to Table 3-1 for statements from other educators who have experienced similar transformations as they implemented inclusion).

Significant positive changes occur when teachers are given opportunities to experience successes with inclusion. However, when individuals are left alone to implement changes, they often talk themselves out of involvement in the innovation (Giles, 1992). Therefore, it is crucial to support and maintain the change as well as to continually improve the implementation.

In order to help bring about congruence between a plan and its practical implementation, a system for evaluation must be in place (Schlechty, 1991). Methods for collecting and sharing data must be built into the system. The resulting information can then be used to refine and improve on the original plan.

For change to be successful it takes strong financial support and "a culture that nurtures competence, morale, and initiative" (Evans, 1993, p. 21). Resources in the form of supplies,

TABLE 3-1 **Educators' comments on their transformations during inclusion.**

- I learned that what I thought were LD traits (poor spelling, lack of organization, immaturity, etc.) were really "kid" traits.
- I noticed that I was removing many of the limitations I had silently placed on some students.
- I worked with four teachers in the classroom. *We* developed wonderful lessons. *We* laughed. *We* argued. *We* gave those kids everything we had. *We* all succeeded in an inclusionary setting.
- I found that [the students] would tailor their own success by making choices. Despite my concerns and the daily frustrations, it was an exciting and rewarding year. It caused me to grow both individually and professionally.
- I no longer question my commitment to the program. There are times that I still wonder when and how the more functional aspects of the students' needs will be met. But when I think about my kids hanging out at the lockers or laughing at the lunch tables like any other students in the cafeteria, I can see that the program is really making a difference to all students.

personnel, and training must be available to support the change and to demonstrate the commitment of the agency to the innovation. Specific proposals should be made for the continuation of the new procedures, and appropriate supports need to be supplied to carry out the plans.

Roles and Responsibilities

> *General educators need the resources which are currently delegated to special education programs to help them adapt and individualize instruction for the diverse student populations found in their classrooms.*
>
> Gersten & Woodward, 1990

When a school makes the change to include students with disabilities in general education classrooms, there are several issues that the change agents (e.g., educators) must face. First, the way in which staff and materials are used needs to be reconfigured. This involves role changes for people resources and distribution of material resources. Staff development that prepares people for new roles is imperative; a change plan that omits ongoing professional development may be doomed from the start. When these types of structures are changed, providing information to parents, students, and other interested individuals such as school boards, community agencies, and business partnerships is necessary. Methods for coordinating curriculum delivery under the new context of a diversified curriculum and techniques for heterogeneous instruction are essential. Change plans must also explicitly address support for individuals. As they change, educators need forums (both formal and informal) in which to share their experiences and accrue personal and professional support.

Another useful activity to help prepare educators for changes in roles and responsibilities is to examine the benefits and challenges of the proposed change from the perspectives of the various stakeholders (special educator, general educator, classroom assistant, administrator, related service provider, parents, etc.). Close examination of their input can help them develop a unified vision as well as identify hurdles that need to be addressed as they shift roles. This information can facilitate the development of a systematic plan for modifying roles and responsibilities tailored to specific student, school, and staff needs.

There are several specific tasks in which school staffs can engage to facilitate the establishment of joint roles and responsibilities. For instance, it is useful for staffs preparing for inclusion to develop a list of roles and responsibilities currently being addressed by each educator separately (see Figure 3-4 for an example). This list can then be used as a springboard for discussion and collaborative decision making on the roles and responsibilities of each team member who is "sharing" a student.

Special and general educators in Maryland who are involved in including students in general education classes shared the role changes that they encountered when implementing inclusion in their schools (see Tables 3-2 and 3-3). These lists highlight the necessity of teamwork and cooperative teaching and planning to accommodate a variety of learners (refer to chapters 5 and 7 for more information on teaming and planning).

	General Educator	Special Educator	Other
Establishing Classroom Routine			
Taking attendance			
Checking homework			
Establishing classroom standards			
Establishing a daily schedule			
Developing and Enforcing Behavior Management			
Establishing classroom rules			
Enforcing classroom rules			
Developing student behavior management plans			
Monitoring student behavior management plans			
Planning and Delivering Instruction			
Deciding on curriculum content			
Lesson planning			
Selecting instructional strategies			
Implementating instructional strategies			
Working with small groups			
Modifying assignments			
Helping students who are having problems			
Selecting IEP goals for students			
Coordinating IEP goals with curriculum			
Monitoring daily student performance and needs			
Completing Paperwork			
Grading assignments			
Reporting grades			
Completing teacher referral reports			
Writing IEPs			
Communicating with parents			

FIGURE 3-4   Roles and responsibilities of team members.

Source: Developed by LRE School Support Team, Montgomery County Public Schools, MD, 1995. Used with permission.

As teachers and administrators act as change agents to facilitate inclusion, they must communicate their vision, set examples, and empower others so that the shared vision of inclusion is accomplished (see Table 3-4 for characteristics of change agents). Educators have a multitude of duties and responsibilities, therefore leaders who maintain the qualities of resiliency, respect, and resourcefulness have a supportive impact as these educators go through the necessary transformations to create inclusive classrooms.

TABLE 3-2   Role changes identified by special educators.

Instructional	Logistical	Personal
Shared instructional responsibility	Being a member of many teams (more team meetings)	Have to come out of isolated area
Having lots of ideas/ materials available to differentiate	Teaching larger groups of students	Advocating for self and teaching self-advocacy to students
Becoming familiar with general education curriculum	Training peers as helpers	Improving communication and organizational skills
Teaching more compensatory skills	Adapting physical space and layouts of general education classrooms	Sharing of resources, space, and responsibility
Creating joint goals with general educators	Using adaptive equipment in the classroom	Letting go of protectiveness of students
Social skills instruction	Finding co-planning time	Not being the sole educator for students with IEPs
Responsibility for general education students	Not having own space—always in someone else's room	"Visiting" your students
Instructional assistants in someone else's class	Someone is there if you have to leave the room	Dealing with other adult personalities
Exposure to new ideas		Becoming one of us rather than one of them
Witness benefits to students		
Special education program is coordinated with general education program		

An Inclusive Transition Experience

The experiences of a large middle school in Montgomery County, Maryland, that changed to an inclusive model clearly indicate the impact of change. The students in this school represent a diverse population both racially and culturally, and about ten percent have disabilities, primarily learning disabilities and emotional impairments.

Our school had been moving in the direction of inclusive services for the students with mild learning disabilities for several years. The special educators and the school administrators were eager to advance the inclusive model to incorporate the students with more intensive learning disabilities who were still in self-contained academic classes all day. Special educators, administrators, and the reading specialist set up a planning meeting and invited all of the other providers of student support services, including the ESL (English for Speakers of other Languages) and the teachers of the children at-risk of academic failure who were not identified to receive special education. There were heated discussions regarding the changes to a more inclusive model. The most resistance came from the ESL teachers who were very comfortable with their current model and felt it was working very effectively. Role change came to the surface immediately as a major concern. The special education

TABLE 3-3   Role changes identified by general educators.

Instructional	Logistical	Personal
Sharing resources	Sharing the classroom	Distinguishing the roles of adults in the classroom
More use of cooperative learning techniques	More use of adaptive equipment and materials	Necessity to plan ahead
Flexibility with short-term and long-term planning	Making space for adaptive equipment	Willingness to change
More interaction with community resource programs	Making time for collaboration	Openness to new ideas and techniques
More differentiated instruction, record keeping, and grading	Accommodating storage needs	Taking joint ownership of students with IEPs
Co-teaching and peer coaching	More meetings to attend	Sharing belief systems
Implementing IEP goals		
Including parents as team members		
Expanding behavior management techniques		
Increase in accountability		
Need to give multiple students simultaneous attention		
Have to learn special terminology		
Use of unfamiliar technology and equipment		
More instructional modifications		
More individualized instruction		

teachers who had been teaching the self-contained classes were also voicing concerns which took two forms. First, they were concerned that the students would not be able to function in the regular classroom because the general educators would not be accommodating enough. Secondly, they were concerned about their ability to team teach in several classrooms with different content and with teachers having different styles. The group met several times to work through these issues and develop a proposal to be presented to the staff for their input.

The Inclusive Model

The model that was presented to the staff was as follows:

- *Assign students with any special need to teams randomly.*
- *Keep the number of students assigned to any team as equitable as possible.*
- *Assign one student support staff member to each team to provide consultation, team teaching, and pullout support for those students who required small group instruction.*
- *Continue ESL classes for those students who required intensive English instruction.*

TABLE 3-4   Characteristics of change agents.

- May come from any level of the organization (top down and bottom up)
- May come from inside or outside the organization
- Are resilient—perceive obstacles as opportunities
- Are creative
- May be perceived negatively or positively
- Consistently focus on their vision
- Seek out supports—empower others
- Solve problems
- Gather energy from many sources

The purposes or goals of the model were to (1) improve the delivery of support services to students with all kinds of special needs, (2) ensure the inclusion of special needs students in the general education classroom to the maximum extent possible, and (3) improve teacher knowledge and skills in differentiating instruction to meet individual needs of students. The model reconfigured the working roles of the general education staff, special educators, ESL teachers, and other special needs staff in the building, and resulted in the development of criteria to measure student success, to provide teacher training, and to determine further adjustments and refinement of the service delivery model. The objectives defined in the model were the following:

1. *To improve the academic achievement of special education ESL and at-risk students*
2. *To increase the services available to students who have not been identified as eligible for special education, ESL support, or at-risk support*
3. *To provide increased opportunities for inclusion in general education classes for those students receiving more intensive special education services.*
4. *To increase the heterogeneous mix of students on teams and increase understanding of individual differences*
5. *To allow for collaboration among and sharing of knowledge between support providers to maximize the level of support available within the building*

The model included planning a series of staff training workshops on differentiated instruction.

Staff Reaction

The model was presented and much discussion and clarification took place. The staff leaders presented the plan to their teams and brought back the general staff reactions for consideration and further planning. The reactions varied widely. Some staff were in favor of the change and open to trying new strategies. Some staff were definitely opposed to the model and communicated that they thought they had no input into its development. Their perception was that the model had been completely planned before it was presented to them and that it was not open to change.

This reaction was very instructive to the administrators and the rest of the planning group. It was clear that a mistake had been made. The planning group should have included a group of general educators, perhaps representing each team, from the beginning of the process. Other reactions focused clearly on role change issues and professional competence issues. Listed below are some of these issues:

- *Teachers were not trained to work with students with more intensive needs and could not be expected to do this.*
- *Students with disabilities would disrupt the class and take time away from the other students.*
- *Teachers were concerned about the level of support they would receive and about the expectations of their adaption of curriculum. Who would be in the room with them? How could they work together? Would the support person be there every day? Would they share the load?*
- *Teachers wanted assurance that students were getting the legally required services to which they were entitled.*
- *Teachers were concerned that the special educators were passing their job off on to the general educators.*

Planning Revisited

The planning continued, this time with representative members of the general education staff. The planning group attempted to address all of the concerns that had been raised. The model was revised to limit the heterogeneity of the students assigned to each team. A time-line of activities was developed. This model was viewed as a multi-year project with the first year containing the bulk of the staff training and substantial model evaluation. As the school year progressed, the planning committee collected staff concerns that needed to be addressed. The following were identified:

1. *The model was implemented with too little training. There was a need for continuing training.*
2. *There were concerns about the behavior and lack of motivation of many students including those identified for support and those who had not been identified.*
3. *There was frustration due to the academic diversity and the need to differentiate instruction. There was a perceived need for increased teacher support.*
4. *There was a need for the development of a plan for crisis intervention for those students who were not having a successful class period or day.*
5. *There was a need to look at both qualitative and quantitative factors when evaluating the model.*
6. *There were both positive and negative experiences occurring within the building. Teams needed to share with each other and benefit from each others' experiences.*

These suggestions came from the staff after having a year's experience with the model:

- *Assign each instructional assistant to a team rather than assigning to random classes.*
- *Separate the students more, especially those with more intense needs; the groups should be more heterogeneous.*
- *Have equal numbers of students with significant problems on each team.*
- *Create a staff position and location for providing crisis support.*
- *Have a flexible pullout support program available if a student needs more than one class period of support.*
- *Provide training on team teaching and teaming with instruction assistants, differentiating instruction, motivating reluctant learners, and effective methods of discipline.*
- *Provide opportunities for staff to observe colleagues to get additional ideas.*
- *Use high school students as volunteer mentors and tutors.*
- *Provide teachers with lists of students and accommodations at the beginning of each year (or grading period if necessary).*

Implications of Change

The original model that was proposed entailed too great a level of change and did not involve general education staff to the optimum extent. After having some experience with the model, suggestions led the planning group back to the originally proposed model the second year. This big leap could not have been taken in the first year, but the staff was ready the second year. There were areas of success and failure. Where staff were willing to try new strategies and the students were more heterogeneously grouped, the model was more successful. The teachers who approached the model positively as well as some of those who were skeptical had a positive experience. Other staff who were dubious about the plan had a very negative experience. These staff have asked to move to a school setting where they do not have to deal with this level of diversity in the classroom. Concerns still remain regarding the need for training and the amount of support teachers will get in their classrooms, as well as the types and severity of the disabilities teachers will be facing in their classrooms in the future. The most crucial factor that impacts successful change seems to be the teachers' willingness to try new things with an open mind. The level of trust between teachers who will be teaming together is also critical. Facing change can be overwhelming and taking change in increments seems to have helped the staff in making the adjustments.

Diane Switlick, Assistant Principal, Gaithersburg, Maryland

Conclusions

Oblivious ... ignorant ... aware ... curious ... full of misperceptions ... fearful ... inadequate ... challenged ... uninvolved ... exploring ... adapting ... This sequence chronicles my feelings about inclusion.

As students with disabilities are more fully included in general education schools and classes, educators are undergoing changes in roles as well as expectations. These changes are felt at a deeply personal level.

However, if the purpose of education is to develop learning communities within schools that mirror what students' living communities will look like in the future, then inclusion needs to occur now. Implementing inclusion requires a shared vision and a solid plan. Attention and support for educators implementing inclusive practices is essential as they develop their vision and implement their plan. Soliciting input from the educators involved, providing information, time, training and resources, and maintaining patience as people adjust to and incorporate a new philosophy and structure is essential for the change to inclusion to be successful.

As the education of students with disabilities becomes commonplace in our general education schools and classrooms, the difference of disability will not be the uncommon and atypical difference it is viewed as today. Disability as a difference will be accepted and appreciated, as recognition is given to each individual's gifts—especially by those students and teachers who have grown up with inclusion.

References

Anderson, B. L. (1993). The stages of systematic change. *Educational Leadership, 51*(1), 14–17.

Battaglia, A. J. (1993). Getting out of the box: The role of leadership. *Chief Executive,* (87), 24–28.

Bradley, D. F. (1993). *Staff training for the inclusion of students with disabilities: Visions from educators.* Unpublished doctoral dissertation. Walden University, Minneapolis.

Bradley, D. F., & Fisher, J. F. (1995). The inclusion process: Role changes at the middle level. *The Middle School Journal, 26*(3), 13–19.

Bradley, D. F., & West, J. F. (1994). Staff training for the inclusion of students with disabilities: Visions from school-based educators. *Teacher Education and Special Education, 17,* 117–128.

Buhler, P. (1993). Vision and the change process in the '90s. *Supervision, 54*(1), 17–20.

Conner, D. R. (1992). *Managing at the speed of change.* New York: Villard Books.

Cyr, J. (1992). Building success through process improvement. *CMA, 66*(2), 24–30.

Evans, R. (1993). The human face of reform. *Educational Leadership, 51*(1), 19–23.

Fullan, M., with Stiegelbauer, S. (1991). *The new meaning of educational change.* New York: Teachers College Press.

Gersten, R., & Woodward, J. (1990). Rethinking the regular education initiative: Focus on the class-room teacher. *Remedial and Special Education, 11*(3), 7–16.

Giangreco, M. F., Dennis, R., Clonninger, C., Edelman, S., & Schattman, R. (1993). "I've counted Jon": Transformational experiences of teachers educating students with disabilities. *Exceptional Children, 59,* 359–372.

Giles, E. L. (1992). *Facilitating change for inclusion.* Unpublished manuscript.

Gutteridge, T. G., Leibowitz, Z. B., & Shore, J. E. (1993). When careers flower, organizations flourish. *Training & Development, 47*(11), 24–30.

Hall, G. E., & Loucks, S. F. (1978). Teacher concerns as a basis for facilitating and personalizing staff development. *Teachers College Record, 80*(1), 36–53.

Harrison, D. B. (1993). A methodology for reengineering business. *Planning Review, 21*(2), 6–12.

Hord, S. M., Rutherford, W. L., Huling-Austin, L., & Hall, G. E. (1987). *Taking charge of change.* Alexandria, VA: Association for Supervision and Curriculum Development.

Hunt, V. D. (1992). *Quality in America.* Homewood, IL: Business One.

Illback, R. J., & Zins, J. E. (1995). Organizational interventions in educational settings. *Journal of Educational and Psychological Consultation, 6,* 217–236.

Joyce, B., & Weil, M. (1986). How to learn a teaching repertoire. *Models of teaching* (pp. 469–489). Boston: Allyn and Bacon.

Loucks-Horsley, S., & Roody, D. S. (1990). Using what is known about change to inform the regular education initiative. *Remedial and Special Education, 11*(3), 51–56.

MacKinnon, J. D., & Brown, M. E. (1994). Inclusion in secondary schools: An analysis of school structure based on teachers' images of change. *Educational Administration Quarterly, 30,* 126–152.

McLaughlin, M. J., & Warren, S. H. (1994). Restructuring special education programs in local school districts: The tensions and the challenges. *The Special Education Leadership REVIEW, 2–2*(1).

O'Neil, J. (1993). Turning the system on its head. *Educational Leadership, 51*(1), 8–13.

Peters, T. (1987). *Thriving on chaos.* New York: HarperCollins.

Rhode Island State Department of Education. (1986). Achieving school effectiveness: Process steps and variables. (ERIC Document Reproduction Service No. ED 298 600)

Rigazio-DiGilio, A., & Beninghof, A. M. (1994). Toward inclusionary educational programs: A school-based planning process. *The Special Education Leadership REVIEW,* 81–92.

Schattman, R. (1992). Inclusive practices transform special education in 1990s. *The School Administrator, 49*(2), 8–12.

Schlechty, P. (1991). *Schools for the twenty-first century.* San Francisco: Jossey-Bass.

Schumaker, J. S., Deshler, D. D., & Ellis, E. S. (1986). Intervention issues related to the education of LD adolescents. In J. K. Torgesen & B. L. Wong (Eds.), *Learning disabilities: Some new perspectives* (pp. 329–365). New York: Academic Press.

Senge, P. M. (1990). *The fifth discipline.* New York: Doubleday.

Smith, B. (1994). Business process reengineering: More than a buzzword. *Human Resource Focus, 71*(1), 17–19.

Sparks, D. (1992–93). 13 tips for managing change. *The Developer,* 1–8.

Stoner, J. (1990). Realizing your vision. *Executive Excellence,* 16–17.

Stump, R. W. (1994). Change requires more than just having a vision. *Human Resource Focus, 71,* 3–4.

Thousand, J. S., & Villa, R. A. (1990). Strategies for educating learners with severe disabilities within their local home schools and communities. *Focus on Exceptional Children, 23*(3), 1–24.

Villa, R. A., & Thousand, J. S. (1992). Restructuring public schools systems: Strategies for organizational change and progress. In R. A. Villa, J. S. Thousand, W. Stainback, & S. Stainback (Eds.), *Restructuring for caring and effective education: An administrative guide to creating heterogeneous schools* (pp. 109–137). Baltimore: Paul H. Brookes Publishing Co.

Volk, D., & Stahlman, J. I. (1994). "I think everybody is afraid of the unknown": Early childhood teachers prepare for mainstreaming. *Day Care and Early Education, 21*(3), 13–17.

Webster's Collegiate Dictionary, 10th Edition. (1993). Springfield, MA: G. & C. Merriam.

Williamson, R., & Johnston, J. (1991). *Planning for success: Successful implementation of middle level reorganization.* Reston, VA: National Association of Secondary School Principals.

Wisniewski, L., & Alper, S. (1994). Including students with severe disabilities in general education settings. *Remedial and Special Education, 15*(1), 4–13.

Zins, J. E., & Illback, R. J. (1995). Consulting to facilitate planned organizational change in schools. *Journal of Educational and Psychological Consultation, 6,* 237–245.

Collaborative Team Building

DIANE M. SWITLICK AND DIANNE F. BRADLEY

◆ ADVANCE ORGANIZER ◆

We strongly believe that collaborative teams are the cornerstone of inclusive planning. This chapter highlights the four categories of essential skills in collaboration.

Personal
Interactive
Process
Dynamics

Descriptions of collaboration, rationale for training of both general and special
educators, and actual training material is presented. Each category contains research,
examples, and practical applications of the skills critical to effective team building for
inclusive planning.

---

*The lesson I learned was that it is essential to establish good communication among
all parties involved in the inclusion process. It can make the inclusion experience more positive for everyone. My story begins just before the 1994–95 school year began. The principal informed me that the parents of a child with autism were interested in having their son
attend a general education first grade class for part of each day. My principal felt that I
would be the best teacher because of the degree I had just received in special education
which emphasized inclusive philosophies and techniques. She asked how I felt about the
idea of having a student with a disability in my classroom for part of the day. I was very*

excited to have the opportunity to put my years of study to use. It seemed ironic that a situation like this would arise so soon after spending two years learning about inclusion. It could not have happened at a better time.

The first thing I did was contact the mother of the student with whom I would be working. Our first phone call was very important. We talked over the phone for quite some time. I introduced myself and told her about my background, my experiences, and my degree in inclusion. Mrs. Ireland was relieved to learn that I was excited about having her son in my class. She told me all about her son Patrick. Mrs. Ireland addressed all of her son's strengths and all of the things he was able to do academically. She also pointed out areas that were difficult for him and the objectives on which he was working. We decided that it would be best to wait a couple of weeks before including Patrick in my class. This would give me a little time to get to know my class first. We agreed to talk again toward the middle of September.

After I had time to establish a routine in my class, I called Mrs. Ireland. She expressed an interest in coming to observe my class to decide if her son would be comfortable in this setting. We arranged a time for her to come in and observe. After the observation, she was pleased and told me how the school year was going for Patrick. I had several questions about his classroom setting, and I expressed an interest in observing him in his classroom and talking with his classroom teacher. We set up a meeting for the following week.

I went to Patrick's school and met Mrs. Ireland, Patrick's teacher, and the school psychologist. We discussed Patrick's Individualized Education Program and Mrs. Ireland shared with us the objectives that she would like me to work on in my classroom. Patrick's classroom teacher talked about the setting in the classroom and what to expect. She also gave me a lot of information about what I could do in my classroom that would help Patrick feel successful. She, too, was excited about the idea of inclusion and her insight was very helpful. The school psychologist offered suggestions and took notes. Then it was time for me to finally meet Patrick. His teacher introduced us, and I stayed to observe. We agreed that Patrick should begin coming to my school the following Monday. Patrick's father would drop him off in the morning just as the other students were arriving. Patrick would stay for one hour, then take the school bus back to his other school. We agreed to begin with one hour to see how it would go.

Prior to Patrick's arrival in my classroom, I did some disability awareness lessons with my class. This helped them to understand what it would be like when Patrick arrived.

After one week of having Patrick in a general education class, I gave the Irelands a report on how Patrick did his first week, and I continue to provide updates on his progress. The Irelands and I are in constant communication. They feel very happy and comfortable with how things are going. Our goal is to continue to increase the time that Patrick stays in the general education class. Inclusion was, and continues to be, a very positive experience for all of us and good communication was an essential factor.

Elizabeth Higgins, first grade teacher, Montgomery County Public Schools, Maryland

---

What no one educator can do alone, we all can accomplish together.

Crucial to the success in meeting the increasingly diverse needs of all students in the general education setting is the development of collaborative relationships among the school staff so that expertise may be shared (Thousand & Villa, 1989). Collaboration has been described in the following ways:

- Sharing plans, instruction, and evaluation responsibilities for students (Thousand, Villa, & Nevin, 1994)
- Pooling talents, joint responsibility and accountability, expending of time, energy, and resources for a worthy goal (Phillips & McCullough, 1990)
- Distributing labor, making decisions through consensus (Giangreco, Cloninger, & Iverson, 1993)
- Coordinating, distributing leadership, creating positive interdependence and parity (Villa, Thousand, Stainback, & Stainback, 1992)
- Cooperating, sharing equal status, making unique contributions (Rainforth, York, & Mcdonald, 1992).

All of these descriptions clearly indicate the need for shared responsibility, mutual planning, joint problem-solving, and interdependent attainment of common goals. The purpose of collaboration is to share knowledge and perspectives and, therefore, arrive at better strategies than would be obtained by working alone (Stainback & Stainback, 1992). The result should be improved learning outcomes for all students.

We believe that collaboration is the cornerstone of inclusion. Productive collaboration requires a set of specialized skills. Technical knowledge and sensitivity in communication is required of teachers working in a collaborative role.

Because most educators do not have a strong background in collaborative techniques, training and skills acquisition in this area is necessary for both general and special educators to serve in collaborative roles (Erchul & Conoley, 1991; Friend, 1984; Thousand & Villa, 1989; West & Idol, 1987). A collaborative role requires specific abilities in working successfully with other adults (Erchul & Conoley, 1991). Therefore, to improve the role of teachers as effective collaborators, they must acquire collaborative skills.

West and Cannon (1988) reported competencies that special educators must have to function successfully as collaborators with general educators. Nine major categories emerged:

- Knowledge of consultation theory and models and the accompanying research
- Practice in consultation
- Personal characteristics of the consultant
- Knowledge and skill in interactive communication
- Collaborative problem solving
- Knowledge of systems change
- Experience and knowledge in equity issues, values, and beliefs
- Skills in staff development
- Ability to evaluate the effectiveness of the collaborative effort

Friend (1984) confirmed the importance of these categories in a study asking general educators what they thought special education teachers needed for effective collaborative consultation. The skills they listed indicated much similarity:

- Evaluating interventions for effectiveness
- Sharing information about students
- Brainstorming to generate solutions to problems
- Using strategies for resolving conflicts
- Observing students

Showers (1990) notes that training must include an understanding of the theory, a visual demonstration of the theory, and opportunities to practice the strategies. Training programs that include these components can more effectively produce teachers with the skills necessary for collaborative planning.

To implement collaborative practices effectively, the teacher must be an artful scientist. He or she needs a combination of technical skills that comprise the scientific aspect of collaboration and the art of utilizing the process of collaborative consultation (Idol, 1990; West, Idol, & Cannon, 1989). Both general and special educators must possess these competencies and join in the process as equal partners. The areas of divergence occur in content expertise versus instructional adaptation and modification expertise. This sharing of diverse competencies results in improved instruction and student performance.

The kind of assistance that general educators have not found helpful in collaborative planning is transplanting traditional special education practices such as individual interventions or remediation within the classroom, into the general education environments. Instead, teachers want full consideration of the context of the general education class. When the support strategies respect the values and needs of the classroom, its students, and the teachers, they are more readily accepted and implemented by general education teachers (Giangreco, Dennis, Cloninger, Edelman, & Schattman, 1993). Thus, technical components of the collaborative process must also include content knowledge, teaching methodologies, and intervention strategies for the classroom teacher to instruct students with disabilities. The collaborators must also demonstrate effective communication, problem solving, and decision-making skills to convey this essential information (Idol, 1990).

Acquisition of Collaborative Skills

> *The good news is that collaborative skills can be learned, and that learning how to collaborate is no different from learning how to play a game, or ride a bicycle built for two.*
>
> Thousand & Villa, 1992

Researchers agree that teachers in the collaborative role need formal training in consultation (Erchul & Conoley, 1991; Johnston, 1990; Showers, 1990; Thousand & Villa, 1989). Gersten, Darch, Davis, and George (1991) found that when teachers are not adequately trained in collaboration skills, they tend to avoid the consultation role. How, then, should educators receive their new training?

To effectively educate students with disabilities in general education classrooms, school staffs must have training in collaboration skills. Thousand and Villa (1990) found that in-service training offers the possibility of establishing a common conceptual framework for special and general educators: "In-service programs are the principal means through which educational agencies change the interaction between teachers and students" (National Joint Committee on Learning Disabilities, 1988, p. 53). Training is necessary for both general and special educators. Any training will be beneficial even if all team members are unable to participate. Each individual is encouraged to pursue workshops, university courses, and professional reading in communication and collaboration. Training should be ongoing, systematic, and meaningful to the educators (Miller, 1990; Phillips & McCullough, 1990; West, 1990).

Essential Skills for Teacher Training

> *When students read about collaborative teamwork but experience only loosely organized multidisciplinary teams in both didactic instruction and practical application, it is unlikely that they will truly understand collaborative teamwork.*
>
> Rainforth, York, & Macdonald, 1992

Four essential categories of skills should be included in staff training to ensure the development and maintenance of effective team relationships:

1. Personal—Relationship building, roles, and personal style, which includes examining the personal characteristics of the participants and how their values and beliefs interact to affect the collaborative relationship.
2. Interactive—Communication skills, which address the interactive process and the interpersonal skills of the participants in communicating content and feelings, respect and empathy.
3. Process—Stages in the collaborative process from problem identification to evaluation and restructuring.
4. Dynamic—Stages in team development and interaction. Each of these areas will be discussed in depth. Sample objectives for each set of skills is presented in Table 4-1.

Personal Skills

> *A team is only as strong as the relationships between its members.*

Developing relationships on a team is part of a change process that is incremental and gradual. It consists of building trust and taking risks. Whenever change and risk taking occur, fear can become a factor. (see Chapter 3 for further information). This sense of fear can create perceptions and initiate behaviors that need to be addressed in a caring and supportive

TABLE 4-1   **Essential skills for teacher training in collaboration.**

Content	Sample Objectives
Personal Skills	
Identify roles and personal styles.	To examine personality types, values, and beliefs
Identify preferences and expectations.	To describe relationship hurdles that would be responsive to collaboration
	To examine consultation readiness
Interactive skills	
Content and feelings	To distinguish content from feeling
Levels of ownership	To facilitate cooperative ownership of issues and goals
Nonverbal communication	To increase understanding of verbal communication
Communicating respect	To enhance problem clarification
Respectful questioning	To acquire skills in respectful questioning
Empathy training	To demonstrate skills in paraphrasing and using empathy statements
Giving feedback	To demonstrate three kinds of I Messages
Process Skills	
Problem identification	To describe the problem and collect student and environmental data from a variety of sources
Data collection and analysis	To enhance observation skills
	To examine a variety of strategies, methods, and materials
	To skillfully restate goals
Strategy selection and implementation	To explore the feasibility of various strategies for use in the classroom
	To acquire skill in conflict management
Evaluation	To enhance skills in evaluating and modifying intervention strategies
Dynamics Skill	
Forming, Storming, Norming, and Performing	To examine group developmental stages and characteristics

Source: Adapted from Bradley. (1994). "A framework for the acquisition of collaborative consultation skills." In *Journal of Educational and Psychological Consultation, 5*(1), 51–68.

manner. Building trust depends on a cooperative goal structure. Each member of the group must be committed to providing help and support for all the other members of the group. This commitment leads to the development of positive *interdependence* which translates into both *resource interdependence,* which capitalizes on the contributions of each member's special skills, and *reward interdependence,* through which each person enjoys the rewards of attaining the objective (Rainforth, York, & Mcdonald, 1992). In order to reach the goal of maximizing the achievement of every student, resource and reward interdependence are vital.

Rainforth, York, and Macdonald (1992) and Bradley (1994) outlined strategies that promote the development of positive interdependence in collaborative teams:

1. *Define the purpose of the team.* Construct a shared mission which clearly defines the goals, processes, and roles of the team members. Within the mission is the theme of mutual support, including both technical and moral support and the general responsibilities and expectations of all team members.

2. *Consider the readiness of the participants to engage in the collaborative relationship.* Analysis of participants' readiness stages can be determined by an instrument such as the Consultation Readiness Scale (Cherniss, 1984). Six levels of readiness for consultation are delineated in the instrument. Familiarity with this scale enables any person in a consultative role to ascertain the readiness level of the consultee. In a team setting, it may promote discussion of the stages of readiness that will help all participants achieve a high degree of readiness.

3. *Determine preferences and expectations.* A variety of attitudes, beliefs, values, and personal characteristics can either bring richness to the collaborative process or impose attitudinal barriers that inhibit this relationship. Often those seeking advice already have in their minds preferences for and expectations of how the team should function (West & Idol, 1987). Differences in expectations can lead to resistance, which can play a key role in the degree of success of the team. Training is necessary to help address this resistance to change (Johnston, 1990; Polsgrove & McNeil, 1989).

4. *Explore expectancy and motivation.* Use of an instrument such as the Consultation Model Preference Scale (West, 1985) can assist teams in their understanding of the various expectations of its members. They can then delineate differences in the expectations of their membership. Discussions that evolve about these differences will assist the team in clearly establishing the roles and responsibilities of each member.

5. *Learn specific skills for dealing with reluctance on the part of any member to collaborate.* All team members need to learn essential communication skills together and to practice them as they work. Members may take turns in observing group process and in giving and receiving feedback.

6. *Build and maintain relationships both socially and professionally.* Collegiality among all members of the school staff must be continuously encouraged and nurtured (West et al., 1989). Team-building activities, time to share strategies that work, and social gatherings can all promote closer relationships among staff and team members. Enhanced relationships can greatly affect team functioning.

Interactive Skills

Effective communication skills are a crucial asset to the collaborative process (Bradley, 1994; Friend, 1984; Gersten et al., 1991; Idol, 1990; Johnston, 1990; West, 1990; West & Cannon, 1988; West et al., 1989). Communication can affect the participants' relationships with each other as well as their commitment to and interest in the collaborative process. Interactive communication skills are among the nine clusters of skills identified in an expert-validated study done by West and Cannon in 1988. Special educators support the belief that communication is a critical aspect of the collaborative role (Friend, 1984). Collaborative teams need opportunities to learn to talk with one another (Miller, 1990). Communication is a two way process that involves verbal and nonverbal cues. Effective collaboration relies on the ability of the collaborators to understand and clarify individual communications. Over the past ten years, the authors of this chapter have taught courses in counseling and collaboration that focus on the following categories of skills:

1. Discriminating content and feeling
2. Determining ownership of feelings
3. Asking respectful questions
4. Using empathy statements
5. Using I messages

These essential skills were first organized into a training program by Fagen and Guedalia in 1977. Since that time the model has been modified for use in consultative and team collaborative situations. Staff training in communication skills has included practice and competency-based requirements with structured feedback to ensure proficiency. Participants have consistently reported a high level of application to their collaborative roles and shown a high level of competency in skill acquisition following the courses (Montgomery County Public Schools, 1984–1991). The courses have given teachers the practice necessary to transfer skills to their school sites. The skills included in these courses are described in the following sections.

Discriminating Content and Feeling

> *There are two parts to every communication—First, what is said or the content and second, how it is said or the feelings.*

If team members are to serve as effective collaborators, they need to be able to interpret some of the more subtle cues that the other participants might convey during a collaborative session. Covey (1989) states that "Communication experts estimate that only 10 percent of our communication is represented by the words we say. Another 30 percent is represented by our sounds, and 60 percent by our body language" (p. 241). Therefore, the content that is stated verbally often needs to be further interpreted for underlying messages. For instance, a positive comment accompanied by a grimace or sarcastic voice tone cannot be interpreted by words alone. The collaborator needs to pay attention to the nonverbal content being conveyed. The use of these skills helps explore feelings (Bradley, 1994).

Three basic points must be considered in all communications: (1) people frequently react to the *way something is said* rather than to what is being said, (2) what people say as well as how they say it can be based on *how they feel* at any given point, and, (3) for individuals to understand why they behave in particular ways, they need to recognize that these *feelings affect their behavior.* Structured practice in listening to both content (what) and feelings (how) is essential. Both parts must be identified and communicated back to the speaker for the speaker to feel completely understood. Because feelings often precipitate behavior, understanding feelings can lead to a more effective decision on how to deal with a concern or situation.

In many situations, it is impossible to remember all of the content, but by restating the essential content, you acknowledge the *uniqueness* of each individual's situation. At the same time, reflecting the feelings communicated helps the speaker see their normalcy and the *universality* of feelings.

Following repeated practice, listening for both content and feelings becomes somewhat automatic. Listening with a discriminating ear and acknowledging content and feelings are valuable skills in nearly all situations, including communicating in emotionally charged situations with team members, students, and parents.

Determining Ownership of Feelings

> *Since ownership goes hand-in-hand with responsibility, all team members must accept ownership in order to successfully implement and follow through on the decisions of the team.*

Having gained the skill of listening for content and feeling, the next step is determining the level of recognition and acceptance, or ownership, of those feelings. Many people learn to disguise or conceal their feelings, especially those of anger or affection. This concealment may become pervasive, as people virtually lose touch with their feelings. When people deny or minimize their feelings or blame others, they have a low level of ownership of their feelings (Fagen & Guedalia, 1977). The low level of ownership indicates that the person is not ready to take responsibility for or actively work on solutions to the current situation.

> *I'll bet the principal sent you down here to help me out. I've been teaching for twelve years, and I can tell you right now, it's not me. It's the way we are expected to teach such a wide range of students. No one can handle this.*

When a team member is experiencing a feeling, but talks about the feeling as though it occurred in the past or was related to some past event, this is partial ownership. If the speaker names the feeling but quickly minimizes it or sloughs it off, partial ownership would also be indicated. Partial ownership indicates that a person can identify the feelings effectively, but is still not ready to take full responsibility (Fagen & Guedalia, 1977).

> *They talked their little heads off again today while I was trying to get James and Eddie started on their assignment. Using multiple groups is too hard. I used to get really upset with them when they were off task, but now I just know what to expect.*

When a team member can clearly identify his or her feelings, express them, and accept them, this indicates a high level of ownership. High ownership indicates that the person is ready to assume responsibility and move on to what they can do to solve the problem (Fagen & Guedalia, 1977).

I am still frustrated, but I'm starting to feel good about the progress. I have tried using three groupings, varied peer helpers, and on occasion totally separate activities. Sometimes everything works great and at other times it falls apart. I'm scared I won't be able to find the strategies that will work.

Practice within the team on determining the level of ownership becomes crucial to effective intervention implementation throughout the collaborative process. Team members will continually need to help each other identify the level of ownership. It may be necessary at times to move to a higher level of ownership to effectively plan for change. Helping a team member move to a higher level is a gradual process that is not fostered by direct confrontation. Helping someone move from low to partial ownership may be accomplished by offering the disguised or externalized feeling as a possibility and by

- asking if he or she has ever seen that feeling in others
- asking if he or she thinks there are ever times when a person should feel angry, upset . . .
- using a similar example, labeling the feelings, and asking if he or she has ever felt like this person

Helping someone move from partial to high ownership requires that the team members emphasize the feelings so the speaker can acknowledge the feelings being minimized.

Asking Respectful Questions

Respect is positive regard and caring for others.

Another important aspect of a successful collaborative relationship is respecting other team members (Erchul & Conoley, 1991; Johnston, 1990; Marvin, 1987; Polsgrove & McNeil, 1989; West, 1990). By offering encouragement and support, mutual respect and expectations can be established. To accomplish this, the team members must be willing to take risks and display openness to the rest of the team. An atmosphere must be created in which both parties feel free to expose and discuss concerns. An aura of trust must be present in the collaborative relationship. Communication of respect can create this nonthreatening atmosphere.

Communicating respect is accomplished by demonstrating interest in others. Listening attentively and asking questions to help clarify the message or increase the level of understanding communicates sincere interest and support. To discover team members' thoughts and feelings about an issue or situation, we need to question them in a way that will enable the entire team to gather information.

There are several types of questions that communicate respect (see Figure 4-1). Questioning in any team setting may begin with surface or ice breaker questions and progress to clarification and involvement questions. Each type of question is described and examples are provided. Clarification questions are designed to facilitate the other team members' understanding of the message being communicated. Asking questions like those listed

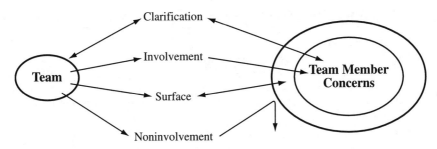

FIGURE 4-1 Respectful questions.

below not only benefits the team, but causes the member with the concern to reconsider what has been said and to think it through one more time.

1. I'm not sure I understand. Could you say a little more about that?
2. What did you mean when you said...?
3. How did it happen?
4. What was different about this time?
5. I missed the last point. Would you mind repeating it, please?
6. Are you feeling angry?

When a message has been clarified, it helps the team to understand a person's orientation and leaves less room for misinterpretation.

Involvement questions serve the purpose of seeking out information about the person's feelings and understanding. They are the kind of questions that get to the core of the concern rather than the surface (Fagen & Guedalia, 1977). There are many kinds of involvement questions, but they usually fall into one of the categories outlined in Table 4-2.

There are also questions that do not communicate respect. Noninvolvement questions are almost rhetorical in nature or may be off the subject completely. These questions do not indicate interest or caring. An example of a noninvolvement question might be to shift the focus to yourself by asking: "That reminds me of a problem I once had. Did I ever show you the chart I used?"

It is important to probe areas of concern without getting sidetracked by surface issues. Surface issues are sometimes raised by the team member to keep the group from focusing on the real issue. An example might be to focus the questions on the students when the team member is angry and blaming the students for the problems (Fagen & Guedalia, 1977). Surface questions often detract from the main issue and keep the team members from getting too close to the core concern.

Using Empathy Statements

Reflective listening conveys respect and empathy to the speaker, and it keeps the channels of communication open.

TABLE 4-2   Involvement questions.

1. Stretch Questions
   a. How do you think the other teachers will react?
   b. What if they are extremely supportive? What might they do or suggest? How would you feel about that?
   c. What if they are extremely angry? What might they do? How would you feel about that?

2. Compare and Contrast Questions
   a. How does this class compare to your other classes?
   b. Have you ever had a student like Susie before?
   c. Have you ever been apprehensive about trying a new strategy?
   d. How did you deal with a similar situation last year?

3. Searching Out Motives
   a. Is there a particular reason you're treating this group of students differently?
   b. Are you feeling pressured to cover more material or maintain better discipline with this class?
   c. Is there something taking your time and energy away from your students?

4. Core Issue Questions
   a. What does it mean to you to make a mistake? What would it mean to you to make a mistake in front of your class?
   b. Are you feeling like you don't know how to make the necessary changes in your classroom arrangement?
   c. Do you feel that you are watering down the content, placing you in accountability trouble?

Another essential skill for collaboration is the ability to convey to others that they are being listened to (Marvin, 1987; Polsgrove & McNeil, 1989; West & Cannon, 1988). The art of reflective listening—whereby the listener maintains attention to the speaker by feeding back feelings, showing respect, and displaying empathy—is an essential competency. It is important to be able to paraphrase and restate the goals and concerns of the participants in order to establish and maintain rapport (Dustin & Ehly, 1984; Egloff & Lederer, 1980; Friend, 1984).

Covey (1989) wrote that the key to effective interpersonal communication is to "Seek first to understand, then to be understood" (p. 237). Although most educators serving in the collaborative role are familiar with reflective listening skills, these are often difficult to put into practice. Team members may see their role as giving advice. However, using the skills of listening and feeding back thoughts and feelings to others can empower *them* to select solutions that will best *satisfy their specific needs*. Use of these skills enables the collaborative team to show encouragement and support in a nonthreatening and nonjudgmental manner.

Empathy is understanding another person, especially what he or she is feeling. It involves going beyond the mere expression of words and intellectual ideas to a deeper level of understanding. When empathy exists for someone else, there is an awareness of an internal frame of reference. Although it is impossible to entirely understand another individual, it is quite possible to strongly identify with his or her feelings and circumstances. Genuine attempts to perceive and verbalize another's feelings can be deeply appreciated. As team members experience the dimensions of respect and empathy, they become more apt to consider alternative strategies and interventions later in the problem-solving process.

Empathic understanding is not characteristic of all people. However, sensitivity to another's thoughts and feelings can be acquired through practice. Teams can practice empathy statements using the rating scale defined in Table 4-3, which has been adapted from Carkhuff (1971).

Using I Messages

> *Negotiation, compromise, and conflict management are useful skills for building a collaborative team.*

To become a true agent of change and still maintain positive relationships with other teachers, team members must be able to provide nonthreatening feedback. Members need the ability to establish cooperative ownership of goals for educating students without offending their colleagues (Bradley, 1994). One way in which this can be done is through the use of assertiveness and confrontation skills (Polsgrove & McNeil, 1989). "I-messages" in which

---

TABLE 4-3   Levels of empathy.

Level 1

Occurs when the team members attempt to be empathic by giving back information or feelings that they have perceived in the interaction. The speaker indicates that these are inaccurate or untrue. The inaccuracy can be due to low ownership on the part of the speaker or to a lack of understanding on the part of the listener. Clarification may need to follow.

Level 2

Occurs when the team members give back the exact content and/or feelings that have been presented. This is sometimes referred to as "mirroring" or "reflective listening." There is confirmation from the speaker that the information is correct.

Level 3

Occurs when the team members present what has been stated with an added element that increases understanding of the situation or feelings communicated by the speaker. This may be achieved by adding a feeling word or a new dimension to the thought or feeling presented. This new information is acknowledged by the speaker as being accurate.

Source: Adapted from Carkhuff, R. (1969). *Helping and human relations.* New York: Holt, Rinehart & Winston.

participants give feedback about themselves by stating their own feelings about behavior and its effect on them can provide nonjudgmental feedback as well as a degree of self-disclosure (Marvin, 1987).

In implementing training with team members, it is useful to emphasize three types of I Messages. Each type has a different purpose (Fagen & Guedalia, 1977).

Disclosure I Messages.   Disclosure messages reveal something about oneself. Messages may relate to past, present, or future experiences. Disclosures indicate a team member has shared similar feelings or has been in a situation that prompted similar feelings. The objective is to confirm the reality or normalcy of another team member's feelings. There are some cautions with disclosure. Team members should take care not to indicate an air of superiority by telling stories about their own great solutions or belittle or minimize another's feelings. An example of a disclosure I Message might be, "I have a lot of difficulty myself handling a wide range of needs in the classroom."

Immediacy I Messages.   Immediacy messages relate to what a team member feels about the person he or she is working with, or what that person is doing at the present time. Immediacy is also promoted by asking questions that deal with the relationship between two or more group members. This is probably the most widely known type of I Message. Examples might be, *"I get annoyed when you come in angry, and it carries over to our discussion of student's needs,"* or *"I'm really glad you feel you can trust me with the information."*

Confrontation I Messages.   Confrontation messages point out discrepancies between what the team member is saying now and what has previously been said or done. These messages also may be used to indicate a lack of correspondence between two different things the person has said or done. Confrontation may involve helpful questioning of the person's perception or interpretation of reality and may encourage the person to see a basis for an alternative viewpoint. This type of message can be difficult to give without becoming blaming or critical. Examples might be: *"On the one hand you said that Tom's mother was totally uncooperative at the conference, and on the other hand you shared three strategies she uses at home that could be of help to us in our planning,"* or *" I was surprised to hear you say that the curriculum modifications we made were a waste of time because I heard you say that Rose stayed on task for five minutes longer today."* Confrontation must be used with care and should only contain items that have actually been reported by the presenter. Confrontation must not be an attack. The major objective is promotion of responsibility and congruence of one's own thoughts, feelings, and actions. Confrontation may be used effectively to deal with two major discrepancies. The first discrepancy is when the team member appears to be more confident or successful than actions indicate, for example, *"I'm getting the picture that the class has adjusted to Tommy's extreme behaviors, and your plans are working well; yet, I saw how tired and worried you looked at the end of the period."* The second discrepancy is when team members present themselves as less confident and capable then their actions indicate. An example is, *"You seem to be feeling as though you will not be able to adapt the materials successfully this time, but I know you have made similar adaptations several times before."*

Process Skills

> *Listening is the ultimate act of empowerment.*
>
>   Blokker, 1994

Experts in the field of educational collaboration identify as many as ten steps in the collaboration process (Bradley, 1994; Erchul & Conoley, 1991; Phillips & McCullough, 1990; Polsgrove & McNeil, 1989). The steps have traditionally followed a problem-solving method that is deficit-based. These can be condensed into four concise stages that encompass the various tasks of the process: (1) problem identification, (2) data collection and analysis, (3) strategy selection and implementation, and (4) evaluation. It is important to consider the purpose of the steps when determining the most effective and productive process to follow. A problem-solving model can be very effective for a specific concern raised by a teacher looking for direct assistance from the team. A problem-solving model may also be effective in conflict resolution between team members. A very closely related model developed specifically for conflict resolution by Blokker (1994) would include (1) accepting feelings about the conflict, (2) determining what is valued and important by both or all participants, (3) agreeing on a problem, (4) determining solutions and consequences, (5) developing and implementing a plan, and (6) evaluating the outcome.

Another process that may prove very useful to any collaborative team is vision-based planning. The team may use this process to plan for team development with the targeted goal being productive and efficient collaboration, or they may use this process model for individual student planning. The essential components of this process are the following: (1) developing a mission or goal statement, (2) collecting data and determining a starting point, (3) determining the specific objectives, (4) developing a timeline and prioritizing the objectives, (5) completing a detailed plan of action with specific responsibilities, and (6) evaluating the effectiveness. This process is described in detail in Chapter 7.

A team must decide which process will best meet the needs of the situation and participants. Once a process is chosen specific roles for each team member can be determined. Since vision-based planning is described in a subsequent chapter, the process section of this chapter will focus on the problem-solving model first discussed in this section so the reader may become familiar with both.

Problem Identification
Problem identification and clarification are essential first steps in the process (Dustin & Ehly, 1984; Erchul & Conoley, 1991; West & Idol, 1987). In this stage, the problem needs to be defined in specific observable behaviors. All team members need to perceive the problem in a similar way to determine the procedures for solving it. For instance, if a teacher describes a student as "inattentive," this description must be clarified. Does the student look out the window? Bother other students? Play with objects? Anecdotal records and specific examples can be provided to help portray a clear picture of the student's behavior. Clarifi-

cation questions can be very helpful in arriving at clear observable statements on the problem. Accurate problem identification is the best predictor of whether the plan will be implemented (Erchul & Conoley, 1991).

Data Collection and Analysis

A second essential step in the collaborative process is data collection (Marvin, 1987; Polsgrove & McNeil, 1989). Data collection begins when the specifics of the problem are discussed and defined. Data must be collected from various sources to obtain numerous perspectives on the problem. In many cases, data collected will define a problem even more clearly or will possibly uncover other problems. Some usual sources of data include formal and informal testing. When formal sources of assessment data are available, such as standardized tests or curriculum-based assessments often called criterion-referenced tests, these may provide valuable insight into the student's current level of performance. When necessary, further data can be collected through behavioral checklists and rating scales. Sociometric data may also be valuable in evaluating social interactions. The list of possible assessments could become rather lengthy (see Chapter 6 for further information).

The data collection phase is a good opportunity for teachers to share information that they have collected about a particular student. Many teachers keep portfolios of student work samples. Work samples provide excellent data on learning styles as well as specific strengths and areas of need. Involvement of the parents and/or the students themselves may be beneficial. Parent interviews often offer a rich source of information about a child. Anecdotal and historical information can be obtained from other school personnel and from school records. Observations of a student in various school environments provide another effective way to gather data (Friend, 1984).

Data collection helps all parties involved assess student strengths and needs by pinpointing specific concerns. Data also help in establishing a measurement procedure that will assist in evaluating the effectiveness of the planned intervention.

Strategy Selection and Implementation

The selection of intervention strategies is a critical step in the collaborative process. Idol (1990) refers to the interventions used in this stage as the utilization of technical skills. Staff training must include specific intervention strategies for team members to share (West & Idol, 1987). Dugoff, Ives, and Shotel (1985) found that classroom teachers described one of the ideal roles of the special education teacher as working with teachers to provide materials and strategies to meet individual needs of the students in their classrooms.

Several effective instructional practices are consistently included in the literature and will be discussed in detail in subsequent chapters of this text (Gersten et al., 1991; Johnston, 1990; King-Sears, Mercer, & Sindelar, 1992; Stainback & Stainback, 1990). Some are listed briefly below:

- Cooperative learning
- Curricular and instructional modifications
- Adaptations of the teaching and learning environment
- Strategy-based instruction

- Inductive thinking
- Peer tutoring
- Curriculum-based instruction and assessments
- Behavior-teaching strategies
- Problem-solving skills
- Metacognitive skills

It is expected that the team members will have varying degrees of expertise in these areas and that they can teach and demonstrate for each other.

Although those serving in the collaborative team role are expected to have a variety of strategies available, it is the classroom teacher who most likely will be the implementor. Often, interventions are not carried out because the teacher does not have the skills or a clear understanding of the recommendations or because the proposed interventions are not realistic or appropriate for the setting. *Therefore, the selected strategies must be realistic and acceptable from the teacher's perspective for them to work.* For instance, Fagen, Graves, and Tessier-Switlick (1984) compiled a number of accommodations for use in the general education classroom with students who have learning disabilities. They field-tested them for "reasonableness" with classroom teachers. Idol and West (1993) developed an "Intervention Feasibility and Effectiveness Scale." Using this scale, team members can identify such factors as impact, adaptation skills, and time needed and then rank them by team consensus. Teams must have the full participation and support of the person who is responsible for putting strategies into practice. These strategies should be cooperatively planned and implemented, and joint or multiple responsibilities need to be defined (Polsgrove & McNeil, 1989).

One way in which support can be engendered for such instrumental strategies as the use of curriculum modifications or adapted teaching methods is through demonstration teaching. This method helps make the intervention realistic and models the correct procedure. This modeling can extend to materials modification and content adaptation. It may take time and several sessions to influence a positive and lasting change.

Evaluation

The purpose of an intervention is to provide positive change benefiting both the teacher and the student. Usually the expected outcome is expressed as part of the strategy, and the desired change is explicit. The measure of the changes occurring and the value of those changes is the evaluation stage of the collaborative process.

If teachers are collaborating to try and reduce the frequency of shouting behavior by a student, they might decide to implement a behavior change strategy that requires the student to record the number of times he or she calls out each day, with the goal being to decrease the number of these incidences. This type of strategy provides immediate feedback to both the student and the teacher, and its effectiveness can be readily evaluated. There is consistent agreement that evaluation is an essential phase of the process (Bradley, 1994; Dustin & Ehly, 1984; Villa, Thousand, Paolucci-Whitcomb, & Nevin, 1990; West, 1990; West & Cannon, 1988).

Although the steps in the collaborative process usually proceed in the order presented, participants may find themselves going back to any of the stages at any point in the process.

The stages must be fluid enough to be able to recycle into any of the other stages. However, ensuring that all stages of the collaborative process are addressed can increase the effectiveness of the intervention and increase the skill level of those who participate in this process when dealing with similar problems in the future (West & Idol, 1987).

Dynamics Skills

> *Regardless of the situation, services for at-risk students are often most effective when professionals pool their expertise and creative energies.*
>
> Knackendoffel, Robinson, Deshler, & Shumaker, 1992

The formation of a collaborative team takes time and work on the part of all team members. Each team becomes a uniquely growing and changing entity. Typically, teams go through several stages before arriving at a truly productive relationship. Tuckman (1972) identified these stages as:

Forming—Searching, testing, wondering
Storming—Conflict, struggle, confrontation
Norming—Progress, organization, cohesiveness
Performing—Innovation, success, celebration

Johnson, Johnson, Holubec, and Roy (1984) also identify four stages of team development:

Forming—Initial trust building
Functioning—Management, organization, leadership
Formulating—Decision making, creativity, task orientation
Fermenting—Using controversy constructively, appreciation of differences

All teams, whether educational, business, or sports go through similar stages. In preparing teams to analyze their own performance and determine their stage of development, the members must be very familiar with the stages of development. The addition of any new member can alter the team's current level of functioning. The stages are described below (Blokker, 1994). Characteristics of each stage are also outlined in Table 4-4.

Forming
At this stage team members have a mixture of feelings ranging from eagerness to begin work and excitement about the new team to anxiety about team members and the usefulness of the team's endeavors. There is a high level of testing behavior, but also a clear dependence on the team leader for direction. The tasks before the team are creating their own structure, defining goals and roles, defining tasks, and assessing skills. The performance level is low and completion of work is very time-consuming. The team leader must assume a highly structured and task-oriented focus.

Storming

During this stage team members experience negative feelings due to the discrepancy between their initial hopes for the team and the reality of their actual level of performance. They may be dissatisfied with their sense of dependence on the team leader's direction. They may even be experiencing anger about the goals, tasks, or action plans that have been produced by the team. There is frequently competition among members for control, power, and attention within the team. The tasks facing the team at this stage are developing collaboration skills, defining roles, determining exactly how they can work together, and handling emotions and emotional blocks to progress. The negative feelings generated during this stage often disrupt group functioning. The team leader must focus on structure as well as relationships during this stage. Conflict resolution is a frequent activity for most teams at this stage. The productivity is typically very low. As the team members increase their functional knowledge of each other, communication skills, and methods of conflict resolution, they begin to develop interdependence, and productivity improves as they move to the next stage.

TABLE 4-4   Team building.

	Forming	Storming	Norming	Performing
Mode	Search	Conflict	Agreement	Production
Stance	Count me in	Who's in charge?	It's coming together	We're good!
Concern	Being included	Control	Communication	Success
Feelings	Wondering Tentative Nervous	Stuck Directionless Frustrated	Optimistic Hopeful	Secure Satisfied Excited Trusting
Relationship to leader	Dependent	Counter-dependent	Independent	Interdependent on team members
Trust	Watchful Guarded Minimal risk taking	Hidden agendas Testing limits	Confiding Sharing	Experimentation Risk taking Division of labor
Participation	Polite Impersonal Tentative	Active Attempts to influence Cliques	Balanced Encouraging	Supportive Open communication
Handling differences	Play down	Expressive Defensive Impatient	Comprise Data flow Active listening	Open to new ideas Respect differences Capitalize on strengths
Ownership	Complaints Blaming	Self-interest Competition	Team sense Cohesive Sense of accomplishment	High commitment Loyalty Flow of leadership

Norming

Dissatisfaction decreases as the teams develop a productive working norm. As productivity increases, the discrepancy between expectations and reality begins to diminish. More positive feelings of harmony and trust emerge as conflicts are resolved. Participants feel better about the team and begin to build confidence in team efforts. This sense of team self-esteem leads to increased flexibility, openness, honest feedback, and even feelings of affection. Goals and purposes become a shared responsibility. The team frequently develops a language of their own and a "culture." The tasks of the team are increasing proficiency in collaborative skills, developing critical and creative thinking skills, providing constructive evaluation, and continuing growth in conflict resolution. The team leader at this stage will relinquish control over the group. There will be a minimum of structure as the leader takes on the role of facilitator. Leadership behaviors focus on managing group dynamics and relationships.

Performing

The team has now reached its peak operating stage. Members are eager to participate and perform with a positive interdependence. The team shares a sense of confidence in producing viable outcomes. There is shared leadership or a true collaborative spirit within the team. The primary focus is on task achievement. As interpersonal issues surface, the team is direct and effective in handling them. Collaborative skills continue to be developed and refined. The performance level is high and time is used efficiently.

The following example provides a look at how the stages of forming, storming, norming, and performing might emerge in a team planning for a newly included student.

Nick, a child with physical challenges, mental retardation, and delayed speech and language, had been educated in a special school for children with disabilities since the age of three. When he was getting ready for first grade, his parents decided that they would like him to attend his neighborhood school. This decision was made for a variety of reasons: (1) They wanted Nick to attend the same school as his brother, (2) Nick was more likely to make friends in the neighborhood, and (3) He would be in a more normalized environment. After they approached the principal of the school, she made arrangements for the team who would be working with Nick to meet on Friday mornings from 8:30 to 9:00 to plan for Nick's school program.

The Friday the first meeting was to take place, Nick's parents arrived early looking anxious and nervous. In the earliest forming *stage of this team, the resource teacher and classroom teacher arrived late to the meeting because they had bus duty on Friday mornings. The principal had an emergency to attend to. Friday was not one of the days that the speech/language pathologist (SLP) was assigned to the school. So the occupational therapist and the parents sat nervously eyeing each other until the other members arrived. However, at 9:00, as the meeting was getting underway, the teacher had to leave the meeting because his children were coming to the classroom. The first meeting lasted for ninety minutes and not much was accomplished.*

As the planning meetings for Nick progressed and Nick entered the class, it looked as though chaos was inevitable. The classroom teacher was resisting writing plans by Friday for the next week because he preferred to do this task over the weekend. The SLP thought the resource teacher should be responsible for seeing that the Individual Education Program (IEP) and accompanying paper work were at the meeting, and the resource teacher thought the principal's secretary should see to that task. After the meetings, the classroom teacher and resource teacher complained in the staff lounge about these crazy parents who insisted that their child with severe disabilities be placed in a general education classroom. It would never work! The teacher even thought about asking for a transfer! The storming *stage was in full swing.*

As the year continued, the principal was able to remove the teachers from bus duty, change the SLP's schedule so she was able to attend on Fridays, and convince the classroom teacher to try for a month having his plans ready by Friday. As the team moved into the norming *stage, service providers took responsibility for making sure the IEP goals for their subjects were at the meeting. They realized some of their goals overlapped and began to plan in a more collaborative manner. Staff members started to listen to parental concerns about why the previous segregated environment was not appropriate for their child.*

Eventually, this group of people was performing *as a team. They had worked together to create plans and adapted lessons that were working for Nick. The educators involved felt secure and were ready to take on future challenges. They had come to see how most of Nick's IEP goals could be accomplished in the classroom. As the year had progressed, the parents' trust in the teachers increased as they saw Nick blossom. They celebrated by bringing refreshments to the team meetings which now were lasting thirty minutes or less. The classroom teacher decided he liked having his plans done by Friday so he could really enjoy his weekends. Most important, all the team members were experiencing the huge amount of progress that Nick was making in his new setting.*

As this group of people moved through the stages of team building, they experienced conflicts, separation, resignation, recognition, coming together, and finally a true celebration of their successes in working together. Each realized they could never have made it through the process without the others. The team solidified as they became interdependent on one another. It is helpful if a team can observe and monitor their own progress through the developmental process. Once team members are aware of the stages, it becomes important to observe the interaction periodically. Table 4-5 contains a Team Observation Checklist that is very useful in providing feedback to a team. It can facilitate discussion and enhance overall functioning. Table 4-6, The Characteristics of an Effective Team, lists the criteria that may be used in evaluating the effectiveness of an established team.

The Home–School Connection

> *When parents are involved in the educational process, their children experience more success in school.*
>
> Guralnick, 1989; Powell, 1989

TABLE 4-5   Team observation checklist.

_____	1. Begins meeting on time
_____	2. Sits in a circle
_____	3. Meetings are on a regular schedule
_____	4. Uses a structured agenda—items, time limit, action/discussion
_____	5. Has agreed to goals
_____	6. Roles are assigned
_____	7. Members express honest feelings
_____	8. Each member participates
_____	9. Feelings are reflected and understood
_____	10. Team discusses interactions
_____	11. Generates and explores multiple solutions
_____	12. Devotes time to positive comments
_____	13. Distributes follow-up equally
_____	14. Accomplishes the set agenda
_____	15. Develops written notes—actions, timeliness, and responsibilities
_____	16. Meeting ends on time
_____	17. Team enjoys meeting

Family participation in educational decision making is not only desirable, it is required by the federal laws concerning children with disabilities. Therefore, it is crucial that educators create a variety of ways to collaborate with families. One way to accomplish this is to maximize the role of families as team members in the group problem-solving process. (See Chapter 5 for more information.) The connection between home and school can be strengthened when the teaching team has an understanding of how the family functions and how family and personal responsibilities impact various members. This knowledge can help facilitate strategies planned for use at school to carry over into the home. A misperception or disagreement about these strategies can create a conflict resulting in a lack of home support (Dunst, Trivette, & Deal, 1988).

Maximizing the involvement of families requires familiarity with some of the factors that both parents and professionals have identified as influencing the quality of home–school collaboration. This section will focus on the factors that influence the effectiveness of communication and collaboration. The actual planning process involving families, and often the students themselves, will be discussed in Chapter 7.

Educators all enter collaborative relationships with perceptions and expectations. When they are planning with family members, their perceptions of "the family" greatly influence their behavior and suggestions. Just as the diversity of students has changed, the structure of the family has changed over the last several years. Collaborative teams must collect information regarding the primary language, cultural beliefs, and family makeup, as well as the time and resources available to the family in a nonthreatening manner (Vincent & Salisbury, 1988). Teams must also be conscious of the fact that family structure and resources change over time. This means that efforts in determining strategies that are con-

---

TABLE 4-6   Characteristics of an effective team.

- Commits to a vision
- Accomplishes change and improvement in task completion
- Communicates personal feelings and attitudes to improve team functioning
- Shares all viewpoints and makes decisions
- Recognizes that all members' opinions are important
- Accepts individual differences, needs, concerns, and expectations
- Focuses the responsibility for success on all members
- Encourages individual freedom of expression
- Uses the unique talents and abilities of each member
- Faces problems and makes modifications
- Handles conflict in a productive fashion

Source: Adapted from Blokker, B. (1994). Team building: Strategies for collaborative decision making and conflict resolution. Unpublished workshop materials, Millcreek, WA.

sistent between home and a school is an ongoing process that requires a great deal of flexibility (Salisbury, 1992). Parents must be the ones deciding on their level of involvement. This level of involvement will widely vary from parent to parent. When a parent makes the decision to have minimal involvement, the team must respect that right. When a parent decides to become highly involved, teams can capitalize on that participation rather than become threatened by it. Collaborative team members must assist each other to remain nonjudgmental and respectful even when there is conflict.

The following suggestions have proven very helpful in relating effectively to families as partners in their child's education:

- Expect conflict to arise.
- Deal with conflict through consensus building.
- Respect and solicit parent input frequently in meetings.
- Expect that you won't have all the answers.
- Begin meetings with ideas—not a completed plan.
- Avoid jargon.
- Communicate frequently with parents and keep many of the communications positive.
- Be patient—Parents may have trouble getting their ideas across to the team, and they may be tense or angry.
- Keep meeting times flexible.
- Use round robin style sharing during the meeting.
- Assist parents with concerns at home whenever possible.

Just as care must be taken to provide options for families to be involved, care must be taken to involve students in the planning process. This involvement becomes increasingly important as students get older. In earlier discussion on the importance of teacher selection of strategies for the classroom and parent selection of strategies for the home, the reader will recall that the student has a significant influence over all strategies to be implemented. If the students have an understanding of their disabilities and give input into the interventions, the likelihood of their success is greatly increased.

Conclusions

Effective collaboration begins with the acquisition of essential skills and an understanding of how relationships are formed and maintained. Teams that work together can, and should, learn and practice these skills together. Throughout the development of the team relationship, care must be taken to observe group process and the stage of group development. Although collaboration skills are not inherent or frequently taught in teacher education programs, they are skills that can be learned by all team members to enhance collaborative team functioning. Building strong teams leads to effective planning. Both collaboration and cooperative planning are critical to the successful implementation of inclusive practices.

References

Blokker, B. (1994). Team building: Strategies for collaborative decision making and conflict resolution. Unpublished workshop materials, Mill Creek, WA.

Bradley, D. F. (1994). A framework for the acquisition of collaborative consultation skills. *Journal of Educational and Psychological Consultation, 5*(1), 51–68.

Carkhuff, R. (1969). *Helping and human relations.* New York: Holt, Rinehart & Winston.

Cherniss, C. (1984). *The consultation readiness scale.* New Brunswick, NJ: Rutgers University.

Covey, S. R. (1989). *The 7 habits of highly effective people: Powerful lessons in personal change.* New York: Simon & Schuster.

Dugoff, S. K., Ives, R. K., & Shotel, J. R. (1985). Public school and university staff perceptions of the role of the resource teacher. *Teacher Education and Special Education, 8*(2), 75–82.

Dunst, C. J., Trivette, C. M. & Deal, A. G. (1988). *Enabling and empowering families: Principles and guidelines for practice.* Cambridge, MA: Brookline Books.

Dustin, D., & Ehly, S. (1984). Skills for effective consultation. *The School Counselor, 32*(1), 23–29.

Egloff, L. J., & Lederer, C. M. (1980). Teacher consultation for mainstreaming: A packet for special educators. *The Pointer,* Spring, 57–66.

Erchul, W. P., & Conoley, C. W. (1991). Helpful theories to guide counselors' practice of school-based consultation. *Elementary School Guidance & Counseling, 25,* 204–211.

Fagen, S., Graves, D., & Tessier-Switlick, D. (1984). *Promoting successful mainstreaming: Reasonable classroom Accommodations for learning disabled students.* Rockville, MD: Montgomery County Public Schools.

Fagen, S. A., & Guedalia, L. J. (1977). *Individual and group counseling: A competency-based manual for in-service training.* Washington, DC: Psychoeducational Resources.

Friend, M. (1984). Consultation skills for resource teachers. *Learning Disabilities Quarterly, 7,* 246–250.

Gersten, R., Darch, C., David, G. & George, N. (1991). Apprenticeship and intensive training of consulting teachers: A naturalistic study. *Exceptional Children, 57*(3), 226–236.

Giangreco, M. F., Cloninger, C. J. & Iverson, V. S. (1993). *Choosing options and accommodations for children: A guide to planning inclusive education.* Baltimore: Paul H. Brookes Publishing Co.

Giangreco, M. F., Dennis, R., Cloninger, C., Edelman, S., & Schattman, R. (1993). "I've counted Jon": Transformational experiences of teachers educating students with disabilities. *Exceptional Children. 59*(4), 359–372.

Guralnick, M. (1989). Recent developments in early intervention efficacy research: Implications for family involvement in PL 99–457. *Topics in Early Childhood Special Education, 9*(3), 1–17.

Idol, L. (1990). The scientific art of classroom consultation. *Journal of Educational and Psychological Consultation, 1,* 3–22.

Idol, L. & West, J. (1993). *Effective instruction for difficult-to-teach students.* Austin, TX: Pro•Ed.

Johnson, D. W., Johnson, R. T., Holubec, E. L., & Roy, P. (1984). *Circles of learning.* Arlington, VA: Association for Supervision and Curriculum Development.

Johnston, N. S. (1990). School consultation: The training needs of teachers and school psychologists. *Psychology in the Schools, 27,* 51–56.

King-Sears, M. E., Mercer, C. D., & Sindelar, P. T. (1992). Toward independence with keyword mnemonics: A strategy for science vocabulary instruction. *Remedial and Special Education, 13*(5), 22–33.

Knackendoffel, E. A., Robinson, S. M., Deshler, D. D., & Schumaker, J. B. (1992). *Collaborative Problem Solving.* Lawrence, KS: Edge Enterprises.

Marvin, C. A. (1987). Consultation services: Changing roles for SLP's. *Journal of Childhood Communication Disorders, 1*(1), 1–15.

Miller, L. (1990). The regular education initiative and school reform: Lessons from the mainstream. *Remedial and Special Education, 11*(3), 17–22.

Montgomery County Public Schools: Annual Reports, In-service Training Unit, 1984–1991.

National Joint Committee on Learning Disabilities. (1988). Inservice programs in learning disabilities. *Journal of Learning Disabilities, 21*(1), 53–55. (Original work published 1981).

Phillips, V. & McCullough, L. (1990). Consultation-based programming: Instituting the collaborative ethic in schools. *Exceptional Children, 56*(4), 291–304.

Polsgrove, L., & McNeil, M. (1989). The consultation process: Research and practice. *Remedial and Special Education, 10*(1), 6–13.

Powell, D. R. (1989). *Families and early childhood programs.* Research monograph of the National Association for the Education of Young Children. Washington, DC: National Association for the Education of Young Children.

Rainforth, B., York, J., & Macdonald, C. (1992). *Collaborative teams for students with severe disabilities.* Baltimore: Paul H. Brookes Publishing Co.

Salisbury, C. (1992). Parents as team members. In B. Rainforth, J. York, & C. Macdonald. *Collaborative teams for students with disabilities: Integrating therapy and educational services.* Baltimore: Paul H. Brookes Publishing Co.

Showers, B. (1990). Aiming for superior classroom instruction for all children: A comprehensive staff development model. *Remedial and Special Education, 11*(3), 35–39.

Stainback, S., & Stainback, W. (1992). *Curriculum considerations in inclusive classrooms: Facilitating learning for all students.* Baltimore: Paul H. Brookes Publishing Co.

Stainback, W., & Stainbeck, S. (1990). *Support networks for inclusive schooling: Interdependent integrated education.* Baltimore: Paul H. Brookes Publishing Co.

Thousand, J. S. & Villa, R. A. (1989). Enhancing success in heterogeneous schools. In S. Stainback & W. Stainback (Eds.), *Educating all students in the mainstream of regular education* (pp. 89–103). Baltimore: Paul H. Brooks Publishing Co.

Thousand, J. S. & Villa, R. A. (1990). Sharing expertise and responsibilities through teaching teams. In W. Stainback & S. Stainback (Eds.), *Support systems for educating all students in the mainstream.* Baltimore: Paul H. Brooks Publishing Co.

Thousand, J., & Villa, R. (1992). Collaborative teams: A powerful tool in school restructuring. In R. Villa, J. Thousand, W. Stainback, & S. Stainback, (Eds.) *Restructuring for caring and effective education: An administrative guide to creating heterogeneous schools* (pp. 73–108). Baltimore: Paul H. Brookes Publishing Co.

Thousand, J., Villa, R., & Nevin, A. (1994). *Creativity and Collaborative learning.* Baltimore: Paul H. Brookes Publishing Co.

Tuckman, B. W. (1972). Developmental sequence in small groups. In R. C. Diedrich & H. Allan Dye (Eds.), *Group procedures: Purpose, Processes and outcomes* (pp. 236–264). Boston: Houghton Mifflin Co.

Villa, R. A., Thousand, J. S., Paolucci-Whitcomb, P., & Nevin, A. (1990). In search of new paradigms for collaborative consultation. *Journal of Educational and Psychological Consultation, 1,* 279–292.

Villa, R. A., Thousand, J. S., Stainback, W., & Stainback, S. (Eds.) (1992). *Restructuring for caring and effective education: An administrative guide to creating heterogeneous schools.* Baltimore: Paul H. Brookes Publishing Co.

Vincent, L. J. & Salisbury, C. (1988). Changing economic and social influences on family involvement. *Topics in Early Childhood Special Education, 8*(1), 48–59.

West, J. F. (1985). Regular and special educators' preferences for school-based consultation models. (Doctoral dissertation, University of Texas, Austin). *Dissertation Abstracts International, 47,* 504A.

West, J. F. (1990). Educational collaboration in the restructuring of schools. *Journal of Educational and Psychological Consultation, 1*(1), 23–40.

West, J. F., & Cannon, G. S. (1988). Essential collaborative consultation competencies for regular and special educators. *Journal of Learning Disabilities, 21*(1), 56–63.

West, J. F., & Idol, L. (1987). School consultation (Part 1): An interdisciplinary perspective on theory, models, and research. *Journal of Learning Disabilities, 20,* 388–408.

West, J. F., Idol, L., & Cannon, G. (1989). *Collaboration in the schools: An inservice and preservice curriculum for teachers, support staff, and administrators. Instructor's manual.* Austin, TX: Pro•Ed.

$$Chapter \quad 5$$

From Isolation to Cooperation in Teaching

DIANNE F. BRADLEY AND DIANE M. SWITLICK

◆ ADVANCE ORGANIZER ◆

Collaboration among educators lends itself to planning and teaching together for the maximum benefit of all students. These arrangements capitalize on the knowledge and skills of the individual educators who influence each student's program. This chapter explores several methods of providing collaborative services to students. The co-teaching arrangements of complementary instruction, supportive learning activities, and team teaching are explored as methods by which services are delivered directly to students by educators working as a team. The indirect services of collaborative problem solving, group problem solving, and peer coaching are also examined. As each model is described, facilitating factors and outcomes of the use of the model are delineated.

Last spring during the yearly sectioning of children into classes for the following year, grade level teachers met, talked, shared, and jostled students from one class to another to formulate classes balanced by race, gender, academic achievement, and social/emotional needs. Although I am a seasoned primary teacher, when I "met," on paper, my first graders whose needs, levels, strengths, and expectations were as varied as their appearance, I knew this year would be different.

With the variety of learning needs in my class (for instance, there were five children who had significant language needs) I realized I would need the support, expertise, and commitment of a specialist to maximize the success of this diverse group of learners. As I thought about preparing a first grade program which would meet the needs of all these stu-

dents, I developed an idea—Could we bring the speech/language program to the children instead of the five students leaving the class at various times of the day? If the speech/language pathologist (SLP) could come into the room to provide service, I could then incorporated her strategies into my teaching throughout the rest of the day. In addition, the students would have the benefit of seeing adults planning and teaching together.

I broached the subject with the SLP, and much to my relief she was open to the idea. We committed ourselves to creating time to examine student needs through IEP goals and objectives and then to team teach these objectives in the regular classroom through the science content. Each lesson taught was designed around both a specific speech/language objective as well as a science objective. What a marvelous experience it turned out to be for all of us! As a regular educator I now have a host of new strategies in my bag of tricks. My teaching partner, the SLP, has a more accurate perspective of what typical learners are capable, of and most importantly, all "our" first graders benefited from having the expertise of both of us.

Bonni Rubin-Sugarman, first grade teacher, Mt. Laurel, New Jersey

---

Teachers working in collaborative models shift the focus of the problems away from the child and move toward changes they can control directly.

Pugach & Johnson, 1990

Best practice guidelines developed for general and special education require that opportunities for collaboration be provided to maximize learning opportunities for all students (Fox & Williams, 1991; Halvorsen & Sailor, 1990; Stainback & Stainback, 1990; Villa & Thousand, 1990). Not only is collaboration encouraged by the school restructuring movement, school improvement reforms, and teacher empowerment efforts (Sailor, 1991; Villa & Thousand, 1992; West, 1990), but there is considerable evidence to support that collaborative teaching models are a fundamental way of successfully serving students with disabilities in the general education setting (Idol, Paoluccci-Whitcomb, & Nevin, 1986; Lew, Mesch, & Lates, 1982; Thousand & Villa, 1989). Encouraging educators from all disciplines to combine their expertise and capitalize on their knowledge and talents can offer **all** students an abundance of learning opportunities.

Many schools have established various collaborative arrangements in an effort to increase their potential for individualizing instruction. Schools have found that there is greater opportunity to use the unique, diverse, and specialized knowledge each team member brings to the learning experience (Bauwens, Hourcade, & Friend, 1989). Collaborative efforts provide many benefits to teachers, which transfer to better teaching of students. Following are some of these:

- An increase in the number of students receiving assistance (Armbruster & Howe, 1985; Pugach & Johnson, 1990)
- An increase in the self-confidence of the teachers in handling classroom problems (Pugach & Johnson, 1988)

- An increase in the tolerance level of teachers working with students with cognitive deficits (Pugach & Johnson, 1988)
- An increase in communication, leadership, and conflict resolution skills among teachers (Johnson & Johnson, 1987)
- An increase in flexibility in scheduling and grouping, allowing for a division of labor in teacher responsibilities (Fox & Faver, 1984; Olsen, 1968)
- An opportunity to work with a wide variety of students and foster sharing of responsibility for all students (Boudah, 1995; Thousand & Villa, 1990)
- An alleviation of the sense of isolation teachers frequently experience (Garver & Papania, 1982; Thousand & Villa, 1990)
- A facilitation of adult stimulation, professional discussion, and interaction (Bauwens et al., 1989; Fox & Faver, 1984; Lieberman, 1986)

In order to meet the true intent of Public Laws 94-142 (The Education for All Handicapped Children Act) and 101-476 (Individuals With Disabilities Education Act), which is to deliver educational services to students with disabilities in the least restrictive environment, a joint effort among educators is essential. The following sections describe various options that educators have available to them to provide collaborative services to students with disabilities.

Teaching widely diverse groups of students is shared work.

MacKinnon & Brown, 1994

Collaborative Service-Delivery Models

Educators are expressing the need for a more comprehensive range of service-delivery options for students with disabilities (Phillips & McCullough, 1990). Embedded in the expectation that general and special educators will team teach and collaborate with each other are a variety of approaches and opportunities for collaborative teaching and service delivery as depicted in Figure 5-1.

Several models of school-based collaboration are available to educators. These include three models of indirect collaborative service delivery: (1) collaborative problem solving, which relies on equal partners sharing their particular expertise with each other; (2) group problem solving, where team members combine their expertise and generate ideas for educating students in the mainstream; and (3) peer coaching, in which teachers work with each other with newly acquired skills through demonstration teaching and observation. There are also several options for implementing co-teaching that offer the direct services of both special educators and general educators to all students. These include complementary instruction, supportive learning activities, and team teaching. Each of these models is described in the following sections.

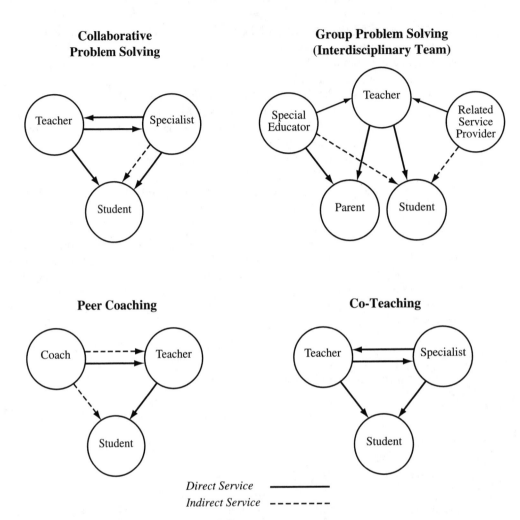

FIGURE 5-1   Service delivery models.

Indirect Service-Delivery Models

Educators who are able to successfully establish a collaborative relationship can focus their efforts on problem-solving strategies. Together they can work through the major steps in the problem-solving process as identified in Chapter 4:

1. Define and clarify the problem.
2. Collect and analyze data.
3. Select and implement a strategy.
4. Evaluate the outcomes.

As both special educators and general educators move through the steps in this process, "the challenge of creating responsive instructional and management approaches is shared, and the expertise of all teachers is maximized" (Pugach & Johnson, 1990, p. 136). This process serves as a comfortable but systematic tool to guide the collaborative effort and is flexible enough to adapt to differing situations.

Collaborative Problem Solving

> *One form of educational support service increasingly used to promote team owner-ship and to assist at-risk and exceptional students in the general classroom involves collaborative consultation or problem solving among teachers, support staff, and administrators.*
>
> West, Idol, & Cannon, 1989

> *Brian is a student with autism who is included in my 5th grade class. He often calls out and makes provocative comments to the other kids. I did not know what to do or how to han-dle the situation. I consulted with the instructional assistant who knows Brian very well and has worked with him in other inclusive classes. She asked me how I would treat the other students if they were engaging in that behavior. She told me to treat him and respond to him just like I would any other fifth grader. "Expect nothing less from him." He immediately responded when I reacted to him as I would any other student. If I had been addressing his behavior in this way from the beginning, and if I had taken more responsibility on myself for seeing him as one of my students, I would have gotten a lot farther with our relationship and my relationship with him as his teacher.*
>
> *Geraldine Guerrier, fifth grade teacher, Thornhill, Ontario, Canada*

Description

School-based collaboration has traditionally taken the form of collaborative consultation in which the consultant becomes a service provider for the teacher who is directly responsible for the students. In the school setting, this indirect service delivery model has evolved to focus on collaborative problem solving between educators to benefit students so that education can occur in the most natural setting—the general education classroom (Graden & Bauer, 1992).

In the collaborative problem-solving relationship, teachers or teacher and specialist interact on an equal basis to benefit the "client" (i.e., the student). In collaborative problem solving, the teacher who provides the direct services takes a more highly involved and active role in the problem-solving process. If this high involvement level is not attained, then classroom adaptations are not likely to occur with successful outcomes in any systematic way (Graden & Bauer, 1992).

Elements essential to successful collaborative problem solving include both interpersonal communication skills and a framework for problem solving (Bradley, 1994; Gutkin

& Curtis, 1990; Idol & West, 1987). Mutual trust, respect, and acceptance between the educators engaged in this collaborative relationship must exist in order for the problem-solving approach to be effective. The development of explicitly defined interventions for students must be a shared responsibility, and both parties must feel they play a significant role in the intervention process, but *the final decisions must be acceptable to the classroom teacher and fit unobtrusively into the natural context of the classroom* (Graden & Bauer, 1992; Martens, Peterson, Witt, & Cirone, 1986).

Often, because of their training, special educators have expertise in adapting curriculum, developing alternative materials, and dealing with behavioral challenges. During the collaborative process, they may be expected to generate intervention strategies. However, effective strategies must be integrated into the curriculum (Rainforth, York, & Macdonald, 1992). This integration highlights the importance of the general educator's content knowledge to the intervention planning process. As this creative process unfolds, it becomes evident that both participants in the collaborative problem-solving relationship bring knowledge and skills to be shared.

Facilitating Factors
Because the special educator serving in the role of collaborator does not have direct responsibility for teaching the curriculum, it is of utmost importance that the expertise of the person who will be implementing the intervention be respected (Marvin, 1987). Educators must be cautioned against "advice giving" sessions and ensure that realistic and workable interventions are mutually selected and defined (Graden & Bauer, 1992).

A major consideration for the success of collaborative problem solving is ensuring that time is available for educators to meet with each other. Schedules should be developed that allow time for educators to share their ideas and expertise. In this way, knowledge of curricula as well as successful adaptations and interventions can be shared to create stronger programs for all students.

Another factor that must be considered when forming collaborative relationships is the right of each person in the relationship to reject or accept the ideas that are generated. When individuals are invested in the practice, there is a greater likelihood that its implementation will be successful (Graden & Bauer, 1992; Martens, et al., 1986; Shea & Bauer, 1987).

Outcomes
Collaborative problem solving partnerships afford participants the opportunity to share in the responsibility for the learning needs of all students and to increase the probability that strategies will be implemented on an ongoing basis (Anderson, Kratochwill, & Bergan, 1986). One of the most important outcomes of this form of peer collaboration is that general educators become more confident and empowered in their ability to handle classroom challenges, both behaviorally and academically (Johnson & Pugach, 1989; Pugach & Johnson, 1990). As a result, the learning and adjustment of students increases (Bergan, 1995). By allowing professionals to engage in a mutual exchange of ideas and resources, useful skills are transferred between educators, and fewer students are referred for out-of-classroom help (Idol, West, & Lloyd, 1988; Pugach & Johnson, 1990).

Because instructional continuity between the content areas and specialized programming is enhanced through the collaborative problem-solving service-delivery model, the following are more likely to occur (Haring, 1988):

- Student achievement is accelerated.
- The diagnosis of learning problems is more effective.
- The students who receive indirect service rather than pullout programming learn to generalize skills in the appropriate social context.

Teachers who work together for the purpose of addressing the needs of students with disabilities demonstrate a positive response to collaborative problem solving as an intervention strategy. As teacher empowerment increases through peer consultation, this can become a preferred and effective model for collaboration (Graden & Bauer, 1992; Gutkin, 1986; Gutkin & Hickman, 1988).

Interdisciplinary Team (Group Problem Solving)

> *Participation on interdisciplinary teams has increased teacher competency for dealing with students with special needs who receive their education in the mainstream.*
>
> Chalfant, Pysh, & Moultrie, 1979

Shannon is a 13-year-old student with Downs syndrome who reads at a second grade level. She enjoys being with people, loves to help others, and takes her responsibilities seriously. Her IEP goals include writing in complete sentences, increasing her vocabulary, and improving her articulation. In world studies, her class is doing a unit on Australia. As part of the unit the students are required to develop an ABC travel information guide. They must select vocabulary words having to do with Australia starting with each letter of the alphabet. They have to research and locate facts and then illustrate each of the words or concepts they select.

The team working with Shannon include the world studies teacher, the resource teacher and the speech/language pathologist (SLP). The three teachers work together to modify the assignment for Shannon. She is paired with another student and assigned only part of the alphabet. She selects her words from a modified list compiled by the world studies teacher. The resource teacher and SLP locate lower level reading materials and coordinate their schedules to provide in-class assistance to Shannon and others who need support with reading and note-taking. Several days a week, one of them listens to Shannon read and dictate what she understands about the vocabulary she is studying. Shannon cuts pictures out of magazines that illustrate her selected words. After working on their own, Shannon and her partner get together to put the ABC book together. They each explain their part to the other.

Michelle Boyer, middle school special education teacher, Rockville, Maryland

Description

School support teams are another type of staffing arrangement that encourages collaboration. Most school systems have interdisciplinary or multidisciplinary teams that are instrumental in making decisions for students requiring special or remedial services. These teams also offer assistance to teachers working with students who present various challenges. Often this team determines eligibility for special education programs as well.

The interdisciplinary team format enables all staff involved with a student to collaborate on a regular basis and to follow a student's progress in an organized way. Although in the past, many teachers saw these teams as the first step toward getting a student out of the general education classroom, these teams have evolved into a group problem-solving model. They provide the opportunity to build a strong interface between instruction in general education classrooms and specialized support programs (Idol et al., 1988). This team format provides an integrated opportunity to plan for the student's success in academics (including curriculum and methodology), classroom environment, social skills, and family support.

As educational programs increasingly become the shared responsibility of classroom teachers, administrators, specialists of all kinds, and families, these individuals with diverse expertise can generate creative solutions to mutually defined problems. In addition, they can better coordinate a variety of services for students who are eligible.

Team members are perceived as equal contributors as they form a collegial relationship. They share a similar base of knowledge and join in exchanging experiences and ideas to solve problems of mutual concern (Phillips & McCullough, 1990). Because inclusion is impossible to do alone, collaboration among team members is the key to successful programming for students with disabilities in the general education classrooms.

Facilitating Factors

There are several factors that must be considered when evaluating the effectiveness of collegial teams. The *selection* of team members, the *role* of each member, and the types of *expertise* required for team members must be determined. In addition, *time* for meetings and other associated team responsibilities must be allocated.

It is essential that team members receive enough training in the group process, including effective *communication* and *conflict resolution,* so that collegiality and the collaborative ethic are maintained (see Chapter 4 for more information). Team members must be apprised of the possibilities of individual interpretations, conflicting viewpoints, and uncertainty about individual responsibilities. Ownership for various facets of a student's program must be clear, especially when the student works with many specialists in addition to a classroom teacher. Often a case manager is selected to coordinate the instructional program. This coordination of services can be challenging when each professional working with a student has to consider the student's *schedule,* his or her own schedule, and the schedule of others in the school with whom the student works. Finally, the group must collectively *evaluate* the effectiveness of their collaboration as well as the effectiveness of the interventions they plan together (Rainforth, York, & Macdonald, 1992).

When considering the makeup of the team, certain factors have to be considered. Many of the specialists and teachers involved already do testing, teaching, and individual consultation with parents and teachers. Frequent meetings can disrupt other activities that they are required to perform. Time must be permitted in the schedules of both specialists and classroom teachers for collaborative problem solving if they are to be part of the team. System-wide support for interdisciplinary team meetings as well as funding for specialized positions are crucial for the success of the group problem-solving model of collaboration (Idol et al., 1988; Schumaker & Deshler, 1988).

Outcomes

When teachers work together to plan programs for students with disabilities, they help each other understand individual youngster's learning and behavioral styles. Inclusion efforts improve because relevant support for individualized instruction is provided in a systematic fashion. Students receive the supports and services that enable them to achieve their objectives in a general education setting.

Participation on an interdisciplinary team for the purpose of problem solving can reduce inappropriate testing, meetings, and pullout programs by implementing prereferral interventions. Participating teachers discuss techniques immediately usable in the classroom setting that promote learning in the least restricted environment.

A major outcome of the group problem-solving approach is that teachers view each other as a primary source of assistance (Johnson & Johnson, 1988). Teachers who were a part of a problem-solving team reported that their best and most innovative ideas came from each other, even when "experts" were present (MacKinnon & Brown, 1994). In buildings in which group collaborative efforts make use of the existing knowledge and talent within the school in a formalized setting, teacher morale increases. Peer support results in increased self-esteem among educators because all professional opinions are given value.

The most beneficial outcome of group collaboration is that it provides a format for establishing a shared ownership for the learning process. Group problem-solving sessions help teachers feel like part of a team and acquire strategies to work with diverse groups of students (MacKinnon & Brown, 1994). Problem identification, setting of goals and objectives, delineating responsibilities, and evaluating the recommended procedures are responsibilities that are shared among team members. The programs of general and special educators are more integrated, and responsibility for programming is shared.

Peer Coaching

Teachers who have participated in the peer coaching model practice new strategies more frequently, use new strategies more appropriately, retain knowledge and skills longer, and understand the purpose and use of the strategy or technique

Joyce & Showers, 1988

I do a lot of cooperative learning in my first grade class. The second grade teacher came to me and said she wanted to learn more about cooperative learning and wanted me to come into her classroom and observe her. I told her I felt uncomfortable in a supervisory role, but how about if we do peer coaching. You come in and observe me and I'll observe you, and we'll share strengths and need areas we both have. I gave her some material to read on cooperative learning and set up a time for her to watch my class. We did mutual observations three times with pre and post conferences, and it worked out well. It was a nice commitment we made to each other. We gave each other good feedback about classroom management and incorporating a variety of skill levels, and the process helped me set goals for developing social skills my students would need as second graders. The other teacher learned to utilize cooperative learning in a variety of content areas and various cooperative learning techniques. It enhanced both of our skills in thinking cooperatively and in our planning for lessons. She became comfortable with the idea of facilitating student learning rather than having most learning teacher directed.

Bonni Rubin-Sugarman, first grade teacher, Mt. Laurel, New Jersey

Description

Peer coaching, as first described by Joyce and Showers (1980), involves the following steps: (1) Theoretical presentation that includes the conceptual framework of the specific teaching technique; (2) modeling and demonstration whereby the "coach" demonstrates the skills in the classroom to facilitate transfer of the technique; (3) practice that includes several applications of the technique made by the teacher in his or her own classroom under the direction and support of the coach; (4) structured feedback that is provided by the coach for each application; and (5) open-ended feedback that is facilitated between the coach and the teacher after each application. Coaching has been defined as "the provision of on-site, personal support, and technical assistance for teachers" (Baker & Showers, 1984, p. 1)

Coaching situations may range from a very structured expert model to a peer learning model. This allows staff in each school the opportunity to decide which model is most appropriate to their needs. Staff members may choose to learn a new strategy and invite an outside coach to provide training and return for structured observation and feedback.

For instance, one school entered into a partnership with a nearby university. A professor well trained in strategy-based instruction presented a seminar for interested staff. Each participant then scheduled observation and feedback sessions monthly with the professor. Each strategic intervention was presented theoretically in the seminar, and teachers discussed how they would implement the strategy in their classrooms. The teachers planned lessons that were formally observed by the professor and were given feedback on their application. Following the seminar, nine out of ten teachers were successfully and appropriately using strategy-based instruction in their classrooms. The probability of their continuing application is greatly improved by their experience in direct application and positive feedback.

As a variation, the staff may participate in a workshop session and follow up by pairing off into peer coaching groups to support the transfer of the new technique. When school-based or commercial workshops present teachers with new ideas and strategies it is helpful to have a buddy with whom to share possible applications. Making a commitment to work with another teacher will ensure that the information is used rather than "put on a shelf." The process can be informal, but necessitates peer classroom visits and feedback sessions. Teachers generally enjoy the experience but find that they must plan carefully and creatively to find the time to implement this method.

Recently, a team of middle school teachers attended a workshop on curriculum modifications. Two members of the team wanted to apply what they learned and decided to work together. They worked on plans and materials first. The first learning that occurred was that each of them had very different ideas about curriculum modifications and what they would actually do in the classroom. To facilitate their work together, they had to spend time talking and reaching agreement on the actual types and extent of the modifications they would use. Once they had reached mutual understanding and goals, they enjoyed the cooperative planning, observations, and reciprocal feedback.

The diversity of staff expertise in most schools provides opportunities for staff members to serve as coaches to each other on various topics and share their expertise. Teachers may voluntarily work on acquiring new skills with a partner if critical time for study, observation, feedback, and moral support are made available (McREL, 1984–85). Studies show that peer coaching increases effective teaching behaviors and enhances teaching skills (Gersten, Morvant, Brengelman, 1995; Hudson, Miller, Salzberg, & Morgan, 1994; Pierce & Miller, 1994).

Facilitating Factors

Professionals in a coaching role need to be aware of several characteristics identified by Neubert and Bratton (1987) that are essential to the creation of an effective coaching partnership. The coach must have the following:

- Thorough knowledge of the technique or strategy
- Credibility in the successful application of the strategy/technique in the classroom
- Skills in giving feedback and support
- An approach that facilitates the teacher's ownership of the lesson, students, and classroom
- Availability for planning, team teaching, conferencing, and personal support

Appropriate training and support is an essential factor to a productive coaching program. When necessary, experts in specific strategies and techniques need to be available. A training program for staff serving as coaches is important to ensure that modeling and feedback are appropriately provided. Essential components of such a training program identified by Morgan, Gustafson, Hudson, and Salzberg (1992) include the following:

- Identifying effective teaching behaviors
- Determining the progress made toward the goal
- Providing positive and constructive feedback
- Communicating in a way that builds a sense of trust and support

There are several conditions that are critical in developing a successful coaching model. The teachers involved must have the autonomy and freedom to direct their own professional growth. The understanding and support of the school-based administrator is essential. Time to plan, observe, and conference is required. Scheduling can be a logistical problem within the current structure of most schools and may require a major departure from traditional school organization. Acquiring the time for coaching activities is a creative endeavor that requires the consideration of such options as (1) larger groups of students with paired teachers and (2) teachers and administrators covering classes for peer coaching teams.

Outcomes

Coaching provides opportunities for both general and special educators to practice and master new skills. The research findings for coaching have been extremely impressive. The transfer of skills from 20 percent (with only the theoretical presentation of techniques) to as much as 90 percent with carefully planned coaching support (Joyce & Showers, 1988; Showers, 1990) demonstrates the high degree of generalization and implementation of skills possible with a coaching model. Not only does peer coaching result in significant increases in effective teaching behaviors (even in content areas other than those in which coaching was being directly conducted), but it also very impressively decreases ineffective teaching behaviors (Englert & Sugai, 1983; Morgan et al., 1992). This may indicate that the effects of a peer coaching model enhance the improvement of teaching performance in general.

Sparks and Breeder (1987) found that the major benefit of a coaching program is the increase in the professional relationships and collegial support that develop between the teachers. Any time new learning takes place that requires changes in comfortable practices, there is some measure of risk and discomfort that can cause teaches to abandon a new technique before it can become established. Peer coaching support facilitates the type and amount of practice, which results in steady and consistent change.

The greatest advantage of peer coaching is increased student achievement. When teachers have opportunities to practice new skills and techniques and receive feedback in a nonthreatening way, their instruction improves and the benefits are transferred to the learner in increased student achievement (Joyce & Showers, 1988; Showers, 1990).

Direct Service-Delivery Models

Cooperative Teaching (Co-teaching)

Amy, a bright student with cerebral palsy, was fully included in my second grade class last year with pullout services for occupational therapy. In November, I asked the occupational therapist (OT) if she would like to team teach with me during her once-a-week sessions since most of the goals on Amy's IEP involved skills we engaged in daily. Her first suggestion was that we work on spatial organization and visual perception. I tried to appear as if I knew what she was talking about and realized that I was going to be learning a good deal from her as well! The OT provided us all with strategies to use to fold a piece of paper, the proper use of scissors, and even informed us of all the muscles we use when we hold a pencil or crayon correctly. She helped us improve our efficiency when we copied words and sentences from the board.

Although Amy has happily progressed to the third grade, I have used the collaborative skills I learned to problem solve with the reading teacher and school counselor, and I have been team teaching with them as well with tremendous success. The children love having another adult in the room, and as the teacher, I love having the opportunity to share my ideas and to receive feedback from professionals whose dedication to teaching all students I greatly admire!

Elizabeth Jardeleza, second grade teacher, Virginia Beach, Virginia

Description

Students with disabilities continue to receive more of their education in general classroom settings, creating a growing demand for instructional arrangements that will ensure success for all students as they are educated together. Because special educators are forming teaching partnerships with general educators, students are taught to generalize their newly acquired skills and behaviors into general education settings and can participate more fully with their typical peers (Adamson, Cox, & Schuller, 1989) thereby making service delivery more effective and efficient (Glatthorn, 1990). In a co-teaching situation, the special educator is not only involved in the planning and evaluation phases, but also in the direct delivery of instruction. This type of service delivery can be accomplished through a variety of teaching arrangements.

Several program options that ensure that both general and special educators are directly involved in the overall classroom instruction process have been identified. They are (1) complementary instruction, (2) supportive learning activities, and (3) team teaching (Bauwens & Hourcade, 1991).

Complementary Instruction.   When teachers are involved in complementary instruction, the classroom teacher is usually responsible for the delivery of the content material and the special educator provides instruction in specific leaning strategies such as summarizing, memory strategies, and organizational skills to all students who might benefit from such assistance. This approach allows the special educator to teach the skills in the environment in which they are to be used, thus increasing the probability that generalization will take place (Bauwens, Hourcade, & Friend, 1989; Bauwens & Robinson, 1995).

Supportive Learning Activities.   Supportive learning activities are those that supplement the essential instructional content of the lesson and provide "multiple pathways" to improve or extend learning (Bauwens & Hourcade, 1991; Bauwens & Robinson, 1995). In this approach, general and special educators determine the instructional goals and content of specific lessons and activities that best reinforce and enrich the content. The general educator assumes the responsibility of presenting the content while the special educator assists students or pulls aside small groups for content enhancement such as review, extra drill, or identification of main ideas.

Team Teaching.   In 1967 Ira Singer defined team teaching as "an arrangement whereby two or more teachers, with or without teacher aides, cooperatively plan, instruct and evaluate one or more class groups in an appropriate instructional space . . . so as to take advantage of the special competencies of the team members" (p. 16). After examining several models of team teaching programs in Vermont, Thousand and Villa (1990) defined team teaching as "two or more members of the school and greater community who distribute among themselves planning, instruction and evaluation responsibilities for the same students on a regular basis for an extended period of time" (pp. 152–153). Although the definition has not changed to a great extent over the last twenty years, the variety of students whose needs must be met in the general education setting has changed significantly.

In the team teaching model, the special and general educator take responsibility not only for the academic subject, but also for all students, with and without disabilities, in the class. Planning, presentation, and evaluation is done together. The responsibility of each teacher depends on expertise and pre-planned agreement. Teachers who have worked successfully in team teaching programs find that not only are the students given an opportunity to achieve to their maximum potential, but that the teachers' expertise increases as well (Stainback & Stainback, 1992).

Team teaching can take several forms. Station teaching takes advantage of the expertise of each teacher who is responsible for stations or centers that focus on a specific piece of the curriculum. Each student participates in all stations. Some teachers find that parallel teaching works best for them. The special and general educator divide the class into two groups to teach the same content. Still others participate in shared instruction during which both teachers are lead teachers, instructing and/or assisting the whole group at the same time.

Often shared instruction works well for teachers who have students with mild to moderate disabilities in their classes. All students can work on the same content with adaptations made when appropriate. Station teaching is effective for students with various ranges of disabilities. Station work can be modified or students can do only selected centers. Parallel teaching is an especially effective strategy to use when differentiated curricula or skills levels are being taught simultaneously.

Facilitating Factors

In order for cooperative teaching to be successful, several essential components must be in place. According to Fuchs and Moore (1988), Garvar and Papania (1982), Olsen (1968), Pugach and Johnson (1990), Villa, Thousand, Stainback, and Stainback (1992), and Thousand and Villa (1990), the development of a co-teaching program works best with the following:

- The full support of the building administrator and the staff who will be involved
- A sense of trust and positive interdependence
- Staff training to acquire skills in communication, shared decision making, perspective awareness, and conflict management
- Flexible scheduling that allows for adequate face-to-face planning time to design, plan, and evaluate program
- Adequate space that can accommodate the numbers of students and teachers on the team

Initially, general educators may perceive the co-teaching arrangement as an attempt to burden them with more responsibility. Simultaneously, special educators often find themselves responsible for participating in different teaming situations with a wide variety of grade levels and teachers. Thus, establishing well-defined roles of each team member and joint responsibility for the content and coordination of services is essential if this model is to be successful. Both special and general educators who are considering undertaking a co-teaching arrangement must be prepared to give up some of the freedom and autonomy that they have when they operate independently. What emerges is stronger, better instruction that differentiates for a variety of needs. Outcomes for both the teacher and the student in a co-teaching arrangement are delineated in Table 5-1.

Outcomes

Successful co-teaching arrangements can provide the teachers involved with numerous benefits. Teachers with varying talents have a natural opportunity to model their skills and to take advantage of the specialized knowledge and instructional approaches of their partners (Thousand & Villa, 1990). Co-teaching naturally lends itself to more adult stimulation and alleviates some of the isolation usually associated with traditional classroom teaching. Teaming also promotes caring and committed relationships. In addition, it can contribute to the development of skills critical for psychological health, including helping others, coping with frustration and failure, controlling anxiety, expressing needs, and managing conflict (Johnson & Johnson, 1989). Co-teaching provides a colleague with whom to discuss curriculum, give and get support, and share instructional ideas.

Co-teaching increases the amount of time that resource personnel are available to team members and identified students (Bauwens, Hourcade, & Friend, 1989). It provides logistical advantages such as being able to carry on with the program during the absence of one team member (Garver & Papania, 1982). Teachers report feeling more supported when they can share their ideas and solutions to problems. Scott and Smith (1988) reported that teachers who work in collaborative school environments tend to enjoy their work and perceive themselves as effective in the delivery of instruction. When general and special educators form a successful team for the delivery of instruction, it reminds educators of their common purpose, increases their appreciation of one another, and generates ideas for a variety of ways of teaching.

While teachers gain more knowledge and skills and experience greater job satisfaction (Chrisco, 1989; Thousand & Villa, 1990), those who benefit the most from a co-teaching arrangement are the students. All students are provided with increased opportunities for a variety of successful learning experiences (Boudah, 1995). Co-teaching may create a lower student/teacher ratio, and students who need more individualized instruction can have more time to interact with an adult. Students are exposed to different teaching styles and can participate in appropriate learning activities, as small and large group activities can be con-

TABLE 5-1   Outcomes of co-teaching.

Outcomes for Students	Outcomes for Teachers
✓ Lower student/teacher ratio	✓ Share skills and materials
✓ Support immediately available	✓ Exposure to varied teaching styles
✓ Varied teaching styles	✓ Increase in knowledge
✓ Don't have to be segregated	✓ Mutual support
✓ All students have access to help	✓ Greater job satisfaction

ducted simultaneously. While minimizing the need for segregated programs for students with disabilities, co-teaching increases and extends the support for students who have learning problems but do not qualify for special programs (Bauwens, Hourcade, & Friend, 1989; Self, Benning, Marston, & Magnusson, 1991).

When special and general educators form successful mergers and share the responsibility for the education of all students, they can bring an impressive combination of skills to the classroom. By using the unique talents of each educator, co-teaching programs can improve the instructional support delivered to students with disabilities in a manner that enhances and supports general classroom content. When general and special educators work effectively together in a co-teaching situation, students are able to receive appropriate academic support as well as specialized instruction without having to be pulled out of the classroom (Thousand & Villa, 1990).

Selecting a Collaborative Model

A variety of factors go into selecting the collaborative model that will be used by a particular group of educators or school staff (see Figure 5-2). The primary factor that must be considered is the range of intensity of student needs in a class, team or school, and accompanying interventions that are appropriate to respond to those needs. Another consideration is the structure of the school. Elementary, middle, and high schools are organized very differently. For example, some schools are already set up in teams that may facilitate further collegial partnerships. Some schools departmentalize for various subject areas. Schools that house only primary students may provide different opportunities for teaming than those with a wider range of grade levels.

The philosophy of the building administrator will also affect the ability and motivation of teachers to form collegial partnerships. When the school principal encourages and facilitates collegial planning and instruction by providing space, planning time, and staff training in team building, successful partnerships are more likely to develop.

Staff collegiality is also affected by the personal and professional relationships of the members of the school faculty. Opportunities for socializing, training, and team building activities promote friendships and working relationships among staff members and serve to facilitate professional partnerships.

Scheduling is another factor to consider when selecting a collaborative model. School-wide scheduling of students with IEPs, the general student population, and special educators is often a challenging task. Unique ways to create opportunities for teachers to plan and teach together must be considered for successful collaborative programming.

Many schools are experimenting with ways in which to provide co-planning opportunities for staff members (Raywid, 1993; Schattman 1992). The following are some of these ideas:

- Build planning time that includes special educators into the master schedule.
- Schedule "specials" such as music, art, and P.E. so that teachers working together are released at the same time.

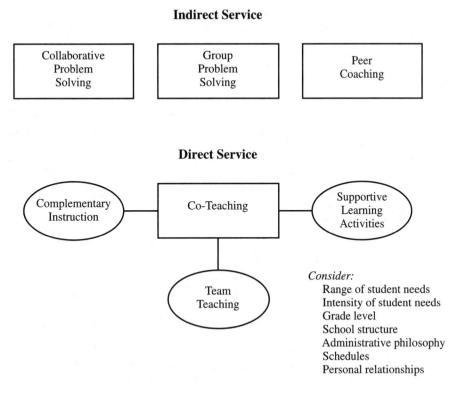

Indirect Service

| Collaborative Problem Solving | Group Problem Solving | Peer Coaching |

Direct Service

Complementary Instruction — Co-Teaching — Supportive Learning Activities — Team Teaching

Consider:
Range of student needs
Intensity of student needs
Grade level
School structure
Administrative philosophy
Schedules
Personal relationships

FIGURE 5-2   Selecting a service delivery model.

- Schedule duties such as hall, lunchroom, and recess so that teachers working together are "duty-free" at the same times.
- Use paraprofessionals, high school students earning service learning credits, and volunteers to monitor noninstructional activities.
- Release team members who work together during schoolwide assemblies and other large group activities.
- Schedule lunch and planning periods of team members at the same time.
- Build "communication time" for team members into staff meetings and staff development activities.

Conclusions

Effective collaboration requires that the professional repertoire of both general and special educators be expanded to incorporate the use of collaborative planning and teaching models. The choice of the most appropriate collaborative model for a particular situation will depend on a variety of factors. Regardless of the model selected, collaborative programming between general and special educators is essential to maximize the success of students with challenging learning needs in general education classrooms.

References

Adamson, D. R., Cox, J., & Schuller, J. (1989). Collaboration/consultation: Bridging the gap from resource room to regular classroom. *Teacher Education and Special Education, 12,* 53–55.

Anderson, R. K., Kratochwill, T. R, & Bergan, J. R. (1986). Training teachers in behavioral consultation and therapy: An analysis of verbal behaviors. *Journal of School Psychology, 24,* 229–241.

Armbruster, B., & Howe, C. (1985). An alternative instructional approach: Educators team up to help students learn. *National Association of Secondary School Principals Bulletin, 69*(479), 82–86.

Baker, R. G., & Showers, B. (1984). *The effects of a coaching strategy on teachers' transfer of training to classroom practice: A six-month follow-up study.* Paper presented at the annual meeting of the American Educational Research Association, New Orleans.

Bauwens, J., & Hourcade, J. J. (1991). Making co-teaching a mainstreaming strategy. *Preventing School Failure, 35,* 19–24.

Bauwens, J., Hourcade, J., & Friend, M. (1989). Cooperative teaching: A model for general and special education integration. *Remedial and Special Education, 10*(2), 17–22.

Bauwens, J., & Robinson, S. (1995, April). *Cooperative teaching.* Paper presented at the Council for Exception Children 1995 Annual Convention "Racing to Excellence," Indianapolis, IN.

Boudah, D. J. (1995). Collaboration: Fostering responsible inclusion through collaborative instruction. *LD Forum, 20*(3), 29–32.

Bradley, D. F. (1994). A framework for the acquisition of collaborative consultation skills. *Journal of Educational and Psychological Consultation, 5*(1), 51–68.

Chalfant, J. C., Pysh, M. V., & Moultrie, R. (1979). Teacher assistance teams: A model for within-building problem solving. *Learning Disability Quarterly, 2,* 85–96.

Chrisco, I. S. (1989). Peer assistance works. *Educational Leadership, 46*(8), 31–32.

Englert, C., & Sugai, G. (1983). Teacher training: Improving trainee performance through peer observation and observation system technology. *Teacher Education and Special Education, 6*(7), 7–17.

Fox, J. F., & Faver, C. A. (1984). Independence and cooperation in research: The motivations and costs of collaboration. *Journal of Higher Education, 55*(3), 43–49.

Fox, T. J., & Williams, W. (1991). *Implementing best practices for all students in their local schools.* Burlington: University of Vermont, Center for Developmental Disabilities.

Fuchs, L., & Moore, L. P. (1988). Collaboration for understanding and effectiveness. *Clearing House, 61,* 410–413.

Garver, A., & Papania, A. (1982). Team-teaching: It works for the student. *Academic Therapy, 8,* 191–196.

Gersten, R., Morvant, M., & Brengelman, S. (1995). Close to the classroom is close to the bone: Coaching as a means to translate research into classroom practice. *Exceptional Children, 62,* 52–66.

Glatthorn, A. A. (1990). Rethinking the regular education initiative: Focus on the classroom teacher. *Remedial and Special Education, 11*(3), 7–16.

Graden, J. L., & Bauer, A. M. (1992). Using a collaborative approach to support students and teachers in inclusive classrooms. In S. Stainback & W. Stainback (Eds.), *Curriculum considerations in inclusive classrooms: Facilitating learning for all students* (pp. 85–100). Baltimore: Paul H. Brookes Publishing Co.

Gutkin, R. B. (1986). Consultees' perceptions of variables relating to the outcomes of school-based consultation interactions. *School Psychology Review, 15,* 375–382.

Gutkin, R. B., & Curtis, M. J. (1990). School-based consultation: Theory, techniques and research. In R. B. Gutkin & C. R. Reynolds (Eds.), *The handbook of school psychology* (2nd ed.) (pp. 577–611). New York: John Wiley & Sons.

Gutkin, R. B., & Hickman, J. A. (1988). Teachers' perceptions of control over presenting problems and resulting preferences for consultation versus referral services. *Journal of School Psychology, 26,* 395–398.

Halvorsen, A. T., & Sailor, W. (1990). Integration of students with severe and profound disabilities: A review of research. In R. Gaylord-Ross (Ed.), *Issues and research in special education* (pp. 110–172). New York: Teachers College Press.

Haring, N. G. (1988). *Generalization for students with severe handicaps: Strategies and solutions.* Seattle: University of Washington Press.

Hudson, P., Miller, S., Salzberg, C., & Morgan, R. (1994). The role of peer coaching in teacher education programs. *Teacher Education and Special Education, 17,* 224–235.

Idol, L., Paolucci-Whitcomb, P., & Nevin, A. (1986). *Collaborative consultation.* Rockville, MD: Aspen Systems.

Idol, L., & West, J. F. (1987). Consultation in special education: Training and practice (Part II). *Journal of Learning Disabilities, 20,* 474–497.

Idol, L., West., J. F., & Lloyd, S. R. (1988). Organizing and implementing specialized reading programs: A collaborative approach involving classroom, remedial, and special education teachers. *Remedial and Special Education, 9*(2), 54–61.

Johnson, D. W., & Johnson, R. T. (1987). *Joining together: Group theory and group skills* (3rd ed.). Englewood Cliffs, NJ: Prentice-Hall.

Johnson, D. W., & Johnson, R. T. (1988). Research shows the benefits of adult cooperation. *Educational Leadership, 45,* 27–30.

Johnson, D., & Johnson, R. (1989). *Cooperation and competition: Theory and research.* Edina, MN: Interaction Book Co.

Johnson, L. J., & Pugach, M. C. (1989). *Enhancing instructional options for students with mild learning and behavior problems.* Final Project Report. Unpublished manuscript, University of Alabama, Area of Special Education, Tuscaloosa; University of Wisconsin, Department of Curriculum and Instruction, Milwaukee.

Joyce, B., & Showers, B. (1980). Improving inservice training: The messages of research. *Educational Leadership, 37,* 379–385.

Joyce, B., & Showers, B. (1988). *Student achievement through staff development.* New York: Longman.

Lew, M., Mesch, D., & Lates, B. J. (1982). The Simmons College generic consulting teacher program:

A program description and data-based application. *Teacher Education and Special Education, 5*(2), 11–16.

Lieberman, A. (1986). Collaborative work. *Educational Leadership, 45*(3), 4–8.

MacKinnon, J. S., & Brown, M. E. (1994). Inclusion in secondary schools: An analysis of school structure based on teachers' images of change. *Educational Administration Quarterly, 30,* 126–152.

Martens, B. K., Peterson, R. L., Witt, J. C., & Cirone, S. (1986). Teacher perceptions of school-based interventions. *Exceptional Children, 53,* 213–223.

Marvin, C. A. (1987). Consultation services: Changing roles for SLP's. *Journal of Childhood Communication Disorders, 1*(1), 1–15.

McREL (Mid-Continent Regional Educational Laboratory). (1984–85). Coaching: A powerful strategy for improving staff development and inservice education. *Noteworthy,* 40–46.

Morgan, R., Gustafson, K., Hudson, P., and Salzberg, D. (1992). Peer coaching in a preservice special education program. *Teacher Education in Special Education, 15,* 249–258.

Neubert, G. A., & Bratton, E. C. (1987). Team coaching: Staff development side by side. *Educational Leadership, 44*(5), 29–32.

Olsen, C. O. (1968). Teaching teams in the elementary school. *Education, 88,* 345–349.

Phillips, V., & McCullough, L. (1990). Consultation-based programming: Instituting the collaborative ethic in schools. *Exceptional Children, 56,* 291–304.

Pierce, T., & Miller, S. P. (1994). Using peer coaching in preservice practice. *Teacher Education and Special Education, 17,* 215–223.

Pugach, M. C., & Johnson, L. J. (1990). Meeting diverse needs through professional peer collaboration. In W. Stainback & S. Stainback (Eds.), *Support networks for inclusive schooling: Interdependent integrated education.* Baltimore: Paul H. Brookes Publishing Co.

Pugach, M. C., & Johnson, L. J. (1988). Peer collaboration: Helping teachers help themselves. *Exceptional Children, 20,* 75–77.

Rainforth, B., York, J., & Macdonald, C. (1992). *Collaborative teams for students with severe disabilities.* Baltimore: Paul H. Brookes Publishing Co.

Raywid, M. A. (1993). Finding time for collaboration. *Educational Leadership, 51*(1), 30–34.

Sailor, W. (1991). Special education in the restructured school. *Remedial and Special Education, 12*(6), 8–22.

Schattman, R. (1992). The Franklin Northwest Supervisory Union: A case study of an inclusive school system. In R. A. Villa, J. S. Thousand, W. Stainback, & S. Stainback (Eds.), *Restructuring for caring and effective education: An administrative guide to creating heterogeneous schools* (pp. 143–160). Baltimore: Paul H. Brookes Publishing Co.

Schumaker, J. B., & Deshler, D. D. (1988). Implementing the regular education initiative in secondary schools: A different ball game. *Journal of Learning Disabilities, 21,* 36–42.

Scott, J. J., & Smith, S. C. (1988). *From isolation to collaboration: Improving the work environment of teaching.* Elmhurst, IL: North Central Regional Educational Laboratory.

Self, H., Benning, A., Marston, D., & Magnusson. (1991). Cooperative teaching project: A model for students at risk. *Exceptional Children, 58,* 26–34.

Shea, T. M., & Bauer, A. M. (1987). *Teaching children and youth with behavioral disorders* (2nd ed.). Englewood Cliffs, NJ: Prentice-Hall.

Showers, B. (1990). Aiming for superior classroom instruction for all children: A comprehensive staff development model. *Remedial and Special Education, 11*(3), 35–39.

Singer, I. J. (1967). What team teaching really is. In D. W. Biggs (Ed.), *Team teaching: Bold new venture.* Bloomington: Indiana University Press.

Sparks, G. M., & Breeder, S. (1987). Before and after peer coaching. *Educational Leadership, 45*(3), 54–47.

Stainback, S., & Stainback, W. (1992). *Curriculum considerations in inclusive classrooms: Facilitating learning for all students.* Baltimore: Paul H. Brookes Publishing Co.

Stainback, W., & Stainback, S. (1990). *Support networks for inclusive schooling: Interdependent integrated education.* Baltimore: Paul H. Brookes Publishing Co.

Thousand, J. S., & Villa, R. A. (1989). Enhancing success in heterogeneous schools. In S. Stainback & W. Stainback (Eds.), *Educating all students in the mainstream of regular education* (pp. 89–103). Baltimore: Paul H. Brookes Publishing Co.

Thousand, J. S., & Villa, R. S. (1990). Sharing expertise and responsibilities through teaching teams (pp.151–166). In W. Stainback & S. Stainback (Eds.), *Support networks for inclusive schooling.* Baltimore: Paul H. Brookes Publishing Co.

Villa, R. A., & Thousand, J. S. (1990). Administrative supports to promote inclusive schooling. In W. Stainback & S. Stainback (Eds.), *Support networks for inclusive schooling: Interdependent integrated education* (pp. 201–218). Baltimore: Paul H. Brookes Publishing Co.

Villa, R. A., & Thousand, J. S. (1992). Student collaboration: An essential for curriculum delivery in the 21st century. In S. Stainback & W. Stainback (Eds.), *Curriculum consideration in inclusive classrooms: Facilitating learning for all students* (pp. 117–142). Baltimore: Paul H. Brookes Publishing Co.

Villa, R. A., Thousand, J. S., Stainback, W., & Stainback, S. (1992). *Restructuring for caring and effective education: An administrative guide to creating heterogeneous schools.* Baltimore: Paul H. Brookes Publishing Co.

West, J. F. (1990). Educational collaboration in the restructuring of schools. *Journal of Educational and Psychological Consultation, 1*(1), 23–40.

West, J. F., Idol, L., & Cannon, G. (1989). *Collaboration in the schools: An inservice and preservice curriculum for teachers, support staff, and administrators.* Austin, Tex: Pro•Ed.

Chapter 6

Assessment

MARGARET E. KING-SEARS

◆ ADVANCE ORGANIZER ◆

Assessment in special education can be conducted for a variety of reasons: eligibility for special education services, progress monitoring of IEP goals and objectives, and documentation about the effectiveness of instructional programs are a few examples. At the same time that general education is seeking alternatives to traditional assessment practices, it is prudent to explicitly plan for and include students with disabilities in new assessment formats. Several recent assessment initiatives in general education are described as are systems currently used within special education. Assessment, regardless of format, is presented in terms of how well it yields useful and relevant instructional information. Emphasis is on curriculum-based assessments that elicit student involvement, assist educators with making instructional decisions, and represent meaningful and functional aspects of students' educational programs.

Ms. Haube, a fifth grade teacher, learned toward the end of last year that she would be receiving one student with learning disabilities, one student with serious emotional disturbance, and one student with moderate mental retardation into her class the next school year. "So much for natural proportion," she thought. Her principal selected her because she was such a good teacher for students who were at-risk. "So much for being a good teacher," she thought. Nonetheless, she was a participant in the planning process for inclusion that occurred at the end of last year, and Ms. Nagle (the special education teacher) seemed like a competent and congenial person that she could work well with. Ms. Haube was able to sit in on and provide input on each student's end-of-year IEP meeting, so she felt like she had some information on the students. Furthermore, Ms. Nagle had orchestrated a preliminary visit to the fifth grade classroom for the students. Ms. Haube was glad to meet them in advance, made them feel welcome (and was actually surprised at how well they were received by her students that year), and definitely ended the school year with conflicting feelings of optimism and anxiety about how the next year would go. Foremost in her mind was how the parents of her typical students (both average and high achievers) would receive and perceive her involvement with inclusion.

One of the summer workshops she attended with Ms. Nagle (which their school system sponsored to better prepare them for inclusive teaching and programming) featured a session on heterogeneous assessment presented by teachers who had already been involved in inclusion for a year. What Ms. Haube found particularly interesting was how these teachers had used a method for separating students' results that was called "HALO" data. "HALO" data represented the way that these teachers had separated classroom assessment data for different groups of students in their classroom so that progress for each group could be determined: H for high achievers, A for average achievers, L for students who were low achievers, or at-risk, and O for other students, which for these teachers were students with learning disabilities. HALO data represented a way to determine how well students from homogeneous groups were progressing when heterogeneous teaching methods were used (the presenters at the session Ms. Haube attended had used a ClassWide Peer Tutoring method for separating their data). The premise for collecting data, and disaggregating it, was that general education teachers needed to know that the teaching methods they were using were comparably effective for students labeled as gifted, typical learners, at-risk, and those with disabilities.

She and Ms. Nagle discussed the HALO technique, and they made plans to start the year gathering HALO data when they used cooperative learning techniques. The possibility of becoming "researchers" with their students was imminent, and their journey as inclusive teachers had begun with a major end point in sight—They would know how well each student was learning.

Assessment results of students in the United States are undergoing scrutiny and controversy about not only how typical students perform on assessments (especially those results that become public), but also the relevance of those test results to meaningful outcomes for the students as citizens and employees in the future (Barnett & Macmann, 1992). For example, even though a desired outcome for students in schools today is for them to develop problem-solving skills, state testing programs rarely succeed in assessing students' thinking skills or their ability to synthesize content or solve problems (exceptions include Vermont, Maryland, and Kentucky) (O'Neil, 1992). Furthermore, even though employers value skills associated with socialization, those skills are infrequently tested or taught in schools.

How do the aforementioned areas affect students with disabilities in state testing programs? Unfortunately, very little effect is discernible because these students are rarely involved in such state testing programs. Students with disabilities are seldom included in the development of statewide assessment programs, and these students are inconsistently included in the assessment standardization procedures as well as in the assessment itself (McLaughlin & Warren, 1994). Given the impact of assessment results and subsequent decisions based on those results, the omission of students with disabilities becomes quite apparent: *If students with disabilities are not included in the assessments, how can they be included in use of the results?*

How assessment results are used must be directly linked to their intended purpose. When used contrary to intended purposes, decisions are made based on incorrect, and sometimes incompatible, information. Given the impact that assessment results can have on school programming, the importance of examining the original intent of tests becomes clear. Educators need to be familiar with the varied reasons that assessments may be given in the first place. Two models are described next: a measurement model and a standards model.

Taylor (1994) distinguishes intents of the major tests (also referred to as "high-stakes" tests) given to students in the United States. One intent is to differentiate among levels of students—measurement that is intended to separate students into percentiles and stanines and standard scores. Ranking of students is desired with the *measurement model.* Frequently, this type of assessment is used when determining student eligibility for special education programs because these assessments depict the performance of a student relative to his or her peers. However, it is questionable, at best, whether an assessment intended to discriminate among students can also be useful for establishing clear standards or expectations for learners. Fuchs (1994) reports that high-stakes testing is a relatively recent phenomenon because testing results today may be used to determine the quality of schools and districts, individual teacher effectiveness, and allocation of funds and personnel. Archbald (1991) notes further that student promotion or retention decisions, student placement into special programs, graduation certification, and school accountability are examples of how test results affect school programs and individuals. Whether these are appropriate, valid, or reliable uses of these tests is beyond the scope of this chapter; their mention here is to briefly familiarize the reader with the "big picture" of assessments as they are used in education today and the significant influence that some of these assessments exert over program planning—and consequently over inclusion of students with disabilities in instructional and assessment decisions.

A second intent of assessment is based on completely different assumptions than the measurement model. The standards model is used to measure students' performance about what they have learned or what they need to know. Taylor (1994) lists four assumptions of standards model testing:

1. Public educational standards can be set.
2. Most students can achieve the standards.
3. Multiple measures can be used to represent diverse ranges of student expectations and performance.
4. Educators can internalize the standards and provide consistent evaluations of student performances.

The third assumption of the standards model holds more promise for inclusive schools since it has the potential to allow flexibility for individual student performances and also may lend itself to the provision of instructionally relevant information for students with and without disabilities. The other assumptions can be reexamined to include the presumption that flexible standards can be set so that each student is able to attain each standard.

One of the driving forces for assessment and instructional practices today are the National Education Goals (see Table 6-1), which were initially developed by the governors

TABLE 6-1   National education goals.

By the year 2000

- All children in America will start school ready to learn.
- The high school graduation rate will increase to at least 90 percent.
- All students will leave grades 4, 8, and 12 having demonstrated competency over challenging subject matter including English, mathematics, science, foreign languages, civics and government, economics, art, history, and geography, and every school in America will ensure that all students learn to use their minds well, so they may be prepared for responsible citizenship, further learning, and productive employment in our nation's modern economy.
- U.S. students will be first in the world in mathematics and science achievement.
- Every adult American will be literate and will possess the knowledge and skills necessary to compete in a global economy and exercise the rights and responsibilities of citizenship.
- Every school in the United States will be free of drugs, violence, and the unauthorized presence of firearms and alcohol and will offer a disciplined environment conducive to learning.
- The nation's teaching force will have access to programs for the continued improvement of their professional skills and the opportunity to acquire the knowledge and skills needed to instruct and prepare all American students for the next century.
- Every school will promote partnerships that will increase parental involvement and participation in promoting the social, emotional, and academic growth of children.

Source: U.S. Department of Education. (1994). *High standards for all students* (p. 7). Washington, DC: U.S. Government Printing Office.

of each state. Madaus (1993) suggests that these goals (requiring assessment at specific grade levels on content linked to world class standards for all students) be cautiously examined relative to intended values and benefits. For example, he questions whether the range of school subjects needed for today's diverse student population will be devalued by a single set of standards that focus on specific subjects and how students who are not college bound or students at-risk will perceive the imposition of these standards. Furthermore, how do students with moderate or severe disabilities fit into a national assessment? Madaus asks, "Who is empowered by the creation of a national testing system?" (p. 14). He suggests that teachers, not assessments, be the cornerstone of any systemic reform (refer to Chapter 3 for more information on systems change) directed at improving our schools. However, present reform policies concentrate primarily on standards and assessments, not on teachers, except insofar as assessments can be used to drive their teaching. Taylor (1994) notes that any new assessment systems must be developed in concert with the goals of that specific reform movement. Reform goals that *explicitly include students with disabilities* will also *quite naturally include these students in the assessment systems* constructed to accompany the goals. The challenge is to ensure that students with disabilities are included in both the reform goals and the assessments. Yet that challenge has historically not been met. Ysseldyke and Thurlow (1994) describe several recommendations on how to include *all* students with disabilities in large-scale national assessments (refer to Table 6-2). Their

TABLE 6-2   Recommendations on how to include students with disabilities in large-scale assessments.

Large-Scale Assessments with All Students Who Have Disabilities

Involvement Needs to Occur at Three Points

1. When large-scale assessment instruments are developed, not after the fact.
2. During the administration of large-scale assessments, which may mean that partial participation occurs and/or alternative assessments are used for some students.
3. When results of large-scale assessments are reported; those results should include all of the students with disabilities who took the test (students not taking the test should receive scores of 0).

Accommodations and Adaptations Should Be Used During Administration

4. Students should be comfortable and secure in the test setting (e.g., should study carrels or a separate room be used?).
5. The validity of the measures should be maintained through the use of large print, word processor, Braille version, etc.

Monitor How These Guidelines Are Implemented So That No Student Who Could Be Accommodated Is Excluded

6. Conduct follow-up studies of excluded students to verify that they were rightfully excluded.
7. Remove incentives for excluding students (e.g., scores of 0 for nonparticipants).
8. Determine areas for further study (e.g., new forms of testing modifications, reasonableness of the requested modifications).

Source: Paraphrased from guidelines developed by Ysseldyke, J. E., & Thurlow, M. (1994). *Guidelines for inclusion of students with disabilities in large-scale assessments.* ERIC Document No. 372 560.

recommendations provide a starting point to address the current dilemma of haphazard or nonexistent inclusion of students with disabilities in high-stakes assessments.

> *Clearly, as movement toward national standards and assessment gains momentum, decisions about including special education students in national, state, and local assessment practices are as important as decisions about including them in instruction in general education programs.*
>
> Poteet, Choate, & Stewart, 1993

Regardless of national, state, or local requirements for assessment, educators in individual classrooms make the ultimate decisions about what content is taught and how it is assessed on a day-to-day basis. Frustration results when educators feel they spend an inordinate amount of time preparing for national or state examinations at the exclusion of what they consider to be the critical instructional content. Similarly, educators and parents who spend a great deal of time constructing IEPs for students with disabilities and then feel the document is not used are discouraged that the procedure has been aimless, except for fulfilling the legal requirement of IEP construction. What's missing is the original intent—and educators' foremost concerns—in using any type of assessments: *Do assessments provide meaningful information that helps to determine student progress and guide teaching?*

> *Evaluators wrote reports that were thorough but provided little information that teachers could relate directly to their educational programs.*
>
> Spruill, 1993

The purpose of this chapter is to describe several types of assessments that can be used to determine progress and guide teaching for students with disabilities. Quite deliberately, parallels to assessment practices in general education are described and illustrated in ways that include students with a range of disabilities. Varied purposes for giving assessments are described, different types of assessments are presented, and examples of how educators are using assessments in inclusive classrooms are identified. Grading practices that can be used in inclusive settings are described and linked directly to the type of assessment and intended outcomes prepared in advance for students.

Purposes of Assessments

Shriner, Ysseldyke, and Christenson (1989) describe five purposes of assessments that relate to the types of decisions made about students. *Screening* decisions are made when an initial assessment is given to a student for the purpose of determining if a student is "significantly different in some way from his or her peers" (p. 161). Typically a screening assessment is used when an educator or parent has concerns about a youngster's performance, whether in academic or behavioral areas. The screening results can provide preliminary information about student performance in basic academic, language, or behavior areas compared to typical peers (norm-referenced tests usually are used to yield this type of comparison information). When screening results indicate that further exploration is warranted, then *referral* assessments, usually referral for possible special education services or another type of specialized services, are conducted. Assessments conducted at the referral stage are often norm-referenced standardized tests given on an individual basis (versus norm-referenced tests delivered to a group). *Classification* decisions comprise the next stage, such as when the results of the previous assessments are used to make determinations about eligibility for some type of program, of which special education programs may be an option (refer to Chapter 2 on Disability for a sequence of the special education eligibility process). For whatever type of educational program a student is a part of, *instructional planning* decisions need to be made about what content students need to be taught and the methods most likely to be successful. Finally, *pupil progress evaluation* decisions are those made based on student progress whether on a daily, weekly, monthly, or yearly time span. The last two types of evaluations are the focus for this chapter. In fact, instructional planning and student progress evaluation are treated as intertwined pieces in this chapter, with one part never functioning separate from the other. Especially in inclusive classrooms, educators, parents, and students should be satisfied that differential instructional planning efforts clearly result in individual student progress.

Types of Assessments

Standardized, norm-referenced group tests are measurement models that require the student to select and mark correct responses. These models typically require the student to respond to questions using a multiple-choice response format. Some of the more popular/prevalent norm-referenced tests include the Comprehensive Test of Basic Skills, California Achievement Tests, and Iowa Test of Basic Skills. Criticisms of standardized, norm-referenced tests may not be entirely attributable to the test and its construction, but to the uses of the results (Herman, 1992; Worthen & Spandel, 1991). Tests are constructed for specific uses, and some of the important areas to be considered are reliability, validity, and the student population from which norms were developed. However, even the best tests can create problems if they are misused (see Table 6-3 for examples of possible misuses of tests' results).

> *Conflict can emerge when a district or school encourages child-centered, needs-based educational programs and services and then advocates norm-referenced testing as an exclusive or primary tool of student evaluation.*
>
> Cullen & Pratt, 1992

TABLE 6-3   Misuses of tests and their results.

1. Using the wrong tests
2. Assuming test scores are infallible
3. Using a single test score to make an important decision
4. Failing to supplement test scores with other information
5. Setting arbitrary minimums for performance on tests
6. Assuming tests measure all the content, skills, or behaviors of interest
7. Accepting uncritically all claims made by test authors and publishers
8. Interpreting test scores inappropriately
9. Using test scores to draw inappropriate comparisons
10. Allowing tests to drive the curriculum
11. Using poor tests
12. Using tests unprofessionally

Source: Constructed from information in Worthen, B. R., & Spandel, V. (1991). Putting the standardized test debate in perspective. *Educational Leadership, 85*(5), 65–69.

Another characteristic of standardized group tests is that they require students to show what they have learned in a relatively narrow way (Armstrong, 1994). Most standardized tests contain linguistic questions or test items that students answer by filling in test bubbles for responses while seated at their desks and within a specified period of time. Standardized, norm-referenced tests are developed to be administered either to a group of students or a one-to-one basis (i.e., individual administration). The type of information gained from these tests are not typically conducive to instructional program planning because the results (e.g., grade level scores, standard scores) do not provide specific information about what the student needs to begin learning.

Criterion-referenced tests are usually more of a standards model intended to give useful information about how a student performs on a prescribed set of objectives. Students are not compared to each other, but their performance is stated relative to accomplishment of a progression of criterion such as: "Student can add a series of two-digit numbers with regrouping involved." These criteria can provide useful instructional information to teachers because there is a specific starting point for what the student needs to learn. However, criterion-referenced tests are not typically administered very frequently (although they can provide an excellent pretest starting point) so that teachers still need to tap into additional sources to gather instructional information while instruction is occurring. When inclusive programming occurs, teachers need to use assessments that not only provide a starting point for instruction (e.g., "What does the student need to learn right now?") but also provide guidance for how well the student is progressing while instruction is occurring (e.g., "Is this teaching method effective for this student?"). Moreover, criterion-referenced tests may not be based on the specific curriculum being taught in a particular school system or relate to the curriculum targeted for a particular student (e.g., a functional curriculum for a student with developmental disabilities).

Performance assessments are designed to assess what the student can do with their learning versus testing separate pieces of information or knowledge (Poteet, Choate, & Stewart, 1993). Marzano, Pickering, and McTighe (1993) define performance assessments as "a variety of tasks and situations in which students are given opportunities to *demonstrate* their understanding and to thoughtfully *apply* knowledge, skills, and habits of mind in a variety of contexts" (p. 13). Coutinho and Malouf (1993) note that in special education the principles underlying performance assessment have been historically used in special education assessment practices (e.g., behavioral, curriculum-based, direct, ecological, functional, and naturalistic assessment). The U.S. Office of Technology Assessment (1992) delineate three common features of performance assessments:

1. Students construct rather than select a response.
2. Direct observation of students' behaviors occurs on tasks resembling those commonly required for functioning in the world outside the school.
3. Clarification of students' learning and thinking processes occurs along with their answers.

For students with severe cognitive disabilities (e.g., mental retardation, multiple disabilities), the use of direct observations on tasks necessary for successful functioning in real life activities is especially appropriate because these students have extreme difficulty in transferring their learning to new situations. Haring and Liberty (1990) discuss the essential nature of teaching and testing students with significant disabilities while they are performing in the real environment. Generalization of learning (that is, taking tasks learned in one setting into other situations or settings) does not naturally occur for many students with disabilities. In the past, educators have taught students skills in one setting and have presumed that students will naturally use those skills or adapt their use of skills when new situations arise; educators today know this is unlikely to happen and so generalization instruction must be built into daily instruction (Ellis, Lenz, & Sabornie, 1987).

> *Strong forms of performance assessments are achievable in the classroom, where teachers have control of instructional outcomes and the instructional environment so that assessment criteria and feedback can be used to enhance learning.*
>
> Elliott, 1994

Elliott (1994), however, cautions that the widescale use of performance assessments to replace traditional multiple-choice tests is currently based more on dogma than data. Although performance assessments are inherently appealing to educators, the wide-scale effects on students are currently unknown. He suggests that educators be particularly mindful of the validity of their assessments, whether these assessments are statewide, teacher-constructed, or classroom-based assessments.

Authentic assessment evaluates students' achievement of realistic tasks set in real-life contexts; performance assessment becomes authentic when it requires realistic demands and is set in real-life contexts (Meyer, 1992). Poteet and colleagues (1993) note that performance and authentic assessment are terms sometimes used interchangeably, but they differentiate between the two by stating that authentic assessment is the "realistic" subset of performance assessment. Elliott (1992) describes authentic assessment as a movement that could increase the acceptance and use of behavioral observation methods and more classroom-based data, directions that have been espoused by a number of researchers and practitioners in special education for years (e.g., Alberto & Troutman, 1995; Deno, 1985; Fuchs & Fuchs, 1985; King-Sears, 1994).

Popham (1993) acknowledges the high cost of scoring authentic assessments. He suggests the use of "genuine matrix sampling," which involves using a smaller sample of both students (who should be representative of the larger group of students) and assessment tasks (which should be representative of the entire assessment) to alleviate the high cost of measuring every student on every task in authentic ways. This type of sampling begins with the development of authentic assessment tasks and then samples those tasks, schools, and students within those schools. There exists within this type of sampling procedure very natural opportunities to include students with disabilities in authentic assessment tasks. The authentic tasks developed can be based on each student's IEP goals and objectives. The end goal is that more appropriate instructional emphases occur in schools—for all students.

Christenson (1992) states that the concepts of authentic assessment seem to be very consistent with empirically-based principles of effective instruction, including: specific objectives for assignments, variety in teaching and practice of skills, an emphasis on student understanding and application rather than solely on memorization, and a process to guide educators' decisions about instructional match by incorporating students' different abilities and interests. There are a variety of ways that student performance is enhanced when authentic assessments are used *because it can be linked to effective teaching principles* such as time on-task, feedback, and student involvement (see Table 6-4).

Armstrong (1994) describes different ways that students can perform the same curriculum (or IEP) objectives by using varied performance methods based on the multiple intelligences theory. Multiple intelligences theory purports that all students have intelligence in a variety of areas, and that some of their areas are stronger than others, and that the type of intelligence that schools historically have chosen for students' demonstration of learning rarely taps into all students' strengths areas. The seven areas of multiple intelligence described by Gardner (1983) include linguistic, logical-mathematical, spatial, musical, bodily-kinesthetic, interpersonal, and intrapersonal. For example, Armstrong identifies varied performance methods that can be used to assess students' knowledge after reading a book: (1) writing a response (linguistic), (2) developing a hypothesis (logical-mathematical), (3) drawing a picture (spatial), (4) building a model (bodily-kinesthetic), (5) creating a song (musical), (6) sharing with a friend (interpersonal), and (7) designing a personalized response (intrapersonal). Although each student may choose the way in which he or she demonstrates their knowledge, each student begins the assessment/instruction portion of the curricular unit knowing what competencies or objectives or goals or criteria need to be demonstrated within the type of project he or she chooses to perform.

TABLE 6-4   **Complements between effective teaching and authentic assessment.**

Enhancing Student Performance

- Use active engagement.
- Consider prior knowledge and tie new learning to existing knowledge.
- Construct personal meaning.
- Engage in self-monitoring of their progress.
- Use others to discuss their thoughts to achieve a deeper level of meaning.
- Have a clear statement of expectations.

Enhancing Student Motivation

- Give students choices in and control over their learning.
- Students believe assigned tasks have personal relevance.
- Students assume personal responsibility for learning.
- Students have a high sense of self-efficacy.

Source: Constructed from information in Christenson, S. L. (1992). Authentic assessment: Straw man or prescription for progress? *School Psychology Quarterly, 5,* 294–299.

In an inclusive classroom, those criteria vary for students such that each student is responsible to a set of criteria that is both realistic and challenging for him or her. A student with developmental disabilities is responsible for a picture that depicts the main idea and primary characters of the story that he or she has seen on videotape. A student with learning disabilities may have listened to the story on audiotape and is responsible for drawing pictures that illustrate the sequence of events in the story. Perhaps another group of students is responsible for reading the story independently and then identifying the passages in the story that depict inferences or foreshadowing. Then that group of students selects how they will demonstrate their knowledge through creating a song or building a model or designing their own format for their response. The key to using multiple intelligence theory with assessment is teachers' extension of traditional ways students' demonstrate their knowledge to include a multitude of ways that students can demonstrate their knowledge. The caution for teachers who use multiple intelligence assessment methods, or any other type of creative, novel, and innovative ways to measure student's learning, is to remember that simply using alternative methods for assessment does not obviate the need to determine beforehand the criteria by which assessment is judged. That is, students who simply complete a different type of assessment must still be aware of the critical dimensions of the learning that must be included in their assessment format. Those dimensions or criteria should be varied for the different students (with and without disabilities) in the inclusive classroom so that they are challenging and realistic for them.

As such, the evaluation standard changes when authentic assessment is used (Elliott, 1992). Traditionally, teachers have used grades to evaluate student progress. However, performance-based grading benchmarks are used with authentic assessments. Students progress toward mastery of the agreed-upon learning outcomes by comparing their work to a standard of performance, instead of to other students. Frequently students are presented with scoring rubrics at the same time that they are presented with learning tasks. Marzano and colleagues (1993) describe scoring rubrics as fixed scales (typically a scale of 1 to 4) with a list of characteristics describing the performance for each point on the scale. The performance descriptions are used to inform students about their quality of performance in relation to a "best" quality. Castner, Costella, and Hess (1993) developed the following rubric to use across schools, grades, and disciplines in their school district:

4 = exemplary (fully meets criteria)
3 = proficient (adequately meets criteria)
_____ *Mastery Line* _____
2 = approaching proficiency (sometimes meets criteria)
1 = evidence of attempt (seldom meets criteria)

A variety of terms can be used (e.g., less-than-satisfactory, satisfactory, strong, and excellent work) as well as criteria that corresponds to each term. By using flexible criteria, a student with learning disabilities can be working toward "exemplary performance" with individualized criteria developed for him or her. Criteria for a student with severe mental retardation also may be differentiated. Regardless of the terms used, the words themselves are not useful until descriptions for, and an understanding of, their meaning are conveyed to students. Frequently, students themselves can be involved actively in developing the standards or criteria for rubrics (which are scoring systems with specific descriptive information given for each standard).

For students with disabilities, the initial objectives and evaluation criteria may be derived directly from the IEP. Possibilities for using the same rubric scoring guidelines for differential assignments are possible, such as when a student with a learning disability has a writing assignment using a computer for spelling difficulties and eye-hand coordination problems, or a student with moderate mental retardation is responsible for writing an assignment featuring possible vocational opportunities instead of Shakespearean history. Differentiated learning outcomes, set up beforehand, as well as the within-student comparison, makes authentic assessment a natural link to evaluation in inclusive settings. Moreover, student self-assessment is incorporated by explaining to students the criteria used to evaluate their work so that they can make decisions about their work quality.

Portfolio assessments contain the observable evidence or products of performance assessment—evidence that may or may not reflect authentic tasks (Poteet et al., 1993). Nolet (1992) distinguishes between "assessment" and "instructional" portfolios. Instructional portfolios are used for motivation, facilitating discussions, or promoting reflection to help the student perform new behaviors. Instructional portfolios contain content decided by the teacher and student, whereas assessment portfolios may contain content decided only by the teacher. Assessment portfolios contain systematically collected information to help the teacher make educational decisions about the effectiveness of instruction. Assessment portfolios contain samples of student work over time and under varying conditions relating to a central content area. Distinctions between the type of portfolio used highlights the degree of student involvement, so the decisions in determining the content and the types of decisions made about the content should be clear to the students. Portfolios can be especially beneficial for students with disabilities when the content, and criteria for the content, is used to provide more concrete information about the learning process and about learning progress. For example, a portfolio that contains writing samples for a student with learning disabilities can provide the student with a clearer perspective on how his or her writing style has improved. However, it is not merely the presence of the work within a portfolio that provides this meaning; the meaning is dependent on how the teacher uses the work samples and products to engage the student in discussion about his or her progress in writing. Paulson, Paulson, and Meyer (1991) describe guidelines for developing and using instructional portfolios that include the following:

- Emphasis on the content, included providing an opportunity for the student to "learn about learning"
- The portfolio as something done by the student, not to the student
- Information that depicts student growth in instructional areas
- Careful delineation of the criteria by which teachers and students determine content to be placed in the portfolio

Furthermore, these criteria may be used flexibly in different ways as the school year progresses. For example, writing samples from a student with learning disabilities may be used to depict "work in progress" initially, and then the final work product may eventually be placed in the portfolio.

> *Teachers need to help their students view ongoing evaluation as part of the process of doing the task and understand that the purpose is to help the student be successful at it.*
>
> Cullen & Pratt, 1992

Functional assessments focus on the context for student behavior in both academic and behavioral areas. A functional assessment includes antecedent (setting events, what happens prior to behavior), behavior (what student behavior occurs), and consequence (what event/result immediately follows the student behavior)—typically called "ABC" data. Functional assessments are particularly necessary when student's inappropriate behaviors are the focus of intervention, and teachers are attempting to figure out what the student is communicating to them through exhibiting inappropriate behaviors. The use of functional assessments has been emphasized in recent years in attempts to elevate teacher assumptions or casual observations of student behavior into a more systematic approach to developing interventions (Kern, Childs, Dunlap, Clarke, & Falk, 1994). Advantages of a functional assessment approach include greater confidence that variables affecting student performance are accurately identified, which logically provides more reliable information that interventions developed to impact on those variables will have a direct, and desirable, effect on student behavior. In short, functional assessment includes developing and testing theories about what is causing student behavior—academic or social—which then lead to appropriate curricular interventions. Functional assessment is especially important for inclusive settings because it acknowledges the significant, and sometimes adverse, effects that environmental or people influences can have on student behavior. For example, the way in which a teacher responds to an inappropriate behavior may be a factor in maintaining the misbehavior. A student who receives negative attention for calling out in class or who succeeds in gaining the teacher's attention through calling out and being recognized is actually reinforced positively (attention) through continuing what the teacher considers to be undesirable behavior. That is, although the behavior is not acceptable to the teacher, the teacher's response maintains the behavior instead of decreasing it. Similarly, a student who causes disruption when faced with completing an assignment that he or she knows they cannot do has used disruptive behavior as an "escape" function that is successful in accomplishing what the student intended: the focus in the classroom is now on the disruptive behavior and not on the student's responsibility to complete the assignment; nor is the focus on teaching the student how to complete the assignment or on rethinking the level of the assignment. Functional assessments can help teachers isolate the variables within the classroom that may be contributing to or sustaining or causing the inappropriate behavior. In some respects, a functional assessment can help teachers focus on the cause of the inappropriate behavior versus the symptoms.

Functional assessments also remove the onus of "problems" from being solely student-based. Equal emphasis is on interactions that occur within the environment. That is, responsibility may rest with the adult's behavior changing in order to bring about more desirable student behavior. The following identifies a compilation of possible antecedents and consequences that can affect student behavior:

> **Antecedents:** *presentation of instruction; teacher directions for completing an activity; level of task difficulty; student interest in the task; student choice in selecting tasks*
>
> **Consequence:** *feedback; reinforcement; avoidance or escape from a task; punishment*

Lentz and Shapiro (1986) suggest that three methods be used to assess the academic environment. First, teacher interviews are used to further identify the problem and to analyze what may be causing the problem (e.g., problem analysis). Next, direct observation during the time period in which the student problem is exhibited can be used to supplement the teacher interview. Because this procedure occurs repeatedly (a minimum of three times is recommended) and is conducted by an outside observer (e.g., not the teacher), more objective information may be gathered as a result. Given a teacher's tasks to engage many different students in instruction, the possibility that a teacher may be missing a key antecedent event is likely. Finally, student work is analyzed to determine error patterns, appropriateness of skill level, and work output.

Curriculum-based assessments (CBA) in special education have been described with a wide range of definitions (Fuchs & Fuchs, 1985; Germann & Tindal, 1985; Salvia & Hughes, 1990). For example, one type of curriculum-based assessment may be described as teacher-constructed pretests and posttests, or solely the posttest (Howell & Morehead, 1987). Another type of curriculum-based assessment might focus on critical skills within a single unit of instruction on a long-term basis (Fuchs & Deno, 1991), while others may focus on critical skills across multiple units of instruction. The next section of this chapter provides a synthesis of the varied interpretations of curriculum-based assessment by focusing on the following characteristics of CBA:

- Direct observation of student performance (may be authentic or simulated situation)
- Frequent collection of data (which may be placed in a student's portfolio)
- Data used to make decisions during instruction (versus "after the test")

APPLY as a Framework for Developing and Using Curriculum-Based Assessments

A framework for developing useful curriculum-based assessments is presented next with the intent of conceptualizing a flexible framework within which any assessment model can be used (see Table 6-5 for a visual display of the framework). A mnemonic, APPLY, accompanies the framework as a memory prompt for the sequence of five steps involved in using CBA (Jorden & Haube, 1995; King-Sears, 1994).

Analysis of the curriculum goals, objectives, outcomes, and intents are a necessary first step. Varied curricula (e.g., vocational, social skills, life skills, strategy, and general education) are available for students with disabilities, and a thorough understanding is necessary to target multiple settings, or contexts, for student performance of targeted curriculum objectives. McLaughlin (1993) describes several of the curriculum options for special education (refer to Table 6-6), and educators should choose from these options the one(s)

TABLE 6-5   APPLY as an assessment development framework.

1. **A**nalyze the curriculum.
2. **P**repare items to meet curriculum objectives.
3. **P**robe frequently.
4. **L**oad data using a graph format.
5. **Y**ield to results—revisions and decisions.

Source: King-Sears, M. E. (1994). *Curriculum-based assessment in special education* (p. 17). San Diego: Singular Publishing. Used with permission of the publisher.

that is appropriate for individual students with disabilities. Note that some students with disabilities may be learning objectives from more than one curriculum option. Consequently, educators and related service personnel need to become familiar with more than one curricula and sometimes more than one grade level. Without this familiarity, the notion of targeting key objectives for assessment will be quite difficult and haphazard.

Educators must target, from the multitude of curriculum objectives available within the curricula their students are working from, those objectives that they believe are the critical

TABLE 6-6   Major curriculum options for special education.

Standard curriculum	The typical curriculum provided by the school system for all students in general education programs.
Standard curriculum with adaptations	Uses the ongoing general education curriculum with modifications in presentation, practice, and evaluation methods that match individual learner needs.
Parallel alternate curriculum	Emphasizes essential objectives from the standard curriculum but structures the curriculum, instructional strategies, and evaluation procedures to accommodate groups of learners with special needs.
Remedial basic skills curriculum	Focuses on identification and intensive instruction to correct specific deficits in basic literacy areas of language arts, reading, and mathematics.
Learning strategies/ study skills curriculum	Emphasizes principles, rules, and techniques that enable students to learn, solve problems, and function more independently in classroom, vocational, and social settings.
Social skills curriculum	Addresses prosocial development and/or identified deficits in basic communication, coping, and survival skills.
Career-vocational education	Encompasses comprehensive experiences through which students learn about and prepare for productive engagement in postsecondary work environments.
Independent living skills curriculum	Emphasizes current skill needs and adult outcomes required for successful functioning in major life domains, environments, and activities.

Source: Adapted from information in McLaughlin, V. L. (1993). Curriculum adaptation and development. In B. S. Billingsley (Ed.) *Program leadership for serving students with disabilities* (p. 152). Richmond, VA: Virginia Department of Education.

ones (i.e., the "benchmarks") for students to learn. Some educators target an objective for a curriculum-based assessment that encompasses several smaller objectives so that when students can accomplish the targeted objective, they have actually also accomplished several "enabling" objectives. In fact, any task is comprised of many smaller objectives. All behaviors will not be measured with a CBA; efficient teachers target the primary objectives that will be measured via the CBA. Curriculum analysis of objectives also includes designating the criteria by which student performance of those objectives will be depicted.

Smith and Dowdy (1992) suggest that educators who work with students with developmental disabilities also consider the future life outcomes of these students when targeting key curriculum objectives. They describe a "future based assessment" profile that includes curriculum, assessment, and instruction that focuses on what a student needs to be able to do in their future, related to not only employment (which is typically addressed on an Individualized Transition Program) but also to critical areas such as independent community living skills, access to relevant community agencies, responsibilities as a citizen within a community, and socialization skills.

Preparing items to meet curriculum objectives is the second step. These items are based both on the objectives and the predetermined criteria set up for performance. Note that these objectives and criteria may vary for individual students in a classroom. Characteristics of those items are that they are as real life and authentic as possible, directly match the curriculum objectives (which may be derived from the IEP), and be directly observable and measurable. Two types of assessments can be developed (preferably these are performance-based). One is a formative assessment that is intended to measure student progress toward objectives, and the other is a summative assessment (which may encompass more cumulative information than formative assessments). Typically with curriculum-based assessments, the focus is on gathering formative assessment data *during* instruction that can inform the teacher when instructional changes need to occur, and results can also inform the student about their expected summative assessment results (e.g., which items are consistently missed on the formative assessment and need to be studied more before the final test). Teachers who plan to use innovative methods of assessment (e.g., based on multiple intelligence theory) may incorporate into this step many ways that students can demonstrate their knowledge of the items or criteria selected. Furthermore, the criteria may vary from student-to-student within an inclusive classroom.

Listed below are some questions teachers can ask themselves as they develop items to meet the curriculum objectives:

1. How much does accuracy count? How much does thoughtful examination count over accuracy?
2. Do the mechanics of accomplishing the objective, such as the mechanics of writing for a report, count a little or a lot?
3. How closely does the item reflect essential content?
4. How authentic can the assessment be made while still retaining the value of instruction on that content?
5. To what extent can the focus of item development be on the critical outcomes versus assessment development solely for the purpose of giving a grade?

If scoring rubrics are used to communicate the performance criteria to students, then descriptions for each of the levels of performance on the rubric scale are developed at this point.

Probing frequently is the third step, and this requires that educators collect intermittent (e.g., daily, weekly) assessment data to determine that students are progressing and that the instructional techniques being used are effective. Frequent probes are especially critical for students with disabilities to ensure that student progress is being made, that the instructional methods are effective, and that the use of instructional time is optimized (e.g., students are working on information that is new and challenging for them). It is essential that teachers are able to inform students who are at any point in completing a long-term project when they are on the right track and when they need to reconsider what they are doing to get on the right track while they are completing the project, not after the project has been turned in three weeks later. Frequent probes that include the predetermined criteria for assessment allows the teacher to discuss critical aspects of the project with the student and to reinforce when students are moving in the right direction. More importantly, frequent probes allow the teacher to reteach or reemphasize key points before the project is turned in for more formal evaluation.

Loading data using a graph format is the fourth step in the APPLY framework. Graphed data make it possible for educators to make decisions by analyzing the data and provide students, families, and other school personnel more of a concrete picture of their progress. Enhanced achievement gains occur (Fuchs & Fuchs, 1985) when teachers *and* students use graphed data:

- Students increase their performance because they now have a tangible image of their progress.
- Self-esteem increases because students can see that their efforts result in improved performance.
- Teachers are more likely to try alternative teaching techniques when they have data that prompts them to make a teaching change.
- Goal-setting by students, even when teachers believe the goal is too high, results in higher achievement than when teachers set goals for students.

Students who have a visual display of their progress are also better able to use teacher feedback during instruction as a means through which they can improve their future performance. Wiggins (1993) notes that "the form and manner in which we report the result, the opportunity to improve through hard work, can provide crucial incentive for the student to give something difficult another go or work a little harder even when improvement does not seem possible" (p. 143).

Yielding to results and making necessary revisions and decisions based on data is the last step. Ideally, those data indicate that teaching is resulting in learning the intended goals and objectives. When data do not indicate that expected progress is occurring, then revisions in instructional procedures, student involvement, materials used, or a multitude of other variables that impact student performance may be necessary. One popular method for making decisions is the use of the "three-day rule." When a student has not made anticipated progress on three consecutive occasions on a curriculum-based assessment, then it's time for the teacher to explore more in-depth reasons why this may be happening. Another decision-making technique is to set an aimline on the graph. To set the aimline, connect the student's initial performance data point across the graph to the intersection point between the session date and the aimed-for data point (see Figure 6-1 for an example of a graph with each part explained).

Decisions made at this point should also prompt educators to reflect on the process of evaluation and how well that process "fits" that student. The following questions can encourage discussion about the wide variety of influences on teaching and learning:

- Do revisions of the targeted curriculum objectives need to occur?
- Does the information from the probe provide sufficient and meaningful data?
- Should an alternative teaching method be used?
- Is the learning environment arranged well for individual learners (e.g., physical arrangement, positive atmosphere, supportive climate)?
- How is the student viewing their CBA progress and relating progress to his or her learning process?
- Is anticipated progress being made?
- Are the targeted objectives challenging enough for individual students?

These questions can be used to promote dialogue among teachers, students, and parents. Moreover, the APPLY framework appears to meet the four criteria set forth by Cullen and Pratt (1992) in their discussion of how evaluation of students in inclusive schools can become more purposeful (p. 177):

1. Determine if objectives were achieved.
2. Assist in the development and implementation of an educational plan that meets student needs.
3. Assist the teacher to determine the direction of the future.
4. Provide information on the quality of the learning environment for specific kinds of learning.

The remainder of this chapter will focus on how to use curriculum-based assessments in ways that capitalize on student involvement, maximize usefulness for teachers, and resemble real-life tasks in real-life contexts. Guidelines for simulating real-life tasks and contexts are given, and ways to manage assessment and instruction in heterogeneous classrooms that include students with a range of disabilities are presented.

> *The exact nature of assessment has changed over the years from a strong emphasis on norm-referenced testing to the current movement to use non-standardized, curriculum based assessment paradigms.*
>
> Smith & Dowdy, 1992

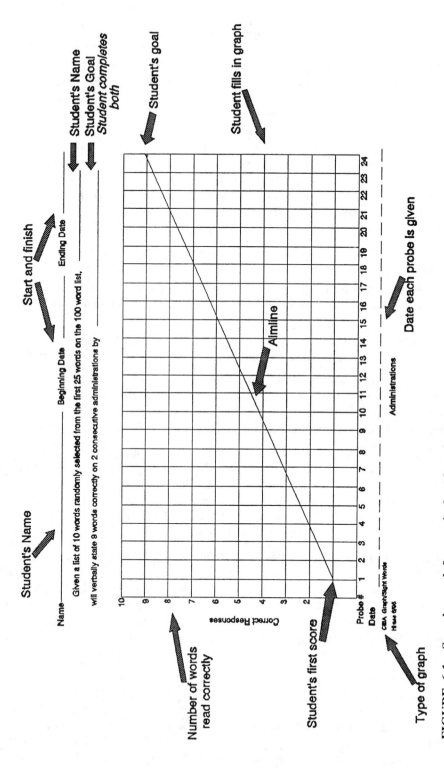

FIGURE 6-1 Sample graph for curriculum-based assessment.

Source: Bui, X., Hlass, J., & Reda, M. (1995). *Using curriculum-based assessment in reading instruction.* Unpublished manuscript, Johns Hopkins University at Rockville, MD.

APPLY Case Study # 1: Fraction Computations and Word Problems

1. Analyze the curriculum. Ms. Hlass and her fourth grade students, including two students with learning disabilities and one student with serious emotional disturbance, are just completing work on computations and problem solving with regrouping in multistep multiplication and division with whole numbers. Ms. Reda, the special education teacher, has been consulting weekly with Ms. Hlass to ensure that the three students with IEPs are progressing satisfactorily in math. So far, the students are doing well with multiplication and division. The fourth-grade students are about to begin a unit on fractions in which the focus is on identifying fractional parts including mixed numbers, adding and subtracting mixed numbers with like denominators, and solving word problems using mixed fractional numbers. Although there are more objectives contained in the math curriculum, Ms. Hlass targets a critical few as benchmarks for her CBA objectives:

> **Objective # 1:** Given pictures representing fractional parts greater than one, students will write the correct mixed number.

> **Objective # 2:** Given mixed fractions with like denominators to add and subtract, students will accurately compute the problem so that the answer is expressed in lowest terms.

> **Objective # 3:** Given a word problem to solve that includes adding and subtracting mixed fractions with like denominators, the students will correctly solve the problem.

2. Prepare items to meet the curriculum objectives. Ms. Hlass develops several forms of a probe that contains three problems of each of the critical objectives she has targeted. She weights each of them differently because they increase in complexity, and she wants her assigned point values to reflect that. Refer to Figure 6-2 for one form she uses with students.

3. Probe frequently. At the beginning of math class at least three days a week, Ms. Hlass distributes the probes to all of her students. Each student then grades his or her own paper (Ms. Hlass monitors closely, but she has also previously discussed with students the importance of being honest and how these scores do not count as test grades). Approximately five minutes of instructional time is allotted for this CBA (Ms. Hlass also uses this CBA activity for a second purpose: promptly orienting students to classwork for the day).

4. Load data using a graph format. Students in Ms. Hlass' class have a portfolio folder in their desk that contains their graphs for various content areas, so they find the one that corresponds to math. Students then calculate how many points they have earned on the probe by multiplying each correct problem by its corresponding predetermined point value (which is also listed on the probe sheet). Each student then graphs his or her score on the graph (see Figure 6-3) and makes a notation about their performance (e.g., improved, declined, stayed the same).

5. Yield to results—revisions and decisions. Ms. Hlass directs students to return to their probe sheet and see if they can figure out how to correct any problems they missed. Students may consult with a neighbor if they need some assistance, but only after they have tried to figure it out on their own. Students then set a goal for the next administration of the probe—each student targets the number they aim to earn the next time the probe is administered by lightly penciling in the number on the graph. Ms. Hlass can then use several methods to get

Name:	Date:	Adding & subtracting mixed fractions with like denominators. **Form A**

Write the correct fraction that goes with each picture:

1. ◆◆◆◆◆◆-

   ◆◆◆◆---   = _____

2. ♣♣♣♣♣♣♣-

   ♣♣♣♣---   = _____

3. ☺☺☺☺☺   ☺☺☺--
   ☺☺---
                    = _____

correct of 1, 2, 3 _____ × 1 = _____

Compute the following, and reduce the answer to lowest terms:

4. $5\frac{7}{8}$
    $+ 1\frac{2}{8}$

5. $13\frac{3}{10}$
    $- 9\frac{5}{10}$

6. $2\frac{5}{7}$
    $+ 3\frac{1}{7}$

correct of 4, 5, 6 _____ × 2 = _____

Solve the following word problems, and reduce the answer to lowest terms:

7. The recipes to make two types of cakes requires $1\frac{3}{8}$ cups of flour for one cake and $2\frac{5}{8}$ cups of flour for another cake. How much flour is needed to make both cakes?

8. The fourth grade Pizza Party began with 5 whole pizzas, and by the time the class had eaten as much as they could there was $1\frac{3}{10}$ pizza left. Some of the pizza that was left over was probably because it had anchovies as a topping. How much pizza did the fourth graders consume?

9. Three cooperative work groups in science need enough sand to complete their laboratory experiment on Thursday. Each group needs to have $2\frac{1}{2}$ cups of sand. How much sand is needed so that there is enough for all three groups?

correct of 7, 8, 9 _____ × 3 = _____

Total # of points earned on this probe: _____

FIGURE 6-2   Probe for fourth grade: Adding and subtracting mixed fractions with like denominators.

an immediate indicator about how many students, and which students, may need reteaching in critical math areas. One method is to ask students to raise their hands in response to what they got correct (e.g., # 1, # 2). Another method is to ask students to give a "thumbs up" or "thumbs down" response to what areas they would like further review in (which does not necessarily mean they got an answer incorrect). A third method is to collect the probes and quickly sort them into piles according to problems correct. Many other methods can be developed by creative teachers, and Ms. Hlass also plans to collect the students' CBA graph folders later in the week so that she can view each student's progress individually. For right now she is concerned about using her instructional time efficiently and eliciting as much active student involvement in their learning as she can.

Objective #1: Given pictures representing fractional parts greater than one, students will write the correct mixed number (3 points possible).

Objective #2: Given mixed fractions with like denominators to add and subtract, students will accurately compute the problem so that the answer is expressed in lowest terms (6 points possible).

Objective #3: Given a word problem to solve that includes adding and subtracting mixed fractions with like denominators, students will correctly solve the problem (9 points possible).

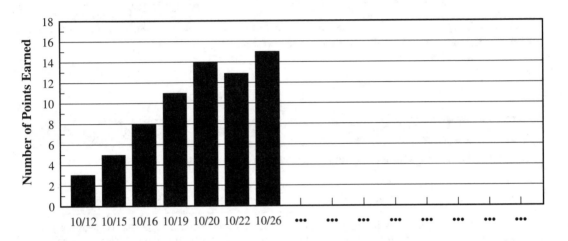

FIGURE 6-3   CBA graph for fractions.

Variations

All students complete math probes at the beginning of the class period, all students graph their earned point values using the same graph format, but the content of math objectives for individual students varies:

1. One student is focusing on identifying fractions for mixed numbers in which he needs to both identify the correct fraction and draw pictures of the fractions when a mixed number is provided.
2. A group of students is working on the same type of objectives, except theirs are for adding and subtracting unlike fractions (a more advanced skill).
3. A student whose instruction is differentiated using a parallel curriculum format receives a probe in which her task is to indicate which of the pair of fractional parts are the same. Another part of her probe requires her to replicate an instructional pattern (found in an example) in a blank shape.
4. Have students make up their own word problems, then solve them.
5. Students write a play that involves several word problems. They perform the play for the class and have the class assist with problem solving during the play.

6. Students develop word problems based on an experience they have really encountered such as fractions used when: figuring how to divide a pizza or pie into identical pieces; weighing fruit at the grocery store; pumping gas at the service station; determining body weight.

APPLY Case Study # 2: High School General Science Class

1. Analyze the curriculum. Ms. Jorden, a high school special education teacher, is team-teaching a tenth grade general science class with Mr. Fiance. Before each unit of instruction Ms. Jorden and the students who may have difficulty with the multisyllable words in the unit (the students include students with learning disabilities, among other students) review the list of words and target those that they do not recognize. Ms. Jorden uses one format of a curriculum-based assessment to determine that the students are acquiring word recognition skills for the unfamiliar science terms. Another form of a curriculum-based assessment will focus on the terms' definitions. Still other formats for curriculum-based assessment can be used for the science unit (refer to other formats and content suggested at the end of this case study), but this scenario describes CBAs that target the following objectives:

Objective # 1: Given twelve biology terms, the students will correctly pronounce each term.

Objective # 2: Given a biology term, the students will correctly explain how it functions or relates to the total body system.

2. Prepare items to meet the curriculum objective. Using the combination of these sources (e.g., the textbook, curriculum guide, and student involvement in identifying unfamiliar science terms), Ms. Jorden develops a probe, or listing, of twelve terms that the students cannot pronounce (refer to Figure 6-4 for a probe sheet). Note that the probe sheet she is using has the words precounted at the end of each line, which makes scoring the number of words correctly pronounced a faster process.

Objective #2 can be demonstrated by students in a variety of ways. Students may choose to build a model that shows how the biology terms function in a body system, or

alveoli artery capillaries cerebellum cerebrum retina esophagus ligaments medulla hormone acoustic villi	12
capillaries cerebellum cerebrum retina esophagus ligaments medulla hormone acoustic villi alveoli artery	24
esophagus ligaments medulla hormone acoustic villi alveoli artery capillaries cerebellum cerebrum retina	36
medulla hormone acoustic villi alveoli artery capillaries cerebellum cerebrum retina esophagus ligaments	48
cerebellum cerebrum retina esophagus ligaments medulla hormone acoustic villi alveoli artery capillaries	60
hormone acoustic villi alveoli artery capillaries cerebellum cerebrum retina esophagus ligaments medulla	72
capillaries cerebellum cerebrum retina esophagus ligaments medulla hormone acoustic villi alveoli artery	84

FIGURE 6-4 Probe: Twelve terms from general science.

they may write a research paper that compares the terms as they relate to human and animal systems, or they may work as a small group to write and perform a skit that portrays the roles and functions of each term. Regardless of the format each student selects, the teachers can use the same curriculum-based assessment probe to document students' knowledge of the information (see Figure 6-5).

3. Probe frequently. Ms. Jorden uses the probe shown in Figure 6-4 to conduct one-minute timings with each student on three occasions during the week. Because she has read through the list herself and finds that she can read words at a rate of seventy-five words per minute, she has an idea of the optimum performance that could be expected for the students. An alternative is to probe typical students in the class and to use that number as the point to aim for with her students—the "aimline" performance indicator.

For Objective #2, during the science class the students inform one of their teachers when they are ready to be probed on the content. For practice, students can work with each other using flashcards that have the term on one side and the definition on the other (making it possible for students to check their partner's answer by referring to the correct definition).

4. Load data using a graph format. Ms. Jorden has set aside a maximum of ten minutes at the beginning of three strategy periods each week for administering all of the curriculum-

Objective #2: Given a biology term, the students will correctly explain how it functions or relates to the total body system.

	Explanation Includes		
	What it is	**What it does**	**How it works in the body**
Term	**Definition**	**Function**	**Relationship to Body System**
alveoli			
artery			
capillaries			
cerebellum			
cerebrum			
retina			
esophagus			
ligaments			
medulla			
hormone			
acoustic			
villi			

FIGURE 6-5 A probe for biology terms.

based assessment probes on biology vocabulary. She is administering the probes with five students. To maximize the use of their time, she has developed a curriculum-based assessment file in the classroom. The CBA file contains probe sheets that are clearly labeled for several curricula and corresponding skill areas. Several laminated probe sheets are in each file so that Ms. Jorden can reuse the sheets. The CBA file also contains a CBA graph folder for each student. The students are familiar with the CBA routine: When Ms. Jorden calls each student to administer the probe, the student finds a probe sheet for his or her use and also a laminated probe sheet for Ms. Jorden to use. The timer is set for one minute, the student reads as many words as he or she can in one minute, and Ms. Jorden marks her probe sheet when errors are made. If the student reaches the end of the sheet before one minute is up, he or she begins reading the list again (this is important when gathering data on both acquisition of terms and fluency rates). After the minute is up, Ms. Jorden gives her sheet to the student, and the student counts the number of correct words, counts the number of errors, and plots each of these numbers on his or her graph. Figure 6-6 displays a graph for the pronunciation rate for one student. Note that the student's performance increases even more during the third week when the unit of instruction in science class begins (Ms. Jorden pretaught the words for two weeks prior to the unit). Each student then reviews his or her errors using a Language Master magnetic card (each term's pronunciation has been prerecorded on a card) and practices the correct pronunciation.

For Objective #2 in the science class, students' number of terms correctly described are graphed. Each student compares their performance to the previous score and sets a goal for

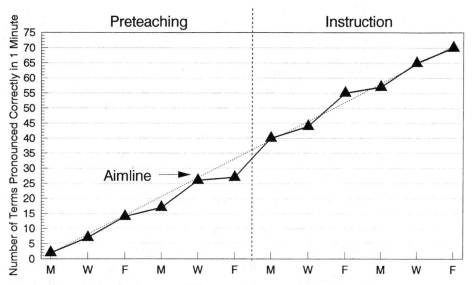

Objective: Given a listing of 12 science terms, the student will correctly pronounce the terms at a rate of ____ words per minute.

FIGURE 6-6 CBA graph of word pronunciation rate.

their next performance. Some students are also able to analyze their score to determine which terms they are consistently missing. Then they know which terms to be particularly mindful of when working on their project.

5. Yield to results—revisions and decisions. Students who are making anticipated progress will be recording data points either slightly above or below the projected aimline. When sufficient progress is not being made, Ms. Jorden and the student discuss ways to increase his or her performance. Sometimes the decisions made include the use of different teaching techniques, the use of more varied review methods for the student, practice with another student who is learning the terms, or listening to the cards on the Language Master more frequently. The possibilities are endless, and the idea of involving the students throughout the CBA process increases their motivation (they typically set goals for themselves for how many words they plan to get right on the next administration) and responsibility (they are aware of what they need to learn, by when, what their current performance level is, and how much progress they make). Active student involvement also provides Ms. Jorden the opportunity to share teaching and learning procedures with the students.

Variations That Can Also Include All Students in the General Science Class

1. Target the terms' definitions and develop/allow varied formats for students showing their knowledge of the terms.
2. Target a biological process that illustrates how the terms are used (the probe could be a checklist of the process steps).
3. Target several key questions from the unit for the students to respond to either verbally or in writing (e.g., "Describe how the cerebrum differs from the cerebellum. Using your knowledge of body systems, discuss what can happen when one body system is not functioning correctly.").
4. Develop a vocabulary definition probe sheet based on terms within a unit of instruction versus a chapter of the unit. In this way, students can be probed about the terms they learned, are learning, and will learn during the unit. Furthermore, the student's retention, or maintenance, of the terms is measured concurrent with instruction on new words.

APPLY Case Study # 3: Fifth Grade Science

1. Analyze the curriculum. Ms. Bui is a fifth-grade teacher who teaches Susan, who has moderate mental retardation, during science. Susan's IEP targets goals and objectives such as increasing verbal and written vocabulary and following two-step directions. The fifth grade general education science curriculum objectives, at first glance, do not appear to lend themselves to including students such as Susan. However, Ms. Bui's colleagues developed a guide for teachers (Hlass, Jorden, Lightner, & Nagle, 1995) that correlates the general education science curriculum to the functional life skills curriculum for students with moderate to severe disabilities (see Table 6-7 for a sample page from this guide). Susan will participate in the science sessions in fifth grade, but her focus will not be identical to that of the other students (this type of differentiation is frequently referred to as a "parallel" curriculum; refer to Chapter 9 for more information on how to differentiate curriculum to facilitate inclusion). Concurrent with her fifth grade peers working on the "Solar Energy" objectives, Susan's focus, and subsequent participation during science lessons, will be on the following objectives (Objective # 1 will be illustrated further in this case study):

> **Objective # 1:** Given two-step directions to follow throughout the day, Susan will correctly follow the directions.

TABLE 6-7   Integration of life skills into the fifth grade science curriculum.

To combine these curricula, collaboration among staff members working with each student is essential. Collaboration must occur weekly, and the team should target long-term objectives as well as weekly objectives.

Solar Energy

Fifth Grade Science Curriculum Objectives	Life Skills Functional Curriculum	Comments
1. Observe and describe heat energy transfer.	1. Identify the colors WHITE and BLACK. Identify the concepts HOT and COLD. Identify the sun and sunny weather.	1. Use pictures, crayons, and objects for colors. Use communication pictures as visual models.
2. Observe and describe the effects of variables on heat energy transfer.	2. Fill buckets with water. Prepare lab trays. Identify the concepts of full and empty using a pitcher and water. Practice pouring from a pitcher with few spills.	2. Use communication pictures as visual cues. Use common household pitchers and cups that the students will recognize and can hold easily in their hands.
3. Use materials to test the effect of a variable on heat energy transfer.	3. Prepare lab trays. Identify the four colors from the box of food coloring. Identify weather and place of experiment in science journals (e.g., sunny/under tree).	3. Students who are unable to write can paste communication pictures of weather in their science journals.
4. Use instruments of science to observe and describe the variables that affect the transfer of heat energy.	4. Pour from a pitcher with few spills. Identify the following: size of cup, the concepts of WET for water, OPEN and CLOSED for the lid of the cup. Identify a thermometer and its purpose.	4. Make sure the pitcher is small enough for the student to manipulate.
5. Design an experiment to test a hypothesis on the material that is most effective in maintaining a liquid at a constant temperature.	5. Prepare lab trays. Identify the concepts of liquid and solid. Identify the textures of the types of insulation used by touching (such as hard, soft, rough, or smooth).	5. Use communication pictures to relate the meaning of the concepts and textures.

Source: Hlass, J., Jorden, J., Lightner, L., & Nagle, D. (1995). *Integration of life skills into the science curriculum.* Unpublished manuscript, Johns Hopkins University, Rockville, MD, p. 59.

Objective # 2: Given objects of various colors that are used during instructional activities of varied content, Susan will correctly identify the color.

Objective # 3: Given demonstrations of the concepts of hot/cold, open/closed, Susan will correctly identify the term that accompanies the concept.

Objective # 4: Given objects with varied textures to feel, Susan will correctly identify if the object's texture is hard/soft, rough/smooth.

2. Prepare items to meet the curriculum objectives. Ms. Bui is able to use the probes developed for the identified curriculum objectives not only in science class, but at other times throughout the day when Susan, and sometimes her classmates, have opportunities to work on them. Again, these opportunities are typically not contrived, but fall naturally within the activities conducted in the 5th grade classroom making them authentic assessments. Refer to Figure 6-7 for a probe related to following two-step directions.

3. Probe frequently. Although there are multiple opportunities during each day to have Susan practice these objectives in naturally occurring activities, Ms. Bui targets Susan's primary responsibility (determined prior to class) during science class as the time to collect data, so that five days of data are collected each week for each of the objectives. Frequently she can enlist the assistance of Susan's peer buddy and cooperative group members (see Chapter 14 on Student Support Networks) to accurately note Susan's performance and record it on the probe sheets.

4. Load data using a graph format. Ms. Bui has developed these probes so that they can also be used as the graphing mechanism. The shaded portions indicate the data point on these probes, providing an immediate visual representation of Susan's progress.

IEP Objective: Given two-step verbal directions to follow throughout the day, Susan will correctly follow the directions.

Date	Context	First direction	Second direction	Level of Prompt		
				Verbal	**Gestural**	**Physical**
1/7	set up experiment	1	2	V	G	P
1/8	cooperative group	1	2	V	G	P
1/9	gather materials	1	2	V	G	P
1/10	distribute materials	1	2	V	G	P
1/11	set up experiment	1	2	V	G	P
1/14	clean up materials	1	2	V	G	P
1/15	cooperative group	1	2	V	G	P
1/16	distribute materials	1	2	V	G	P
1/17	set up experiment	1	2	V	G	P
1/18	clean instruments	1	2	V	G	P
1/21	gather materials	1	2	V	G	P

FIGURE 6-7   **Probe and graph for following directions.**

5. Yield to results—revisions and decisions. Susan is making anticipated progress on most objectives, and for those areas Susan will continue to practice while adding more difficult concepts to extend the objectives (e.g., other vocabulary, additional concepts, use of concepts in new situations). However, she is having difficulty accurately following verbal two-step directions, although she is making progress. Ms. Bui needs to consult with Susan's peers and her special education teacher, Ms. Hamilton, to inquire further about the types of directions and vocabulary used for the two-step directions. The following questions can be used to guide decisions and revisions that may assist Susan's teachers and peers with boosting her performance:

- Is vocabulary that Susan is not familiar with being used?
- Does the person giving the direction have Susan's attention first?
- Should pictures be used along with—or instead of—the physical/gestural/verbal prompts to convey the meaning to Susan?
- Would it help for Susan to repeat the directions before beginning the task, and then to verbalize the direction as she is completing the task?
- Is Susan being reinforced immediately after she correctly follows the directions?

Variations

1. A student whose disability prevents him or her from verbally responding may use a communication board to indicate responses.
2. Some students may be learning to increase their proficiency in using technology such as computers with eye-gaze response capabilities or a touch-response computer.
3. Involve the students themselves in noting the occurrence of their performance. Checklists with pictures could enable students to know what to do (e.g., which direction to follow) independently (similar to self-management procedures).

APPLY Case Study # 4: Geometry

1. Analyze the curriculum. Students in Mr. Michael's eighth grade math course are beginning a geometry unit. Within this class, Mr. Michael has students with learning disabilities, emotional or behavioral disorders, students at-risk, and students who have not received any label thus far in their school career. Mr. Michael considers this class to be far more heterogeneously grouped than other math classes he teaches, and so he spends a great deal of time developing CBA probes that allow him—and his students—to demonstrate knowledge of math concepts in a variety of ways. The targeted objective for one of the CBAs he will be using in this unit is:

Objective: Given each of fourteen geometry terms, the student will define the term by correctly (1) stating its definition, (2) drawing a picture of what the term looks like, and (3) using the pictures of all terms in an illustration.

2. Prepare items to meet the curriculum objective. Mr. Michael has actually embedded into his targeted objective criteria statement a variety of items that can demonstrate students' understanding of geometry terms. He lists several ways that students can demonstrate their knowledge on chart paper in the classroom and then elicits from them additional ways that he had not yet thought of. The chart paper lists the following ways in which students can show they know these terms:

> *match terms to definitions; write definitions from memory; given a term to draw,*
> *student will draw an example; given a picture, student will circle eight examples*
> *of geometry terms then identify those terms to a peer; from a picture map they drew*
> *of their bedroom the students will develop a quiz for peers to take about examples*
> *of geometry terms found on their map; choose an object found in the classroom*
> *and identify all examples of the geometry terms found on that object*

3. Probe frequently. Mr. Michael is teaching the geometry unit over a three-week period so he lets students know that on at least five occasions during the unit they need to let him know they are ready to note their performance on the probe for terms. Several versions of the probe are available for Mr. Michael to use and for students to choose from (see Figure 6-8 for an example of one probe). Students are encouraged to choose the probe format that is the most challenging and realistic for them, and sometimes students can be involved in developing the probe formats.

Objective: Given listings of fourteen geometry terms and their definitions, the student will match the term to the correct definition.

1. ray		a. a line that goes up and down when compared to the horizon
2. perpendicular		b. a mirror image of a figure, as if the figure is "flipped" over
3. congruent parts		c. a set of points; a straight path with no beginning and no end
4. intersecting lines		d. a line which is parallel to the horizon
5. vertex		e. parts that are the same or identical
6. angle degree		f. a straight path connecting two points
7. line segment		g. a line that divides the figure into two congruent parts
8. point of intersection		h. has a starting point and the straight path never ends
9. horizontal line		i. lines that intersect at one point
10. line		j. the place where lines meet
11. parallel lines		k. the number of degrees that describes how close together lines are
12. line of symmetry		l. lines that intersect at right angles to each other
13. vertical line		m. the point where two rays meet
14. reflection		n. lines that never meet because they do not intersect

FIGURE 6-8   Geometry terms and definitions; CBA probe sheet for matching terms and definitions.

4. Load data using a graph format. The graph in Figure 6-9 is used to depict student performance on key geometry terms and concepts throughout the instructional unit. Mr. Michael oversees the probe sessions for each student, but expects all students to graph their results and review their performance before discussing their progress with him. On at least two occasions during the unit the students are responsible for setting up a five-minute conference time with Mr. Michael to discuss their progress. Available times are posted on the bulletin board, and students sign up as they feel ready to have a private feedback conference with Mr. Michael.

5. Yield to results—revisions and decisions. Mr. Michael feels most comfortable making decisions about student performance during the conference sessions in which he can dialogue with the students about how well they're doing in his class. Additionally, for students who are not yet performing at their goal, he can assist them in pinpointing specific areas they need to concentrate on, methods for improving their performance, and also reinforce the progress they have experienced thus far.

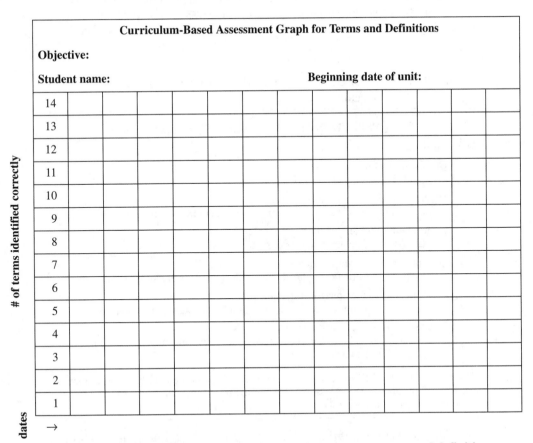

FIGURE 6-9 Curriculum-based assessment graph for geometry terms and definitions.

Variations

- Students use rubric scoring guidelines for self-evaluation of responses.
- Selection of illustrations to place in students' portfolios occurs between the teacher and the student.
- Students' portfolios also contain photographs and three-dimensional items that relate to the geometry concepts.
- Development of multiple assessment formats includes student input, and the teacher uses clear criteria for judging the quality of projects.

Evaluating How USEFUL Assessments Are

Once educators have developed a variety of assessments that they feel successfully accomplish intended goals and outcomes from curricula, there needs to be a "checkpoint" for them to validate that the assessments are USEFUL (see Table 6-8). Understanding of the assessment purposes and results on the part of students, other teachers, and parents should be evident. If people do not understand why an assessment is given or what the results mean, then redevelopment or refinement may be necessary. Synthesis of critical instruc-

---

TABLE 6-8   USEFUL as a framework for determining functionality of developed assessments.

USEFUL: Determining Functionality of Assessments

Is the assessment...

Understood by others?
   Students, Parents, Educators

Synthesize and communicate meaningful feedback?
   Leads to future learning, builds on previous learning, improves current learning

Evaluate critical objectives of the curriculum?
   Long-term, short-term, higher-order thinking skills, strategies

Fill a present void/need within assessment?
   Helps with instructional planning and selection of methodologies

Use frequently to maximize instructional time?
   Student involvement, increased time on-task, increased motivation

Link assessment data to instruction?
   Data used to make decisions about methodologies, student progress, and performance; data decision rules are used

Objective: Given the USEFUL framework for evaluating a curriculum-based assessment, teachers will evaluate their CBAs so that each of the six components of the framework is successfully fulfilled/accomplished.

Source: King-Sears, M. E. (1994). *Curriculum-based assessment in special education* (p. 31). San Diego: Singular. Used with permission of the publisher.

tional goals should also occur. It is no longer possible to teach, nor test, everything there is to know. Educators use their expert judgment of what they consider to be the critical content when developing assessments. Evaluation of those outcomes occur when solid assessments are developed. Filling an existing void in relation to currently used norm-referenced testing is possible with curriculum-based assessments. If CBA represents just another useless item for teachers to do, then the true potential, and probably correct application, of CBA is not being realized. Use of CBA frequently assists teachers with maximizing instructional time because it is clear when students are ready to move on to more challenging material, or when they need additional assistance. Linking CBA to instruction and instructional decision making is critical.

Grading Practices in Inclusive Settings

Grading practices in elementary, middle, and high school classrooms vary widely among and across grade levels and teachers. Elementary teachers give grades based on more informal evidence and observation, and they are more likely to include improvement and effort when assigning grades; middle level teachers rely more on observation of student participation in class, motivation, and attitudes than on tests; high school teachers assign grades based primarily on paper-and-pencil test results and as a method of informing other students, colleges, and teachers about student performance (Brookhart, 1994; Ornstein, 1994). As was noted in the introduction of this chapter, what is most important is that individual teachers are clear on why they are giving grades and ensure that the reasons match the assessment, or grading, practices. Furthermore, "fairness" issues regarding grades also require that students are informed about what components of grades will be (Jongsma, 1991; Redding, 1992; Wiggins, 1988).

> *Distributing grades fairly, as rewards and punishments for student effort and achievement, is a large part of the grading task and at the same time a classroom management function.*
>
> Brookhart, 1994

A synthesis of research on grading practices and purposes reveals the following major reasons for assigning grades to students (Ornstein, 1994, p. 56):

1. Assurance that students have mastered specific content or achieved a certain level of accomplishment
2. Selection or identification or grouping of students for certain educational paths or programs
3. Direction or providing information for diagnosis and planning
4. Motivation or emphasizing specific material or skills to be learned and helping students to understand and improve their performance

> *... students see that even teachers next door to each other, teaching different sections of the same course, employ different standards. ... For most teachers, grading is a private affair. ... A grade is usable by students only if the criteria behind it are explicit and put in descriptive terms.*
>
> Wiggins, 1988

A major concern of educators involved in inclusive settings is how to grade students in a single classroom when the students are working on different learning outcomes. Although the answer to that is quite simplistic in words, that is, that grades are based on the different learning outcomes for individual students, it can be a more complex procedure in its operationalization because it requires a high degree of organization and flexibility to monitor an individual student's performance. Perhaps a beginning comfort level in differentiation of grading practices is a realization and acknowledgment that teachers have always differentiated their grading, even when they had relatively homogeneous groups of students in their classrooms. For example, all fourth grade teachers do not teach and grade reading the same, all tenth grade world studies teachers—even if they are from the same school or school district—do not teach and grade that content the same, and all special educators who teach vocational life skills to secondary students do not teach the same content nor give the same types of tests to students to determine grades in the same way. Teachers already vary in their grading practices. Grading in inclusive settings is merely an extension of the individualized way that individual teachers are already grading students. Inclusive programming expands the individualized nature of grades to include other students (e.g., students with mental retardation) and content (e.g., a functional life skills focus).

> *Assigning grades to students' schoolwork is inherently subjective, regardless of the method used.*
>
> Ornstein, 1994

Grading in inclusive settings can be compared to other changing paradigm struggles educators confront. Oakes and Lipton (1992) note that as detracking classes has become more prevalent in schools (challenging the traditional, yet erroneous, practice that homogeneous classes are best), educators who simply mix classes and teach all students the same way set themselves up for frustrating, counterproductive, and short-lived reform. Similarly, grading practices in inclusive heterogeneous classes cannot follow the same grading practices that were used in separate homogeneous classes; educators should expect to experience a paradigm shift away from traditional grading practices and toward more flexible (and more realistic) standards and guidelines (see Chapter 3 for more information about paradigm shifts). The use of alternative types of testing, observations of students conducting science experiments, and collection of portfolio samples of work in progress as well as work completed can provide educators with differential grading systems that reflect individual achievement and effort compared to self instead of comparison to peers. The paradigm shift to alternative grading systems can be more easily accomplished when teams of teachers work together to develop grading criteria for assignments/course competencies, generate a variety of ways in which students can show their performance, and set aside the necessary amount of time to provide meaningful feedback to students. Report card grades can be determined not by merely adding together numerical scores based on in-class tests and assignments, but also by incorporating additional and meaningful performance indicators such as cooperative work with other group members toward the completion of a project (e.g., "What was my significant contribution to the group effort? How would I rate my performance? How would I rate my other group member's performance in relation to mine?") and self-assessment of progress based on both external- and self-determined standards (e.g., "My progress was good because I showed improvement on. . ."); the attainment of goals set at the beginning of the course or unit (e.g., "A month ago I targeted for myself the 'exemplary' standard for this project. I met the exemplary standard through my depiction of. . ."). Admittingly, there is a significant investment of time for teachers to construct and use more meaningful assessments.

Encouragingly, creative educators are developing more and more solid formats for assessing performance and determining grades for students that focus on salient and meaningful student outcomes and that are conducted within the scope of class activities. Resourceful teachers are not considering this a "do alone" task, but are meeting as teams (note that teams do not have to be restricted to educators at one school site. Many teachers are beginning to share their ideas via e-mail systems and other efficient tools that allow fairly immediate connections), and they are also allowing their students to become part of the team. Students who assist in developing both the criteria for their performance and the selection of performance tasks they would like to do are more motivated toward responsibility for their learning.

Brookhart (1994) notes that grades can be used to provide more information to students by using grades and other assessment feedback not only to judge the quality of student work, but also to explain what the student needs to do better. How often do students look at their letter grade or number grade and react to that score before (if ever) looking more in-depth to see what they need to improve, why they need to improve in that area, and how they can improve their performance? If students receive information with grades that helps them make progress, then motivation should increase, which should subsequently enhance future performance.

Ornstein (1994) suggests the following guidelines for grading students (p. 63):

1. Explain your grading system to the students.
2. Base grades on a predetermined set of standards.
3. Base grades on the student's degree of progress.
4. Base grades on a variety of sources.

Those guidelines do not change in theory when used in inclusive settings, but the practice of using the guidelines based on a single set of systems, standards, sources, or students does change. That does not mean that a high school teacher who works with 140 different students across six class periods will develop 140 different grading criteria; it does mean that six (or fewer) grading criteria that were previously used for each of the six class periods will no longer suffice. Table 6-9 identifies some practices that can assist teachers in the development of alternative grading structures based on these guidelines. Furthermore, student involvement in developing and using varied grading procedures and practices can (1) enrich their involvement in their learning, (2) provide opportunities for student choice of assignments, (3) make the process of grading and learning and teaching more of a shared responsibility, and (4) result in more meaningful and diversified grading practices.

TABLE 6-9   Suggestions for alternative grading practices.

Explain your grading system to the students.

1. Develop a syllabus for each course with grading systems described.
2. Provide examples of work products so that students can refer to models.
3. Discuss grading criteria at the beginning of the course or unit or grading period.

Base grades on a predetermined set of standards.

1. Know going into a course or unit how flexible you are willing to be about how students can accomplish standards that have been set by outside sources (e.g., the school system curriculum, norm-referenced assessments).
2. Clearly communicate those standards *and* their rationale to students at the onset of the course or unit.
3. Develop a variety of ways that students can inform you of how they have accomplished those standards.

Base grades on the student's degree of progress.

1. Conduct some type of pretest so that you know what the student's current level of performance is.
2. Emphasize that the pretest does not count toward the final grade.
3. Change student's paradigm of thinking about assessments so that the traditional way of viewing assessments as summative evaluations that count for a grade are well-balanced with the use of formative evaluations that inform and guide teaching practices and learning opportunities from feedback.
4. Discuss pretest results with the student at the beginning of the course or unit of instruction.
5. Have students set goals for the grades they want to work toward and how they would like to accumulate those points.
6. Periodically during the unit or course have students self-evaluate their progress in relation to the pretest score and the goal they set for themselves.

Base grades on a variety of sources.

1. Paper-and-pencil tasks	9. Song or musical rap
2. Observation	10. Write and direct a play
3. Projects	11. Self-assessment
4. Research	12. Journal
5. Role-playing	13. Conference with teacher
6. Community service	14. Develop a commercial
7. Teach someone else the content	15. Combine the above
8. Verbal assessments	16. Develop your own method!

Conclusions

Assessment and instruction in inclusive settings must provide connections for students and educators about the learning process. These connections are directly linked to meaningful and relevant outcomes that students are expected to demonstrate both today in the classroom and tomorrow in their community. Consequently, each student's content for the connections need to be realistic, challenging, and pertinent to his or her future performance as a productive citizen. Furthermore, students need to be involved in their learning and to take responsibility for their progress early on in the school years so that they acquire the skills and thinking patterns necessary for them to solve problems and set goals and improve their performance in their future work settings. Educators and families have a limited amount of time during the school years, and over the school years, to maximize teaching and learning opportunities. Students with disabilities are capable of learning so much in inclusive settings, where they have access to and interactions with people whom they learn with, or next to, today, and will be neighbors with tomorrow. Appropriate and diverse assessment methods combined with powerful instructional techniques can reflect those capabilities and enhance the possibility of improved performance in the future. The challenge for educators, parents, and students is to ensure that these combinations of instruction and assessment occur every day, for every student.

References

Alberto, P. A., & Troutman, A. C. (1995). *Applied behavior analysis for teachers.* Columbus, OH: Merrill Publishing.

Archbald, D. A. (1991). Authentic assessment: Principles, practices, and issues. *School Psychology Review, 46,* 279–293.

Armstrong, T. (1994). *Multiple intelligences in the classroom.* Alexandria, VA: Association for Supervision and Curriculum Development.

Barnett, D. W., & Macmann, G. M. (1992). Decision reliability and validity: Contributions and limitations of alternative assessment strategies. *The Journal of Special Education, 25,* 431–452.

Brookhart, S. M. (1994). Teachers' grading: Practice and theory. *Applied Measurement in Education, 7,* 279–301.

Bui, X., Hlass, J., & Reda, M. (1995). *Curriculum-based assessment and reading.* Unpublished manuscript, Johns Hopkins University at Rockville, MD.

Castner, K., Costella, L., & Hess, S. (1993). Moving from seat time to mastery: One district's system. *Educational Leadership, 51*(1), 45–50.

Christenson, S. L. (1992). Authentic assessment: Straw man or prescription for progress? *School Psychology Quarterly, 5,* 294–299.

Coutinho, M., & Malouf, D. (1993). Performance assessment and children with disabilities. *Teaching Exceptional Children, 25*(4), 62–67.

Cullen, B., & Pratt, T. (1992). Measuring and reporting student progress. In S. Stainback & W. Stainback (Eds.), *Curriculum considerations in inclusive classrooms* (pp. 175–196). Baltimore: Paul H. Brookes Publishing Co.

Deno, S. L. (1985). Curriculum-based measurement: The emerging alternative. *Exceptional Children, 52,* 219–232.

Elliott, S. N. (1992). Authentic assessment: An introduction to a neobehavioral approach to classroom assessment. *School Psychology Quarterly, 5,* 273–278.

Elliott, S. N. (1994). *Creating meaningful performance assessments: Fundamental concepts.* Reston, VA: Council for Exceptional Children.

Ellis, E. S., Lenz, B. K., & Sabornie, E. J. (1987). Generalization and adaptation of learning strategies to natural environments: Part 2: Research into practice. *Remedial and Special Education, 8*(2), 6–23.

Fuchs, L. S. (1994). *Connecting performance assessment to instruction.* Reston, VA: Council for Exceptional Children.

Fuchs, L. S., & Deno, S. L. (1991). Paradigmatic distinctions between instructionally relevant measurement models. *Exceptional Children, 58,* 488–500.

Fuchs, L. S., & Fuchs, D. (1985). Effectiveness of systematic formative evaluation: A meta analysis. *Exceptional Children, 53,* 199–208.

Gardner, H. (1983). *Frames of mind: The theory of multiple intelligences.* New York: Basic Books.

Germann, G., & Tindal, G. (1985). An application of curriculum-based assessment: The use of direct and repeated measurement. *Exceptional Children, 52,* 244–265.

Haring, N. G., & Liberty, K. A. (1990). Matching strategies with performance in facilitating generalization. *Focus on Exceptional Children, 22*(8), 1–16.

Herman, J. L. (1992). What research tells us about good assessment. *Educational Leadership, 49*(8), 74–78.

Hlass, J., Jorden, J., Lightner, L., & Nagle, D. (1995). *Integration of life skills: General education curriculum and functional life skills curriculum.* Unpublished manuscript, Johns Hopkins University at Rockville, MD.

Howell, K. W., & Morehead, M. K. (1987). *Curriculum-based evaluation for special and remedial education.* Columbus, OH: Merrill Publishing.

Jongsma, K. S. (1991). Rethinking grading practices. *The Reading Teacher, 45,* 318–320.

Jorden, J., & Haube, A. (1995). A *guide to using curriculum-based assessment: Do you know what your students know?* Unpublished manuscript [videotape & guide], Johns Hopkins University at Rockville, MD.

Kern, L., Childs, K. E., Dunlap, G., Clarke, S., & Falk, G. D. (1994). Using assessment-based curricular intervention to improve the classroom behavior of a student with emotional and behavioral challenges. *Journal of Applied Behavior Analysis, 27,* 7–19.

King-Sears, M. E. (1994). *Curriculum-based assessment in special education.* San Diego: Singular.

Lentz, F. E., & Shapiro, E. S. (1986). Functional assessment of the academic environment. *School Psychology Review, 15,* 346–357.

Madaus, G. F. (1993). A national testing system: Manna from above? An historical/technological perspective. *Educational Assessment, 1*(1), 9–26.

Marzano, R. J., Pickering, D., & McTighe, J. (1993). *Assessing student outcomes: Performance assessment using the dimensions of learning model.* Alexandria, VA: Association for Supervision and Curriculum Development.

McLaughlin, M. J., & Warren, S. H. (1994). Restructuring special education programs in local school districts: The tensions and the challenges. *The Special Education Leadership REVIEW, 2*(1), 2–21.

McLaughlin, V. L. (1993). Curriculum adaptation and development. In B. S. Billingsley (Ed.), *Program leadership for serving students with disabilities* (p. 152). Richmond, VA: Virginia Department of Education.

Meyer, C. A. (1992). What's the difference between authentic and performance assessment? *Educational Leadership, 49*(8), 39–40.

Nolet, V. (1992). Classroom-based measurement and portfolio assessment. *Diagnostique, 18,* 5–26.

Oakes, J., & Lipton, M. (1992). Detracking schools: Early lessons from the field. *Phi Delta Kappan, 73,* 448–454.

O'Neil, J. (1992). Putting performance assessment to the test. *Educational Leadership, 49*(8), 14–19.

Ornstein, A. C. (1994). Grading practices and policies: An overview and some suggestions. *NASSP Bulletin, 78*(561), 55–64.

Paulson, F. L., Paulson, P. R., & Meyer, C. A. (1991). What makes a portfolio a portfolio? *Educational Leadership, 49*(8), 60–63.

Popham, W. J. (1993). Circumventing the high costs of authentic assessment. *Phi Delta Kappan, 74,* 470–473.

Poteet, J. A., Choate, J. S., & Stewart, S. C. (1993). Performance assessment and special education: Practices and prospects. *Focus on Exceptional Children, 26*(1), 1–20.

Redding, N. (1992). Assessing the big outcomes. *Educational Leadership, 49*(8), 49–53.

Salvia, J., & Hughes, C. (1990). *Curriculum-based assessment: Testing what is taught.* New York: Macmillan.

Shriner, J. G., Ysseldyke, J. E., & Christenson, S. L. (1989). Assessment procedures for use in heterogeneous classrooms. In S. Stainback, W. Stainback, & M. Forest (Eds.), *Educating all students in the mainstream of regular education* (pp. 143–158). Baltimore: Paul H. Brookes Publishing Co.

Smith, T. E. C., & Dowdy, C. (1992). Future based assessment and intervention for students with mental retardation. *Education and Training in Mental Retardation, 27,* 255–260.

Spruill, J. A. (1993). Secondary assessment: Structuring the transition process. *Learning Disabilities Research & Practice, 8,* 127–132.

Taylor, C. (1994). Assessment for measurement or standards: The peril and promise of large-scale assessment reform. *American Education Research Journal, 31,* 231–262.

U.S. Department of Education. (1994). *High standards for all students.* Washington, DC: U.S. Government Printing Office.

U.S. Office of Technology Assessment. (1992). *Testing in American schools: Asking the right questions, OTA SET-519.* Washington, DC: U.S. Government Printing Office.

Wiggins, G. (1988). Rational numbers: Toward grading and scoring that help rather than harm learning. *American Educator, 12,* 20–25, 45–48.

Wiggins, G. (1993). *Assessing student performance.* San Francisco: Jossey-Bass.

Worthen, B. R., & Spandel, V. (1991). Putting the standardized test debate in perspective. *Educational Leadership, 85*(5) 65–69.

Ysseldyke, J. E., & Thurlow, M. (1994). *Guidelines for inclusion of students with disabilities in large-scale assessments.* ERIC Document No. 372 560.

Team Planning for Individual Student Needs

DIANE M. SWITLICK AND JULIE STONE

◆ ADVANCE ORGANIZER ◆

Effective planning to meet the individual needs of all students in the general education setting is possibly the greatest challenge facing educators today. This chapter explores the planning process and its application to the school-wide and classroom setting. A comprehensive planning process is presented that can be used by a school system or a team for students with a range of disabilities at different severity levels. Examples show the relationship between long-range planning and the development of the Individualized Education Program. Planning forms that may be adapted to specific school settings are included.

Like most parents, I did not enter willingly into the labyrinth known as "Special Education." That my son had special needs was not in dispute, but I was merely the mother. I felt confident that the school "system" would do for my child what it was supposed to do: namely, "fix" him.

My confidence ebbs away as I sit, outnumbered ten to one, at a conference table full of "professionals." These people speak in low, assured tones, one after another, and I listen, bewildered, to: Woodcock, WISC, Matrix Analogies, scores, indicated strengths and needs, projected start dates, short-term instructional objectives. Everyone nods and smiles. I sign here, initial there, and am ushered out. I cry in the car before I start the engine. Where is my child in all this data?

I wish for one person, who knows my child, who cares deeply about his daily experiences as well as his future, someone who understands the terminology and the options and could be useful in such a meeting. These professionals wanted what was correct, certainly, but they also wanted expediency. Who would protect my child in all of this, who could help him achieve the vision that we have for him?

What I discovered was, no matter how skilled a teacher, how intuitive a therapist, how caring a principal, no one can know, nor have as much stake in the unique entity that is our child, as we as parents can. Therefore, we must enter into a partnership with the school system, become familiar with the terminology and knowledgeable about our rights and responsibilities. Having entered into this partnership, I feel confident, caring, effective, responsible, resourceful, and certainly more courageous. It's not always easy, but it is always necessary. Education is a process and we are all involved, whether we want to be or not. We will make mistakes along the way, but we cannot remain bystanders. There may be no perfect placement, no magic answers, and each year will bring a new challenge.

Stacey Roy, Parent

> *... life is not tried; it is merely survived if you're standing outside the fire.*
>
> Brooks, 1994

Inclusive education requires far more than individuals with and without disabilities participating as much as possible in the same classroom. It requires specific planning to ensure that this participation is meaningful for all of the members of the classroom grouping. Inclusion is built on the underlying belief that all children need to participate in the general classroom together. In our day-to-day life, we are not classified into ability groups. As adults, we must have the skills to interact with a wide range of individuals. The appreciation of and ability to handle diversity must begin as early as possible. Inclusive education does not mean that when all students join together in the classroom they learn the same things. It means that when all students are in the general education setting together they learn content and skills appropriate for them in the same classroom.

Teachers attempting to implement inclusion in their classroom need support and assistance. Quality instruction for a highly diverse group of students requires collaborative teams to develop and implement educational programs designed to meet the needs of each student as an individual. While this is a massive undertaking, it becomes more manageable when a planning process is used. Any planning process relies on consideration of each student's total character. Target outcomes or goals are determined not only in terms of specific objectives, but are based also on the impact the program will have on the individual's future goals and ultimately the quality of life (Giangreco, Cloninger, & Iverson, 1993).

In the past, educational planning sessions considered only the current needs and what the child should accomplish next (e.g., during this school year). In recent years, educational planning has taken on a more comprehensive character. Current plans begin with creating a vision for the future. Where do we want this child to be when he or she leaves school? For persons with more severe disabilities, this visioning focuses on creating a future of integrated life and determining ways to realize the goals established (Mount, 1987; O'Brien & Lyle, 1987). The specific objectives are stepping stones to independent living. This planning method is decidedly different than planning models of the past that were solely deficit-based (Hammill & Bartel, 1975; Salvia & Ysseldyke, 1985). Planning has taken on a broader focus to encompass the end result or final outcomes. We no longer focus on what the child cannot do, but rather on what the students will need to do now to prepare them for productive adult life. Learning is framed in the context of the real life situation or in the application of the skills. For instance, a child with a deficit in grammar would not be taught grammar rules. The rules would be included in the context of everyday writing. The child would learn a rule as needed in developing writing pieces. This way the instruction takes on meaning. A second change in emphasis is that family and friends are playing a larger role in the planning process (Forest & Lusthaus, 1987; Mount & Zwernik, 1988; O'Brien, 1987). They join in the actual goal setting and plan the annual educational goals and objectives. With the current emphasis on long-range goals, the family participation is imperative.

Selecting and adapting a planning process to each unique school setting requires a basic understanding of planning and knowledge of the existing planning processes available. It is the focus of this chapter to review existing planning models and to provide an adaptable model for readers to implement in their school settings. Examples are provided to indicate how the model can be used differently for students with varying strengths and needs.

Planning Is Pervasive

> *Implementation of inclusive education can be most successfully accomplished by following a long-term strategic planning process.*
>
> Rigazio-DiGilio & Beninghof, 1994

The idea of planning is not new or specific to education. Planning takes place in every aspect of life. You may recall that Chapter 3 illustrated that all change requires a plan. Stephen Covey (1989) writes that we must "Begin with the end in mind" (p. 97). He states that this idea is based on the principle that "... all things are created twice. There's a mental or first creation, and a physical or second creation to all things." (p. 99). We all must think it before we do it. This is true whether you are developing a blueprint, planning a presentation, planning a family vacation, or planning a student's educational program. Stoner (1982) states that "... planning is the basic process we use to select our goals and determine how to achieve them" (p. 99).

Covey takes the concept a step further and distinguishes between the concepts of leadership and management. They are not the same. Leadership includes a long range vision of the following: Where am I going? What do I want to accomplish? Management, however, entails the detailed plans for achieving the goal—How will I get there? What's the best method to use? In educational planning, a child's needs have always shaped a teacher's plans. In general education, teacher planning has typically targeted the middle range of the children in the classroom. Special education has tended to concentrate only on the individual student needs. However, all these needs have been evaluated in the short range, that is, What will my students achieve this week or this year? Instructional planning has been typically managerial in nature. Covey uses an example that illustrates very clearly the differences between leadership planning and managerial planning, "The leader is the one who climbs the tallest tree, surveys the entire situation, yells, 'Wrong jungle!' But how do the busy efficient producers and managers often respond? 'Shut up! We're making progress'" (p. 101). Without the long-range view, we may end up quite efficiently at the wrong destination. As we apply this concept to education, we must constantly ask ourselves "For what are we preparing these students?" The planning process discussed in this chapter is based on planning that encompasses both leadership and managerial characteristics. It has grown out of the strategic planning used in the business world. While the plans are for individual students, a major emphasis in the general education classroom must be an underlying acceptance of differences and the celebration of a diversity that provides students with the permission to be unique and different.

Results of education have been called into question for several years (Adler, 1990; Goodlad, 1984). These questions revolve around concerns about graduates acquiring a solid base of knowledge, their ability to integrate it, apply it, manage it, build on it, and put it to use in a meaningful way (Ford, Davern & Schnorr, 1992). This failure, at least in part, is a result of limited vision, deficit-based planning, and targeting short-term goals. This limited vision can be seen in both general and special education. In Individualized Education Program (IEP) development, short-term goals and objectives have tended to focus on the development of specific skills and only rarely on the application of these skills in the general education classroom or in real life situations. An example that can be readily observed in many settings is the focus on basic math facts and computation skills. When an inordinate amount of time is spent on computation alone, the student never learns how and when to apply the concepts of mathematics to their daily living. Even when math problems include real life situations, the conceptual learning is lost to the practice of specific computation skills. In those cases in which a calculator would serve as an appropriate accommodation, the teacher and students can be released from skill practice and can concentrate on the patterns and underlying "rules" of mathematical thinking. Solid planning for effective achievement of annual goals and objectives is essential, but may be totally misdirected if the future life goals are not the basis of the initial planning.

Flexibility in planning is critical. Plans must be constantly changed and reevaluated to ensure that both the short-term and the long-term goals are attained and that the instruction is meaningful in future application.

The Planning Process

> By referencing the student's educational program to the characteristics of a good quality life, we remain mindful of our shared desire that the lives of children we teach be bettered as a result of their having been in school.
>
> Giangreco, Cloninger, & Iverson, 1993

Since planning is so critical to achieving success, it is crucial to look at the attributes of a comprehensive plan. While specific definitions of planning may vary, there is agreement on the basic attributes of the planning process (Kaufman & Herman, 1991; Mauriel, 1989; Nebgen, 1991; Rigazio-DiGilio & Beninghof, 1994; Stoner, 1982).

1. Uses fundamental value-based questions that establish the mission or final outcome
2. Provides a framework for more specific planning to follow, including objectives and performance criteria
3. Involves a long-range time frame
4. Provides a sense of coherence and momentum to the planning actions and decisions
5. Involves those who will be responsible for and manage the implementation of the plan and attainment of the goals

Although there are many commonalities, all plans are different. They can differ in their purpose, the process used for development, the format, and the specific components. Frequently, the sequence starts by asking a series of questions. The answers are used to develop a mission or goal statement. Data are systematically gathered that will assist in decision making. All possible strategies, steps, or interventions are identified and evaluated, leading to a process of prioritizing that determines the smaller steps or objectives. This process is strikingly similar to some of those described in Chapter 4, but the outcomes vary with different models.

The questions asked during the development of a plan must render answers that are specific to the intended purpose and the individual(s) involved. For instance, where do we stand on the way to our goals? What are the current strengths and needs? What are the next steps that must be attained? Throughout this process, participants must continually consider the long-range outcomes that emerge and impact the current plans.

Overview of Existing Individual Planning Processes

> *Program modification begins and ends with values.*
>
> Rigazio-DiGilio & Beninghof, 1994

In looking at the planning process for children with disabilities, it is immediately apparent that several models are currently being used. Any of these models will render an appropriate plan for a student. Each process has its own strengths. Any process may be used that satisfies the student and staff needs. Each process is based on the underlying family values and final outcomes identified for the individual student. The following descriptions provide background information on some of the more widely disseminated plans.

Life-Style Planning

The Life-Style Planning process was developed by O'Brien and Lyle (1987). This process requires that teachers, service providers, and family members engage in the planning together. There are three basic components of the process:

1. Determining a desirable future for the child or adult
2. Outlining the activities and describing the supports that are necessary to move toward the desired goals
3. Taking responsibility for organizing the resources available and analyzing what may not be available

The entire planning process focuses on five outcomes that are critical in achieving an acceptable quality of life. These outcomes are called accomplishments (O'Brien, 1987; Mount & Zwernik, 1988):

- Community presence
- Choice
- Competence
- Respect
- Community participation

The process is designed for persons with severe disabilities and relies on the team's abilities to design specific plans.

McGill Action Planning System

The McGill Action Planning System (MAPS) was developed at McGill University by Marsha Forest (1987). MAPS is a systematic approach for developing plans for the inclusion of children with very challenging needs into age-appropriate general education classrooms. This planning process is founded on the belief that all children belong and that all children should learn alongside one another. MAPS emphasizes a team approach. Teams typically include family, friends, peers, professionals, and the child. Vandercook, York & Forest write: "MAPS is a way to operationalize the assertion that all children belong in a school community and to promote the establishment of relationships with others in the school community. Communities are built upon relationships" (1989, p. 45). "Relationships" takes on a heightened importance because they serve a function in social and cognitive development (Lewis, 1982). These relationships represent the context in which competencies as well as resources emerge to assist in this learning process (Hartup, 1985).

The basic assumptions of the MAPS process are integration, individualization, teamwork and collaboration, and flexibility. There is commitment to ongoing problem solving (Vandercook et. al., 1989). The inclusion of peers without disabilities was first emphasized in the MAPS process because peers play a significant role of support in the plan's execution. At a meeting in which all team members are present, sitting in a half-circle, a facilitator asks a prescribed series of questions. The facilitator's responsibility is to ensure that everyone participates. All answers to the questions are recorded on chart paper. The result of the process is a shared vision with specified goals and the identification of the supports or resources required to achieve them. The guiding questions for the MAPS process are (Vandercook et. al., 1989) the following:

1. What is the individual's history?
2. What is your dream for the individual?

3. What is your nightmare for the individual?
4. Who is the individual?
5. What are the individual's strengths, gifts, and abilities?
6. What are the individual's needs?
7. What would the individual's ideal day look like, and what must be done to make it happen?

Choosing Options and Accommodations for Children: A Guide to Planning Inclusive Education

Choosing Options and Accommodations for Children (COACH) originated in 1982 as a planning tool to develop individualized habilitation plans for adults with disabilities. It was revised and implemented by public schools in 1985. Several versions have been published to date. There are six assumptions underlying the COACH process: (1) pursuing valued life outcomes is crucial to educational success; (2) family members and situations are relevant to educational planning; (3) collaborative team work is crucial; (4) coordinated planning depends on shared goals; (5) problem-solving methods are necessary for effective planning; and (6) special education is a service, not a place (Giangreco, Cloninger, & Iverson, 1993). The following are major life goals or outcomes that focus the planning process:

1. Having a safe, stable home both now and in the future
2. Having access to a variety of places and engaging in meaningful activities
3. Having a level of personal choice and control that is age appropriate
4. Being safe and healthy

The authors emphasize that COACH is both an assessment and planning tool for use in developing educational programs that are implemented in general education settings for children with disabilities. Family input is considered critical in determining educational priorities. These priorities are then sorted into IEP goals and objectives not present in the curricula or are targeted for instruction within the natural delivery of the curricula. The COACH process continues by identifying the supports necessary to facilitate success. Student or professional support becomes a part of a specific student's plan. Collaborative teamwork among school and family members and commitment to the long-range goals are vital throughout the comprehensive planning process to ensure a meaningful plan that can be implemented in the classroom.

Each process outlined for individual educational planning thus far focuses on children with significant disabilities. Presently, teachers and other professionals are faced with a wide range of student needs. This makes it crucial to have access to a planning process that can accommodate the needs of students with mild disabilities. To that end, one more planning process is presented that is more general in nature, but has many similar qualities to those already reviewed.

It is clear that any model selected for use must be both comprehensive and feasible to operate successfully in the dynamic setting of a school. After working with each of these planning models, the authors have synthesized the elements into an individual planning process. This process may be used with students experiencing mild to severe learning difficulties. While it is not as specific as COACH, it may be used in conjunction with COACH when plans are developed for a child with severe disabilities. The steps in the process are outlined in Figure 7-1. As the diagram indicates, the process is cyclical, and any step may be revisited at any time during planning. An overview of the model is presented along with four cases to serve as examples. Blank planning forms are found at the end of the chapter for adaptation or use within your school or program.

Student Planning Process

The student planning process is a team-based approach to individual student planning. Team membership varies for each individual student and is determined by current levels of performance and areas of need. These factors change over time and thus, so may the specific team participants. Possible team members may include but are not limited to:

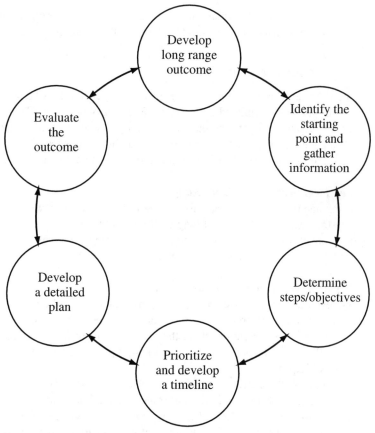

FIGURE 7-1   The planning process.

- General education teacher(s)
- Special education teacher(s)
- Related service providers or specialists

Speech-language pathologist	Occupational therapist
Physical therapist	Reading specialist
Counselor	Psychologist
Audiologist	Auditory specialist
Vision specialist	Nurse/health technician

- Community agency representatives
- Administrator
- Instructional aides
- Mental health professionals
- Peers
- Family members
- Student

As the team begins their planning, they gather all of the pertinent information and follow the basic steps in the planning model. Collaborative planning takes place at a group meeting.

Steps in the Planning Process

The steps serve as an outline guiding the planning meeting. All team members come to this meeting having completed their Profile Planning Worksheet. This form contains specific areas to consider in defining the current strengths and needs of the student (see Form 7-1). During the meeting, the Programming at a Glance form is completed. It provides a concise record of the planning decisions made during the meeting (see Form 7-2).

Step 1—Determine the Long-Range Outcome:
Think about where you want this student to be at age 21 as well as where you want to be sure they are not. Where will they be living, working, and playing? What are the critical components to achieve this outcome? *This long range outcome should be clearly written on the bottom of the Program at a Glance form.*

Step 2—Identifying the Starting Point
Ask each participant to share the strengths they identified on the Profile Planning Worksheet. Record all responses on a piece of chart paper labeled strengths.

Ask each participant to share the needs they identified on the Profile Planning Worksheet. Record all responses on a piece of chart paper labeled needs. Circle the priorities by each participant.

Discuss all the circled needs and reach consensus on five to seven priorities. As necessary, restate or refer to the long-range outcome. *Record these briefly in the appropriate curriculum area in the Priority Needs section of the Program at a Glance form.* Once the priorities have been identified, write the objectives for the IEP. These objectives are necessary to continue with the decision making process.

FORM 7-1　Profile Planning Worksheet.

CURRICULUM AREAS	STRENGTHS	NEEDS	PRIORITY AREAS
ACADEMIC			
Reading: Decoding, word recognition, comprehension			
Writing: Process, usage, grammar punctuation, capitalization, size, spacing			
Math: Concepts, computation, application, problem solving			
Science/Social Studies: Content, participation			
COMMUNICATION			
Speaking, adaptive technology needs, augmentative communication needs			
SOCIAL SKILLS			
Friendship skills, peer relations, expresses feelings, makes requests, takes risks			
BEHAVIOR			
Respect for self and others, attention span, activity level			
WORK STUDY SKILLS			
Organization, on-task behavior, follows directions, working with peers, task completion			
MOTOR			
Fine Motor: Writing-formation of letters or numbers, size, spacing, cutting			
Gross Motor: Trunk strength, ascending/descending stairs, age-appropriate physical skills			
FUNCTIONAL			
Survival language, travel training, money, shopping, daily living skills			
RECREATION & LEISURE			
Long-term age-appropriate hobbies, activities, or interests			

continued

FORM 7-1 Continued

CURRICULUM AREAS	STRENGTHS	NEEDS	PRIORITY AREAS

VOCATIONAL

Job skills, positive work habits,
   on-site training

TRANSITION SERVICES

Adult services, job supports, social
   supports or community living
   supports

PERSON COMPLETING FORM: **TITLE:**   **DATE:**

Step 3—Determine the Steps to Achieve the Outcome

Remind all participants about the concept of least restrictive environment. This can be facilitated by having an excerpt from the Individuals with Disabilities Education Act, Federal Law 101–476 originally 94–142:

> *"Each public agency shall ensure:*
>
> *(1) That to the maximum extent appropriate, children with disabilities, including children in public or private institutions or other care facilities, are educated with children who are nondisabled, and*
> *(2) That special classes, separate schooling or other removal of children with disabilities from the regular educational environment occurs only when the nature or severity of the disability is such that education in regular classes with the use of supplementary aids and services cannot be achieved satisfactorily." (§ 300.550)*

The law further defines the continuum of alternative placements that must be available:

> *(a) "Each public agency shall ensure that a continuum of alternative placements is available to meet the needs of children with disabilities for special education and related services.*
> *(b) The continuum required under paragraph (a) of this section must:*
> *(1) Include the alternative placements listed in the definition of special education under § 300.17 (instruction in regular classes, special classes, special schools, home instruction, and instruction in hospitals and institutions), and*
> *(2) Make provisions for supplementary services (such as resource room or itinerant instruction) to be provided in conjunction with regular class placement." (§ 300.551)*

Having reviewed the above law, discuss whether all or some priority instructional needs can be met in the regular education classroom. What types of supports and services

FORM 7-2   Programming at a Glance.

Physical Features		Priority Instruction Needs	Groupings
Regular classroom	%	Academic	Heterogeneous
Special education (in class)	%		Homogeneous
Special education (separate class)	%	Communication	Cooperative
Accessibility issues:			Peer tutoring
• ramps	Y/N	Social skills	• same grade
• elevators	Y/N	Behavior	• cross grade
• class arragement	Y/N		
• bathroom	Y/N	Work study skills	
• equipment	Y/N	Motor skills	
Services/Staffing			**Preparation and Procedures**
Administrator		Functional skills	Staff training
General educator		Recreation/leisure	• staff
Special educator			• students
Speech/language pathologist		Vocational skills	• community
Occupational/physical therapy			Behavior plans
Reading specialist		Transition skills	Medical/health plans
Psychologist/counselor			Emergency plans
Instructional assistants			
Nurse			

Long-Range Outcome:

are necessary? Would special education direct services be necessary? If so, how much? Is a self-contained special education classroom required to meet one or more of the priority needs? If so, how will it be ensured that the student will be educated with peers without disabilities? *Record the percentages in each environment in the Physical Features section of the Program at a Glance form.*

Do any of the following accessibility issues need to be resolved? Circle the appropriate response (Y/N) in the Physical Features section of the Program at a Glance form.

- Are ramps or elevators required for this student to access all areas of the building?
- Should special consideration be made when physically arranging the classroom environment?
- Do arrangements need to be made in order for this student to use the bathroom?
- Is any special equipment (chairs with arms, different type/size desk, etc.) required?

Consider all the existing staff in the building. Who will need to be involved, for any purpose, with this student? Place a checkmark next to their title under the Services/Staffing section of the Program at a Glance form.

With what mixture of peers should this student be educated? When and for how long should this student be with peers without disabilities? What types of peer supports need to be built in order to facilitate success? Record responses in the Groupings section of the Program at a Glance form.

Identify the training (staff, students and/or community) that will need to be completed in order to successfully implement this student's program. Write the name and position of the person responsible for coordinating this training in the Preparation and Procedures section of the Program at a Glance form.

Consider any other plans that need to be made before the arrival of this student. For example, how will fire drills, bathrooming, or other health related issues be handled? Record this information of the Preparation and Procedure section of the Program at a Glance form.

Step 4—Establish A Timeline
Using the Program at a Glance form, determine what necessary follow-up tasks are required for program implementation. Record all necessary actions/responses on the Follow-Up form (see Form 7-3). Note that timeline issues also are required to complete the IEP.

Step 5—Plan The Details
Using the Program at a Glance form and the objectives written for each priority identified for the IEP, check to ensure that the objectives are consistent with the long-range outcome. Transfer the objectives to the IEP. Discussion of specific implementation strategies for the IEP objectives should take place to determine which can be met in the regular classroom

FORM 7-3   Follow-Up Form.

Actions/Responses	Person Responsible	Timelines

and which require a special class or a community setting. Who is responsible for this implementation also needs to be determined. Programming on a day-to-day basis in the classroom is the next step in planning.

Step 6—Evaluation

Evaluating the effectiveness of the planning process on a regular basis is essential. The majority of the evaluation will come from daily planning to implement the instructional objectives and related curriculum-based measures. Logistical issues that require problem solving and ongoing communication arise regularly. Periodically and at least annually, the overall planning process must be examined in total. Copies of the planning forms are provided here for reference. Full page copies for use and adaptation to each setting are provided at the end of the chapter.

A Taste of Planning

> *We have only begun to discover the myriad of beneficial possibilities created when teams collaborate to teach diverse groups of students.*
>
> Giangreco, Cloninger, & Iverson, 1993

The best way to understand and analyze the usefulness of any planning procedure is by using it. To that end, case studies offering a range of disabilities have been included. These cases will not only provide concrete examples of the process, they will include also specific examples of the IEP objectives that emerge from the planning. These IEP objectives will be related to classroom implementation on a broad basis. More specific information and examples of classroom programming can be found in Chapter 9.

Amanda: Case Study #1

Amanda is currently a fourth grader. She has been included in general education classes since the first grade. She spent kindergarten in a self-contained special education class. Amanda is diagnosed as having mild mental retardation, Downs syndrome. Amanda had a history of early cardiac problems that were corrected by surgery. She has had no further significant health problems. She is farsighted and wears glasses. She receives a combination of services provided in the general education classroom through adapted curricula and materials and direct support from a special educator or an instructional assistant. When in-class support is provided the special educator also assists other students in the room with similar needs. Amanda also receives services in a special education classroom. She works with both a special educator and a speech/language pathologist during this time. Amanda's general education teacher also receives regular consultation from an occupational therapist.

Amanda's progress in elementary school has indicated steady academic increases and the development of strong social skills. She is outgoing and well liked by her peers. She has many friends. Her fellow students are accustomed to providing support for her. They frequently assist and motivate her to do well and work hard.

The planning conference for Amanda is conducted to plan for her fifth grade school year. Present at the conference are this year's and next year's general education teachers, the special educator, the speech/language pathologist, the occupational therapist, and Amanda's mother. Each member of the planning team has completed a Profile Planning Worksheet and has brought it to the meeting. An illustrative copy is provided in Chart 7-1, but it is a summary of all of the information from the forms brought to the meeting.

The meeting agenda follows the planning process.

Step 1—Determine the Long-Range Outcome

The long-range outcome has been determined for Amanda in previous planning meetings. It is reviewed to determine if changes are necessary. The components of the goal are independence, maintaining relationships, and having a job. All participants feel that changes are not necessary.

CHART 7-1   Profile Planning Worksheet: Amanda.

CURRICULUM AREAS	STRENGTHS	NEEDS	PRIORITIES
ACADEMIC			
Reading: Decoding, Word Recognition, Comprehension	Uses packets effectively Verbalizes ideas Ending punctuation Recognizes first word	Phonic decoding Reading comprehension Attending to read alouds Generalize strategies	Reading skills
Writing: Process, Usage, Grammar Punctuation, Capitalization, Size, Spacing	Uses picture cues Short term memorization Comprehension good Writes own sentences	Punctuation Capitalization Developing independence	Writing process
Math: Concepts, Computation, Application, Problem Solving	Place value 10s Uses calculator Time (hour and half hour) Computation and graphing	Build confidence Problem solving, money Telling time (5-minute intervals)	Problem solving Time and money
Science/Social Studies: Content, Participation	Hands-on, group projects Good attitude	Basic facts (+ and -)	
COMMUNICATION			
Speaking, Adaptive Technology Needs, Augmentative Communication Needs	Articulation, gets concern across, expresses needs Very verbal	Formal communication Oral reports, keep oncentration	Formal communication
SOCIAL SKILLS			
Friendship Skills, Peer Relations, Expresses Feelings, Makes Requests, Takes Risks	Won't tolerate mistreatment Friendly, sense of humor Initiates relationships with older and younger peers	Sorting fact from fiction Response strategies to insults Problem solving Lets peers do for her	Develop a "Circle of Friends" Social problem solving

CHART 7-1   Profile Planning Worksheet: Amanda.

CURRICULUM AREAS	STRENGTHS	NEEDS	PRIORITIES
BEHAVIOR			
Respect for Self and Others, Attention Span, Activity Level	Developing sense of responsibility Persistent, follows rules and routines	Low attention on things doesn't like	
WORK STUDY SKILLS			
Organization, On-task Behavior, Follows Directions, Working with Peers, Task Completion	Completes homework Follows 1 or 2 step directions Organized, cooperative	Decrease dependency on peers, remember materials Transition to different activities	Transition
MOTOR			
Fine Motor: Writing—formation of letters or numbers, size, spacing, cutting	Works at writing skills Writes well, cuts well	Spacing words Assistance holding pencil Manipulating objects	Spacing Manipulating obj. Keyboarding
Gross Motor: Trunk strength, ascending/descending stairs, age-appropriate physical skills	All strengths	Sitting upright to write	
FUNCTIONAL			
Survival language, travel training, money, shopping, daily living skills	Good functional language Daily living done at home	Enhance daily living Money, time	Applying money concepts
RECREATION & LEISURE			
Long-term age-appropriate hobbies, activities, or interests	Likes outdoor activities Roller skating, swimming, bowling, bike riding	Balance arm strength	Girl Scouts
VOCATIONAL			
Job skills, positive work habits, on-site training	Follows directions, takes pride in work Interest in waitress job	"Work ethic' task endurance	
TRANSITION SERVICES			
Adult services, job supports, social supports or community living supports	N/A		

Summary from regular class teacher, special educator, speech/language pathologist, mother, and occupational therapist.

PERSON COMPLETING FORM: **TITLE:**   **DATE:**

Step 2—Identify the Starting Point

Each participant shares the strengths they have identified on the Profile Planning Worksheet. Looking at the current strengths and needs should give all of the information necessary to begin the planning process. It is usually beneficial to let the parent report first. This ensures that they are actively involved from the beginning. It is good to return to them after others have presented since they know the child better than anyone else. The reporting of strengths is a time to enjoy the growth and progress made by the student.

Each participant shares the needs they have recorded. Once all needs are collected, they are recorded on the Programming at a Glance form, discussed, and prioritized (see Chart 7-2). Five to seven of the priority needs are selected for the development of the IEP objectives. The priority needs identified for Amanda are reading skills, writing skills, math problem solving, time and money, formal oral communication, social problem solving, transition from one activity to another, and keyboarding skills. The priority need in the recreation and leisure category is a community objective that can be met through participation in a local Girl Scout troop. This will be met by the family and will not be a part of the IEP.

CHART 7-2   Programming at a Glance: Amanda.

Physical Features		Priority Instruction Needs	Groupings
Regular classroom	83%	Academic: Reading fluency and comprehension—consistent application of strategies; writing process; capitalization; punctuation; math problem solving; money	Heterogeneous (for most of day)
Special education (in class)	50%		Homogeneous (some reading, writing)
Special education (separate class)	17%		Cooperative (facilitate content science and social studies)
Accessibility issues:			Peer tutoring
• ramps	N	Communication: Topic maintenance; formal presentation skills	• same grade
• elevators	N		• cross grade (consider as tutor for younger students)
• class arragement	N	Social skills	
• bathroom	N	Behavior: Increased independence	
• equipment (computer)	Y		

Services/Staffing		Work study skills: task endurance	Preparation and Procedures
Administrator	Y	Motor skills: Writing (proper size and spacing)	Training: Y
General educator	Y		• staff
Special educator	Y	Functional skills: Time and money	• students (Circle of Friends)
Speech/Language Pathologist	Y		• community
Occupational/Physical Ther.	Y	Recreation/leisure	Behavior plans N
Reading Specialist	N	Vocational skills	Medical/health plans N
Psychologist/Counselor*	Y*	Transition skills	Emergency plans N
Instructional Assistants	N		
(may not all be necessary depends on school)			

Long-Range Outcome: Independent, happy, healthy life with fulfilling relationships and a job.

Following further discussion to define the areas of need, the planning team writes the objectives for inclusion on the IEP.

1. To increase reading comprehension:
   - Use phonic techniques for decoding unfamiliar words.
   - Use context clues to increase passage comprehension.
   - Use strategic reading skills such as summarization, picture clues, and prediction.

2. To increase independence and effective use of grammar in writing assignments:
   - Use all steps in the writing process.
   - Use correct capitalization and punctuation in sentence writing and paragraph writing.
   - Use proper size and spacing of letters in writing.
   - Write organized paragraphs containing a topic sentence and the supporting details.

3. To increase math skills in daily living applications:
   - Use basic math facts of addition and subtraction in real life problem-solving situations.
   - Tell time in five-minute intervals.
   - Add and subtract money.
   - Make change from $1.00 to $10.00.

4. To improve organization and oral presentation skills:
   - Use an outline to organize an oral presentation containing three main points and supporting details.
   - Use effective oral skills in classroom presentations.

5. To increase understanding of problem solving in social situations:
   - Develop a "Circle of Friends" to provide social support.
   - Model problem-solving using situational activities.
   - Apply problem-solving process and skills to real life situations.

6. Decrease the amount of time necessary to transition from one activity to another:
   - Develop a signal indicating a transition is approaching.
   - Use a checklist to quickly get needed materials set up or packed to go home.
   - Use self-monitoring techniques to decrease dependence on peers in transition.

7. To increase proficiency in keyboarding:
   - Learn proper fingering techniques.
   - Gain speed and accuracy in keyboarding.
   - Use the computer for writing pieces.

Step 3—Determine the Steps to Achieve the Outcome

Each of the objectives identified for the IEP must now be analyzed to determine if the objective can be attained in the general education classroom or if a specialized setting is necessary. The discussion of Amanda's goals indicate that the majority of these goals can be met in the general education classroom. The special educator will assist the teacher in adapting materials and lessons in reading, writing, and math. The special educator will meet with Amanda once a day for an hour to provide additional support in phonics decoding, to supplement time on the writing process, and to introduce keyboarding. The speech/language pathologist will work with the special educator on the writing process and provide direct assistance in oral communication. This would entail about one hour a day, twice a week. Some of this time with the special educator and some in the general education classroom. The counselor will collaborate with the special educator to set up a Circle of Friends and to model social problem solving. This will be accomplished during a lunch meeting each week.

The results of this discussion can be recorded on the Programming at a Glance form in the Physical Features and the Services/Staffing sections. Since most of the objectives can be achieved in the general education classroom, the percentage of time should be very high. This does not mean that the special education services are not being provided during that time. The special educator may be present in the room or may help with adapting the class materials. These activities both qualify as special education services. The percentage of in-class special education services should also be relatively high.

Grouping strategies can also be completed from the information discussed. Since most of the day is spent in the general education classroom, heterogeneous groups would be appropriate for the majority of the time. Homogeneous grouping would be used for reading, writing, and oral communication with the special educator and speech/language pathologist when services are provided in a small group setting outside of the classroom. Cooperative group activities are most appropriate for those content-based activities in which Amanda needs peers to assist with difficult and abstract content such as science and social studies. The Circle of Friends would also be a cooperative activity. A discussion focusing on the benefits of having Amanda service as a tutor for younger children is held. It is decided that serving as a tutor would foster independence and increase her self-esteem.

The final section of the Program at a Glance form can now be completed. In reviewing the services for Amanda, the only training that is required is for the students who will participate in the Circle of Friends.

Step 4—Establish a Timeline

Using all of the information recorded on the Program at a Glance form, a plan for follow-up is developed using the Follow-Up Chart (see Chart 7-3). It is best to be specific in the items listed and helpful to staple this form on the inside cover of the student folder so it is easy to check. The first item in follow-up is always completion of the IEP. Items will vary from student to student. Amanda's services will require some preplanning for the next school year. This would involve possible orders for new materials. In August, specific planning for daily activities will need to be scheduled. The counselor will need to complete some preplanning for the Circle of Friends. Many items for follow-up will need to be completed in August just before the beginning of a new school year. The follow-up list is vital in picking up all of the pieces after the long summer break.

Step 5—Plan the Details

In preparing to plan the final details, it is wise to check the plans and the IEP objectives to ensure that they are truly directed at the long-range goal or target objectives that have been

CHART 7-3   Follow-up Form: Amanda.

Actions/Responses	Person Responsible	Timeline
Complete development of the IEP	Special educator and mother	30 days
Meeting to discuss curricular and materials details	Special educator, speech/language pathologist, occupational therapist, general educator	30 days
Select students for "Circle of Friends"	Counselor	By end of year
Training of students for circle	Nurse	September
Inclusion in the cross-age tutoring program	Special educator administrator	August/September

identified. Most of this discussion will finalize the information that is required for the IEP such as the criteria for mastery of each objective and the person(s) responsible. The discussion may get as specific as instructional strategies and activities that work well for Amanda, if time allows.

Step 6—Evaluation

The plan will be evaluated throughout the year. It is wise to set specific dates to monitor progress as a group. Some teams like to note these follow up meetings on the Follow Up Chart.

Darrell: Case Study #2

Darrell is currently a seventh grader. He has been included in general education classes since kindergarten. Darrell is diagnosed as having spina bifida. He is in a wheelchair. He also has a specific learning disability that manifests itself mainly in the language area. Darrell has had a history of medical problems most of which have been related to his spina bifida. He has had several surgeries and gets frequent infections. He has been hospitalized about once a year for kidney infections for the last several years.

Darrell currently receives a combination of services in general education and special education classrooms. In math class, a strength area, he works on grade-appropriate material. Some test formats are adapted for him. In science and English class, he has a special educator present to assist him with activities, comprehension, and directions. In physical education, he participates in most activities with frequent and sometimes significant adaptations. The physical therapist consults weekly with the teacher. He receives two classes each day with the special educator that focus on reading, written language, organization skills, and generalized academic support such as homework planning, review of material, and extended practice sessions. He takes computer keyboarding for one class period each day. He is on a self-catheterization program that is supervised by the school nurse. This process must be completed twice each day during school hours. Concerns have been raised because of the time lost from the instructional program.

The planning conference for Darrell is conducted to plan for his eighth grade school year. Present at the conference are the general education team leader, counselor, special educator, physical therapist, nurse, Darrell's parents, and Darrell. Each member of the planning group have completed a Planning Profile Worksheet. The team leader present, who will work with Darrell next year, has a copy that was completed by this year's team and has discussed the items with that team. An illustrative copy of Darrell's profile is included here as Chart 7-4, but it is a summary of information from all of the forms.

The meeting agenda follows the basic planning process.

CHART 7-4　Profile Planning Worksheet: Darrell.

CURRICULUM	STRENGTHS	NEEDS	PRIORITIES
ACADEMIC			
Reading: Decoding, word recognition, comprehension	Reads 4th grade independent Uses context clues Listening comprehension Verbalizes ideas, story plots Short-term memorization Short term memorization Writes paragraphs	Reading comprehension text material Reading for enjoyment Generalize strategies Punctuation, capitalization, and sentence length Use of computer to write	Reading skills Writing longer pieces Proofreading Keyboarding
Writing: Process, usage, grammar punctuation, capitalization, size, spacing			
Math: Concepts, computation, application, problem solving	Multiplication and division Uses calculator Reads graphs and charts	Problem solving Word problems Application of concepts	Problem solving Real life application using word problems
Science/Social Studies: Content, participation	Group projects Good attitude	Resists written tasks	
COMMUNICATION			
Speaking, adaptive technology needs, augmentative communication needs	Very verbal and social		
SOCIAL SKILLS			
Friendship skills, peer relations, expresses feelings, makes requests, takes risks	Good social skills Friendly, sense of humor Initiates relationships	Overly social	
BEHAVIOR			
Respect for self and others, attention span, activity level	Very respectful Follows others Decrease hallway passing time	Manipulates with charm Attention to task (writing) Work avoidance	Behavior contract

CHART 7-4 Profile Planning Worksheet: Darrell.

CURRICULUM	STRENGTHS	NEEDS	PRIORITIES
WORK STUDY SKILLS			
Organization, on-task behavior, follows directions, working with peers, task completion	Works well with peers Follows directions On-task in math Cooperative	Task completion Remember materials Organization Homework	Organization skill Contract for homework
MOTOR			
Fine Motor: Writing-formation of letters or numbers, size, spacing, cutting		Messy writing Keyboarding	Spacing Manipulating objects Keyboarding
MOTOR			
Gross Motor: Trunk strength, ascending/descending stairs, age-appropriate, physical skills	Upper body strength Swimming	Adaptive physical education Stretching, movement of lower extremeties	Swimming, weight training Wheel chair activities
FUNCTIONAL			
Survival language, travel training, money, shopping, daily living skills			
RECREATION & LEISURE			
Long-term age-appropriate hobbies, activities, or interests	Likes outdoor activities Swimming	After school activities Clubs and hobbies	
VOCATIONAL			
Job skills, positive work habits, on-site training	Follows directions Good people skills	Work ethic Pride in work Explore job interests	Begin career exploration
TRANSITION SERVICES			
Adult services, job supports, social supports or community living supports	N/A		

Summary from regular class teacher team, special educator, counselor, nurse, mother, father, Darrell, and physical therapist.

PERSON COMPLETING FORM: **TITLE:**   **DATE:**

Step 1—Determine the Long-Range Outcomes

This is the first time Darrell's family has completed this kind of planning process. Time is spent during the meeting discussing what Darrell's parents and Darrell see as his long-range goals. Darrell wants to go to college, but he does not know what type of job interests him yet. He wants to live by himself and be independent. He wants to have a car and drive himself to work. He wants to make a lot of money. His parents want him to have a close group of friends and be happy and productive. The long-range goals decided upon are to attend college, maintain relationships, and live independently.

Step 2—Identify the Starting Point

Each participant shares the strengths they have listed on the Profile Planning Worksheet. These are noted as they are shared on the Programming at a Glance form (see Chart 7-5). Darrell receives quite a bit of positive reinforcement for his progress.

Each person shares the needs that are also recorded on the Programming at a Glance form. The parents and Darrell share theirs' first. Then the rest of the team members each

---

CHART 7-5   Programming at a Glance: Darrell.

Physical Features		Priority Instruction Needs	Groupings
Regular classroom	85%	Academic: Reading comprehension, text materials, attitude, written language, punctuation, capitalization, sentence length, math problem solving, word problems	Heterogeneous (most of day)
Special education (in class)	55%		Homogeneous (reading, organization)
Special education (separate class)	15%		Cooperative (whenever poss.)
Accessibility issues:			Peer tutoring
• ramps	Y		same grade
• elevators	Y		cross grade
• class arrangement	N	Communication	
• bathroom	Y	Social skills	
• equipment (computer)	Y	Behavior: Manipulates, resistance to tasks, attention to tasks	
Services/Staffing		Work study skills: Organization, task completion, homework	**Preparation and Procedures**
Administrator	Y		Training: Y
General educator	Y	Motor skills: fine-spacing, keyboarding, gross-upper strength, lower stretching	• staff
Special educator	Y		• students (consultation)
Speech/language pathologist	N	Functional skills	• community
Occupational/physical therapist	Y	Recreation/leisure	Behavior plans Y
Reading specialist	N		Medical/health plans Y
Psychologist/counselor	Y	Vocational skills: Career exploration	Emergency plans Y
Instructional assistants	Y		
Nurse	Y	Transition skills	

Long-Range Outcome: To attend college, maintain relationships, live independently

share their list, commenting briefly on similar items and explaining new and different items. The need areas are discussed, and priorities are selected for the development of IEP objectives. The priority areas for Darrell are reading skills, writing skills, math problem solving, behavior (task completion), organization, keyboarding, fine and gross motor training, and career exploration. Some areas Darrell is pleased with, especially the career exploration, and some he is not, such as the behavior contract. Discussion is focused on why these areas are important to his long-range goal. Following this discussion, the planning team writes the objectives for inclusion on the IEP.

1. To increase reading skills and comprehension:
   - Use text organization, picture clues, bold print, and target vocabulary to increase comprehension using expository reading selections (including grade level texts).
   - Increase the amount of time spent reading, and improve attitude toward reading using student selected books and books-on-tape.

2. To consistently use the writing process to produce independent writing samples:
   - Use correct punctuation and grammar in the writing process.
   - Write complex sentences and organized paragraphs.
   - Write longer and more complex stories.
   - Write expository and persuasive pieces.
   - Use word processing and spell check as a part of the proofreading process.

3. To improve math skills:
   - Construct equations from and complete word problems.
   - Apply math concepts to real life situations.

4. To develop and use a behavior contract to increase time on task, assignment and homework completion:
   - Develop a contract with the general and special educator.
   - Take responsibility for the contract.

5. To develop and use a checklist and improve organizational skills:
   - Increase organization of notebook and materials.
   - Increase memory for homework and classroom materials.

6. To increase fine motor skills:
   - Increase readability of handwriting.
   - Increase proficiency in keyboarding skills.

7. To increase stretching and movement of lower extremities:
   - Participate in swimming for at least twelve weeks during the year.
   - Improve upper body strength in weight training.
   - Improve flexibility with stretching of lower extremities.

8. To complete an interest inventory and career exploration activities.

Step 3—Determine the Steps to Achieve the Outcomes

Each of the objectives prepared for the IEP must be analyzed to determine if it can be met in the general education classroom or if a specialized setting is required. This discussion reveals that many of the objectives can be implemented in the general education setting. The reading objective can be implemented in the English class but will require extended practice and specialized support in a special education setting. The same is true for the writing objective. Individualized assistance with word processing would also require some specialization. The team agrees that the math objective can be met in the general education classroom and only requires monitoring by the special educator. The behavior contract and checklists will be developed and revised as necessary by the special educator and Darrell with input from the team of teachers who will be working with Darrell next year. The fine motor skills can be monitored by the special and general educator working collaboratively. The gross motor objective can be implemented through the physical education program with regular consultation from the physical therapist. Finally, the career exploration objective can be implemented by the counselor in collaboration with all of Darrell's teachers. Any necessary specialization or individualized follow up can be planned in collaboration with the special educator.

An area of concern that is discussed but not included as an IEP objective is the need to decrease the amount of time Darrell misses from classes for catheterization. The counselor will look at arranging classes to minimize travel in the building, and Darrell agrees to decrease socializing in the halls on his trip to the Health Room. This item will also appear on the contract to be developed to facilitate close monitoring. All team members agree that missed time from classes will have a major impact on Darrell's overall academic performance.

The results of this discussion facilitate the completion of the Programming at a Glance form. Since nearly all of the objectives can be attained in the general education classroom with adaptation of instruction and materials, the percentage of time in the regular classroom should indicate at least 85 percent. A special educator will need to be present in two to three academic classes, and the physical therapist will work with the physical education staff. This indicates that the in-class special education services should be at least 50 percent. Only one class period of special education support will be required in a special class setting so that percentage should be no more than 15. The Physical Features section also contains information on accessibility. Since Darrell uses a wheelchair, most of these areas are marked yes.

The Services/Staffing section can also be completed by marking all of the staff needed to develop an appropriate program for Darrell. The services are varied and complex. The Groupings section may be completed simply by marking which grouping practices already discussed will be most effective for Darrell. A lengthy discussion is focused on the items in the Preparation and Procedures section of the form. There is minimal need for training. The new team of teachers will require awareness of Darrell's strengths and needs as well as the catheterization requirements. The behavior plan is noted with a yes and some discussion of the elements takes place. The nurse is monitoring a health plan, and she discusses that briefly. Emergency plans are discussed. Since the school which Darrell attends is a two-story building, an emergency evacuation plan must be developed in case of fire and the elevator cannot be used. There is a plan on file now. Problems that arise during the year are noted to help in planning for next year.

Step 4—Establish a Timeline

With all of the information now recorded on the Programming at a Glance form, a plan for follow-up can be developed using the Follow-Up Chart (see Chart 7-6). The first step in follow-up is to complete the IEP. Other items are also listed such as conducting a team meeting with the team of new teachers to raise their awareness of Darrell's strengths and needs. The development of an emergency plan is noted to be completed by the special educator and the grade level administrator. The nurse feels it will be important to contact Darrell's doctor in August to check his current medical status, and this is noted on the form. The development of the behavior plan is also noted since it is to done early in September.

Step 5—Plan the Details

The team takes a final look at the objectives they have written for the IEP. They discuss whether these objectives are going to focus Darrell on the right path to attain his long-range goal. They also begin to define the specific criteria for measuring mastery of the objectives and assigning persons responsible. Little time is devoted to discussion of specific adaptations to classroom activities. This is planned for an August meeting of the teaching team following their discussion of Darrell's needs.

Step 6—Evaluation

The team decides to review the plan at the end of each marking period to make adjustments. The examples described for both Amanda and Darrell provide an in-depth overview of the details of the planning process. Two more examples are provided in an abbreviated format. The sample forms summarizing the programming decisions are provided as well.

Nancy: Case Study #3

Nancy is a five-year-old kindergartner. She was born prematurely. She has spina bifida. She wears glasses and can see little without them. She is very small in stature compared to the other students. She frequently drags herself from one center to another on the floor. Her favorite activities have been singing, looking at picture books, and playing with blocks. She is socially immature and becomes overstimulated at times.

CHART 7-6   Follow-Up Form: Darrell.

Actions/Responses	Person Responsible	Timeline
Complete development of the IEP	Special educator and parents	30 days
Team meeting with new teachers	Special educators and team leader	August
Develop an emergency evacuation plan	Special educator and administrator	August
Confer with doctor regarding health issues	Nurse	August
Develop behavior plan	Special educator and Darrell	September

During the year, she has been fully included in a general education class with twenty-three other children, one student with physical disabilities and one student who is hard of hearing. A special education teacher and an instructional aide have been working with the general education teacher. Nancy has had a very successful year. The planning team feels that most of her needs can be met in the general education setting. The areas of need that have been identified on the Profile Planning Worksheet are communication, social skills, motor skills, and bathrooming (see Chart 7-7). The related services of speech/language,

CHART 7-7   Profile Planning Worksheet: Nancy.

CURRICULUM AREAS	STRENGTHS	NEEDS	PRIORITY AREAS
ACADEMIC			
Reading: Decoding, word recognition, comprehension	Comprehension is good if interested Recognizes letters	Letter sounds Comprehension questions Fine motor	Phonics training, reading readiness
Writing: Process, Usage, grammar, punctuation, capitalization, size, spacing		Writing practice	Letter formation, writing skills
Math: Concepts, computation, application, problem solving	Counting, identifies numbers	One-to-one correspondence Problem solving	Addition Subtraction, problem solving
Science/Social Studies: Content, participation	Focuses on lessons	Participate more	
COMMUNICATION			
Speaking, adaptive technology needs, augmentative communication needs	Articulation, tells stories	Expand ideas Speaking when called on-related to topic Immature syntax	Speak out in class Raise hand to answer question
SOCIAL SKILLS			
Friendship skills, peer relations, expresses feelings, makes requests, takes risks	Beginning to raise hand Wants to interact more with classmates Is well liked Imaginative play	More interaction Make new friends Initiate conversation	Circle of Friends Brownies
BEHAVIOR			
Respect for self and others, attention span, activity level	Very caring Wants to please others Respectful	Independent work completion Focus attention	Increase time on task
WORK STUDY SKILLS			
Organization, on-task behavior, follows directions, working with peers, task completion	Likes to clean up Follows directions with assistance	Follow multistep directions Needs routine Task completion Ask for help Work with peers	Follow multistep directions

CHART 7-7 Profile Planning Worksheet: Nancy.

CURRICULUM AREAS	STRENGTHS	NEEDS	PRIORITY AREAS
MOTOR			
Fine Motor: Writing-Formation of letters or numbers, size, spacing, cutting	Emerging skills Cuts with adaptive scissors, Coloring, Writes name	Letters, shapes, and numbers	Writing skills Establish hand dominance Pincer grip
Gross Motor: Trunk strength, ascending/descending stairs, age-appropriate physical skills	Wants to do it herself Uses walker for short distance Good strength for wheel chair	Strengthen upper body to use walker more	Upper body strength Expand reach
FUNCTIONAL			
Survival language, travel training, money, shopping, daily living skills	Clearly communicates wants and needs	Daily living skills	
RECREATION & LEISURE			
Long-term age-appropriate hobbies, activities, or interests	Enjoys books and people Loves dolls Likes movies Loves to sing	Expand community activities	Community activities Brownies
VOCATIONAL			
Job skills, positive work habits, on-site training			
TRANSITION SERVICES			
Adult services, job supports, social supports or community living supports			

Summary from regular class teacher, special educator, speech/language pathologist, parents, occupational therapist, and physical therapist.

PERSON COMPLETING FORM: **TITLE:**   **DATE:**

occupational therapy, and physical therapy will need to be provided, preferably in the general education setting. As the Programming at a Glance, Chart 7-8, indicates, several needs have been targeted for work in the first grade year:

- Establishing hand dominance
- Learning writing skills

CHART 7-8   Programming at a Glance: Nancy.

Physical Features		Priority Instruction Needs	Groupings
Regular classroom	100%	Academic: Addition, subtraction, problem solving, writing, reading readiness, phonics	Heterogeneous all day
Special education (in class)	70%		Homogeneous
Special education (separate class)	%		Cooperative
Accessibility issues:		Communication: Speaking out in class, raising hand to answer questions	Peer tutoring
• ramps	Y		same grade buddy system
• elevators	N		cross grade
• class arrangement	Y	Social skills Social interaction, Circle of Friends, Brownies	
• bathroom	Y		
• equipment (computer)	Y	Behavior	
		Work study skills: Follow multistep directions, time on task	
Services/staffing			**Preparation and Procedures**
Administrator	N	Motor skills: Hand dominance, letter and number, shapes, upper body strength	Training:
General educator	Y		• staff (regular educator)
Special educator	Y		• students (buddy)
Speech/language pathologist	N	Functional skills	• community
Occupational/physical Therapist	Y	Recreation/leisure time in community	Behavior plans N
Reading Specialist	N		Medical/health plans Y
Psychologist/Counselor	N	Vocational skills	Emergency plans Y
Instructional Assistants	Y	Transition skills	
Nurse	Y		

Long-Range Outcome: Live and work independently, maintain relationships

- Using addition, subtraction, and learning how to solve problems
- Increasing social interactions at school (Circle of Friends)
- Increasing social interactions in community (Brownies)
- Training in phonics, reading readiness
- Following multistep directions
- Speaking out in class, raising hand to answer questions
- Increasing time-on-task and task perseverance
- Increasing upper body strength

The Follow-Up Form, Chart 7-9, lists the activities that must be completed in preparation for the coming school.

Elliot: Case Study #4

Elliot is an 18-year-old who is going into the eleventh grade in the fall. Elliot is diagnosed as having spastic quadriplegic cerebral palsy. He uses a motorized wheel chair to move

CHART 7-9   Follow-Up Form: Nancy.

Actions/Responses	Person Responsible	Timelines
Develop fine motor tasks that fit into the class	Occupational therapist	By September
Set up a Circle of Friends	Classroom teacher	Begin in September
Join Brownies	Parents	As soon as possible
Set up tour of first grade	Classroom teacher	As soon as possible
Perform strengthening exercises	Physical therapist	Give to parent for summer
Plan for classroom set-up	Classroom and special education teachers	August

through the school and community. He can move forward independently and backward with assistance. He uses eye gaze and vocalizations to communicate. Students who have worked and socialized with Elliot can interpret his vocalizations. Those who have no experience with Elliot require training to understand him. He can use a head pointer and communication board to form sentences. Elliot has significant physical and occupational therapy needs because he gets tense with intentional movement attempts and requires assistance to relax. He also requires support at the shoulder to successfully move his arms.

Elliot has received a large portion of his early education in a special school. He has attended his neighborhood school since seventh grade. Because of previous Circle of Friends efforts, he has a solid social group. He responds to these students eagerly when he sees them. The areas of program concentration determined by the Profile Planning Worksheet, Chart 7-10, for completion during this school year are the following:

- Communicating his likes/dislikes and needs for assistance effectively
- Continuing expressive language development and acclamation to new technology that can assist Elliot with his needs to communicate
- Expanding reading skills and sentence writing
- Increasing knowledge of business math concepts and personal math applications
- Maintaining social relations through participation in two general education classes, English and art (using computerized graphics programs), and through his Circle of Friends activities
- Gaining job skills such as assisted machine copying and date stamping mail in a large office with the assistance of a job coach
- Using a communication device to use prerecorded messages in the community e.g. for ordering in a restaurant

As the Programming at a Glance, Chart 7-11, indicates, Elliot will receive most of his education in the general education setting and the community. About 30 percent of his time will

CHART 7-10   Profile Planning Worksheet: Elliot.

CURRICULUM AREAS	STRENGTHS	NEEDS	PRIORITY AREAS
ACADEMIC			
Reading: Decoding, word recognition, comprehension	Reads at 4th grade instructional level	Independent and expository reading experiences	Expand reading skills
Writing: Process, usage, grammar, punctuation, capitalization, size, spacing		Augmentive device for sentence construction	Augmentive communication devices
Math: Concepts, computation, application, problem solving	Basic computation	Business and personal math applications	Expand math skills
Science/Social Studies: Content, participation			
COMMUNICATION			
Speaking adaptive technology needs, augmentative communication needs	Uses head pointer and communication board Use of prerecorded messages	Explore use of computer-generated speech technology	Community use of prerecorded messages Use of technology
SOCIAL SKILLS			
Friendship skills, peer relations, expresses feelings, makes requests, takes risks	Maintains peer relationships with Circle of Friends	Express feeling, likes, dislikes, and makes requests	Clearly communicate needs
BEHAVIOR			
Respect for self and others, attention span, activity level	Very respectful Good attention to task	Control excitement	
WORK STUDY SKILLS			
Organization, on-task behavior, follows directions, working with peers, task completion			
MOTOR			
Fine Motor: Writing–formation of letters or numbers, size, spacing, cutting			
Gross Motor: Trunk strength, ascending/descending stairs, age-appropriate physical skills	Attempts movement Turns head 45 degrees	Positioning shoulder support to move arms Relaxation assistance	Assistance in movement
FUNCTIONAL			
Survival language, travel training, money, shopping, daily living skills	Good money usage Travel trained for shopping	Continue daily living Travel training-job Community communication	Community participation

CHART 7-10   Profile Planning Worksheet: Elliot.

CURRICULUM AREAS	STRENGTHS	NEEDS	PRIORITY AREAS
<u>RECREATION & LEISURE</u>			
Long-term age-appropriate hobbies, activities, or interests	Excellent artist using computer graphics	Art class	
<u>VOCATIONAL</u>			
Job skills, positive work habits, on-site training	Limited but successful work experience	Daily work program	Job skills
<u>TRANSITION SERVICES.</u>			
Adult services, job supports, social supports or community living supports			Begin planning for adult service needs

Summary from Elliot, parents, special educator, speech/language pathologist, occupational therapist, and physical therapist.

PERSON COMPLETING FORM: **TITLE:**   **DATE:**

CHART 7-11   Programming at a Glance: Elliot.

Physical Features		**Priority Instruction Needs**	**Groupings**		
Regular class/community	70%	Academic: Reading development and business math and personal applications	Heterogeneous (classes/community)		
Special education (in class)	70%		Homogeneous (therapies, technology)		
Special education (separate class)	30%	Communication: Communicate needs clearly	Cooperative		
Accessibility issues:			Peer tutoring		
• ramps	Y	Social skills: Maintain social relationships	same grade		
• elevators	Y		cross grade		
• class arrangement	Y	Behavior			
• bathroom	Y	Work study skills			
• equipment	Y	Motor skills: Supported movement, therapy needs			
Services/Staffing		Functional skills: Community, restaurant, travel	**Preparation and Procedures**		
Administrator	Y	Recreation/leisure: Continue computer graphics	Staff training:		Y
General educator	Y		• staff		Y
Special educator	Y	Vocational skills: Supported employment	• students		Y
Speech/language Pathologist	Y		• community		Y
Occupational/physical therapist	Y	Transition skills: Begin planning for adult service needs	Behavior plans		N
Reading specialist	N		Medical/health plans		Y
Psychologist/counselor	N		Emergency plans		Y
Instructional assistants	Y				
Nurse	Y				

Long-Range Outcome: Assisted community living arrangement, paid employment, job coach.

CHART 7-12 Follow-Up Form: Elliot.

Actions/Responses	Person Responsible	Timelines
Conduct training with teachers and students in English and art classes	Special educator, speech/language pathologist, and physical therapist	August and September
Train job coach	Special educator, speech/language pathologist, and physical therapist	August and September
Conduct training at job site	Special educator, speech/language pathologist, and physical therapist	August and September
Explore new communication technology and adaptive devices	Speech/language pathologist, occupational and physical therapists	Ongoing
Develop a detailed plan for positioning, bathrooming, and therapy	Occupational and physical therapists with special educator	August

be spent in a special class learning to work with augmentative communication devices and with other related services. Training will be necessary for the students who have not known Elliot before and for the employees of the office where he will have his worksite training. The Follow-Up Form, Chart 7-12, outlines the responsibilities for the training and information gathering that must take place before Elliot's program can be implemented.

The four cases indicate the range in grades and disabilities that can be addressed with the planning process. Teachers field testing the process found it to be flexible and easy to use. However, the process is very dependent on the expertise of the professionals working with students to identify the range of issues to be addressed as the teams moves through the process. These details are not spelled out in the planning process itself.

Conclusions

Adequate planning requires a comprehensive but easy to use planning process. Teams should agree on the process and adapt the specifics of their chosen process to meet their own school needs. Once selected, the process should be followed without fail to prevent oversights in the plans. Any planning process selected by a team will require periodic updating and revision. Once individual plans are developed for each student, it is easy to see that the IEP is only a part of this overall plan. In the school setting where time becomes a priceless commodity, efficiency in planning is essential. Planned follow-up is crucial, and the need for ongoing communication and adaptation is essential to successfully including students with disabilities in the general education program.

References

Adler, J. (1990). Creating problems. *Newsweek* (Special Edition—Education: A consumer's handbook). Fall/Winter. 16–22.

Brooks, G. (1994). Standing outside the fire. *The Hits.* Blue Rose. Nashville, TN: Liberty Records.

Covey, S. R. (1989). *The seven habits of highly effective people: Restoring the character ethic.* New York: Simon & Schuster.

Ford, A., Davern, L., & Schnorr, R. (1992). Inclusive education: "Making sense" of the curriculum. In S. Stainback, & W. Stainback (Eds.), *Curriculum considerations in inclusive classrooms: Facilitating learning for all students* (pp. 37–61). Baltimore: Paul H. Brooks Publishing Co.

Forest, M. (1987). *More education integration: A further collection of readings on the integration of children with mental handicaps into regular school systems.* Downsview, Ontario: G. Allen Roeher Institute.

Forest, M., & Lusthaus, E. (1987). Promoting educational equity for all students: Circles and MAPS. In S. Stainback, W. Stainback, & M. Forest (Eds.), *Educating all students in the mainstream of regular education* (pp. 43–58). Baltimore: Paul H. Brookes Publishing Co.

Giangreco, M. F., Cloninger, C. J., & Iverson, V. S. (1993). *Choosing options and accommodations for children: A guide to inclusive education.* Baltimore: Paul H. Brookes Publishing Co.

Goodlad, J. I. (1984). *A place called school: Prospects for the future.* New York: McGraw-Hill Book Co.

Hammill, D. D., & Bartel, N. R. (Eds.). (1975). *Teaching children with learning and behavior problems.* Boston: Allyn and Bacon.

Hartup, W. W. (1985). Relationships and their significance in cognitive development. In R. A. Hinde, J. Stevenson-Hinde, & A. N. Perret-Clermont (Eds.). *Social relationships and cognitive development* (pp. 66–82). New York: Oxford University Press.

Kaufman, R., & Herman, J. (1991). *Strategic planning in education: Rethinking, restructuring, revitalizing.* Lancaster, PA: Technomic Publishing Co.

Lewis, M. (1982). The social network system model: Toward a theory of social development. In T. M. Fields, A. Houston, H. C. Quay, L. Trowl, & E. Finely (Eds.), *Review of human development* (pp. 180–214). New York: Wiley Interscience.

Mauriel, J. (1989). *Strategic leadership of schools.* San Francisco: Jossey-Bass.

Mount, B. (1987). Personal future planning: Finding direction for change. (Doctoral dissertation, University Of Georgia). Ann Arbor, MI: *UMI Dissertation Information Services.*

Mount, B., & Zwernik, K. (1988). *It's never too early, it's never too late.* St. Paul, MN: Metropolitan Council, Publication No. 421–88–109.

Nebgen, M. (1991). The key to success in strategic planning is communication. *Educational Leadership,* April, 26–28.

O'Brien, J. (1987). A guide to life-style planning. In B. Wilcox, & G. T. Bellamy (Eds.), *A comprehensive guide to the activities catalogue.* Baltimore: Paul H. Brookes Publishing Co.

O'Brien, J., & Lyle, C. (1987). *Framework for accomplishment.* Decatur, GA: Responsive Systems Associates.

Rigazio-DiGilio, A., & Beninghof, A. (1994). Toward inclusionary educational programs: A school-based planning process. *The Special Education Leadership REVIEW,* 81–92.

Salvia, J., & Ysseldyke, J. E. (1985). *Assessment in special and remedial education.* Boston: Houghton Mifflin Co.

Stoner, J. (1982). *Management.* Englewood Cliffs, NJ: Prentice-Hall.

Vandercook, T., York, J., & Forest, M. (1989). The McGill Action Planning System (MAPS): A strategy for building the vision. *Journal of the Association for Persons with Severe Handicaps, 14*(3), 205–215.

Chapter 8

Integrated Therapies

THOMAS J. O'TOOLE AND DIANE M. SWITLICK

◆ ADVANCE ORGANIZER ◆

Integrated therapies focus on the inclusion of related service providers into the comprehensive educational plan. This chapter provides an historical perspective on related services and the rationale for current and changing service delivery models. Highlighted are speech/language, occupational, and physical therapies. The transdisciplinary service delivery model is emphasized because it is consistent with inclusive philosophy. Therapeutic classroom practices are shared along with examples of curriculum-based therapy goals and objectives.

I was verging on miffed last June, when I was assigned to a school housing the Total Inclusion program. I decided to gather up the fledgling pieces of experience I had accumulated delivering speech/language support to students in a center-based program for students with significant disabilities, where I felt these students really belonged. That my program had been finally shut down after years of threats by the powers that be was still feeling unreal to me. I was grieving the loss of a close-knit, caring staff and was being forced into the real world that we feared for our students. I acknowledge now the sense of fear I had about the change I was about to undergo.

All of my students were very needy, thus requiring a highly structured setting with integrated related services. On my caseload that year was a young man who had been receiving special services since 1985, when he enrolled in a preschool program. He went to a private learning center and later transferred to public school in the learning center. Among his needs were cognitive, speech language, and gross and fine motor, but the most educationally impacting concern that year was his behavior. His outbursts frequently resulted in his removal from the room, after being unable to remain in time out in the classroom.

In September of 1992, we were reunited. Frankly, I was flabbergasted. In a million years, I never would have expected this student to have been considered for total inclusion in the regular classroom. Despite his academic needs, I was far more concerned with his history of vastly inappropriate behavior.

To say that I was impressed by what I saw, at least by October, is a gross understatement. He was staying in line in the hallway with his sixth grade class. He was interacting with peers. He was interacting with adults. By spring, I noticed some awesome academic gains, as well. He reads functionally, though some two years below grade level; he does basic math calculation easily; he can solve simple math word problems with minimal cuing. He read his oral report from a piece of paper, not unlike other students in the class, and even made occasional eye contact. To see him working independently in the classroom, staying on task without constant prompting, and interacting with peers was proof positive that inclusion works. Watching him has proven to me that social skills are an integral part of being a member of our society and functioning side by side in the real world must have its foundation when these students are young. Had someone not been willing to take a risk with this student, we never would have been able to witness these gains.

Bambi Lowry, speech/language pathologist

A successful, long-term collaborative teaching arrangement necessitates a paradigm shift that lends itself to a shared ownership and commitment by professionals to educate all students.

Ferguson, 1992a

Including related services in a comprehensive educational program is crucial to effective instructional planning for students with disabilities. As educational programs have become more inclusive, related services have also been encouraged or even required to take steps toward inclusion. There are many types of related services that are described in Federal Law. General educators have frequently had difficulty trying to understand exactly what a related service actually is—its purpose and goals. Although the concept of related services can be confusing, a key point is that related services are those services that are necessary to assist a student to benefit from his or her special education program. These services are supportive and are not provided alone. The concept clearly indicates that without these services a student would not benefit from the special education program. Thus, the idea of integrating these services along with special education into general education seems to make sense.

Related services are listed and defined in Public Law 94–142 and its recent reauthorization, PL 101–476. They are as follows:

§ 300.16 Related services
(a) As used in this part, the term "related services" means transportation and such developmental, corrective, and other supportive services as are required to assist

a child with a disability to benefit from special education, and includes speech pathology and audiology, psychological services, physical and occupational therapy, recreation, including therapeutic recreation, early identification and assessment of disabilities in children, counseling services, including rehabilitation counseling, medical services for diagnostic or evaluation purposes. The term also includes school health services, social work services in schools, and parent counseling and training. (Federal Register, 1992, p. 44803)

While this listing is helpful, a brief definition of some of these related services may be even more meaningful:

- Physical therapy—Focuses on physical functions that include gross motor skills, positioning of the body or limbs, handling techniques, muscle tone, range of motion, muscle strength, joint mobility, endurance, flexibility, lower limb bracing/splinting/casting, mobility training, transfer techniques, and prevention of loss of physical function. Support may take the form of consultation and training of teachers, parents, or instructional aides, development of functional activities, development and use of adaptive equipment, and direct therapy.
- Occupational therapy—Focuses on functional participation in instruction, which includes use of the upper extremities, fine motor skills, muscle tone, range of motion, posture, visual–motor skills, e.g., eye–hand coordination, oral motor skills, e.g., feeding, and prevention of loss of functioning. Support may take the form of consultation and training of teachers, parents, or instructional aides, development of functional activities, development and use of adaptive equipment, and direct therapy.
- Speech/language therapy—Focuses on communication skills, which may include assessment of the communication demands in all instructional settings, social interactions, receptive and expressive language skills, articulation, fluency, voice quality, neuromotor factors relating to oral musculature, respiration/phonation, and use of augmentative communication devices. Support may take the form of consultation and training of teachers, parents, or instructional aides, development of instructional activities, development and implementation of augmentative communication devices, and direct therapy.
- School health services—Focuses on all health-related concerns or needs, which may include tube feeding, catheterization, suctioning, administering medications, safety issues, and limitations due to health or physical impairment. Support may take the form of consultation with doctors, hospitals, teachers, parents, direct care providers, or administering medication and other medical treatment.
- School psychological services—Focuses on social emotional issues, which may include assessments, counseling services, behavioral analysis and consultation, and interpretation of testing information. Support may take the form of consultation and training for teachers, parents, or instructional aides, student assessment, instructional consultation, family or student counseling, referral, or consultation on psychological data.
- Audiology—Focuses on hearing and aural rehabilitation, which may include assessment, consultation on hearing aids, instructional implications, consultation with

medical personnel, and family consultation. Support may take the form of consultation with teachers, parents, doctors, or instructional aides, collaboration with interpreters, assessment of auditory functioning, and consultation regarding hearing devices.

- Other consultants—A range of specialists may provide input and services to a planning team, family, or student. These specialists may include orientation and mobility, vision, hearing, and dual sensory impairments (deaf-blind). Consultants may provide support in a range of areas such as assistive technology, rehabilitation, leisure activities, community involvement, instructional consultation, direct therapy, and teacher and parent training.

Because this list is extremely lengthy, this chapter will focus primarily on the related services of speech/language therapy and occupational and physical therapy. These are the most frequent related services provided in the school setting. Some examples of related services have already been discussed in Chapter 7, including school health and counseling although they were not specifically labeled as related services. This chapter will provide many further examples of the three services targeted.

Historical Perspective

> *Service delivery is an evolutionary process. The approaches that were appropriate at one time we no longer use.*

With the passage of Public Law 94–142 in 1975, related service providers such as speech/language pathologist, occupational and physical therapists, psychologist, counselors, nurses and health technicians, parent educators, and social workers found themselves not only in more demand, but with more directives on where and how they would deliver their services. Speech/language pathologists, counselors, psychologists, nurses, and social workers were already working in many public school buildings in addition to working in clinical settings such as hospitals, universities, rehabilitation facilities, public agencies, and private practices. In contrast, occupational therapists, physical therapists, and rehabilitation counselors were largely assigned to special schools or centers where students with severe physical disabilities were clustered. The therapists were also found in hospitals, rehabilitation facilities, and community developmental centers. Passage of PL 94–142 brought a rapidly growing demand for related services personnel in public schools to work in the regular school building and often in the classroom.

In 1986, with the passage of Public Law 99–457, the Early Education of the Handicapped Act, there was another increase in the demand for these specialized personnel. Many of the children requiring these services were in the public school setting. During this same time period at the university training level, there was little evidence of change in how therapists were prepared to work in the school environment. It soon became apparent that related service providers of all kinds needed to know more about the schools. Conversely, school personnel had little knowledge of what many of these service providers were trained to do. Magnotta (1991) noted that fifteen years ago she completed graduate training in the field of speech/language pathology and entered the workforce in the public school setting. One of the most significant attitudes she encountered was "overcoming my own traditional training influenced by a medical model as opposed to one influenced by an education model" (p. 171). The medical model refers to a deficit model that diagnoses a problem and plans interventions to *treat* or *cure,* the underlying cause of the problem. The education model refers to curriculum-based interventions designed to help a student *benefit* from their overall education. Curriculum-based interventions may involve new learning or compensatory skills. The medical model was emphasized in training despite the fact that many of the training programs had a public school connection because they were located in teacher training institutions. The impact on the physical and occupational therapists who rarely received their training in teacher training institutions was even more pronounced. Blossom and Ford (1991) noted that in a clinical setting, the physical well-being of the child is the primary objective of treatment. However, in the school, the child's educational achievement is the primary focus. The primary objective had a dramatic effect on the choice of intervention. It became clear that the education focus had to be addressed by all three related service disciplines. In looking back, Ottenbacher (1991) noted that the major change in occupational therapy services was a much expanded need for services in school settings.

Presently, there is a clear indication that many changes have occurred. There are more service providers in school settings. The therapists are familiar with the educational curricula, and a range of service providers are now included on educational teams in the schools (Rainforth, York, & Macdonald, 1992). However, it is still more commonplace to find these related service providers on teams serving students with severe disabilities whereas the majority of students requiring help for educational reasons have less severe disabilities.

Service Delivery Options

> *If you walked into one of our schools, you would see a wide variety of collaborative/ consultative models in place. Sometimes we team teach, side by side in the classroom with our colleagues in special education or regular education. We provide direct instruction or monitor groups doing follow-up work.*
>
> Montgomery, 1992

Models for service delivery of related services have greatly expanded over the last ten years. The impetus for such changes has come as a result of changing interpretations of legislation and from the professional organizations representing the service providers. The result has been increased effectiveness in the service outcomes (Smith, 1990). The specific means of change will be discussed for each service provider, but the parallels are apparent.

Speech/Language Pathology

Speech/language pathologists have traditionally provided services within the public school setting using a variety of service delivery mechanisms. In 1991, the Committee on Language Learning Disorders of the American Speech-Language Association noted that: "In the most common service delivery method, speech/language pathologists work independently as they pull students out of the regular classrooms for individual or small group treatment sessions. However, recent emphasis on whole language approaches to instruction, least restrictive educational settings, and better generalization of treatment results, demand the consideration of alternative service delivery options for public school speech and language intervention" (p. 44).

In 1993, the American Speech and Hearing Association (ASHA) published *Guidelines for Caseload Size and Speech-Language Service Delivery in the Schools.* Table 8-1 shows the service delivery model options discussed in the ASHA guidelines. As the figure indicates, these service delivery options vary widely. Collaborative consultation is a delivery

TABLE 8-1   Speech/language service delivery options.

Collaborative Consultation

The speech-language pathologist, general and/or special educators, and parents work together to facilitate a student's communication and learning in educational environments. It is essential that the administrator allow the speech/language pathologist and the other collaborators to have a regularly scheduled planning time through the duration of service.

Classroom-Based

This model is also known as integrated services, curriculum-based transdisciplinary, interdisciplinary, or inclusive programming. The emphasis is on the speech/language pathologist providing direct services to students within the classroom and other natural environments. Team teaching by the speech-language pathologist and the general and/or special educator is frequent.

Pullout

Services are provided to students individually and in small groups in the speech room. Some speech/language pathologists may prefer to provide services within the physical space of the classroom, but the therapy is separate from the classroom.

Self-Contained Program

The speech-language pathologist is a special class teacher responsible for providing academic instruction and intensive speech/language remediation in a separate classroom setting.

Source: Adapted from American Speech and Hearing Association. (1993). Guidelines for caseload size and speech-language service delivery in schools. *Asha,* 35(Suppl. 10), 33–39.

option that requires no direct service to the student by the speech/language pathologist. The service is provided instead by the general and special educators after consultation with the speech/language pathologist. The classroom-based model emphasizes a team teaching approach in which the speech/language pathologist works directly in the classroom along with the general or special educator. This teaming situation may occur daily or on a more limited basis. Pullout programs typically involve the speech/language pathologist removing students from the classroom in small groups to work on specific skills. This instruction is rarely linked to the classroom instruction. The self-contained program refers to a rather intensive service-delivery model. Those students who require extensive language development work in a self-contained setting work with the speech/language pathologist as their primary teacher. Instruction in several academic subjects may occur with the speech/language pathologist. The constant focus is on language development.

Service delivery is a dynamic concept that changes as the needs of the students change. No one service delivery model can be viewed as adequate. Eger (1992) points out that the change to more flexible service delivery is a result of the collaborative nature of program planning today. The speech/language pathologist is no longer the sole determiner of the child's program. Others are involved in program planning, such as the school board, the parents, the teacher, and the students themselves. Even the approach to assessment has become more functionally-based and can be conducted within the classroom, for example, by observing speech patterns in a play ground social setting or buttoning a coat at dismissal time.

Huffman (1992) lists numerous points that enable the speech-language pathologist to become a true partner with the educational team working in the general education setting. (See Table 8-2 for a summary of these points.) These points emphasize the comprehensive nature of the role and highlight the need for flexibility. The functional references in the figure clearly indicate the classroom-based focus of the instruction.

Lozo (1993) presents a similar list of implications related to inclusion in which he promotes an expanded role for the speech/language pathologist. This role expansion includes such activities as increased involvement in curriculum planning, prevention activities, and work with at-risk populations. These changes in the role of the speech/language pathologist result in a larger number of students being served and increased therapy in the classroom environment. Since language and communication skills are the foundation of all learning, the speech/language pathologist is in a unique position to enhance all students language skills. Today an increasing number of speech/language pathologists are using classroom-based services and are making connections with the general education curriculum (ASHA, 1992).

Occupational Therapy

Ottenbacher (1991) stated that for occupational therapists several different approaches to service delivery can be identified in school environments. Three stand out as the most common, but they vary in their underlying assumptions. These three systems are the medical approach, the functional approach, and the developmental approach. He notes that each of these approaches is associated with a distinct philosophical orientation.

TABLE 8-2   School-based role: Speech/language pathologist.

- Address student needs in a variety of settings
- Enhance generalization by using the natural setting
- Teach, model, prompt, and reinforce vocabulary and other specific skills
- Allow teachers to observe strategies used by the speech/language pathologist
- Assess the student in the functional use setting
- Enable students to use newly acquired skills with his or her peers
- Teach the classroom teacher to model appropriate "teacher talk" within the classroom
- Promote transdisciplinary planning and ownership among staff in achieving curriculum goals
- Use augmentative and alternative communication tools within the functional setting
- Focus on classroom and social communication, such as how to initiate conversation, to take turns, to maintain a topic, and to end a conversation
- Focus on using body language, "reading the situation," sending signals of understanding or misunderstanding
- Visit worksites and work with employers

Source: Adapted from Huffman, N. P. (1992). Challenges of education reform. *Asha,* November, 42–43.

The medical models have diagnostic testing as an essential component. Much emphasis is placed on the evaluation process and the skills of the evaluator to interpret assessments and then select an appropriate treatment plan. The emphasis is on treating the causes of the problem and ultimately focusing on the patient's physical well-being. An example might be working on exercises to increase hand strength to improve writing skills. The medical model is not easily adapted to inclusive settings because interventions require more creativity to make curricular connections.

Ottenbacher (1991) notes that the functional model focuses on the ability to perform a specific task in the setting in which it is most frequently carried out. The emphasis is on identifying skills needed to function in a specific environment. For example, if a child is learning to fasten buttons, then teach that skill using the child's clothing. This model is more easily integrated into the classroom because many real life opportunities arise during the school day.

The developmental model emphasizes the acquisition of skills following a developmental sequence. The occupational therapist determines the current developmental level of the child and then teaches skills that follow in the developmental sequence even if they are not age appropriate or available in the school environment. This model may be compatible with the general education classroom when the skills are age appropriate and school activities mesh with the necessary environment for teaching the skill.

Ottenbacher (1991) further discusses service delivery models for occupational therapists by describing four types of team functioning. These are unidisciplinary, multidisciplinary, interdisciplinary, and transdisciplinary. Table 8-3 gives the characteristics of these team approaches. The unidisciplinary approach is completely isolated therapy. This approach would be most compatible with the medical model discussed above.

The multidisciplinary and interdisciplinary models are somewhat collaborative but still fragmented. The multidisciplinary team approach frequently is based on the medical model. The team members having very different expertise work independently with a student. Overlaps in services are not apparent due to the independent nature of the therapy. As each service provider assesses a student in isolation, inaccurate results may occur, and the recommendations for the classroom may be too numerous or complex to actually implement. The interdisciplinary team approach improves service delivery by ensuring that formal communication between team members occurs. Typically a case manager performs the function of coordination between the team members. This eliminates duplication of services and overlapping recommendations. However, services are still largely provided to the student in isolation (Smith, 1990).

The transdisciplinary approach has become very popular because it represents a true collaborative or shared expertise among professional team members. The traditional boundaries of professional roles are broken down as service providers teach each other and plan together. This truly collaborative role is currently the preferred method for students with moderate and severe disabilities (Smith, 1990). (Refer to Chapter 7 for more information on team planning.) The parallels between these service delivery models and those

TABLE 8-3   Team roles for occupational therapists.

Team Approach	Evaluation	Team Activity/Planning	Implementation
Unidisciplinary	Done by individual in isolation	Each discipline develops own goals and objectives	Treatment implemented by discipline member
Multidisciplinary	Done by individual in isolation with shared results to the team	Each discipline develops own goals and objectives that are shared with the team	Treatment implemented by discipline member
Interdisciplinary	Done by individual in isolation with shared results to the team	Each discipline develops own goals and objectives; attempt made to coordinate treatment goals when convenient	Treatment implemented by discipline member within the same physical setting
Transdisciplinary	Done by disciplines in joint effort with joint evaluations	Goals and objectives developed to student needs, not discipline needs	Treatment implemented in natural setting by a team

Source: Adapted from Ottenbacher, K. J. (1991). School-based practice for related services. *AOTA: Self Studies Series.* Rockville, MD: American Occupational Therapy Association.

described in Table 8-1 for speech/language pathologists are readily apparent indicating a range of services from pullout and self-contained to classroom-based integrated services.

Dunn (1988) also describes three methods of service delivery: direct services, monitoring, and consultation. Most service providers are trained to provide direct services by working directly with the student daily or weekly. In monitoring, the occupational therapist would train another staff member who then carries out the procedures with the child. The role of the occupational therapist becomes one of monitoring the progress of the therapy. Consultation fits well into a transdisciplinary or classroom-based approach. The service provider meets periodically with the team and discusses the needs of the student and suggests interventions. The occupational therapists also assist in developing goals and objectives, suggest methods of instruction, and monitor the outcomes.

In order to better prepare occupational therapists for role changes, the American Occupational Therapy Association (AOTA) is revising its list of competencies for the school setting. These competencies clearly emphasize collaboration as critical. Other skills mentioned are the ability to engage in consensual decision making, consultation, and flexibility to develop, implement, evaluate, and modify their program. Chandler (1992) also stresses the importance of collaboration and teaming for occupational therapists by noting that the IEP should not have separate sections for each related service, but rather, it should focus on all interventions as supportive of the educational goals.

Physical Therapy

In 1990, the American Physical Therapy Association (APTA) published guidelines for physical therapists that placed special emphasis on the need for cooperation among the providers of educational and related services. Several broad competencies for school physical therapists relate to curriculum, teaching, and the classroom. These are listed below:

- Administer "time and cost-appropriate" evaluative procedures in a natural setting.
- Record outcomes and prioritize results.
- Collaborate with the classroom teacher, special educator, parents/guardian, psychologist, principal, occupational therapist, and speech-language pathologist.
- Design, implement, and evaluate physical therapy in coordination with the student's educational progress.
- Teach or train appropriate staff to integrate the physical therapy into the educational program.

Physical therapists realize the need to emphasize intervention strategies and to identify ways that team members can use the child's daily routines, when such things as postural control, mobility, and sensory processing are required (APTA, 1990). They conduct observations in the educational environment, including the classroom, as a part of the screening and assessment process. Working as a team member, the physical therapist may find that criterion-referenced assessments provide more useful diagnostic and prescriptive information that the norm-referenced assessments. (See Chapter 6 for further information on assessment)

In 1990, the ATPA described models of service delivery in the schools as direct and indirect. The direct model could take place in the therapy room or in the classroom. An example of direct therapy in the classroom that could lead to incorporating a skill into the student's daily routine would be sitting on the edge of a story circle and working arms and legs as the child listens. Indirect services could focus on intervention activities developed with other educational team members and carried out by those team members. An example would be teaching handling, lifting, and positioning skills required in the classroom. The teacher or instructional aide would then perform the actual service delivery.

This review of service delivery models clearly defines the need for collaboration as a recurring theme. A gradual shift to classroom-based therapies, whether they are direct or indirect services is occurring. The service delivery models are taking on an increasing transdisciplinary flavor.

Transdisciplinary Models and Integrated Therapies

> *When transdisciplinary team members teach each other to implement both therapeutic and educational interventions, children receive their related services throughout the day, not just in a separate room during a scheduled isolated therapy time.*
>
> Gallivan-Fenlon, 1994

The transdisciplinary approach is a truly collaborative model for the delivery of related services. This model has primarily been implemented with children having severe disabilities. It is characterized by information sharing across traditional discipline boundaries. The team members share information on several levels: information about the child, about their discipline and therapy, methods of instruction for specific skill enhancement, and methods of observation and assessment of progress. This sharing promotes consistency in program implementation, a sharing of outcome goals, and role release for the service providers. Role release means that the functions normally performed by one service provider are "released" to be performed by other service providers, the special educator, or the general educator. This role release is dependent on a teaching and learning process whereby the team members teach each other the new skills necessary to provide the required related services to a specific student (Rainforth et al., 1992; Smith, 1990).

The use of transdisciplinary service provision has resulted in definite benefits for children. However, there was an essential element missing in its early conceptualization, the concept of context for service provision. Context refers to the "where" or the place where services will be provided and the "conditions" or the circumstances where the service provision will be most useful and generalize most broadly to the everyday life settings. As teams began to consider context in service delivery, the integrated therapy model became a natural outgrowth of the transdisciplinary approach. Integrated therapies ensure that objectives are taught throughout the student's day in real life situations to improve the student's performance and participation in school and community-based activities (Rainforth et al., 1992; Smith, 1990). The benefits of therapy are enhanced when services are provided in real life settings. The team identifies the context in which emerging skills can best be used and then designs the interventions to enable the desired performance. This assures generalization to relevant contexts instead of leaving generalization to chance. School and community settings are rich in opportunities to integrate communication, social, and motoric learning. Students do not have to be removed from the educational setting. The daily routines that occur everyday in school, such as entering school from the bus loading area, transitions between activities or classes, lunch, recess, art, or physical education, provide the context for related service delivery. Finally, as students learn in everyday contexts, they also learn to respond to natural cues that exist in their home, classroom, or the community. Thus, students learn the skills in the setting in which they will be used and become acclimated to the natural cues that will promote continued use of the skills (Rainforth et al., 1992).

There has been some reluctance on the part of related service personnel to get into the classroom. Their concerns and fears can be characterized by such questions as: How will I coordinate services in all the different classrooms? Do teachers really want me there? What can I do about philosophical differences with administrators, teachers, parents, and other related service personnel? Who is ultimately responsible for the child's special needs? Will I have time to meet with other staff members? Parents? Is this movement to integrated therapies really administration's way of dealing with personnel shortages or is it truly a move to provide a better product? Will we be allowed to develop flexible schedules? Is it possible to measure student performance based on real classroom outcomes?

In order to make the transition to the classroom setting, related service providers must receive training and support. They need to know something about teaching and teaming. The inclusive education movement is shifting the traditional attitudes about roles and responsibilities. This, in turn, is placing a focus on the use of integrated therapy. Giangreco (1986) states that:

> Transdisciplinary teaming is enhanced through the use of integrated related services or integrated therapy, which refers to the incorporation of educational and therapeutic techniques employed cooperatively to assess, plan, implement, evaluate and report progress on common needs and goals (p. 205).

Gallivan-Felton (1994) notes that for preschool aged children with multiple disabilities, the use of an integrated therapy model makes instruction more meaningful. This is because

> When transdisciplinary teams integrate related services into the classroom, they teach communication and motor skills within the context of many typical preschool activities and routines that occur throughout the day. In this way, the child has repeated opportunities to practice and learn in natural environments where they will be used and needed. Related services delivered in this fashion take on increased relevance to the educational program and function as they are intended to assist a child to benefit from his or her educational program. (p. 17)

Putting an integrated therapy program into practice can be initially confusing for all of the educators involved. Writing goals and objectives that reflect the student's need in a format that all team members can understand and implement, however, is crucial to successful teamwork. Actually looking at some objectives from integrated IEPs may prove helpful. Some examples are provided in Table 8-4.

TABLE 8-4   Sample IEP goals and objectives.

Traditional Service Provision	Integrated Service Provision
Physical Therapy	

1. Will demonstrate improved strength and flexibility
    assume and maintain supine flexion position for 20 seconds
    assume and maintain prone extension position for 20 seconds
    will perform a sit-up
    will perform a wheelbarrow walk with support at ankles
2. Will demonstrate improved balance
    will stand on one foot
	1. Using a proper grip with right hand, stabilizing paper with left, and sitting upright, will write legibly using proper form and spacing
	    upper and lower case letters
	    first and last name
	    shapes using oblique lines
	    numbers 1 to 10
	2. Climb on and off playground equipment independently
	3. Will sit squarely in chair with trunk erect during classroom activities

Occupational Therapy	4. Will move through hallways and up/down the stairs keeping up with classmates and not stepping out of line

1. Improve shoulder to finger movement patterns
    demonstrate spontaneous supination and midposition of forearm in tasks
    demonstrate wrist rotation in writing with shoulder and elbow isolation and fixation
	5. Will draw characters from books or stories read in class with nine or more body parts
	6. Will use attending behaviors (look, listen, body still with back straight) when verbal directions are given to small or large groups

Speech/Language Therapy	7. Will participate appropriately, using intelligible speech and increased sentence length, In group discussions when called on by the classroom teacher

1. Will demonstrate improved articulation skills
    will produce /v/ in the medial and final word position at the sentence level
    will produce O singly in all word positions
2. Improve expressive vocabulary, morphology, and syntax
    will verbally label trained nouns
    will stabilize use of pronouns and copula in structured sentences and spontaneous speech
	8. Will increase intelligible and spontaneous language use in classroom group discussions
	9. Will answer questions about story problems using intelligible speech and improved grammar, e.g., subject/verb agreement, past tense verbs

The traditional goals and objectives are categorized by discipline and filled with jargon known only to the professional in that field, for example, maintain supine flexion position. The integrated goals are overlapping with school curriculum and contain language that any person reading the IEP could readily understand, for example, sit squarely in chair with trunk erect during classroom activities. If we expect all team members to work on all goals, the first step is to ensure that the IEP can be understood by all. Two case studies have been included to illustrate how a transdisciplinary team might work together integrating therapy into the classroom, one at the elementary level (Figure 8-1) and another at the secondary level (Figure 8-2). As teachers share their expertise, they will increase their repertoire of techniques to use with students with disabilities, obtain more ideas for implementing IEP objectives in general education environments, and extend what they learn to other students in their classes.

Mary is a fourth grade student who is friendly and enjoys being around people. Her IEP goals include improving:

1. *Gross and fine motor skills*
2. *Expressive language skills, including appropriate verbal interactions with peers*
3. *Short-term memory*

The classroom teacher, PE teacher, occupational therapist, and speech/ language pathologist meet to discuss implementation of the goals. They find out that in PE Mary will be working on dribbling. They determine that in PE the motor, communication, and listening goals ran be addressed. The speech/language pathologist finds out from the PE teacher the steps in dribbling when playing basketball and discusses verbalizing the steps with Mary and the importance of having her her repeat the directions. She will continue to consult with the PE teacher on Mary's progress and occasionally observe Mary in PE. The occupational therapist decides to work with Mary's dribbling partners two times a week to assist with the skills. They decide the students should be in groups of three for this activity so they can practice passing as well. To address her communication goal she will compliment her peers when they accomplish the skill. She can further work on her socialization skills of negotiating in groups (who will be first, how many times to dribble, taking turns, etc.). Through interaction with her peer group she will observe modeling of staying on task, taking turns, and complimenting others. In addition, her peers can remind her of the sequence of steps.

In this way, the PE teacher is sharing her skills of how to play basketball. The speech/language pathologist is transferring her knowledge of the importance of reauditorizing directions and is able to give specific techniques for doing this. The occupational therapy goals are addressed through the PE curriculum and direct services occur in the context of the PE class. Socialization goals occur in the natural environment with feedback from peers.

FIGURE 8-1   Case study: Elementary.

Carlos is an eighth grader with good memory for simple tasks and events who loves to draw. He has low cognitive functioning resulting in reading and writing levels that are significantly below grade level. In addition, he is working on increasing his vocabulary and speaking more clearly.

His history class is getting ready to write detailed biographies of famous Black Americans using multiple sources. His history teacher, special education resource teacher, and speech-language pathologist meet to discuss program modifications. Together they set expectations that Carlos will find ten facts and write them down. In addition, he will give a short oral report on the facts he has gathered. They decided that the history teacher will give Carlos a choice of several people about whom to write his report. The resource teacher will then help Carlos select a book or two on his level. The resource teacher will conduct a short pullout program for students who need strategy instruction in note-taking. During this session a peer buddy will be trained for Carlos to help him write down the facts from the books. Once the note-taking is finished, the resource teacher will come into the classroom and help Carlos and other students organize their notes. All the students will be required to give short oral presentations on their biographies. The speech/language pathologist will help Carlos and other members of the class select relevant facts for presentation, sequence them, and rehearse their presentations. She will draw on Carlos's strengths of memory of simple facts and drawing. Carlos will include visuals in his presentation and be encouraged to volunteer to draw visuals for other students' reports as well.

As these teachers coordinate their efforts, they learn to use each others' skills effectively without requiring that all of them be in the classroom every moment. The resource teacher and the speech/language pathologist can integrate their objectives into the required tasks of the classroom. When these specialists work in the classroom, they are available to help typical students who need assistance, or they can pull groups of students to work on strategies or organizational skills related to classroom content. The use of students as helpers alleviates the classroom teacher from having to do it all. In addition, Carlos' strengths are drawn on to help others.

FIGURE 8-2   Case study: Secondary.

Integrating Therapy and Curriculum

We use children's literature, science, and social studies content material in a writing process approach to teaching oral and written language skills (speaking, listening, thinking, writing). Literature sometimes is used to introduce science and social studies topics or simply to enjoy imaginative stories. We engage in hands-on experiences related to the topic (e.g., cooking, field trips, science experiments, or interviewing).

Ferguson, 1992b

To link therapy to the curriculum, new approaches and modifications are necessary to allow the curriculum to become more child-centered. Nelson and Kennucan-Welsch (1992) note that curriculum modification is not sufficient by itself but must be part of overlying themes that encompass instructional issues such as scheduling, planning, and role issues for all staff involved. While some related service providers may feel the need for security and wish to go into the classroom each time with a detailed lesson plan, this is not necessarily the most effective way to work. Others are more comfortable going into the classroom and informally "picking up on" the instructional techniques the teacher is using. These authors also indicate that as a teaming relationship develops and matures there is a decrease in the amount of time necessary for planning.

One method of integrating related services is to analyze the child's daily activities and look for opportunities to address specific objectives within this framework. Huffman (1992) provides an excellent example using the related service goals common to speech-language therapy. Table 8-5 describes the daily links. The activities that typically occur during the school day are listed. The types of activities and interventions that could occur during these time periods are described. For example, during homeroom the student can focus on following directions. The IEP for this student may specifically list "following multistep directions" as an objective. The chart provides one method a team may use in determining when and where objectives can be addressed in a natural setting.

TABLE 8-5   Opportunities for daily intervention.

Daily Activities	Types of Intervention
Arrival	Conversation, communication, cycle intelligibility, handling transition
Homeroom	Comprehension of and following directions, organizing for the day, planning
Social studies	Using texts and units for vocabulary expansion and word meaning, intelligibility, thought organization
Math	Categories, quantitative terms, synonyms, opposites, time, logic, cause-effect, prediction, closure
Reading	Listening, phonic comparisons, sound symbol relationships, retelling prediction, wh-concepts in stories, pronunciation
Language arts	Sentence construction, verb agreement, thoughts to writing, words saying what you mean, topic selection, description
Science	Prediction, cause-effect, attributes, categorization, sequencing, questioning, quantitative–qualitative concepts
Hallway transitions	Managing time, conversation, organizing, social skills
Dismissal	Sequencing, planning organization, social rules

Source: Adapted from Huffman, N. P. (1992). Challenges of education reform. *Asha,* November, 42–43.

Creativity is the key to linking related service therapy to the curriculum. Some examples of extension activities taken from the experiences of the speech-language pathologist to enhance student communication skills are the following:

- Encourage students to become involved with the school newspaper.
- Assign pen pals between classes or schools.
- Initiate with the English teacher a persuasive writing project using a real life topic within the school or community.
- Co-teach a telephone communication unit.
- Preteach social communication skills appropriate for a field trip, visit to a restaurant, store, or museum.

As related service providers link therapeutic intervention to the curriculum, they need to collaborate with the classroom teacher who has overall responsibility for what instructional activities occur in the classroom. Successful classroom interventions must be flexible and fit the overall climate and structure of the classroom (Chandler, 1992). The importance of observing the students in their natural environment cannot be stressed enough. It's here where meaningful assessment of the student's educational needs can best be achieved. It's here that interactions between the student and teacher and the student and his/her peers can be observed. The classroom is the ideal place for educational/therapeutic interventions to take place. Chandler describes an example of how the occupational therapist can adapt the therapeutic plan to the situation of the moment.

> *Sam is a kindergarten student with cerebral palsy. A functional and educationally relevant goal for Sam is to be able to sit in a bolster chair and attend to seat work (coloring, pasting, drawing, copying letters) for 20 minutes. Occupational therapy may work with Sam to increase range of motion in the hips and shoulders and strengthen trunk extension (among other goals) to contribute to the functional goal of sitting and attending in the classroom. Due to the itinerant schedule, the occupational therapist arrived at the school just after lunch. Ms. Baker, Sam's classroom teacher, had always read to her students while they "rested" in their seats after lunch. After speaking together about the therapeutic activities for Sam, Ms. Baker decided to have the children sit on the floor during story time. The occupational therapist sits behind Sam and does relaxation and ranging activities with him while he listens to the story. Brief periods of listening in prone and then in long and tailor sitting follow the ranging. Facilitation to the back can be done in these positions also. Sam and his therapist are seated on the outside of the circle so that their movement is not distracting to the other children (although the other kindergarten children are not immobile!). The advantages of intervention done in this manner include:*

> - *The child participates in the regular class activity at the regular time.*
> - *The child does not miss any class activity due to therapy time.*
> - *No time is lost in transfer to another location.*
> - *There is increased time for the therapist to observe the classroom routine and how children respond to it.*

- *The teacher has an opportunity to observe what the therapist is doing with the child.*
- *There is a sense of shared responsibility for the child's progress.*
- *The occupational therapist does not have to work in the storage room (under the stairwell, in the "sick" room, behind the bleachers, etc.)." (p. 22)*

The role of the physical therapist in instructional planning is focused in the areas of gross and fine motor development, mobility, and activities of daily living. This could take the form of helping the teacher find ways to include motor skill practice and instruction in the everyday classroom routine. Areas of expertise that a physical therapist brings to classroom planning are outlined by Rainforth and colleages (1992, p. 35) as follows:

- Sensory factors related to posture and movement
- Muscle tone
- Range of motion
- Muscle strength
- Joint flexibility
- Endurance
- Flexibility
- Posture/postural alignment
- Balance and automatic movement
- Functional use of movement

  1. Mobility such as walking
  2. Recreation/leisure

- Adaptive positioning equipment
- Lower limb bracing/splinting/inhibitive casting
- Task adaptation

When looking over this list it is obvious that a physical therapist provides services both for students with physical challenges and for students with more significant multiple disabilities. Some specific examples might include how a child will handle or grasp manipulatives used in any instructional activity a class is completing.

- When crayons, markers, or pencils are using during small group activities, the student will use the palmar grasp for all objects.
- When reminded before a presentation, student will grasp cards/papers using a thumb–fingertip grasp.
- When reminded before activities, student will assume a sidesitting position on the floor and maintain the position for a minimum of three minutes without additional cues.
- When physically assisted to position forearms, student will hold large objects (toys, bins, books) with two hands and carry them at least ten feet.

The physical therapist will collaborate with the classroom teacher as to whether sitting, standing, or using adaptive devices are necessary for or preferable for a student given the type of classroom activity. The physical therapist can also assist in planning what the peers will be doing and whether peer assistance is valuable or necessary during the classroom activities. This type of planning can maximize the level of participation for the student with disabilities. Some examples of integrated physical therapy objectives taken from IEPs might be:

- Classroom performance/academics

    1. When writing, will sit squarely in chair with trunk erect
    2. Given a picture cue taped to the desk, will sit with a still body, straight back, and eyes on the speaker to improve ability to follow directions

- Follow school/classroom rules and routines

    1. Will independently take chair off the desk in the morning and put it back on the desk in the afternoon
    2. Will remain in position in line when moving through the hall with classmates (keep pace with other students, without tripping, safely ascend and descend stairs)

- Social skills/friendship development

    1. During recess, will climb on and off playground equipment safely and independently
    2. Using a ten-inch ball, will play catch with friends
    3. While playing basketball with a minimum of three friends, will bounce a ball and run

During physical education and/or recess, the physical therapist can co-teach. This enables the therapist to ensure the participation of the student with physical challenges in the class and also enables the therapist to work with small groups of students who may benefit from additional skill development. For example, during physical education, the class is learning to play soccer. The physical therapist may pull a group aside to demonstrate kicking and practice the skill. Another opportunity to integrate therapy is during transition times in the classroom. When the students are moving about the room, they may be changing the type of materials they are using or moving from one activity to another. These transitions can be busy and confusing for all of the students. The assistance of the physical therapist with logistics is often helpful. Direct service during such times can ease the stress for a student with disabilities as well as the other participants in the class.

Integrating Therapy as an Evolutionary Process

Related service delivery is currently in an evolutionary process, and the approaches that are being used are changing in response to legal, social, and economic issues. The movement to integrated related services should allow the related service personnel to do their jobs with increasing effectiveness. More importantly, as teachers and administrators see the value of this evolving approach, they will welcome the new models, and the benefactor in all of this will be the students. Giangreco (1990) offers a caution however, that we do not assume we have reached the ideal point on related service-delivery decision making. He says, "It is conceivable that our current practices...have become so commonplace that we have neglected to study carefully how such decisions are made, how we might improve them, and what impact such decisions have on students, families, and professionals" (p. 30). Transdisciplinary and integrated related services have appeared in educational literature since the early 1980s. Although much has been written about these models, only 10 percent of the training programs for service providers incorporated preservice experiences in a team or collaborative setting (Roth & Miller, 1991). Thus, most related service providers are learning to integrate related services in the educational setting. As they take jobs within a school system, they begin to provide services using a "pullout" model. As the related service providers learn more about the educational setting, the classroom, and the curriculum, they begin to see the benefits of providing services in a more collaborative manner. Teaming becomes the norm, and the service providers begin to use a "plug-in" model. Opportunities for integration become more obvious, enabling therapists to deliver services that are compatible with the classroom activities. As time in the collaborative role progresses, the related services become increasingly embedded in the daily routine of the classroom, and the therapies become truly integrated. This evolution is portrayed in Table 8-6 as it was conceptualized by Moore (1993).

TABLE 8-6   Evolution of school-related services delivery.

The Traditional Role "Pullout Model"	Transitional Role "Plug-in Model"	Integrated Related Services Model
Works from a medical model-evaluates the students	Works from an educational model	Works from the curriculum
Diagnoses individuals	Screens and evaluates groups and individuals	Uses formal and informal assessments of areas in need of support
Prescribes developmental tasks	Participates as active member of curriculum development team	Therapists learn curriculum . . . become integral members of the team
Works on IEP developed for "Therapy"	Works to integrate IEP into classroom task demands	Therapist and regular and special educators collaborate to write goals and objectives and blend them with the curriculum
Works with clinical models	Works with a variety materials of delivery models in the classrooms and resource rooms using classroom text and assignments	Modify and adapt curriculum as needed to ensure IEP goals are met; uses appropriate grade level material
Works until patients are "cured" of their pathology	Works to help student become "effective students" by developing the requisite communication skills	Works to enhance the students performance on their educational and therapeutic goals using classroom activities

Source: Moore, J. (1993). Continuum of school or school-based therapy delivery and cooperative teaching planning sheet. Preconference Workshop Materials. Council for Learning Disabilities, Baltimore, MD.

The stages in this evolutionary process were outlined originally by the United Cerebral Palsy Association in 1976. The specific activities required for a team's progress through the evolution are the following:

1. Role extension: Designing and implementing objectives that are discipline-specific
2. Role enrichment: Designing and implementing objectives that cross discipline lines
3. Role expansion: Designing and implementing objectives that are derived from a sharing of knowledge across all disciplines
4. Role exchange: Implementing objectives and strategies learned from other team members
5. Role release: Designing and implementing objectives and strategies effectively without regard to discipline lines
6. Role Support: Providing ongoing support to each other as objectives and strategies are implemented in the real-life setting collaboratively

As teachers spend more time planning together, it may be helpful to have a form to facilitate the planning and recording of individual responsibilities. Figure 8-3 is a sample planning form that which was developed by Moore and which can be used or adapted to any transdisciplinary team. It allows the team members to define specific areas that they each will address, the IEP objectives that will be attained, the areas of joint involvement, and the materials and techniques that will be used.

Student's Name: _____		D.O.B. _____	From _____ To _____		
	Curriculum Area/Goals	**Need from IEP**	**Joint Goals**	**Mat'ls**	**Tech.**
Classroom teacher					
Special Ed teacher/other					
Speech/language pathologist					
Other therapist (e.g., OT, PT)					
Comments					

FIGURE 8-3   Cooperative teaching planning sheet.

Source: Morris, J. (1993). Continuum of school or school-based therapy delivery and cooperative teaching planning sheet. Preconference Workshop Materials. Council for Learning Disabilities, Baltimore, MD.

If related services are a particular area of interest, the reader is referred to Rainforth and colleages (1992) for a more comprehensive picture of integrated related services. This book provides more in-depth information, and forms and addresses quite thoroughly the issue of collaboration.

Conclusions

The delivery models for related services vary widely. The evolution over time has been dramatic. Today it is apparent today an increasing number of therapists see the value of classroom and curriculum-based related service delivery. It is also obvious that the professional organizations representing these service providers strongly support collaborative and classroom-based interventions. Within the last few years, many examples of integrated related services have begun to emerge. The benefits of these methods are already becoming strongly evident.

Increasing numbers of related services personnel are joining the reform movement to ensure the continuation of appropriate related services to students. They are finding that their approaches can work well in an integrated setting. They are welcoming the focus on quality management and outcome-based education, and they are seeing the value of collaborating with parents, families, community members, and other educators. They are seeing the benefits of integrated therapies and committing to this evolving model, which promises to prepare today's children and tomorrow's adults to participate more fully and function more effectively in an ever changing society.

References

American Occupational Therapy Association: Guidelines Committee. (1989). *Guidelines for occupational therapy services in the public schools* (2nd ed.). Rockville, MD: Author.

American Occupational Therapy Association. (1994). *Standard of practice*. Commission on Practice. Rockville, MD: Author.

American Physical Therapy Association. (1990). *Physical therapy practice in educational environments: Policies and guidelines*. Alexandria, VA: Author.

American Speech and Hearing Association. (1991). A model for collaborative service delivery to students with language-learning disorders in the public schools. *Asha, 3*(33) (Suppl. 5), 44–50.

American Speech and Hearing Association. (1992). Trends and issues in school reform and their effects on speech-language pathologists, audiologists, and students and communication disorders.

Ad Hoc Committee on Changes in Education Policies and Practices, 1–23.

American Speech and Hearing Association. (1993). Guidelines for caseload size and speech-language service delivery in the schools. *Asha, 35*(Suppl. 10), 33–39.

Association for Persons with Severe Handicaps. (1986). *Position statement on the provision of related services*. Seattle, WA: Author.

Bennett, S. (1993). Classroom collaboration: Some good ideas. *Clinically Speaking, 10,* 9.

Blossom, B., & Ford, F. (1991). *Physical therapy in public schools*. Roswell, GA: Rehabilitation Publications and Therapies.

Chandler, B. (1992). Classroom application for school-based practice. *AOTA self study series*. Rockville, MD: American Occupational Therapy Association.

Dunn, W. (1988). Models of occupational therapy service provision in the school system. *American Journal of Occupational Therapy, 42*(11), 718–723.

Eger, D. L. (1992). Why now? Changing school language speech-language service delivery. *Asha,* November, p. 40.

Federal Register, 57(189), Sept. 29, 1992. Rules and Regulations, 34 CFR, Parts 300 & 301.

Ferguson, M. L. (1992a). Clinical Forum: Implementing collaborative consultation: An introduction. *Language, Speech, and Hearing Services in Schools, 23,* 361–362.

Ferguson, M. L. (1992b). Clinical forum: Implementing collaborative consultation: The transition to collaborative teaching. *Language, Speech, and Hearing Services in Schools, 23,* 371–372.

Gallivan-Fenlon, A. (1994). Integrated transdisciplinary teams. *Teaching Exceptional Children,* Spring, 16–20.

Giangreco, M. F. (1986). Effects of integrated therapy: A pilot study. *Journal of the Association for Persons with Severe Handicaps, 11*(3), 205–208.

Giangreco, M. F. (1990). Making related services decisions for students with severe disabilities: Roles, criteria, and authority. *Journal of the Association for Persons with Severe Handicaps, 15*(1), 22–31.

Huffman, N. P. (1992). Challenges of education reform. *ASHA,* November, 42–43.

Lozo, D. (1993). Inclusion: Implications for speech-language programs in the schools. *Practically Speaking,* Fall, 4.

Magnotta, O. H. (1991). Looking beyond tradition. *Language, Speech, and Hearing Services in Schools, 22,* 150–151.

Montgomery, J. K. (1992). Clinical Forum: Implementing collaborative consultation: Perspectives from the field: Language, speech, and hearing services in schools. *Language, Speech, and Hearing Services in Schools, 23,* 363–364.

Moore, J. (1993). Continuum of school or school-based therapy delivery and cooperative teaching planning sheet. Preconference Workshop Materials, Council for Learning Disabilities, Baltimore, MD.

Nelson, N. W., & Kennucan-Welsch, K. (1992). Curriculum-based collaboration, What is changing? *Asha,* November, 46.

Ottenbacher, K. J. (1991). School-based practice for related services. *AOTA: Self Study Series,* Rockville, MD: American Occupational Therapy Association.

Rainforth, B., York, J., & Macdonald, C. (1992). *Collaborative teams for students with severe disabilities.* Baltimore: Paul H. Brookes Publishing Co.

Roth, M., & Miller, S. (1991). Transdisciplinary teaming in preservice special and adapted physical education: Practicing what we preach. *Teacher Education and Special Education, 14*(4), 243–247.

Smith, P. (1990). *Integrating related services into programs for students with severe and multiple handicaps.* Kentucky Systems Change Project. U.S. Office of Education

Task Force Report, New York State Speech/Language Hearing Association. (1993). Recommendations for speech-language service delivery models in the schools. *NYSSLHA Communicator.* May-June, p. 7.

United Cerebral Palsy Association. (1976). *Staff development handbook: A resource for the transdisciplinary process.* New York: Author.

Chapter 9

Curriculum Modifications and Adaptations

DIANE M. SWITLICK

◆ ADVANCE ORGANIZER ◆

There are a multitude of ways to modify the curriculum and daily instructional activities to enable the teacher to meet individual needs and increase the performance of students in the classroom. This chapter will explore methods to modify both curricular focus and instructional practices to meet individual student preferences and those needs that result from a disability. The following types of modification will be defined, and examples of each will be provided:

Accommodation
Adaptation
Parallel instruction
Overlapping instruction

During my second year of teaching, I became involved in a mainstreaming program with the special education teacher in my school. The idea was for her to send to my fifth grade science class two children with learning disabilities. I wasn't thrilled. It was just more work for me, and these kids probably wouldn't get anything out of my class. But, she was insistent, so I agreed. And my life changed.

Joey had severe learning disabilities. He could read hesitantly on a second grade level and wrote at about first grade level. He had a strange, high-pitched voice and would cry when frustrated. But I was stuck with him, and I had the systems of the body to cover. So I taught and he sat. On the third day into the skeletal system, Joey came to my desk and shyly offered me a sheaf of crumpled papers. "These are for you," he said. "I wrote the names of all the bones in the body and where they go." I looked at his painstaking printing and nearly cried. During the circulatory system, he brought me his own blood sample on a slide. He raised brine shrimp and grew sugar crystals. And he learned! I gave him tests orally and he answered every question with great accuracy. The other children envied his ability to learn so quickly. Suddenly, I saw Joey for what he was—a student in my class, and he was learning.

The following fall I enrolled in a university master's program in special education. The focus of this program was inclusion. This is for you, Joey, I thought.

Inclusion is a relatively new concept. Some educators believe that it's no different from mainstreaming or integration. But it surpasses these concepts by its simplicity. And it works! I know because I'm doing it. I "borrowed" a fifth grader, Chrystal, from her special classroom and brought her into my fifth grade room for three hours a day. She had a partner, and she worked with a cooperative group. According to her IEP, she had specific learning disabilities. The IEP further explained that she was unable to retain short-term memory items, and she had low comprehension in reading and math. She had been in a special class since second grade.

At first, Chrystal tried to disappear into the woodwork. She was understandably shy and intimidated. I left her alone; gave her time to adjust. By the third week, she started timidly raising her hand with an answer. By the following week, she was coming to the board to do math problems. On a fraction quiz, she got the highest score. This raised her self-esteem and further encouraged her to try. Chrystal required few accommodations. I let her use a multiplication chart, and she did much of her work with a partner. She was part of a class of her peers and she was accepted by them.

Janet Johnson, fifth grade teacher, Montgomery County Public Schools, Maryland

---

The presence of a student with significant disabilities often becomes the catalyst for teachers to critically examine instructional purposes, methods, and outcomes for all children.

Udvari-Solner, 1996

The characteristics of our classrooms are changing at a rapid pace. Teachers are facing increasing ethnic and cultural diversity, with minority populations growing rapidly. Accompanying these changes are new models of assessment, instruction, and curriculum design. Debates are occurring around the extent to which "reductionistic" approaches such as teacher-directed instruction and diagnostic/prescriptive methods should be used with students with disabilities. Currently, more "holistic/constructivist" models are being emphasized, such as whole language and performance-based education, where learning becomes an individual learner's construction of meaning in the context of his or her own experience (Poplin & Stone, 1992; Tarver, 1992). Cooperative and democratic techniques of teaching and discipline appear as alternatives to individualistic instruction and applied behavior management systems (Putnam, Spiegel, & Bruininks, 1995). Keeping up with instructional changes is a challenge. In reflecting back to Chapter 3 on change, we recall that teachers who are already overloaded view change with skepticism. Diversity in the classroom has increased to the point at which most students with disabilities currently are educated in the general education classroom for at least some portion of the school day. All of these factors serve to increase the challenge of teaching today. Teaching "to the middle" is no longer a feasible instructional approach. Many students cannot keep pace with the curriculum as it is structured in the general education setting. If curricular adaptations are not made for individual students, these students may suffer a different kind of segregation. While in the general education classroom sitting beside their peers, they may be denied the basic right to learn. Thus, curriculum modification has become a requirement in today's classroom.

One of the most basic assumptions of inclusive education is that students with disabilities in a general education classroom will have an instructional program based on their individual strengths and needs—that the students' instructional program will extend beyond social integration and address the students' academic areas of need directly. Instructional differentiation is possible, desirable, and perhaps more difficult than was originally believed (Fuchs, Fuchs, Hamlett, Phillips, & Karns, 1995; Janney, Snell, Beers, & Raynes, 1995; Schumm et al., 1995).

Systematic Adjustments to Curriculum in the Classroom

> *Teachers who successfully include students with diverse learning characteristics are constantly making decisions about what will be adapted, adjusted, reconfigured, streamlined, and clarified in their curriculum and instruction.*
>
> Udvari-Solner, 1996

Curricular and instructional adaptation relies on the teacher's ability to analyze the strengths, needs, and learning characteristics of students as individuals and to plan for instruction based on the needs of individual students. Once instruction begins, the teacher makes judgments about the success of the individual lessons and adjusts subsequent lessons. A prevalent belief is that curricular and instructional adaptation that is responsive to student needs is related to student gains in learning (Corno & Snow, 1986). Special education research has supported this belief. When special educators continually adapt instruction to individual needs, students learn very consistently (Fuchs, Fuchs, Hamlett, & Ferguson, 1992; Wesson, 1991). However, the issue becomes how well this responsive instruction, which is individualized, meshes with both the curriculum goals and the instructional methods commonly found in the general education classroom. Previous studies have indicated that general educators tend to plan for the class, not the individual student. Early in the year, teachers develop their approach to instructional and management routines that continue for the remainder of the school year (Clark & Elmore, 1981). While these routines tend to ensure classroom order and efficiency, routines also need to be flexible and responsive to meet individual needs. Ysseldyke, Thurlow, Wotruba, and Nania (1990) analyzed adapted instructional techniques. They found a marked difference between elementary and secondary teachers. Elementary teachers shared a more positive attitude toward instructional adaptation. These teachers favored alternative methods in managing student behavior, using alternative methods to instruct students who were failing, such as altering goals and modifying tasks, using different classroom materials, and using alternative group placement. Both elementary and secondary teachers viewed the following modifications favorably: modifying the lesson pace, informing students frequently of their needs and performance, and holding students accountable for high quality work. Secondary teachers actually made fewer changes in their instructional methods and made less use of other adults in the classroom.

Fuchs and colleagues (1995) examined instructional adaptation from two perspectives: routine and specialized. *Routine adaptations* were those adaptations that are group-oriented and encompassed materials, grouping arrangements, and outcomes that teachers establish on an ongoing basis when they anticipate the need for differentiated instruction. Techniques such as cooperative learning, peer tutoring, and the use of alternative materials fall into this category. For example, a teacher about to teach the elements of fiction by reading and analyzing a novel may select two different novels based on the reading levels of the students in the class. The concepts would be discussed in two separate groups during class using the examples from each story. The materials have been changed, and the students have been subgrouped for instruction. *Specialized adaptations* are defined as those that result from a student's inability to learn or handle the difficulty of the content. These interventions tend to be student-specific, such as differentiating outcome objectives, changing teaching methodologies, or restructuring the organization and environment in the classroom. For example, students are already subgrouped for novel study, but three students are still unable to take part in the activities. The teacher must further differentiate due to the severity of the needs or the student's emphasis of instruction. One student is a nonreader. This student requires using a tape-recorded version of the novel and instructional modification to simplify all of her assignments. Two other students are learning strategic reading techniques. They are reading one of the novels, but their assignments are completely different since their need is to focus on applying the reading strategies and not on the elements of fiction. Baker and Zigmond (1990) found very little evidence that general educators implemented any specialized adaptations Fuchs and colleagues (1995) found that teachers working with students with learning disabilities were open to making routine adaptations, and when these teachers were specifically prompted and supported, they did make specialized adaptations. Additionally, once teachers had experience with specialized adaptations, they began to think differently about their instructional program and their students. Janney and colleagues (1995) found that teachers who were including students with moderate to severe disabilities were successful in adapting the program with the assistance of the special educator because they gradually made changes in their physical, social, and academic classroom activities. Interestingly, direct experience with a student with significant disabilities was more influential in the change process than was in-service or preparatory training. Thus, research clearly indicates that general educators are able to make specialized adaptations with support and assistance from special educators that enable students with disabilities to become successful learners in the general education classroom.

The Classroom Planning Process

> *The real voyage of discovery consists not in seeking new landscapes, but in having new eyes.*
>
> Proust

Teachers must make many decisions when planning instruction in their classroom. The organization and the content of the curriculum are only the starting place. Much of the content is typically dictated by state mandates. Given this basic curriculum content, where do we go from there? Schumm and colleagues (1995) described a basic planning format to analyze what students with learning disabilities can expect to find in the general education classroom. This model is useful in determining the major points of decision making for the teacher in adapting the instructional program. Table 9-1 summarizes the planning process. There are three basic stages in the process: preplanning, interactive planning, and postplan-

TABLE 9-1   The planning process.

	Teacher Role	Environment	Student
Preplanning	Direct instruction vs. facilitator—How will the teacher function during this unit? Percentage of time spent in different roles.	Environment and resource planning—How will the classroom be organized? What materials will be used?	Student behavior and learning outcomes—Can students attain the goals of the curriculum? How will students approach learning and respond to the activities? What alternative goals are necessary?
Interactive planning	Role changes in implementation—How is instruction proceeding? Is more direct instruction necessary? Is reteaching needed?	Environmental and resource adaptation—Are student responding well to the materials and the methods of instruction? Is more or less group work needed?	Student reactions, needs, and supports—Are the students attaining the goals? Do some students require individual adaptation of the materials or concepts? Are unanticipated needs being met?
Postplanning	Effectiveness of teacher roles and behavior—-Was the teacher role effective? What changes to the role were necessary during instruction? What should be changed for the next unit?	Effect of changes in environment and resources—What activities seemed to work best? What groupings were most effective? What materials were too difficult or too easy? What should be changed?	Student performance—How did students perform on assessments? Is reteaching necessary? Will continuing adaptation be necessary for the next unit?

ning. During each stage three factors must be analyzed: the teacher's behavior, the environment, and the student behaviors and needs.

Preplanning

Preplanning is the initial stage in the planning process. The teacher begins by reviewing the goals of the curriculum and reading relevant background material. Typically, during this phase of planning, teachers must write objectives, outline classroom procedures, predict student outcomes, and devise evaluation methods. Teachers plan for routine adaptations such as cooperative learning, peer tutoring, and alternative materials. Teachers determine, based on individual student needs, what parts of the curriculum can be met by the majority of the students, where small group supports and differentiated materials are necessary, and where students can handle more complex content and a broadening of the required content.

Preplanning typically occurs for the year, for each unit, and it may also occur on a weekly basis. Some questions that may facilitate adaptive preplanning are found in Table 9-2 and are also provided in Checklist 9-1 at the end of this chapter.

Interactive Planning

Interactive planning typically occurs during the time a unit or group of lessons is conducted. The teacher monitors the lessons and evaluates student progress on a daily basis. Adaptations are continually made based on student performance. Individual or small group instructional adaptations are most likely to occur during this time. Teachers monitor whether students understand a concept. Those students mastering the material can move on to new material while those who require further instruction are retaught. Planning for this reteaching or the restructuring of subsequent activities is the focus of interactive planning. No matter how thorough a teacher has been during the preplanning stage, there are always unanticipated reactions from the students to the planned lessons, needs that arise, and problems with student groups or materials. The interactive phase resolves these problems through specific adaptations that typically focus on individual students or on small groups of students. These specific changes may occur spontaneously during the actual teaching period.

Postplanning

Postplanning focuses on what has been learned during the delivery of instruction and the evaluation of student performance. It is a process of reflection that involves the teacher in actively analyzing the entire teaching and learning experience. Using the knowledge gained in this reflection is the focus of postplanning. Thus, it merges with the preplanning process for the next unit. The teacher may reflect on a range of elements within instruction during the postplanning process. Possible areas for reflection are listed in Table 9-3. An example may clarify how teachers use this planning process and how modifications to curriculum and instruction are a part of the planning process.

Mr. Drew is planning a brief unit on the study of Agriculture in China. He is implementing the planning process and begins by determining the concepts he wants to empha-

TABLE 9-2 Preplanning questions.

I. Content:

1. What are the content requirements of the curriculum?
2. Which objectives are most essential?
3. Which students require a functional curriculum and need parallel instruction (same basic content but on a less taxing conceptual level)?
4. What alternative materials ar available (Including audiovisual materials)?
5. What rubrics will be used to measure student performance?
6. What role will students play in suggesting activities or the unit?
7. Will this material motivate students who are not usually interested in school?

II. Student Concerns:

1. Which students can effectively learn the material with little adaptation?
2. Which students require basic instruction on only the essential components?
3. Which students require alternative reading materials or taped readings, but can handle the concepts intellectually?
4. Which students can master the objectives and will require more depth or breadth in their study?
5. What behaviors will the students engage in during the unit activities?
6. Will personal assistance or natural supports be necessary for any students?

III. Instructional Methods:

1. Which instructional approaches are going to be most effective with the content?
2. Where will group activities fit into the plan?
3. Which student will benefit from peer tutoring and being a peer tutor?
4. How will the room arrangement affect the instructional plan?
5. How will groupings be determined?
6. What purpose will groupings serve?
7. How will student interest be sparked in introducing the unit?
8. Will students have an opportunity to interact?
9. What role will the teacher play during instruction (direct teaching, tutoring, facilitating, observing, etc.)?
10. What behaviors will the student engage in during the unit activities?
11. How will IEP goals and objectives be met through the planned activities?
12. How will student progress be monitored and evaluated (daily, weekly, for the unit)?
13. How will outcome expectations be communicated to the students?

size. By looking at how Mr. Drew uses the planning process, teachers may form ideas of how they use the process or could improve their current planning practices. Mr. Drew has selected the effect of weather and the concept of supply and demand. While there are many other concepts that could be included, he has selected these points of emphasis because they will complement learning in other units. Once he has written his objectives, he selects appropriate materials. He selects articles, excepts from textbooks, and mini-lesson topics for direct instruction. He plans the daily classroom activities including a simulation activity that involves the students in a cooperative experience where they play the role of farmers.

TABLE 9-3   Postplanning: Areas of reflection.

Teacher Factors	Environmental Factors	Student Factors
• Attitudes and beliefs that were or were not supported by student outcomes • Methods of instruction and their effectiveness • Adaptation to instruction • Knowledge of the concept • Knowledge of student needs	• Demands for content coverage • Flow of the activities • Classroom climate • Arrangement of the classroom • Organization of student groupings • Social and behavioral influences • Appropriateness of the materials • Need for additional materials to fill in gaps or address student individual needs • Adaptive equipment • Feasibility of implementing adaptations in the classroom setting • Timing of activities and the timeframe of the unit	• Time on-task during each activity • Interest in the unit • Effectiveness of learning strategies and interventions for individual student outcomes • Motivation level of class and individuals • Behavior patterns • Response to adaptations • Performance on evaluation activities • Interaction and social skills • Learning styles and responses to particular activities • Future student needs

The groups plan their planting and receive information on weather conditions and yields. They also get market prices and must determine how well their crops did and their income. He considers all of his students and whether alternative materials will be necessary for some students. He plans to have group work focused on one of the readings because it is difficult. He plans alternative activities for two of the daily lessons for one student who has mental retardation and needs to focus on basic word recognition using similar materials instead of on the complex concept of supply and demand. He structures group roles to the strengths of the students. Once this is completed, he is ready to implement. He moves from preplanning to interactive planning.

The unit is in full swing. The students are performing well with most of the daily lessons. Mr. Drew sees that he has a small group of students that requires extended direct instruction on supply and demand. He selects a reading for the rest of the class to broaden their knowledge, and he structures a small group instructional session for the students requiring extended direct support. Once he is satisfied that all students have a basic understanding of the effect of weather and the laws of supply and demand, he begins the simulation experience. Students respond well to the activity. They develop questions that require completing the simulation of a number of years. Mr. Drew extends the activity by several days to allow for this succession of annual planting. He had not anticipated this interest of the students or the need to see the long-range effect of the factors on the life of the farmer. During the extension of the simulation, Mr. Drew finds that he must plan separate activities for his student with mental retardation who does not comprehend the conceptual learning.

As the unit draws to a close, Mr. Drew is pleased with the overall performance of the students. As he enters the phase of postplanning, he reflects on the changes he made during the delivery of instruction. He determines if these changes have implications for the next unit he has planned. He already sees the need to adjust his time frame because the previous unit took three days longer than anticipated. Mr. Drew is also reflecting on the way he structured the group activity, which focused on a very difficult reading assignment. This structure allowed the students to read and discuss the major content of an assignment that most of the students could not handle independently. He is now thinking that this can be used again in the future.

Analyzing Student Preferences for Learning

> *Sandy, an elementary student, is struggling with the concept of multiplication. Because she is talented in art, her teacher askes her to create visual representations of the times tables. Sandy dives into the task with relish, drawing configurations of objects to depict "two times three," and so on. When she is finished, she understands multiplication, because the concept has been expressed through visual images.*
>
> Association for Supervision and Curriculum Development, 1994

To analyze student preferences, teachers must see students as individuals. Their strengths and needs must be explored on many levels. Each person has different preferences, interests, dominant sensory channels, and specific abilities that are stronger than others. Teachers learn a great deal about their students through reviewing records and IEPs, talking with previous teachers and families, and through their daily contact with the student.

Sensory Preferences

Every person has a preferred channel through which information is received. Teachers are familiar with the many references to visual learners and auditory learners in the literature. Although each individual has a dominant channel, he or she still takes in information through all of the other senses. Some individuals learn best by seeing, some by hearing, and some by doing. As teachers plan for their students, it is important to use as many sensory channels as possible, as frequently as possible, to maximize learning for all students.

Student Interests

Many teachers have learned firsthand that incorporating student interests into their lessons has a significant impact on student motivation. General knowledge of student interests and hobbies can serve as a point of personal contact between the students and the teacher. Asking students about the sports they play or the dance class they are taking sparks meaningful social interaction. A personal exchange serves as a basis for developing a strong interpersonal relationship that motivates not just the student but the teacher as well.

Using student interests in instructional planning is a more challenging endeavor. Teachers use varied methods to involve students in lesson planning, such as having them suggest activities to be included in the unit. However, this method may not be effective if students have little prior knowledge of the topic on which to base their suggestions. When units of study happen to mesh with the interests of some students, these students may bring in items or share information, which in turn sparks the interest of other students in the classroom.

There are many units that do not easily connect with students' personal interests and hobbies, and teachers must build student interest to foster motivation. Since motivation has such an impact on student performance, teachers can structure the initial introduction to a unit to peak interest. Checking student background knowledge of the content through brainstorming can be a natural beginning point. A variation may be to give students the topic, such as "weather," and have them bring in items related to the topic. One student may bring in an umbrella, another a weather map, and another may bring in a backyard rain gauge. Each item can be used to collect background knowledge from the class, and these items may also serve as objects of interest during the unit. Once students have shared or recorded what they know about the content, they can specify what they would like to know. This information can be used to develop activities and also can be developed into personal learning objectives for each student. The students are accountable for the essential learning objectives and for their personal learning objectives. The students may even develop the rubrics, models for appropriate or well-constructed responses, for the evaluations they must complete. (See Chapter 6 for more information on assessment and rubrics.)

One of the most popular frameworks for analyzing student preferences and strengths is the theory of multiple intelligences, which Gardner presented in 1987. Gardner has argued that our traditional concept of intelligence encompasses only two of the forms of intelligences, and each person excels at one or more of the seven possible types. Each type is described briefly in Table 9-4.

Gardner urges educators to take the differences in students quite seriously and to design activities, projects, and evaluations with multiple intelligences in mind. Including all seven in every lesson or unit would be next to impossible, but inclusion of as many as possible is desirable. Often it is helpful to have students analyze their own strengths and weaknesses in each type of ability. They may then use this knowledge in suggesting personal objectives and project ideas for a unit. The following is an example of a lesson including these intelligences:

> In teaching about photosynthesis...(Mr.) Campbell might have his students **read** about the concept (linguistic), use **diagrams** (spatial), **analyze** the sequence of the process (logical-mathematical), **dramatize** the process or **manipulate** fact cards

TABLE 9-4   Gardner's seven types of intelligences.

Spatial: Ability to perceive the visual-spatial world accurately and see transformations

Bodily-Kinesthetic: Ability to use body to express ideas especially using hands to construct, shape, and transform

Musical: Ability to discriminate sounds, pitch, and express content and feelings through music

Linguistics: Ability to use language or language, either verbal or written to express ideas

Logical-Mathematical: Ability to use numbers, problem solve, and reason

Interpersonal: Ability to perceive intention, feelings, and reactions of others

Intrapersonal: Ability to understand self, act according to strengths and weaknesses, and maintain self-discipline

Source: Adapted from Gardner, H. (1987). *Frames of mind.* New York: Basic Books.

> *(bodily-kinesthetic), create a **song** about it (musical), work in groups (interpersonal), and do a **reflective** activity, such as comparing photosynthesis to a change in their own lives (intrapersonal). (ASCD Update, 1994, p 5.)*

Accommodating student learning styles has permeated educational literature for over twenty years. Many preferences have been described in the literature ranging from one's comfort in environmental conditions such as temperature and light, to a preference for the type and amount of interpersonal interaction. Many theories of learning styles have been proposed and studied. Each theory is actually an attempt to describe how individuals think (Gregorc, 1985; Holland, 1973; Renzulli & Smith, 1978; Sternberg, 1994). Sternberg writes: "A style is a preferred way of using one's abilities. It is not in itself an ability but rather a preference. Hence, various styles are not good or bad, only different" (p. 36). While the research on learning styles is less than conclusive, this information indicates that strict adherence to a limited view of the learner can hinder student learning and success. Research does support the use of a continuum of approaches in the classroom.

Modifying Curriculum and Instruction

> *All students can learn and succeed, but not on the same day in the same way.*
>
> Spady

Modifying the curriculum content or the instructional methods in any general education classroom can be accomplished through creative thinking and diligent effort, whether the modification is to meet different needs related to learner preferences or to disabilities (Giangreco, 1993). General educators working in collaboration with special educators *can* make appropriate adaptations for individual students with and without disabilities, but this effort requires guided support. Once teachers gain some experience with modifying the curriculum goals or instructional techniques, they also begin to think differently about instruction and are able to make modifications more independently (Fuchs et al., 1995; Janney et al., 1995). This necessitates not only understanding individual differences, but also having a flexible view of curriculum and instruction. Teachers must determine what comprises the essential conceptual information within a unit of study and then plan its delivery through multiple approaches. The basic curriculum is much like a lump of clay in the hands of the teacher. If it is not manipulated and shaped, it becomes a hardened rock. When clay is shaped, molded, and stretched, it becomes more pliable and easier to work. Just as with the clay, the more teachers work at making adaptations the easier curriculum becomes to adjust. The range and complexity of adaptations made by the teacher increases.

What Is Modification?

To facilitate general educator's implementation of modified curriculum and instruction in the classroom, models and definitions are helpful. The purpose of a modification is to enable an individual to compensate for intellectual, physical, or behavioral challenges. The modification allows the individual to use existing skill repertoires while promoting the acquisition of new skills or knowledge. A concept frequently associated with modification is partial participation, which implies some level of active involvement in a task or activity. This concept acknowledges that some students, particularly those with more severe disabilities, may never learn the same material and skills as the majority of the class participants, but that it is still appropriate for them to participate in the general education classroom (Ottlinger & Kohlhepp, 1992).

Who Selects the Modification?

Before looking at models for modification, it is crucial to remember that the general educator who will implement the modification must be the person who selects the adaptations. Since the general and the special educator frequently plan together, it becomes crucial that the general educator make the final decisions on adaptations, especially if they are the primary implementor. For any modification to be effective, it must **FLOW**:

- **F**it into the classroom environment
- **L**end themselves to meeting individual student needs
- **O**ptimize understanding for each student
- **W**ork well with the activity planned for the lesson

These are valuable criteria that may assist in selecting modifications that can be successfully implemented.

Types of Modifications and Adaptations

> *Support in the form of adaptive teaching methods, repetition and analysis, and multi-model, multi-level sources of information are front loaded during curriculum planning, rather than provided in a remedial or catch-up method as the unit progresses.*
>
> Heron & Jorgensen, 1995

As teachers view the curriculum and the diversity of the student needs in the classroom, they are sometimes bewildered about what can be changed. A synthesis of the types of changes that can be made in the classroom is useful in determining how to approach modifications (Ottlinger & Kohlhepp, 1992; Wood, 1992). The instructional program may be changed in the following ways:

- **Size:** Shorten the length of an assignment, limit the number of problems, or shorten the length of a reading assignment.
- **Time:** Lengthen the time given to complete a task or assignment, shorten an activity, or divide the activity into two or more segments.
- **Input:** Change the form or complexity of the information delivered to the learner (e.g., use books on tape, assign a reader, use a computer program, study in cooperative groups, use large print materials, use audiovisual materials, provide additional structure through the use of graphic organizers, outline material, or use step-by-step installments).
- **Output:** Change the form or complexity of the learner's response (e.g., use oral responses instead of written, demonstrate with explanation, draw, sing, graph, chart, web, tape response, or use a computer).
- **Conceptual/skill difficulty:** Change the skill level or the conceptual difficulty of the activity (i.e., use high-interest/low reading level materials, present with audiovisual support, read only for main idea instead of details, assign basic math problems instead of geometry, require in-depth study, perhaps by writing a play rather than reading a play).
- **Support:** Increase or decrease the amount of teacher and or student/peer support in the classroom (e.g., assign a note taker, assign a peer tutor, assign independent work, assign a cooperative group project with specialized roles, or provide cues and reminders).
- **Expectations:** Change the outcome expectations while using similar or same materials (e.g., write a short story instead of a play, write a sentence not a paragraph, identify number names instead of completing addition problems, name main character and setting instead of achieving comprehensive understanding of a story).
- **Alternative curriculum:** Use IEP goals and objectives as curricula that may widely vary from traditional academic curricula (e.g., use of adaptive switch, change body posture, practice life skills within the classroom such as buttoning, putting on coat/hat, tieing shoes, practice social skills during cooperative groups).

Modifications and adaptations have been used for many years in education, in the community, and in vocational settings. Another method of defining modifications is through the following five categories:

1. Using varied materials and devices
2. Adapting skill levels
3. Providing personal assistance
4. Adapting rules, requirements, or instructions
5. Adapting the physical environment

TABLE 9-5   Types of instructional modifications.

Use Materials and Devices

Use portable devices or materials which enhance an individual's performance. Items may be commercial or teacher made. Adaptive devices and communication tools as well as alternative text materials fall into this category.

Adapt Skill Sequences

Change the steps in a task to simplify or rearrange activities, take a long-term project and break it down into small pieces with a timeline, change the sequence in a job, rearrange the tools necessary for a job.

Use Personal Assistance

Use any type of verbal, physical, or supervisory support, peer buddies, tutors, personal assistants. The assistance may be necessary for long or short periods of time.

Adapt Rules

Modify the typical practices or procedures in an environment, complete every other problem on the math worksheet or dictate an answer, share a task or a job.

Adapt the Environment

Change the actual physical environment, move furniture, obtain smaller chairs, ramps, or wheel chair accessible facilities.

Source: Adapted from Ottlinger, K., & Kohlhepp, P. (1992). *Curricular adaptations: Accommodating the instructional needs of diverse learners in the context of general education.* Kansas State Board of Education.

Table 9-5 provides several examples of each type of modification.

Each model suggests several kinds of changes that can be made within the general education classroom. The list can become long and difficult to remember. One framework developed by Switlick and Stone (1992) has been useful to special educators in expanding their knowledge of the types of modifications and to general educators as they have developed and implemented modifications in their classrooms. The model contains four basic types of curricular and instructional modifications:

- Accommodations
- Adaptations
- Parallel instruction
- Overlapping instruction

Table 9-6 contains a concise definition and examples of each type. More lengthy discussion will be provided in the following sections. Examples will be provided to indicate how teachers can implement each type of modification in their classroom.

Accommodations

An accommodation is a modification to the delivery of instruction or a method of student performance that does not significantly change the content or the conceptual difficulty of the curriculum. Accommodations tend to be easier to make and implement within the general education classroom. Generally, accommodations will benefit many students within the class. Examples of accommodations for students with learning disabilities and behavior concerns abound. One excellent source is *The Pre-referral Intervention Manual,* which covers a range of observable classroom behaviors and provides lists of accommodations (McCarney & Wunderlich, 1988). One of the most complete sources of accommodations for students with learning disabilities is found in Fagen, Graves, and Tessier-Switlick (1984). In this study of accommodations, the authors surveyed over 200 general educators for "reasonableness." Reasonable was defined as including both the characteristics of feasibility and effectiveness. Since students with learning disabilities are found in general education classrooms with the highest frequency, a checklist of accommodations for students with learning disabilities, Checklist 9-2, can be found at the end of the chapter. Some helpful examples are provided in Table 9-7.

Accommodations can also be made to the physical environment and classroom activities that enable students with physical challenges to participate. This account from Laurie Dotterweich is very focused on accommodations for a student, Staci, with physical challenges.

As it turned out, Staci was a very independent, strong-willed child. She was able to tell us how to adapt each center for her. We lowered the art easel and bought lighter weight paint brushes. We poured glue onto a lid and used a q-tip to apply it to her art projects. She pushed the hollow blocks with her walker and then a friend would lift them for her. She lay on the floor to stack and build with the unit blocks and rolled to where she wanted to be. In housekeeping, she moved with her walker or held onto furniture to move around. In sand, she used her standing box to balance her as she stood and played. When she went to a center, she had her friends help her figure out ways to participate. She never had trouble participating.

During movement activities, she moved any way she could. She danced, wiggled, shook, and used her walker to move around. Though her movements were sometimes slow, she was always moving with us. We would always give her that little extra time if she needed it. After a while, the children knew to count slower or wait a minute more for Staci to catch up. It was so natural for them to do so. They would never think of playing a game or doing a movement activity without Staci.

TABLE 9-6   Curricular and instructional modification.

Accommodations

Definition: A modification to the delivery of instruction or method of student performance that does not significantly change the content or conceptual difficulty of the curriculum.

Examples:

- Listening to a taped recording of a novel.
- Circling every other word problem on a math worksheet.
- Providing for oral performance instead of written.

Adaptations

Definition: A modification to the delivery of instruction or method of student performance that changes the content or conceptual difficulty of the curriculum.

Examples:

- Providing picture word cards for key words in a story.
- Using a calculator to complete a math assignment.
- In a story activity the group reports on the main character, plot, subplots, setting, problem, resolution—this student reports on main characters and setting.

Parallel Instruction

Definition: A modification to the delivery of instruction or method of student performance that does not change the content area but does significantly change the conceptual difficulty of the curriculum.

Examples:

- Students are reading a story—this student is given a sheet with all or part of the story and asked to circle the A's or perhaps target words.
- Students are completing a math worksheet on fractions—this student is completing a counting from 1 to 10 worksheet.
- Students in citizenship/current events class are orally reading the newspaper and answering questions—this student orally reports three things remembered from listening to the others read.

Overlapping Instruction

Definition: A modification to the student performance expectations while all students take part in a shared activity or delivery of instruction that changes the content area and the conceptual difficulty of the curriculum.

Examples:

- Students are tape recording a rough draft of a play they are creating—this student uses an adaptive switch to activate the recorder and is working on holding up his head for increased amounts of time.
- Students are conducting a chemistry experiment in groups of six—this student is responsible to make sure everyone has a test tube and a worksheet.

Staci could write well. She was my best story writer because she would actually write sentences using inventive spelling. She used a marker instead of crayons because they required little pressure. She could move and pick up small objects and turn pages in a book. Again, it took slightly longer to do, but she was usually able to keep up. The children naturally waited for her before continuing.

TABLE 9-7   Reasonable classroom accommodations for students with learning disabilities.

Accommodations to modify the delivery of instruction:

- Use a multisensory approach.
- Use a highly structured format for presentation.
- Keep copy clear in printed materials.
- Assign a buddy reader or note taker.
- Review key points frequently.
- Reduce visual distractions.
- Use color coding to match materials and concepts.
- Provide students with a copy of the teacher's presentation notes.
- Highlight sections of text.
- Explain the purpose for reading.
- Post frequently misspelled words.
- Group operations in math or color code operations.
- Use manipulatives, pictures, life experience connections.
- Use oral and written directions.
- Talk slowly.
- Reduce writing requirements.
- Use a word bank.

Accommodations to assist students with organizational problems:

- Provide consistent daily routines.
- Keep work area clear.
- Record homework.
- Provide samples of finished product.
- Explain changes in routine.
- Provide transition time (time to organize).
- Assist with notebook organization and clean out.
- List materials needed.
- Review notes daily.
- Use graphic organizers.

Accommodations for student performance:

- Provide peer tutors for study.
- Use assisted writing, dictation.
- Allow for explanation during evaluation.
- Use self-checking and self-monitoring strategies.
- Use multisensory approaches in evaluation.
- Extend time.
- Use short answers, cues, word lists.
- Skip lines in draft or final copy.

Source: Adapted from Fagen, S., Graves, D., & Tessier-Switlick, D. (1984). *Promoting successful mainstreaming: Reasonable classroom accommodations for learning disabled students.* Rockville, MD: Montgomery County Public Schools.

Staci is very verbal and communicates well. She can work a computer and read simple books. She has wonderful math skills. She loves art and physical education. She loves playing on the playground most of all. The slide and tunnel are her favorites. She does need assistance, but we are more than happy to help her because she is so active and loves school. I wouldn't want her to just sit and watch and not want to do anything.

I quickly realized that I had worries because I did not know what to expect from Staci. I had no knowledge of physical handicaps. As soon as I met Staci and saw her in action, I knew I had nothing to worry about. I learned a great deal from Staci. She showed me that having a handicap does not mean you can't participate in an activity. It just means that you may do the activity in a different way. I did not change my class routine or the activities because of Staci. I didn't have to. Staci showed me how she could participate. She was my best resource. She did everything and as much as her classmates did last year. She had a typical kindergarten experience with her neighborhood friends.

I never saw Staci as different. She would not have allowed that. She was just another student in my class of twenty-five. Making accommodations became matter of fact. We didn't even think twice. There was nothing she wouldn't try to do. Her classmates accepted her completely. They often chose her to play with, wanted to sit with her at snack or circle time, invited her to birthday parties, and included her in all their activities.

Accommodations may also be made for students with behavioral challenges. Some examples are listed below:

- Provide a low rate of criticism. (Focus on positive feedback that is very specific for the individual assignment or behavior.)
- Provide information and behavioral specific feedback. (Make use of a checklist that is attached to the student's desk or that the student completes periodically during the class. A contract with specific behaviors listed may also be marked for each class or hour of the school day.)
- Use positively stated classroom rules that are taught and enforced. (Post in the room all of the things that students should do, such as stay in your seat, bring your materials to class, respect others while they are speaking, etc.)
- Employ time-out, occasional walks, and preventive behavior management strategies. (Assist the students to determine those times when they feel uncomfortable or possibly explosive, then provide them with a quiet setting, a walk, have them run an errand, or arrange a visit to the counselor. If the students can begin to identify when these behaviors will occur and preventive actions or strategies may be put in place, outbursts can be avoided. A time-out may be necessary when an outburst has occurred and the student needs to regain self-control. The time-out should be temporary and may, in some cases, need to be supervised by crisis support staff.)
- Establish predictable classroom routines. (Follow an agenda for the day that is posted in the room. When possible, keep the activities in a consistent order. Notify students before transitions so they will be prepared for the change.)
- Establish a procedure to deal with stress in the classroom. (Teach visual imagery techniques, send the student to visit the counselor or other mental health staff.)

Adaptation

Adaptations are modifications that change the content or the conceptual difficulty of the curriculum and extend to the instructional methodology as well. The extent of the change is greater and typically more time-consuming than accommodations which tend to change only the instructional methods. Adaptations can be made for many purposes. Selecting one or two basic concepts from a unit of study for a student with intellectual challenges involves changing the conceptual difficulty as well as some of the content. Changes such as this require the teacher to make further adaptations in the form of activities, the logistics within the classroom, and the student interactions. Adaptations rarely affect only one aspect of the classroom. An adaptation designed for behavioral reasons often involves shortening activities and adding variety in approaches to instruction. The adaptation may prove helpful to several students in the class, but would not be necessary for all of the students. Teachers must consequently subgroup students within the classroom enabling those who can progress to move on to the next activity or concept. This kind of organization is frequently present in the elementary classroom, but many times it is lacking in the secondary setting where students move through a series of different classes over the course of each day. At the middle school level, teachers have made great strides in varying activities within the class period more frequently and in planning for connections between the separate content areas. Both at the high school and at the middle school level, there still tends to be one lesson plan for the class. If variety exists in activities, it is planned for everyone (Fuchs et al., 1995; Ysseldyke, et al., 1990).

The actual differentiation of lessons for small groups and individual students is necessary to adapt effectively. Clearly the organizational structure of secondary school can limit the teacher's ability to make individual adaptations. It may be difficult to deliver three different lessons during a forty-five-minute period! The movement toward more flexible scheduling (double periods and academic blocks of extended time) for interdisciplinary teams that cross traditional content barriers can and will continue to do much to facilitate basic differentiation.

Adaptations vary widely depending on the needs of the students. Making adaptations to the academic program, especially given the current emphasis on educational accountability, makes teachers very uncomfortable. Teachers feel that all students in the class must reach the outcomes mandated by the state or required by Board of Education policy developers. Administrators have to assist teachers as they work with students with disabilities to determine which students require differentiated outcomes and will not be held responsible for the entire range of curricula. IEP goals and objectives may be used to measure student progress. Using the outcomes included on the IEP creates different expectations for student performance and accountability. The following examples indicate clearly that adaptations can be more time-consuming and complex, but are necessary for some students to be successful.

1. Individualized learning objectives for one or more students: Because learners acquire and apply knowledge at different rates and levels, small groups for instruction may be necessary as well as differentiated activities, homework, and evaluations.

2. Adapted or different instructional materials: Teachers use a variety of materials in the classroom. When text materials are too difficult, the teacher may have to search for materials at a lower reading level or rewrite portions of materials to enable some students to work independently in the classroom. The use of materials on tape and audiovisual materials to supplement the text materials may also be an option. Peer helpers can also be a support.

3. Spontaneous assistance is provided when students make a request: Students may need items read to them, or they may need to dictate a response during a class. Identifying a peer helper, instructional assistant, parent volunteer, or special educator to assist is helpful and may become critical in some instances. Providing prompts and cues that are built into the lesson can greatly improve student performance. Some students, due to organizational or behavioral difficulties, may need direct support during some activities that fellow classmates can complete independently.

4. Create an alternative activity when the planned lesson is too difficult or too easy for some of the students: This can be easy to do if students have been taught how to work in groups fairly independently. Implementing alternative activities may occasionally require an additional adult or peer helpers when groups need assistance.

An example of an adapted reading lesson that Bonni Rubin-Sugarman (1994) implemented with her second grade class may be helpful.

> *All of the students are reading the same literature-based story. Following the reading, students work in cooperative groups of three or four students. Each group gets comprehension questions ranging from recall through higher level thinking skills. Each student has one or two questions that are tailored to their own specific needs. As the group answers the questions, they are also sequencing the story. Once students have answered their own individual questions on a card in complete sentences, they share their answers with their group members. This is a way of checking their answers and getting feedback. The group's responsibility is to sequence the answers so they are retelling the story. Group work is shared with the class.*

A planning format may be useful to teachers making adaptations in the classroom. Figure 9-1 contains an example of an adaptation as well as a format that may be used or adapted to any classroom.

Parallel Instruction

Parallel instruction is actually a form of adaptation used to incorporate a functional curriculum approach into the classroom. Functional curricula includes teaching survival and life skills to students with mental retardation. (See Chapter 10 for further information on functional curricula and parallel instruction.) Students with cognitive challenges such as mild to moderate mental retardation may require a very basic academic program. Many basic academic activities can easily be implemented in a regular classroom. Parallel instruction requires that the basic content area be maintained for all students, but goes a step beyond what is usually considered when adapting instruction. For instance, as the class is reading a play and analyzing the characters, plot, setting, and the time period of the play, a student

Classroom Activities	Adaptation Analysis	Adaptations/Alterations

Example:
Date: Oct. 10 (weekly)
 	
Instructional Methods:
  Introduce vocabulary,
  peer practice
Instructional Staff: Teacher
	☐ No Changes
	☑ Instructional Methods
	☐ Environmental Conditions
	☑ Curricular Objectives
	☑ Instructional Materials
	☑ Personal Assistance
	☑ Alternative Activity
		Teacher distributes words, peers practice. Separate word lists for groups, Letter list for Julie, peer helper reviews letters with Julie, students find words in reading material, Julie finds letters in short paragraph and then copies the letters

Classroom Activities	**Adaptation Analysis**	**Adaptations/Alterations**
Date: Instructional Methods: Instructional Staff:	☐ No Changes ☐ Instructional Methods ☐ Environmental Conditions ☐ Curricular Objectives ☐ Instructional Methods ☐ Personal Assistance ☐ Alternative Activity	
Classroom Activities	**Adaptation Analysis**	**Adaptations/Alteration**
Date: Instructional Methods: Instructional Staff:	☐ No Changes ☐ Instructional Methods ☐ Environmental Conditions ☐ Curricular Objectives ☐ Instructional Materials ☐ Personal Assistance ☐ Alternative Activity	

FIGURE 9-1   Adaptation planning worksheet.

Source: Adapted from Ottlinger, K., & Kohlhepp, P. (1992). *Curricular adaptations: Accommodating the instructional needs of diverse learners in the content of general education.* Kansas State Board of Education.

or students may have the task of listening to the entire play, or a portion of the play, and determining who the main characters are and some basic identity characteristics. Another student may work on letter or word identification using excerpts from the play. As is readily apparent, the logistics of organizing the various activities can be challenging. Another adult or a peer helper may occasionally be necessary to provide an appropriate amount of personal support.

Another example might involve pairs of students working on math word problems. The students must read the problem, set up the mathematical equation, and solve the problem. In some of the pairs, students with mental retardation listen to the problem; their partner sets up the equation. The students with mental retardation solve the problem using only the information in the ones column. Their partner completes the problem (Rubin-Sugarman,

1994). The students are working with the same materials. However, one student is working on basic academics while the other is working on grade level curriculum.

As the teacher is demonstrating and teaching the students to write using cursive, he is also using parallel instruction. The majority of the students are watching the demonstration and practicing letter formation. Two students with physical challenges are watching the demonstration. Since they do not write, they are learning to read cursive. A word in manuscript is presented to them. Then the same word is presented in cursive. The students talk through the cursive letter formation and compare the two words.

Overlapping Instruction

Overlapping instruction is the modification of outcome objectives or expectations for students. As students participate in class activities, several students in the class may have totally different outcomes. Thus, the curricular goals are changed. The basic content may not be the same for all of the students. An example is a student in a high school biology class who has an objective to complete during a lab activity. Her objective is to distribute equipment, count the materials as they are distributed, and engage in positive social interactions as the tasks are completed. These objectives are vocational and social. All of the students are involved in the same classroom completing the same lab activity, but some have vastly different expectations. This concept of differentiation was developed by Giangreco (1993) who refers to it as *curriculum overlapping*. He describes a problem-solving process that can be used to creatively develop the interconnections necessary to plan for students with vastly different objectives within the same classroom. Giangreco also promotes student involvement in the creative problem-solving approach. Many activities, such as leaning to use adaptive equipment, may appear to have little to do with the curriculum in reading. Through overlapping the different outcomes in a common activity, the unnatural connections become natural and normal. The connection must be creatively developed. The example used in Table 9-6 indicates that as students follow along with a story on tape, the student with disabilities is learning to use an adaptive switch to activate the tape recorder for the group.

Differentiation of outcomes as is characteristic of overlapping instruction can be particularly helpful when a teacher is including students with significant disabilities into the classroom. A student whose objective is to make eye contact and acknowledge an interpersonal interaction using audible sounds can work on this task as other students are learning math. For example:

> *Jamie has a tray on his wheelchair. He holds on his tray the manipulatives the students are using during math. As students pick up their materials, they speak to Jamie. Jamie looks at each student and acknowledges the greeting with an audible sound. The same interaction occurs as students exchange materials and return materials.*

Overlapping instruction may occur in the classroom when students have any sort of different outcomes. This technique can be used when students with mild disabilities are present. For example, if a student with learning disabilities has been learning reading strategies, the outcome for this student may be to independently use the strategies. In history class, students are reading a letter written by a soldier during the Civil War. The majority of the students are completing the activity with the objective of understanding when, where, and how this first-hand account relates to their prior knowledge of the war. The student with learning disabilities is applying the strategies to the reading activity. The outcome for this student is analyzing their use of the strategies and exploring additional uses. The material is the same, but the objective is vastly different and may not involve the same type of content mastery.

CHECKLIST 9-1   Teacher Preplanning Questions.

I. Content:
1. What are the content requirements of the curriculum?
2. Which objectives are most essential?
3. Which students require a functional curriculum and need parallel instruction (same basic content but on a less taxing conceptual level)?
4. What alternative materials are available (including audiovisual materials)?
5. What rubrics will be used to measure student performance?
6. What role will students play in suggesting activities for the unit?
7. Will this material motivate students who are not usually interested in school?

II. Students Concerns:
1. Which students can effectively learn the material with little adaptation?
2. Which students require basic instruction on only the essential components?
3. Which students require alternative reading materials or taped readings, but can handle the concepts intellectually?
4. Which students can master the objectives and will require more depth or breadth in their study?
5. What behaviors will the students engage in during the unit activities?
6. Will personal assistance or natural supports be necessary for any students?

III. Instructional Methods:
1. Which instructional approaches are going to be most effective with the content?
2. Where will group activities fit into the plan?
3. Which students will benefit from peer tutoring and being a peer tutor?
4. How will the room arrangement affect the instructional plan?
5. How will groupings be determined?
6. What purpose will groupings serve?
7. How will student interest be sparked in introducing the unit?
8. Will students have an opportunity to interact?
9. What role will the teacher play during instruction (direct teaching, tutoring, facilitating, observing, etc.)?
10. What behaviors will the students engage in during the unit activities?
11. How will IEP goals and objectives be met through the planned activities?
12. How will student progress be monitored and evaluated (daily, weekly, for the unit?)
13. How will outcome expectations be communicated to the students?

Another example of overlapping instruction is portrayed below:

Kalli's learning outcomes emphasized her language and communication. While her academic goals related to the same content, they were less complex in nature. These goals included: (a) demonstrating her knowledge by selecting line drawings representing elements of the rainforest by eye-pointing to the desired option, (b) "reading" taped material aloud by activating a tape player with a pressure sensitive microswitch, (c) "presenting" information summarized by members of her group by recording, then playing back their responses. (Udvari-Solner, 1996, p. 251)

CHECKLIST 9-2   Reasonable Classroom Accommodation Checklist.

Accommodations to assist teachers in modifying the delivery of instruction:

_____ Use a multisensory approach.

_____ Use a highly structured format for presentations.

_____ Keep copy clear in printed materials.

_____ Assign a buddy reader or note taker.

_____ Present material in small, sequential steps.

_____ Review key points frequently.

_____ Reduce visual distractions.

_____ Use color coding to match materials and concepts.

_____ Seat student close to board or screen.

_____ Provide a quiet work area.

_____ Provide students with a copy of the teacher's presentation notes.

_____ Highlight sections of text.

_____ Teach book format.

_____ Explain the purpose for reading.

_____ Post frequently misspelled words.

_____ Group operations in math or color code operations.

_____ Verbalize steps in computation, discuss how answers were derived.

_____ Post a problem-solving sequence chart.

_____ Turn lined paper sideways for columns or use graph paper.

_____ Use a calculator.

_____ Use manipulatives, pictures, life experience connections.

_____ Use oral and written directions.

_____ Talk slowly.

_____ Use tape recorded directions, books, and other material.

_____ Reduce writing requirements.

_____ Use a word bank.

_____ Discuss written responses.

_____ Use graphic organizers.

CHECKLIST 9-2   Reasonable Classroom Accommodation Checklist.

Accommodations to assist students with organizational problems:

_____ Establish a daily routine.

_____ Keep work area clear.

_____ Record homework and post in room in a consistent spot.

_____ Provide samples of a finished product.

_____ Provide a list of all assignments given in each unit.

_____ Construct a timeline for long-term assignments.

_____ Allow time to get organized.

_____ Color code bookcovers.

_____ Assist with notebook organization.

_____ List materials needed for class and for assignments.

_____ Review notes daily.

_____ Provide a study guide.

_____ Teach strategies for reading and writing.

_____ Explain changes in routine.

Accommodations for student performance:

_____ Provide peer tutors for study.

_____ Use cooperative learning techniques.

_____ Use small group discussion.

_____ Assist with writing, dictation.

_____ Allow for explanation during evaluation.

_____ Use self-checking and self-monitoring strategies.

_____ Use multisensory approaches in evaluation.

_____ Extend time, and give untimed tests.

_____ Use of short answers, cues, word lists.

_____ Skip lines in draft or final copy.

_____ Allow class time to begin assignments.

_____ Give specific feedback.

_____ Use models or rubrics.

_____ Review before a test, give frequent quizzes, give sample questions.

_____ Provide a proof reading checklist.

_____ Use oral reports and other multisensory options for projects.

_____ Reduce writing requirements.

_____ Read the test to the student.

_____ Accept print or cursive.

_____ Tape answers to test.

_____ Orient to test format.

Conclusions

A great deal of thought and planning must be directed toward curricular and instructional modification, which begins with creativity and ends with logistics. The range of modification necessary in any one classroom can vary widely. The diversity in today's classroom mandates curricular and instructional modification to ensure successful achievement. There is an almost unlimited variety of modifications available to the teacher. Selection of appropriate modifications is dependent on individual student needs. However, the modifications made for one student usually benefit several students in the classroom. As teachers begin to learn about a practice modifying the curriculum and the methods of instruction, they begin to see the multitude of possibilities and begin to truly shape their classroom.

References

Association for Supervision and Curriculum Development. (1994). The well-rounded classroom: Applying the theory of multiple intelligences. *ASCD Update, 36*(8) 3, 5–6.

Baker, J., & Zigmond, N. (1990). Are regular education classes equipped to accommodate students with learning disabilities? *Exceptional Children, 56,* 515–526.

Clark, C., & Elmore, J. (1981). *Transforming curriculum in mathematics, science, and writing: A case study of teacher yearly planning.* (Research Series No. 99), East Lansing: Michigan State University, Institute for Research on Teaching. ERIC Document Reproduction Services No. ED 205 500.

Corno, L., & Snow, R. (1986). Adapting teaching to differences among individual learners. In M. Wittrock (Ed.), *Third handbook of research on teaching.* New York: Macmillan.

Fagen, S., Graves, D., & Tessier-Switlick, D. (1984). *Promoting successful mainstreaming: Reasonable classroom accommodations for learning disabled students.* Rockville, MD: Montgomery County Public Schools.

Fuchs, L., Fuchs, D., Hamlett, C., & Ferguson, C. (1992). Effects of expert system consultation within curriculum-based measurement using a reading maze task. *Exceptional Children, 58,* 436–450.

Fuchs, L., Fuchs, D., Hamlett, C., Phillips, N., & Karns, K. (1995). General educators' specialized adaptations for students with learning disabilities. *Exceptional Children, 61,* 440–459.

Gardner, H. (1987). *Frames of mind.* New York: Basic Books.

Giangreco, M. (1993). Using creative problem-solving methods to include students with severe disabilities in general education classroom activities. *Journal of Educational and Psychological Consultation, 4,* 113–135.

Gregorc, A. (1985). *Inside styles: Beyond the basics.* Maynard, MA: Gabriel Systems.

Grigorenko, E., & Sternberg, R. (1994). Thinking styles. In D. Saklosfske, & M. Zeidner (Eds.), *International handbook of personality and intelligence.* New York: Plenum.

Heron, E., & Jorgensen, C. (1995). Addressing learning differences right from the start. *Educational Leadership, 52*(4), 56–58.

Holland, J. (1973). *Making vocational choices: A theory of careers.* Englewood Cliffs, NJ.: Prentice-Hall.

Janney, R., Snell, M., Beers, M., & Raynes, M. (1995). Integrating students with moderate and severe disabilities into general education classes. *Exceptional Children, 61,* 425–439.

Jenkins, J., Jewell, M., Leicester, N., O'Connor, R., Jenkins, L., & Troutner, N. (1994). Accommodations for individual differences without classroom ability groups: An experiment in school restructuring. *Exceptional Children, 60,* 344–358.

McCarney, S., & Wunderlich, K. (1988). *The prereferral intervention manual.* Columbus, MO: Hawthorne Educational Services.

Ottlinger, K., & Kohlhepp, P. (1992). *Curricular adaptations: Accommodating the instructional needs of diverse learners in the context of general education.* Kansas State Board of Education.

Poplin, M., & Stone, S. (1992). Paradigm shifts in instructional strategies: From reductionism to holistic/constructivism. In W. Stainback & S. Stainback (Eds.), *Controversial issues confronting special education.* Boston: Allyn & Bacon.

Putnam, J., Spiegel, A., & Bruininks, R. (1995). Future directions in education and inclusion of students with disabilities: A delphi investigation. *Exceptional Children, 61,* 553–576.

Renzulli, J., & Smith, L. (1978). *Learning styles inventory.* Storrs, CT: Creative Learning Press.

Rubin-Sugarman, B. (1994). Personal correspondence.

Schumm, J., Vaughn, S., Haager, D., McDowell, J., Rothlein, L., & Saumell, L. (1995) General education teacher planning: What can students with learning disabilities expect? *Exceptional Children, 61,* 335–352.

Sternberg, R. (1994). Allowing for thinking styles. *Educational Leadership, 53*(3), 36–40.

Switlick, D., & Stone, J. (1992). Curriculum modification. Unpublished course materials. Johns Hopkins University.

Tarver, S. (1992). Direct instruction. In W. Stainback & S. Stainback (Eds.), *Controversial issues confronting special education.* Boston: Allyn & Bacon.

Udvari-Solner, A. (1996). Examining teacher thinking: Constructing a process to design adaptations. *Remedial and Special Education, 17,* 245–254.

Wesson, C. (1991). Curriculum-based measurement and two models of follow-up consultation. *Exceptional Children, 57,* 246–257.

Wood, J. (1992). *Adapting instruction for mainstreamed and at-risk students.* New York: Macmillan.

Ysseldyke, J., Thurlow, M., Wotruba, J., & Nania, P. (1990). Instructional arrangements: Perceptions from general education. *Teaching Exceptional Children,* Summer, 4–8.

Chapter 10

Integrating Specialized Curricula

DIANE M. SWITLICK

◆ ADVANCE ORGANIZER ◆

Integrating specialized curricula may become necessary and appropriate when a teacher has students for whom the general education curriculum is not appropriate. Within the classroom, the student outcomes for those students with more intensive needs typically may be very different. This chapter highlights three major areas of specialized curricula: functional or fundamental life skills curricula; strategically delivered curricula; and social-emotional curricula, which include conflict resolution. Each curriculum area is described, and sources are provided for the reader. Examples of integrated activities are included to serve as models and to foster ideas for integration.

Once there was a little caterpillar who lived in an oriental rug. As he crawled around the rug, he heard other caterpillars discussing the relative merits of specific colors and lines on the rug. Some caterpillars claimed that red was the most beautiful color and that it held the key to solving the pattern. Others insisted, "Oh no! Green is the key." The discussions became heated, and caterpillars with similar views banded together to exalt their viewpoints and to put down viewpoints. The little caterpillar was confused by all the discussion and unable to decide which group was right. As he nestled in his cocoon, he still heard their voices shouting. "Red!" "Green!" "Brown!" Oh, how he wished he knew which group was right!

Soon, the little caterpillar became a butterfly. He flapped his wings and began to rise above the rug. As he approached the ceiling, he looked down. He was amazed! On the rug, he saw a beautiful design. Although some colors and lines were more prominent than others, he noticed that all parts were essential to make the design complete.

Educators, like caterpillars, often focus so intently on one part of the instructional design, that they forget the relevance of the other parts. If we, like the caterpillar, achieve the level of maturity required to rise above the ideological debates, perhaps we can appreciate the value of integrating a variety of approaches to make the instructional design complete.

Mercer, in press

The parameters of any student's education can be broadly characterized by the environment in which learning occurs (e.g., general education class, community), the student's program (e.g., learning outcomes, curricular content), and instructional supports (e.g., personnel, peer tutoring, materials, equipment, instructional approaches/adaptions).

Giangreco & Putnam, 1991

Curricula are often viewed as lengthy documents developed at the local or state level that define the scope and sequence of content identified as appropriate for typical students at each grade level. In addition to the curricula developed for students without disabilities, there are numerous curriculum packages available commercially for both students with and without disabilities, but few have a solid research base. Curricula addressing a range of content have been specifically designed for students with more specialized disabilities whose needs differ significantly from typical students and for whom traditional curricula is ineffective or inappropriate. When teachers provide instruction in a heterogeneous classroom, the needs of individual students may extend beyond that which can be addressed through modifications to the traditional content-based curricula such as history, science, and English. Specialized curricula may be a functional or community-based curriculum for students with mental retardation (Brown et al., 1979), strategy-based curricula for students with learning disabilities (Deshler & Schumaker, 1988), or social skill and behavioral curricula for students with emotional disabilities (Heflin, Borenson, Grossman, Huette, & Ilgen, 1993).

The student's planning team comprised of the general and special educators as well as other service providers must determine the extent of integration possible when meshing content-based curricula with a student's need for specialized curricula. Specialized curricula should be considered only for those students that cannot benefit from the general education curricula or require a supplement to meet the goals on their IEP. The team must determine an individual curriculum for each child and then decide how this curriculum overlaps with the general education curriculum and what opportunities are present or can be created to integrate the two. These decisions must be made on an individual basis for each student. Some of the specialized curricula may be presented to students in a special class setting. However, the links to the general education setting must also be present to ensure the generalization of the learning to this real life setting.

Chapter 9 describes several methods of modifying the curricula for students with disabilities. This chapter will emphasize parallel instruction and overlapping instruction as a primary means of linking specialized curricular needs to the general education classroom. The reader may recall that parallel instruction is a form of adaptation used to incorporate a functional curriculum approach into the classroom. Overlapping instruction is the modification of outcome objectives or expectations for the students. Several examples are shared to spark ideas, provide models, and suggest sources for further study. The focus of this chapter is not to mandate that specialized curricula be integrated totally into the general education setting. Some portion of a student's school day, the maximum amount appropriate, should be spent with age-appropriate peers in general education. For students with severe disabilities, this percentage may range between 30 and 100 percent of the school day. The percentage varies as the student progresses from elementary to middle school and from middle to high school.

Specialization versus Integration

> *The increasing diversity of learners in general education requires a variety of instructional methods to address individual needs. Ideological rigidity that prevents teachers from exploring and implementing instructional options reduces the chances for student success. In contrast, employing a range of instructional approaches empowers teachers and students with choices that promote learning.*
>
> Mercer, Lane, Jordan, Allsopp, & Eisele, in press

The mixture of general education classroom instruction and specialized instruction outside of the general education setting must be flexible and may vary widely both over time and based on individual needs. For example, a child with moderate to severe mental retardation may participate in the general education setting 100 percent of the time during the elementary school years with significant modification of the general education curricula. Related services such as speech/language, occupational, and physical therapy may well be integrated into the classroom activities, recess, and special subjects such as art, music, and physical education. Functional curriculum goals such as communication skills, social skills, and daily living skills may be effectively blended into the daily classroom instruction and routines. When this child reaches middle school, some specialized instruction may take place in the community (life skills in a restaurant or grocery store), on the way to school (travel training), or in the school office (vocational skills). In high school the primary focus of instruction may be life skills and vocational training with the student attending only two to three general education classes. Integrating the objectives of the specialized curricula into the general education setting remains crucial to the attainment of the desired adult outcomes. During the final years of public education, which usually occurs during the age range of 18 to 21, the student focuses almost totally on independent living and vocational goals. At this point integration goals are focused on the community.

A very different pattern may occur for a student with learning disabilities. This child may spend the primary years of elementary school in the general education program. Before the disability is identified, the student may have benefited from the adaptations made by the teacher in the general education classroom. Once the academic workload becomes more demanding and a lack of progress is identified even with these accommodations, the student may be identified for special education services and provided with a specialized strategy-based instructional program for a part of the school day. This may begin in the upper elementary grades. The separate instruction may continue into middle school and high school. It is essential that the strategies taught in the specialized setting be incorporated into the general education setting to ensure generalization and appropriate application. During the high school years, the specialized instruction should also include self-advocacy training. As the student's ability to apply the strategies increases, less time needs to be spent in the specialized setting.

Another possible pattern may exist for a student with serious emotional disturbance. A student may again begin school unidentified in the general educational program. If the student becomes withdrawn or aggressive and the general education setting is deemed inappropriate, the student may be removed for part or all of the school day. Some students require a therapeutic milieu, a safe and stable environment, to learn coping behaviors and expand their behavioral repertoire, while others require a highly structured setting where social and behavioral skills are taught explicitly and consequences are immediate. As growth and improvement is documented the student may be moved back to the home school, but may still spend a large portion of the day in a structured environment. As confidence grows, the student spends more time in the general education classroom with specific provisions for crisis intervention, support, and mental health services.

Each example presents a flexible system of moving in and out of the general education setting. This flexibility is not easy to achieve. It is dependent on several factors:

- Teacher attitude toward the disability (especially emotional disabilities)
- Team teaching and collaboration between the general educator and the special educator
- Student-centered (not content-centered) instruction in the general education setting
- Integration of specialized curricular objectives in the general education setting

Functional Curricula

> *Meeting functional curriculum needs in general education classes requires team effort, creativity, and flexibility.*
>
> Field, LeRoy, & Rivera, 1994

Functional curricula refers to instruction that is age-appropriate and functional or useful in daily living. Most functional curricula are designed to meet the needs of students who have moderate to severe mental retardation, but many teachers have seen the benefit of functional approaches for a range of students, even those without disabilities. The functional curriculum has a major advantage over more developmental approaches because it incorporates higher expectations for students with disabilities (Rainforth, York, & Macdonald, 1992). Developmental approaches tend to teach tasks in a developmental sequence whether or not they are age-appropriate. The functional approach tends to focus on the usefulness or application of age-appropriate content and skills. There is an underlying theme of functionality that allows for the development of units such as domestic skills, basic academics, daily living skills, and vocational skills. However, the specific content for any one student is largely idiosyncratic. There are no established criteria for selection of relevant units or activities. Many curricula have been formally validated for use with children and adults with disabilities. Validation typically means that the content was found to be usable and the objectives were achievable (Rainforth et al. 1992). Most curriculum models focus on knowledge and skills and leave the selection of the methodology for instruction and the environment for teaching entirely up to the student's planning team. Some of the better known models include a community-referenced curriculum, *Teaching to Transition,* (Smith & Schloss, 1988); *Community Living Skills: Taxonomy* (Denver, 1988); *Hawaii Transition Project* (1987); and *Life Centered Career Education (LCCE) Curriculum Program* (Brolin, 1991). The *Life Centered Career Education Curriculum Program* may be the most comprehensive package available to the secondary teacher. The model is organized around three major domains: Daily Living, Personal-Social, and Occupational Guidance and Preparation. The curriculum targets a total of twenty-two adult living competencies. Many of the commercial curricula available focus on students with severe disabilities and assume that the general education curricula is appropriate for all others (Clark, 1994).

However, many teachers would welcome ideas and activities designed for students with mild to moderate cognitive disabilities. Selection of appropriate units and activities from any curriculum is best determined using an ecological approach. This approach reflects characteristics of both the individual student and the environment in which the skills will be used (Brown et al., 1979). Planning always begins with the targeted life goals for the individual student as the final outcome as outlined in Chapter 7. The student's planning team must then determine available environments, which may include the school, the home, the community, or the work site. Strengths and weaknesses are considered along with necessary next steps to reach the desired outcome. Table 10-1 provides a description of various environments or the setting for instruction along with the domains or content areas most appropriate for study. Consideration of these environments opens our minds to a wide range of instructional opportunities and to the concept that these sites may be equally applicable to all students. The major difference resides in the fact that students with mental retardation require direct instruction in the setting in which the skill will be used to gain proficiency. Preparing students for adult life after leaving school is dependent on real life, community-based experiences that ensure learning and generalization. Activities are planned with family for application in the home environment and with general educators for generalization to the school setting. Only through this multiple application is generalization realized.

Several examples are provided to define various methods of curriculum integration. Examples are described at the elementary, middle, and high school level. This organization

TABLE 10-1　　**Ecological approach to curricula development.**

Environment	Description
Domestic	Student's life in and around his or her home—may include maintaining a home as in cleaning, cooking, clothing care, or using facilities; self-care and personal hygiene; personal health and safety; hobbies and backyard activities
School	Students between the age of 5 and 18—general education classroom; activities and skills as well as content in typical curricula and basic academics; consider also library, office, health room, hallway, playground or gymnasium, sports, school dances, clubs; Students over age 18—community college; communication, interpersonal, and vocational skills
Work site	Environments in which people of the same age without disabilities are employed; vocational, job skills, responsibilities and social skills; supported employment
Community	Environments include transportation systems, streets, sidewalks, businesses, public service agencies, stores, churches, arcades, malls and other community centers, sports facilities; may differ according to age or priority for instruction; Travel training, money skills, shopping, communication skills, citizenship, following directions, hobbies, entertainment

is used only to facilitate application to the school organization itself, which differs at these age levels, not to indicate functional curricula is differentiated by grade level or by school level.

Elementary Level

Comparing the environments described in Table 10-1 to the elements of instruction in the typical curricula may seem difficult. There may not be readily obvious connections. Examples are helpful to begin to see that there is a great deal of overlap, and thus, there are many opportunities for integration. Table 10-2 depicts events in a kindergarten classroom and the specific examples of functional activities that have been integrated into the school day. The similarity in content and routines for general education and the functional activities is striking at this age level. However, the differences in curricular emphasis increase markedly as students get older.

Table 10-3 outlines activities in a fifth grade classroom where students are engaged in highly academic tasks. Two students following the functional curriculum are involved largely in basic academics using similar content and materials. Examples of parallel instruction occur in language arts and reading and in math. The differentiation of activities is facilitated through grouping practices, adult and peer support, and the occupational therapist who is present in the room during social studies. During social times, social objectives are the focus. Science serves as an example of overlapping instruction when typical students are learning scientific method and conducting experiments and the two students with disabilities are participating in the same activity, but they have different objectives such as following directions, communication skills, and behavioral expectations.

TABLE 10-2   Kindergarten program.

Time	General Education Activities	Functional Skills
8:30	Arrival, hang up coats, free play, using bathroom, teacher greets students	Walk independently from bus to room, button, zip coat, place gloves and hat in cubby, greet other students and teacher, use bathroom, wash hands
9:00	Opening activity (whole group) take attendance, calendar, weather, sharing, classroom jobs, unit theme	Maintain eye contact with teacher, listen without distracting self or others, demonstrate good posture, respond when spoken to
9:20	Story reading by teacher, discussion	Listen without interrupting, show understanding of names, objects, people, and animals, respond when spoken to
9:40	Art, music, or PE activities—rotation of courses	Speak clearly and audibly, name body parts, use action words, match colors and shapes, express feelings appropriately, participate in exercise, express preferences for hobbies and interests, participate in group activities, use a variety of art materials
10:30	Table time (group work) hands-on cutting and pasting, sequencing, fine motor	Work appropriately in group with a partner, greet other students, fine motor skills, apply paste
10:40	Snack—wash hands, prepare snack, set up table, share, use manners, help clean up	Wash hands, prepare snack, set up table, share, use manners, help clean up, initiate conversation
11:10	Recess/free play–choose indoor activity or go outside, preparation for dismissal	Play independently and with others, share toys, express feelings, use social skills, use bathroom, wash hands, collect items to take home, get hat, gloves, and coat, dress, button, zip, walk independently to the bus

Middle School Level

The middle school provides a blend of experimental academics, exploratory arts electives, with a student-centered team support approach. This environment allows for the integration of functional skills in the general education classroom as well as in the community setting. Close collaboration is a necessity between the general and special education teachers. Many schools have developed their own version of a curriculum matrix to plan for the integration of the functional curriculum. Table 10-4 provides an example of a matrix (Field et al., 1994). The matrix can be designed and adapted to the school and individual student easily. Across the top, the activities that occur each day are listed. Along the side, the actual IEP objectives may be listed. The resulting boxes may be as large as necessary to contain checks or specific notes on implementation plans if desired. Fields and colleagues describe the day as follows:

TABLE 10-3   Fifth grade program.

Time	General Education Activities	Functional Skills
8:15	Arrival	Greetings, social skills, hang up coat, preparing materials
8:30	Language arts and reading Reading groups and LA Centers	Following directions, basic academics, letter formation and identification, word identification, survival reading signs and symbols, peer reading and listening skills
10:30	Current events, sharing, discussion	Listening skills, presenting to a group, awareness of weather and news
11:00	Lunch	Hand washing, following directions, eating independently, cleaning up, social skills
11:25	Recess	Dressing (coat), gross motor skills, leisure activities and sports, group games, communication skills
11:45	Math centers and small group instruction	Number identification, money identification
12:45	Social-studies centers and small group discussion	Occupational therapist works on fine motor activities—cutting, coloring, letter formation using classroom materials
1:30	Science experiment and lab log completion	Communication skills, participates in group, listening, following directions, taking turns, appropriate behavior and verbal response
2:15	Clean up, preparation for dismissal	Washing, cleaning up, dressing, communication skills, following directions

1. Homeroom is a time for peer support, getting organized, and collaboration between the general and special educator to prepare accommodations. A Circle of Friends is built into this time. (See Chapter 14 for more information on Circle of Friends.)
2. Content area integration relies on the use of accommodations and adaptations to the content in the general education instruction. The adaptations may be any of the following:

   • Different format for presentation
   • Same content, but less covered
   • Abbreviated sequence in content
   • Partial participation or supported participation in selected activities
   • Target the same skills but use different materials
   • Different skill level using the same materials
   • Participate in the same activity with different objectives or outcomes

Communication between the teachers and the home is critical in promoting the development and generalization of the daily living skills. Family input on skill attainment is a critical element in assessing progress. Field trips into the community two to three days a

TABLE 10-4 **Middle school curriculum matrix.**

IEP Goals	HOMEROOM	ENGLISH	SOCST	PHYSED	LUNCH	READING	ART	SCIENCE	MATH	MEDIA	TRANS	STORE	OFFICE
	General Education Program									Other Environments			
Speak in front of group	X	X	X					X					
Initiate peer conversations	X	X	X	X	X	X	X	X	X	X	X	X	X
Build money skills	X			X				X			X	X	
Ride bus independently											X		
Basic reading		X	X			X				X	X	X	X
Basic writing	X	X	X			X				X	X		X
Math calculation			X	X	X		X	X	X			X	
Gross motor coordination				X	X								

week facilitate community-based skill development as well as generalization and application of basic academics and daily living skills.

Because the general education curriculum divides information into separate content areas, the interdisciplinary approach to content delivery has become increasingly popular in middle schools to enhance learning outcomes for all students. The interdisciplinary approach mirrors more closely the real life application of knowledge. Some teachers have taken this approach one step further and incorporated community-based lessons for all of their students. This allows spontaneous real life problem solving to naturally arise that can only be simulated in the classroom. Beck, Broers, Hogue, Shipstead, & Knowlton (1994) developed a model for community-based instruction involving all students. Based on individual needs, students with and without disabilities participate in small group excursions into the community. The content themes covered during these trips range from safety, shopping, comparing prices, money skills, appropriate behavior, and courtesy. The special educator accompanies the small groups into the community with differentiated objectives for the participating students. Whole class trips are also planned to the zoo and to a farm. The benefits of this program were increased motivation for the students without disabilities, increased interaction between students with and without disabilities, and positive responses from teachers and parents (Beck et al., 1994).

High School Level

Once students reach high school age, the majority of the instructional time may be spent in community settings. Integration of the functional skills into the general education program is still a crucial factor in maintaining social relationships and ensuring generalization of the skills being taught. Table 10-5 provides an example of a weekly schedule for a high school student with mental retardation. The student participates in a general education schedule through lunch time each day. The student's schedule includes several classes that are part of the general education curriculum. The teachers adapt the instruction in collaboration with the special educator to foster the development and application of the functional curriculum. During horticulture, the student learns basic care of plants and types of plants. The course materials are adapted to facilitate practice of basic academics. Similar or the same materials are used for basic reading. Some activities are adapted for basic math practice. The goal of following oral directions is also emphasized. In home economics, the student takes part in cooking activities with a group of students to facilitate practice of measuring, kitchen safety, survival skills, and cooperation in a group. When the class moves on to sewing, the student will have a specialized project designed for him to learn darning and button sewing. In physical education, the student participates in the activities along with other students. The games and sports are adapted by the physical therapist in collaboration with the teacher. Similar activities are reinforced in a community setting during the afternoon leisure activities. Changing and personal hygiene become another focus during physical education class. During the fourth period, the student has varied work experiences within the school.

TABLE 10-5   High school program: Semester I.

Periods	Monday	Tuesday	Wednesday	Thursday	Friday
Homeroom 7:25–7:40	Homeroom: Organization, dressing, locker				
Period 1 7:45–8:30	Horticulture (basic academics)	Horticulture	Horticulture	Horticulture	Horticulture
Period 2 8:35–9:20	Home economics (cooking, sewing basic academics)	Home economics	Home economics	Home economics	Home economics
Period 3 9:25–10:10	Physical ed. (gross motor, dressing, hygiene)	Physical ed.	Physical ed.	Physical ed.	Physical ed.
Period 4 10:15–11:00	Work experience—office (basic academics, communications, folding, stapling)	Work experience—Office (basic academics, communications, folding, stapling)	Work experience Biology lab (basic academics, sorting, counting)	Work experience Library (basic academics, sorting, filing, communications)	Work experience Library (basic academics, sorting, filing, communications)
Lunch 11:00–11:30	Lunch at school (social skills)	Lunch at school (social skills)	Lunch at restaurant (social skills, money)	Lunch at school (social skills)	Lunch at school (social skills)
Community 1:35–3:00	Community-based Instruction (travel training, work in office at medical center)	Community-based Instruction (travel training, work in office at medical center)	Community-based instruction (travel training, domestic-cleaning shopping, cooking)	Community-based Instruction (travel training, leisure activities recreation center)	Community-based instruction (Travel training, variable activities trips, chores)
After school		Special Friends Club		Swim Team Manager	

Basic academics and following procedures and directions are emphasized. Lunch is also an instructional activity for the student that involves using money, counting change, selecting nutritious meals, and using effective communication skills. The afternoon community-based activities are varied and involve a range of community activities and work experiences. Using public transportation and independence in the community are emphasized as is problem solving in real life situations.

After school the student participates in extracurricular activities. He is manager of the swim team, which allows for social time, communication skills, counting activities, distributing equipment, following directions, and swimming.

Some schools have implemented programs to facilitate communication and social time between students with and without disabilities. One method of accomplishing this is to establish a Circle of Friends for the student with disabilities and promote after school outings with the members of their circle. Another method is to provide an elective subject for students without disabilities to increase their understanding of disabilities. Students taking this class can join a Special Friends Club, which meets weekly and fosters interaction between students with and without disabilities.

A different approach has been taken in some schools in which the staff has incorporated life skills instruction into academic classes for all students. An example of a high school science course was developed by Helmke, Havekost, Patton, & Polloway (1994). They were interested in creating innovative curriculum options for students with learning disabilities, mental disabilities, and behavioral disorders. They began with science because life skills integration in that content area was most obvious to them. Some topics included were locating and using weather information, learning about illness and treatment methods, and a range of topics on physical and emotional health. Problem-solving skills and occupations in the health field were also emphasized. "Life skills instruction can occur in any instructional setting, should be a part of all students' program, and should reflect their transition needs" (Helmke, et al., 1994, pp. 52–53).

Strategically Delivered Curriculum

> *Only if teachers and students learn new strategies, develop new attitudes, and cooperate can the inclusion of all students in regular secondary classrooms benefit everyone.*
>
> Schumaker & Deshler, 1995

To enable students to become self-directed learners, teachers must provide opportunities for students to learn strategies and then become proficient in understanding where, when, and how to use them. This involves students in monitoring their own performance, becoming more aware of their relevant existing knowledge, and using an array of effective learning strategies (Wood, Woloshyn, & Willoughley, 1995). Students with learning disabilities lack knowledge of necessary strategies for learning and are primarily passive learners who lack the process skills necessary to handle the large quantities of information, required especially at the secondary school level (Schumaker & Deshler, 1995). Students can learn to be strategic learners when direct instruction is provided in the learning strategies in their special and general education classes (Deshler & Schumaker, 1988). Strategic learning objectives becomes specialized curriculum when the objectives for student achievement become the strategy itself and not the curriculum content. This is crucial for some students. (For further information on the research and methods of designing strategy-based instruction the reader is directed to Chapter 11.) The critical point emphasized here is the need to integrate strategy-based instruction as an effective teaching methodology in the general education classroom. While all students benefit from strategically delivered instruction, students with learning disabilities may require much more extensive instruction in this area outside of their general education class. The strategy must be presented, modeled, and a substantial number of opportunities must be provided to practice and master the strategy. Figure 10-1 outlines the process of explicit instruction necessary for strategic learning. This chart was developed as a teacher training tool by Bergman & Schuder (1986). There is clear evidence that learning strategies will not have a significant impact on a student's success if the instruction is not intensive and extensive (Pressley, Goodchild, Fleet, Zajchowski, & Evans, 1987; Slavin, 1989). The direct instruction must be followed by discussion on the usefulness and application of the strategy. Students have to understand what a strategy is and why it is useful. This knowledge provides the basic motivation for students to learn and internal-

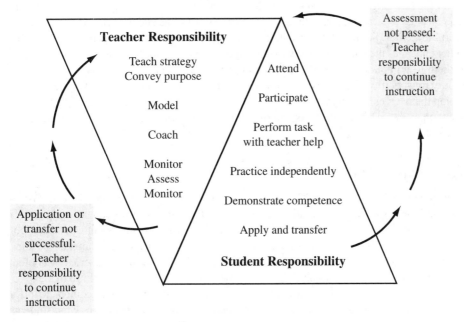

FIGURE 10-1   Model for strategy-based instruction.

Source: Adapted from Bergman, J., & Schuder, T. (1986). Unpublished training materials. Rockville, MD: Montgomery County Public Schools.

ize the strategy. Accompanying this direct instruction is the need to apply the strategy in content-based classes. Without this direct application, the strategy is not effectively generalized to settings other than special education. Thus, the general educator must become a process teacher as well as a content teacher (Deshler & Schumaker, 1988; Weinstein, Ridley, Dahl, & Weber, 1989).

Most strategies are a highly organized and sequential group of skills combined to facilitate the understanding, organizing, and remembering of information. Because of the organized nature of the strategy, it must be embedded in content delivery, use, and evaluation. This is not always an easy task for the teacher. Communication among staff is crucial to the integration of learning strategies in the general education setting. The optimum situation occurs when a school staff as a collaborative group determine the strategies to be emphasized and agree to integrate strategies consistently. If each teacher implements their own set of strategies, the benefits will be sorely diminished due to the lack of consistency. A multitude of learning strategies are described in the literature. Many of these strategies are more simplistic then the strategy-based instruction discussed in Chapter 11. However, they represent strategies that should be a part of effective instruction in all classrooms. Some are specifically designed for students with disabilities. Several examples of possible strategically delivered curricula are outlined below along with ideas for integration.

The types of learning strategies that are frequently taught in schools include paraphrasing, summarizing, visualization, thinking aloud, problem solving, decision making, transforming information into a new form such as chart or graph, and using compare and contrast methods. An example of strategic instruction might be, "while presenting information on the defining characteristics of colonization, the social studies teacher can prompt students to use a paraphrasing strategy to renew the key points and a visual imagery strategy to form a mental picture of representative colonies" (Schumaker & Deshler, 1995). This teacher enhances the students ability to understand and remember the information by teaching them to paraphrase the reading into their own words. The teacher also enhances the memory for specific colonies by attaching the name to some mental picture that the students develop themselves. Thus, the teacher has incorporated two learning strategies directly into the lesson to facilitate the students continued use of the strategies and to increase mastery of the content.

Organizational Strategies

Many students who are behaviorally and cognitively challenged have great difficulty organizing and understanding information. The *Content Enhancement Series* was designed for this specific purpose. The use of graphic and advance organizers, unit organizers, and highlighters can significantly improve student performance (Lenz, Brogrin, Schumaker, Deshler, & Bowdah, 1994; Schumaker, Deshler, & McKnight, 1991). By using a series of content enhancers, teachers are able to organize and present course content in a fashion that explicitly teaches organization of information. The framework connects new content to prior knowledge and builds in concept mastery. Teachers must think deeply about what students need to know, select the central concepts that provide the best organization for the information, identify the relationships among the concepts, select and use instructional techniques that enhance content, and present the content in a manner that actively involves the students.

The *Content Enhancement Series* (Lenz, Marrs, Schumaker, & Deshler, 1993) includes the following materials:

- The Lesson Organizer Routine
- The Unit Organizer Routine
- The Course Organizer Routine
- The Reorganizer Routine
- The Chapter Survey Routine
- The Concept Mastery Routine
- The Concept Anchoring Routine
- The Concept Comparison Routine
- The Recall Enhancement Routine

The materials contain visual organizers that display the information considered important. Teachers not only use the structured materials to plan, but they also present the routines to the students and use them frequently in class. These techniques allow teachers to highlight the critical points within the content and to link related points. Students begin to use organizers of their own following extended exposure, discussion, and use of external organizers.

Reading Strategy

> *Seeing high-risk students select and use appropriate strategies while reading independently is tremendously satisfying...*
>
> Bergman & Schuder, 1993

When students understand the reading and thinking process, they become more effective readers. The importance of reading and writing instruction cannot be underestimated. Much of today's performance-based assessment is based on the students ability to use strategic learning behaviors. Dixon and Rossi (1995) have developed a reading strategy that can be implemented in any general education classroom. An overview of the strategy is depicted in Figure 10-2. The teacher introduces the strategy and then picks a short reading selection. The students read the selection and generate questions. The questions serve as the material to be sorted and labeled. Students receive direct instruction in the types of questions as the teacher presents the types and models the sorting process.

During the second phase, the teacher models a discussion group. The students have already read a selection and generated questions. The discussion is used to categorize and label the questions. Social skills or discussion group etiquette is presented and modeled during this phase. Modeling may continue for two weeks to two months depending on the progress of the students.

Phase III allows students to work independently in small groups to apply the strategy. Groups share their results. If the students have difficulty, the group may return to Phase II. Students with learning disabilities may require additional practice either in the classroom

Phase I

　Learn to ask and label questions.

What	Fact
Where	Inference
When	Opinion
How	
Why	

Phase II

　Model role of discussion leader

　　Read question.

　　Ask what type of question.

　　Ask how do you know, give reason.

　　Ask can we agree on the label for the question.

　　Summarize group discussion.

Phase III

　Students operate independently in small groups.

　　Ask questions.

　　Discuss and analyze questions.

　　Share discussions.

FIGURE 10-2   Implementation process: Reading strategy.

Source: Adapted from Dixon, J., & Rossi, J. (1995). Directors of their own learning: A reading strategy for students with learning disabilities. *Teaching Exceptional Children, 27* (2), 10–14.

or in a specialized setting to achieve mastery. The students lean to analyze reading material. Comprehension is increased, and the follow-up may take any form. This reading strategy can be applied to any reading selection the teacher is using in any content area.

　Another example of a reading strategy is the Students Achieving Independent Learning (SAIL) program (Bergman & Schuder, 1993). This strategic learning model is designed to explicitly teach students how to read. Strategies were taught to mesh with the stages of reading: getting ready to read, before reading, while reading, and after reading.

　Getting ready to read involves students in setting personal goals for reading and provides a basic understanding of the reading process. Reading for gist is emphasized to ensure that students understand that comprehension is a major focus of the reading process.

　Before reading students are involved in selecting their own reading material. They are introduced to different types of text, story structure, and genre. In approaching difficult text, students are encouraged to use background knowledge and text context clues in predicting the content of the story or reading selection.

　While reading students are taught a set of four monitoring strategies: Predict-verify-decide, visualize-verify-decide, summarize-verify-decide, and think aloud. As students apply these strategies, teachers ask students to support their responses with examples from the text along with their rationale. Because the goal is independent reading, students are taught strategies to use in decoding difficult words. The three strategies taught do not interfere with the flow of reading and thus, are less likely to interrupt the reading process. These strategies are guess the word, ignore the word and continue reading, or go back and reread the section.

After reading students are taught to evaluate how well they achieved their purpose for reading. They must decide what they will do if they have not met their purpose. They are also asked to determine what they learned in both the area of comprehension of information and application of the process.

Writing Strategy

> *Only when strategies are integrated within the curriculum will adolescents gain the experience needed to become effective self-regulated learners.*
>
> Wood, Woloshyn, & Willoughby, 1995

A cooperative revision strategy developed by MacArthur (1994) is another strategy that can be integrated into writing instruction. The strategy was devised to be used in conjunction with Atwell's Writing Workshop model (1987). This strategy is based on the finding that students with learning disabilities have less knowledge of what good writing is, and this limits their ability to revise their own writing. These students also tend to view revision primarily as the correction of mechanical errors and have learned few strategies for revising content. This strategy model also uses word processing to eliminate recopying and messy erasures, but word processing is not necessary to implement the strategy. The use of peers to teach the strategy served to increases the effectiveness. Five steps are involved in the revision process:

1. The editor listens to the writing piece as it is read by the author.
2. The author tells the editor what she or he thinks the paper is about and what she or he liked best about the paper. (The two students switch roles and repeat the first two steps.)
3. Each student works independently with each other's draft. They make notes and suggestions directly on the paper. They look for anything that is unclear and places where information or details could be added.
4. The students meet to discuss the suggestions and ask each other questions. This must be a two-way exchange. The decisions on whether to make the changes belong solely to the author.
5. The students work independently on their own papers, making revisions.

The beauty of this strategy is that students who are good writers can be taught the strategy relatively quickly. These students then teach it to their peer partners. The focus for revision can also be tailored to various types of writing. If the writing is fiction, it can target specific parts of a story. If the students are working on persuasive writing, it can focus on the argument and supporting facts.

Deshler, Schumaker, and colleagues at the University of Kansas Center for Research on Learning have developed a strategy intervention program which is certainly one of the best validated for use with older students (Deshler & Schumaker, 1986; Kline, Deshler, & Schumaker, 1992; Schmidt, Deshler, Schumaker, & Ally, 1988; Schumaker & Deshler, 1992). This *Learning Strategies Curriculum* covers a range of strategies for studying, reading, and writing. The strategies are highly structured and sequential. Specific training for teachers is required before teaching the strategies to students, and using the strategies in classes outside of the special education classroom is essential for generalization. The strategies use mnemonic devices to help students remember the steps involved in each strategy. Several mnemonics are summarized in Table 10-6.

TABLE 10-6   Learning Strategies Curriculum: Writing strategies.

I. Sentence Writing (**PENS**)

Pick a formula to write your sentence.
Explore words to fit the formula.
Note the words.
Search for the verb(s) and subject(s).

II. Paragraph Writing (**SCRIBE**)

Set up a diagram.
Create the title.
Reveal the topic.
Iron out the details.
Bind it together with a clincher.
Edit your work.

III. Error Monitoring (**WRITER**)

Write on every other line of paper using PENS.
Read for meaning.
Interrogate yourself using COPS (Capitalization, Overall
    appearance, Punctuation, and spelling).
Take the paper to someone for help.
Execute the final copy.
Reread the paper.

IV. Theme Writing (**TOWER**)

Think of ideas.
Order ideas.
Write ideas in connected paragraphs (introductory, detail, and concluding).
Error monitoring (COPS).
Recopy.

Mathematical Strategies

> *Two important features shared by these successful strategy interventions are explicit teaching of the strategy and extended practice on the use of that strategy.*
>
> d'Ailly, 1995

The use of strategies instruction in math has gained in popularity in recent years. The study of mathematics has moved from calculation to problem solving. A range of strategies are beneficial in enabling students to effectively use a model for problem solving. Mayer (1987) described the process components of problem solving as follows: problem translation, problem integration, solution planning and monitoring, and plan execution. Each component requires specific skills and background knowledge. Students require explicit instruction in these components as well as practice in strategically approaching each step in the process. The first step is to check for understanding of the problem. Restating or paraphrasing is effective for understanding most problems. In the case of more complex or abstract problems, charting or diagramming information may be useful. Visualization is another technique that aids in comprehension.

In approaching a problem, students will require explicit instruction on the types of problems, how to determine the appropriate procedure, and how to determine what information is missing. Good problem solvers have this skill (Low & Over, 1990; Silver, 1981). In addition to direct instruction, teacher modeling through the use of think aloud is crucial to student acquisition of problem-solving skills.

As students engage in solution planning and monitoring, eight different types of activities can be identified: Reading, understanding, analyzing, exploring, planning, implementing, verifying, watching, and listening. These activities involve an ongoing interplay of cognitive and metacognitive behaviors (Artzi & Armour-Thomas, 1992). One effective method to teach and practice these identified activities is through the use of reciprocal teaching (Campione, Brown, Reeve, Ferrara, & Palincsar, 1991). This method of instruction involves modeling of expert performance through think aloud techniques and students later serving as teacher to continue the modeling process. The procedure forces a high level of student engagement. The students and the teacher take turns being "learning leaders" and "supportive critics" who are responsible for leading discussion. This forces externalization of the specific strategies, the monitoring process, and the methods of constructing meaning.

Social Skills and Conflict Resolution

Social skills, conflict resolution strategies, and direct behavioral instruction may be beneficial to all students, but they are a necessity for many students with severe emotional disturbance, conduct disorders, and some students with mental retardation. Most educators would agree that of all students, youngsters with emotional and behavioral problems are the

Effective teaching practices reduce the likelihood of minor behavior problems occuring but are not sufficient to meet all the needs of children and youth with E/BD [Emotional/Behavioral Disorders]. Direct instruction in the area of social skills and individual behavior change programs will still be a necessary component of the educational program of children and youth with E/BD.

Lewis & Bello, 1993

least accepted and most feared by teachers in the general education setting. They may disrupt the education of others as well as distract themselves. General educators lack tolerance for behavior that is noncompliant or aberrant, and they feel unqualified to handle these problems (Gersten, Walker, & Darch, 1988; Guetzloe, 1993; Lewis & Bello, 1993; Safran & Safran, 1988). Yet, more students are at risk for mental illness today than ever before (Department of Health and Human Services, 1989). Statistics indicate that the majority of the students with severe emotional disturbance are educated in segregated programs, separate classes, and separate schools, and that less than half of the students with severe emotional disturbance are reintegrated for any portion of their school day into general education (Downing, Simpson, & Myles, 1990; Peterson, Smith, White, & Zabel, 1980; Rock, Rosenberg, & Carran, 1995; U S Department of Education, 1990). Few studies have isolated specific variables that promote the return of these students to the general education setting (Schneider & Byrne, 1984). The factors that favorably influence the return of these students described very recently by Rock and colleagues (1995) are programs that are in a regular school or as close as possible to the general education setting, multiple options for mainstreaming and reintegration, special educator selection of the mainstream site and situation, schoolwide reintegration procedures, flexibility and positive attitude of the general educator, and available training and support. Also, students with severe problem behaviors who also have cognitive disabilities are rarely educated in the general education setting. Oregon has been identified as a state having one of the highest inclusion rate with these students (Danielson & Bellamy, 1989). Horner and Brazeau (1992) studied the reasons for this high rate of inclusion and found that the most frequent support was to assign an instructional assistant to the classroom. This provided essential one-to-one support, crisis intervention, and behavioral monitoring. The teachers involved were largely pleased with the results of their inclusion but stated that ongoing training and collaborative consultation for problem solving would be a welcome addition.

Given the fact that few children with severe behavioral and emotional problems are presently educated in the general education setting, it is apparent that *personnel support* and *curricular support* play a vital role in the successful reintegration efforts. Direct instruction in appropriate social and behavioral skills as a part of the general education curricula is a method of preventing future occurrence of behavioral problems and may create a more conducive environment for the return of students with behavioral and emotional problems. Social skill competence has a significant impact on successful performance in the classroom (Bryan, 1991). Curriculum integration efforts should not only include behavior management, but also social skills, self-control techniques, and direct behavioral instruction

(Lewis and Bello, 1993). Many student who participate in general education programs for much of their school day have objectives on their IEPs that cover social and behavioral skills. Even students whose primary disability is not severe emotional disturbance may have objectives that fall into the following categories:

- Taking responsibility for own behavior
- Initiating social interactions
- Maintaining social relationships
- Using appropriate behaviors to ask for help in the classroom
- Maintaining attention to task
- Practicing appropriate classroom behaviors

These students may receive direct and intensive instruction in social and behavioral skill in a special class setting. When these students return to the general education setting, the integration of these skill areas into the instructional program is crucial to the successful maintenance of learned behaviors (Fad, Ross, & Boston, 1995). Examples of several curricula with integration suggestions as well as sources for further information are provided in the follow section. (See Chapter 12 for further information on behavior management.) The major content areas in these curricula rather consistently include the following:

- Understanding feelings
- Focusing and concentration
- Communication skills
- Understanding stress
- Understanding conflict
- Problem solving
- Learning and practicing prosocial behaviors
- Self-esteem

Elementary Curricula

> *In effective classrooms for young children—both with and without disabilities—teachers routinely teach social skills as an integrated part of the school curriculum.*
>
> Fad, Ross, & Boston, 1995

Social skills instruction should be an integral part of any educational program because it helps to improve the self-esteem of the students. A classroom with a positive, nurturing atmosphere that accepts and positively embraces the uniqueness and individual differences in children will facilitate growth in self-concept. Borda and Borda (1982) have indicated that classrooms that are most effective in enhancing self-esteem are those that include the following characteristics:

- Students perceive a sense of love and warmth.
- Students are respected as individuals.
- Students can express ideas, feelings, and opinions.
- Students have consistent limits, rules, and standards.
- Students learn to work together and to trust, help, and share with each other.
- Students learn skills for responding to conflict in a supportive community.
- Students have a chance to succeed at their own level.

These characteristics can be built into the organization and procedure of any classroom, and they can be emphasized through the use of specific classroom activities. Curricula for elementary students provide structured activities. Some of these are *Teaching Children Self-Control: Preventing Emotional and Learning Problems in the Elementary School* (Fagen, Long, & Stevens, 1975), *Skillstreaming for the Elementary School Child* (McGinnis & Goldstein, 1984), and *Games Children Should Play: Sequential Lessons for Teaching Communication Skills in Grades K–6* (Chad & Heron, 1980). Teachers can and frequently do develop their own activities for use in the classroom. A key element in designing activities is to mesh these with some theme into the existing curriculum. This enhances the curriculum, and the teachers are not burdened with "add-ons" to the already substantial curriculum load. Figure 10-3 depicts an interdisciplinary web of connections to the content areas of the

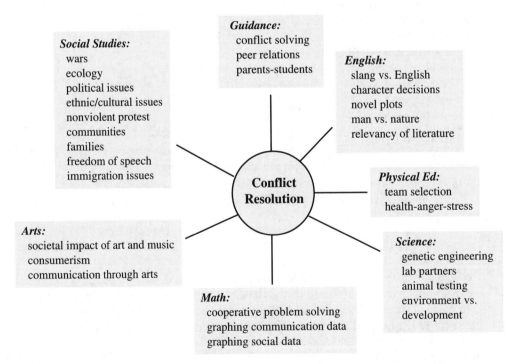

FIGURE 10-3 Interdisciplinary web: Elementary.

general education curriculum. A blank web may serve as a helpful planning guide to teachers who wish to make their own content connections.

Understanding Feelings

A frequent beginning point in social skills instruction is the area of understanding feelings. This process may begin with developing familiarity with feeling words and personal experiences with feelings. Brainstorming feeling words may be used to introduce the topic. The teacher may supplement the students list. Using stories or current events in discussion of feelings becomes a likely content connection and next step. Linking feelings and behavior would serve as the next activity. Moving from stories to the student's personal experience possibly in similar situations allows the students to see the connection between literature and their own lives. Care must be taken not to force students to share any personal situation they are not comfortable sharing. Discussions or writing activities can be used to enhance learning about the connection between feelings, both negative and positive, and behavior.

Building on this introduction to feelings, teachers can develop appropriate coping behaviors by designing activities that teach methods of dealing with anger and frustration. The concept of behavior and consequences can be emphasized. Again, children's literature that is part of the existing curriculum can be used to highlight these points, explore behavioral alternatives, and introduce problem solving. As the content is presented, it is essential to emphasize explicitly the connections of behavior and consequences. This means that social skills and behaviors become the "content" of process learning much the same way learning and thinking strategies were directly taught processes in the earlier section of this chapter. Discussion and writing activities serve as methods to expand knowledge and extend application of the learning to the student's personal experiences. One area crucial to the development of an individual student's self-esteem is the ability to accept criticism and correction. Components of instruction might include understanding that there is a difference between correction and insult, that there are feelings involved, and that behaviors or responses result from these feelings. Examples can be developed from classroom situations, the student's personal experience, and literature.

Friends

Activities designed to identify the characteristics of friends and friendly relationships can enhance student learning on making and keeping friends. Webbing can be used to graphically represent these characteristics. When students with disabilities are present in the class, a Circle of Friends activity can be incorporated into this study for a specific student or as another way for students to understand the types of friends they have in their lives. Children's stories can be used to analyze friendly and unfriendly behaviors as well as how these behaviors affect the feelings of others. Social studies content can extend this concept to friendly and unfriendly relationships between countries.

The concept of maintaining friendships can be used to reinforce appropriate friendly behavior, practice specific communication skills, and to introduce conflict resolution. Important emphasis can be placed on understanding that we are all different, but we can still get along, teach each other new things, and iron out our differences when conflict arises. Specific strategies may include using a Venn Diagram to list characteristics of You, Me, and

Us. Situations involving student-generated dilemmas and examples from literature or current events may prompt discussions, writing activities, or problem solving.

Helping Behaviors

With the increased use of cooperative learning in education, helping behaviors among students have greatly increased. It is necessary to teach students communication skills and group etiquette to maximize the effectiveness of these cooperative activities. Johnson and Johnson (1989), who have written extensively on the effect of competition versus cooperation in the classroom, recommend direct instruction in communication. In addition, students need to learn about helping. There are many facets of helping. Students must be comfortable asking for help. They must be able to determine when they need help and overcome any negative feelings about asking for help. We tend to assume that students know how to ask for help, but many students are uncomfortable. Direct instruction focused on knowing when to ask for help, understanding the feelings related to asking, and acceptance of the idea that it's okay to ask for help can have a lasting impact on developing a sense of community and caring in the classroom. Once students are comfortable asking for help, instruction needs to extend to accepting or refusing help, appropriately, and providing help to others. The concepts of feelings-behavior-consequences can be reinforced during this process. Emphasis may be placed on the appropriate and inappropriate ways of accepting or refusing help as depicted in Table 10-7. When students with severe disabilities are

TABLE 10-7   Ways students accept or refuse help.

Appropriate responses:

    Accepting help:

        Thanking the person offering to help

        Explaining specifically what help you need

        Working together with the person

        Using a polite tone of voice

    Refusing help:

        Explaining why you don't need help

        Using a polite tone

        Demonstrating you can solve the problem yourself

        Thanking the person for offering help

Inappropriate responses:

    Accepting help:

        Allowing others to do things that you can do yourself

        Making rude comments to helper (It's about time you got here)

        Criticizing the helper for the was help is given

    Refusing help:

        Making rude comments

        Yelling, raising your voice, using an angry tone

        Ignoring the offer of help

        Not explaining why you don't need help

present in the classroom, this discussion may consider examples related to helping this individual student as well as exploring other kinds of helping behaviors. Real life examples from the students' experiences can serve as a starting point. Literature may provide further examples, and the concept may be extended to the study of helping careers and even the study of heroes.

Secondary Curricula

> *Teaching social skills in natural settings yields the greatest generalizations.*
>
> Fad, Ross, & Boston, 1995

The social skills themes that flow through the secondary curricula are very similar to those already described for elementary students. Some examples of these curricula are: *Conflict Resolution: A Secondary School Curriculum* (Sadulla, Henriquez, & Holmberg, 1987), *Managing Conflict: A Curriculum for Adolescents* (Copeland, 1989), *Skill Streaming The Adolescent: A Structured Learning Approach to Teaching Prosocial Skills* (Goldstein, Sprafkin, Gershaw, & Klein, 1980), and *Metacognitive Approach to Social Skills Training: A Program for Grades 4 through 12* (Sheinker & Sheinker, 1989). One major difference at the secondary level is the increased importance of adopting a schoolwide approach to social skills and conflict resolution. Students at this level travel to as many as eight different classes in a day and may have as many as sixteen different teachers over the span of a single year. A school supported model facilitates integration of the content included in a specialized curriculum across the various content areas. The topics of prosocial skill, conflict resolution, and assertiveness can be handled differently by different teachers, but the students gain an understanding of how the concepts are pervasive and applicable in multiple situations. Figure 10-4 illustrates some of the many content connections secondary teachers may be able to make.

Conflict management serves as the major framework for many secondary social skills and behavioral curricula. The major content themes may be organized in a similar fashion to the example outlined in Table 10-8, which is taken from Sadulla and colleagues (1987).

Several of the following examples of interdisciplinary applications for conflict resolution are adapted from *Conflict Resolution Tools: Teaching Through the Curriculum* (Montgomery County Public Schools, 1993). These suggested activities serve as models for the wide range of possible applications. Understanding the links between feelings-behavior-consequences is an underlying concept in conflict resolution. This linking process can be expanded at the secondary level to include the following:

- Action—the incident or event
- Thoughts about what happened
- Feelings about what happened
- Reaction to what happened
- Consequences

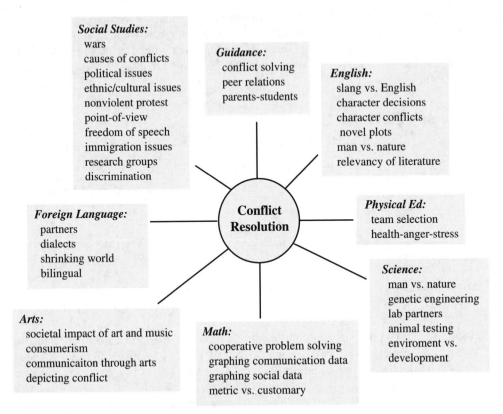

Social Studies:
wars
causes of conflicts
political issues
ethnic/cultural issues
nonviolent protest
point-of-view
freedom of speech
immigration issues
research groups
discrimination

Guidance:
conflict solving
peer relations
parents-students

English:
slang vs. English
character decisions
character conflicts
novel plots
man vs. nature
relevancy of literature

Foreign Language:
partners
dialects
shrinking world
bilingual

Conflict Resolution

Physical Ed:
team selection
health-anger-stress

Arts:
societal impact of art and music
consumerism
communicaiton through arts
depicting conflict

Math:
cooperative problem solving
graphing communication data
graphing social data
metric vs. customary

Science:
man vs. nature
genetic engineering
lab partners
animal testing
enviroment vs. development

FIGURE 10-4   Interdisciplinary web: Secondary.

Discussion of this chain of occurrences can include the statements of "It wasn't my fault." "He made me do it." "I couldn't help it." Students may share personal examples or items from the newspaper may be used to focus discussion on personal responsibility. In social studies, students may use this concept to describe the situation in South Africa related to apartheid or perhaps to a world trade situation. English teachers may relate the concept to a novel or biography that is being read on a similar theme.

"Triggers," sometimes called stimulus or antecedents, are verbal and nonverbal actions that can stimulate a confrontation between two people. There is some commonality in the actions that cause anger. These can be discussed. When students gain an understanding of what these "triggers" are, they can learn not only to avoid them but also how to respond more appropriately or cope with situations involving triggers. Activities can include identifying and sharing triggers that each person has experienced, describing anger and how it feels, and how to tell when another person is angry. Students can explore their own coping mechanisms as well as the consequences of their coping behaviors. This concept can be extended into science by analyzing the physical effects of anger and stress on the body. In social studies, the concept can be linked to Hitler's concept of the Aryan race. In English, the concept may be applied to a novel. An example might be to apply the analysis to Chapter 19 of *Tuck Everlasting*. Students can determine the trigger words that led Mae

TABLE 10-8   Conflict resolution: Curriculum components.

1. Understanding conflict
   - Definition of conflict
   - Connotations of conflict
   - Common societal messages about conflict
   - Major kinds of conflict

2. Conflict styles

   Three basic styles of resolving conflicts and effectiveness
   - Avoidance
   - Confrontation
   - Problem solving

3. Communication
   - The communication process
   - Factors that influence communication

4. Skills for effective communication
   - Barriers to communication
   - Active listening
   - Nonverbal communication
   - Sending clear messages: I Messages

5. Resolving conflicts
   - Collaboration conflict resolution process
     - planning and reflection
     - surface issues and underlying issues
     - positions and interests
     - the conflict resolution environment
     - problem solving
     - formal negotiation
   - Third-party conflict resolution processes
     - conciliation
     - mediation
     - arbitration
     - judicial resolution

Tuck to act the way she did or the nonverbal behaviors of the man in the yellow suit that angered Mae Tuck. Students may write a personal example or develop a fictional short story depicting triggers and the events and feelings surrounding them.

The following examples are adapted from *The C.A.L.M. Approach: An Anger Management Resource Book for Teachers* (Prince George's County Public Schools, 1993). Students ownership of their behavior is a crucial concept in dealing effectively with anger. Having students discuss the statement, "What I do is my choice, and I will accept the consequences for my actions," serves as an introduction activity to accepting responsibility. Students can discuss this statement by comparing when they accepted responsibility and when they did not. Teacher-developed scenarios or excerpts from fiction, current events, or biographies can be used to develop discrimination skills. The concept can be expanded to science by considering questions of ethical responsibility for scientific advances, such as genetic research or expansions in technology and personal privacy issues.

Stress management is a topic that has significant impact on behavior. Students can be taught to recognize the signs of stress. In science, students can relate the concept of physical stress to psychological stress. Social studies can emphasize the effect of societal concerns or stress and its relationship to psychological stress. In physical education, students can explore stress management strategies, including physical exercise, relaxation, and leisure activities.

Being assertive and resisting peer pressure is a topic that takes on significance in middle school and extends into high school. The following activities are adapted from *Coping With Tension, Frustration, and Change: A Social Skill Program for Mid-Level Students* (Montgomery County Public Schools, 1991). Teaching students to say no is a basic assertive technique. The ability to say no in a peer pressure situation that may include inappropriate behavior, clothing, drugs, or simply something the student would rather not do can be more easily accomplished if saying no is a well-practiced behavior. Direct instruction on how to say no may include:

- Say "No Thanks".
- Provide a reason or an excuse.
- Repeat "No".
- Walk away.
- Avoid the person or situation.
- Change the subject.
- Join with others who say no.
- Ignore the person or situation.

Students can be given a series of situations to role play or write descriptions of appropriate ways to say no. Students can think of personal example to share or look for current events articles exemplifying why its important to say no. Students can change roles with parents or teachers and practice saying no. The act of playing a different role may enhance understanding of the consequences and reasons to say no.

Another aspect of assertive training is learning to discriminate between assertive and aggressive behavior. Both fiction and nonfiction provide a multitude of examples for discussion. Students may also benefit from direct instruction about their right to be assertive. The following list of situations is not all inclusive but may be used to illustrate this point and serve as examples for discussion or topics for writing:

- The right to make or refuse requests
- The right to express your opinion
- The right to initiate conversation
- The right to give compliments and express appreciation
- The right to share feelings about a person or situation
- The right to judge your own actions and to be responsible for the consequences
- The right to make mistakes
- The right to report harassment or abuse of any kind

Students may reflect on times when they said no and were glad they did and times when they did not say no, and they wish they would have. Writing a procedural piece on the "art of saying no" is another type of activity to expand application of this skill.

The curricular applications described are only a few of the possible methods of teaching appropriate behavior and social skills to students. Teachers are encouraged to review the curricula mentioned as well as others that may be available and begin to integrate these skills into their classroom instruction on a regular basis.

Conclusions

Integrating specialized curricula into the daily general education program of studies is essential when the student needs dictate a substantially different set of outcomes than the general education population and are critical to ensure generalization of newly learned skills. Teacher flexibility and creative thinking are required to achieve an integrated program. Once achieved, an integrated program will enhance the general education curriculum, provide new opportunities and environments for learning, and benefit all students.

References

Artzi, A., & Armour-Thomas, E. (1992). Development of a cognitive-metacognitive framework for protocol analysis of mathematical problem solving in small groups. *Cognition and Instruction, 9*(2), 137–175.

Atwell, N. (1987). *In the middle: Writing, reading, and learning with adolescents.* Portsmouth, NH: Heinemann.

Beck, J., Broers, J., Hogue, E., Shipstead, J., & Knowlton, E. (1994). Strategies for functional community-based instruction and inclusion for children with mental retardation. *Teaching Exceptional Children, 26*(2), 44–48.

Bergman, J., & Schuder, T. (1993). Teaching at-risk students to read strategically. *Educational Leadership, 50*(4), 19–23.

Bergman, J., & Schuder, T. (1986). Unpublished training materials. Rockville, MD: Montgomery County Public Schools.

Borda, M., & Borda, C. (1982). *Self-esteem: A classroom affair.* San Francisco: Harper and Row.

Brolin, D. (1991). *Life centered career education (LCCE) curriculum program.* Reston, VA: The Council for Exceptional Children.

Brown, L., Branston-McLean, M., Baumgart, D., Vincent, L., Falvey, M., & Schroeder, J. (1979). Using the characteristics of current and future least restrictive environments in the development of curricular content for severely handicapped students. *AAESPH Review, 4*(4), 407–424.

Bryan, T. (1991). *Defining learning disabilities specialists responsibilities in the social domain.* Paper presented to the International Conference of The Council for Exceptional Children, Atlanta, GA.

Campione, J., Brown, A., Reeve, R., Ferrara, R., & Palincsar, A. (1991). Interactive learning and individual understanding: The case of reading and mathematics. In I. Landsmann (Ed.), *Culture, schooling, and psychological development, Vol. 4: Human development* (pp. 136–170). NJ: Ablex Publishing Corp.

Chad, M., & Heron, B. (1980). *Games children should play: Sequential lessons for teaching communication skills in grades K–6.* Chicago: Scott, Foresman and Co.

Clark, G. (1994). Is a functional curriculum approach compatible with an inclusive education model? *Teaching Exceptional Children, 26*(2), 36–39.

Copeland, N. (1989). *Managing conflict: A curriculum for adolescents.* NM: New Mexico Center for Dispute Resolution.

d'Ailly, H. (1995). Strategies in learning and teaching algebra. In E. Wood, V. Woloshyn, & T. Willoughby (Eds.), *Cognitive strategy instruction for middle and high schools* (pp. 137–170). Cambridge, MA: Brookline Books.

Danielson, L., & Bellamy, G. (1989). State variation in placement of children with handicaps in segregated environments. *Exceptional Children, 55,* 448–455.

Denver, R. (1988). *Community living skills: A taxonomy.* Washington, DC: American Association on Mental Retardation.

Department of Health and Human Services. (1989). *Year 2000 national health objectives.* Washington, DC: Author.

Deshler, D., & Schumaker, J. (1988). An instructional model for teaching students how to learn. In J. Graden, J. Zins, & M. Curtis (Eds.), *Alternative educational delivery systems* (pp. 391–411), Washington, DC: National Association of School Psychologists.

Deshler, D., & Schumaker, J. (1986). Learning strategies: An instructional alternative for low-achieving students. *Exceptional Children, 11*(3), 20–24.

Dixon, M., & Rossi, J. (1995). Directors of their own learning: A reading strategy for students with learning disabilities. *Teaching Exceptional Children, 27*(2), 10–14.

Downing, J., Simpson, R., & Myles, B. (1990). Regular and special educator perceptions of nonacademic skills needed by mainstreamed students with behavioral disorders and leaning disabilities. *Behavioral Disorders, 15*(4), 217–226.

Ellis, E., Deshler, D., Lenz, B., Schumaker, J., & Clark, F. (1991). An instructional model for teaching learning strategies. *Focus on Exceptional Children, 23*(6), 1–24.

Fad, K., Ross, M., & Boston, J. (1995). We're better together: Using cooperative learning to teach social skills to young children. *Teaching Exceptional Children, 27*(4), 28–34.

Fagen, S., Long, N., & Stevens, D. (1975). *Teaching children self-control: Preventing emotional and learning problems in the elementary school.* Columbus, OH: Charles E. Merrill Publishing Co.

Field, S., LeRoy, B., & Rivera, S. (1994). Meeting functional curriculum needs in middle school general education classrooms. *Teaching Exceptional Children, 26*(2), 40–43.

Gersten, R., Walker, H., & Darch, C. (1988). Relationship between teachers' effectiveness and their tolerance for handicapped students. *Exceptional Children, 54,* 433–438.

Giangreco, M. (1993). Using creative problem-solving methods to include students with severe disabilities in general education classroom activities. *Journal of Educational and Psychological Consultation, 4*(2), 113–135.

Giangreco, M., & Puttnam, J. (1991). Supporting the education of students with severe disabilities in regular education environments. In L. Mercer, C. Peck, & L. Brown (Eds.), *Critical issues in the lives of people with severe disabilities* (pp. 245–270). Baltimore: Paul H. Brookes Publishing Co.

Goldstein, A., Sprafkin, R., Gershaw, N., & Klein. (1980). *Skill streaming the adolescent: A structured learning approach to teaching prosocial skills.* Champaign, IL: Research Press.

Guetzloe, E. (1993). Inclusion of students with emotional/behavior disorders: The issues, the barriers, and possible solutions. In L. Bullock, & R. Gable (Eds.), *Monograph on inclusion: Ensuring appropriate services to children and youth with emotional/behavioral disorders* (pp. 21–24). St. Louis: Council for Children with Behavioral Disorders.

Hawaii Transition Project. (1987). Honolulu: Department of Special Education, University of Hawaii.

Heflin, L., Borenson, L., Grossman, M., Huette, J., & Ilgen, J. (1993). Advocate, not abdicate. In L. Bullock, & R. Gable (Eds.), *Monograph on inclusion: Ensuring appropriate services to children and youth with emotional/behavioral disorders* (pp. 21–24). St. Louis: Council for Children with Behavioral Disorders.

Helmke, L., Havekost, D., Patton, J., & Polloway, E. (1994). Life skills programming: Development of a high school science course. *Teaching Exceptional Children, 26*(2) 49–53.

Horner, R., & Brazeau, K. (1992). Educational support for students with severe problem behaviors in Oregon: A descriptive analysis for the 1987–1988 school year. *Journal of the Association for Persons with Severe Handicaps, 17*(3), 154–169.

Johnson, D., & Johnson, R. (1989). *Cooperative and competition: Theory and research.* Edina, MN: Interaction Book Co.

Kline, F., Deshler, D., & Schumaker, J. (1992). Implementing learning strategies instruction in class settings: A research perspective. In M. Pressley, K. Harris, & J. Guthrie (Eds.), *Promoting academic competence and literacy in school* (pp. 361–406). San Diego: Academic Press.

Lenz, B., Brogrin, J., Schumaker, J., Deshler, D., & Bowdah, D. (1994). *The Content Enhancement Series: The unit organizer routine.* Lawrence, KS: Edge Enterprises.

Lenz, B., Marrs, R., Schumaker, J., & Deshler, D. (1993). *The Content Enhancement Series: The lesson organizer routine.* Lawrence, KS: Edge Enterprises.

Lewis, T., & Bello, K. (1993). Including children with emotional/behavioral disorders in general education settings: Issues and practical strategies. In L. Bullock, & R. Gable (Eds.), *Monograph on inclusion: Ensuring appropriate services to children and youth with emotional/behavioral disorders* (pp. 11–16). St. Louis: Council for Children with Behavioral Disorders.

Low, R., & Over, R. (1990). Text editing of algebraic word problems. *Australian Journal of Psychology, 42,* 63–73.

MacArthur, C. (1994). Peers + word processing + strategies = A powerful combination for revising student writing. *Teaching Exceptional Children, 27*(1), 24–35.

Mayer, R. (1987). *Educational psychology: A cognitive approach.* Boston: Little, Brown and Co.

McGinnis, E., & Goldstein, A. (1984). *Skillstreaming for the elementary school child.* Champaign, IL: Research Press.

Mercer, C. (in press). *Students with learning disabilities* (5th ed.) (203) Englewood Cliffs, NJ: Merrill/Prentice-Hall.

Mercer, C., Lane, H., Jordan, L., Allsopp, D., & Eisele, M. (in press). Empowering teachers and students with instructional choices in inclusive settings. Englewood Cliffs, NJ: Merrill/Prentice-Hall.

Montgomery County Public Schools. (1993). Conflict resolution tools: Teaching through the curriculum. Rockville, MD: Copyrighted, unpublished curriculum materials.

Montgomery County Public Schools. (1991). Coping with tension, frustration and change: A social skills program for mid-level students. Rockville, MD: Unpublished curriculum materials.

Peterson, R., Smith, C., White, M., & Zabel, R. (1980). Practices used in the reintegration of behavior disordered children in three midwestern states. Paper presented at the National Topical Conference on Seriously Emotionally Disturbed, The Council for Exceptional Children, Minneapolis. (ERIC Document Reproduction Services No. ED 201 122).

Pressley, M., Goodchild, F., Fleet, J., Zajchowski, R., & Evans, E. (1987). What is good strategy use and why is it hard to teach? An optimistic appraisal of the challenges associated with strategy instruction. Unpublished manuscript, Department of Psychology, University of Western Ontario, London, Ontario.

Prince George's County Public Schools. (1993). The C. A. L. M. approach: An anger management resource book for teachers. Upper Marlboro, MD: Unpublished curriculum materials.

Rainforth, B., York, J., & Macdonald, C. (1992). *Collaborative teams for students with severe disabilities: Integrating therapy and educational services.* Baltimore: Paul H. Brookes Publishing Co.

Rock, E., Rosenberg, M., & Carran, D. (1995). Variables affecting the reintegration rate of students with serious emotional disturbance. *Exceptional Children, 61*(3), 254–268.

Sadulla, G., Henriquez, M., & Holmberg, M. (1987). *Conflict resolution: A secondary school curriculum.* San Francisco: The Community Board Program.

Safran, S., & Safran, J. (1988). Perceptions of problem behaviors: A review an analysis of research. In R. Rutherford, C. Nelson, & S. Forness (Eds.), *Bases of severe behavioral disorders in children and youth* (pp. 132–138). Boston: College-Hill Press.

Schmidt, J., Deshler, D., Schumaker, J., & Alley, G. (1988). Effects of generalization instruction on written language performance of adolescents with learning disabilities in the mainstream classroom. *Journal of Reading, Writing, and Learning Disabilities International, 4*(4), 291–309.

Schneider, B., & Byrne, B. (1984). Predictors of successful transition from self-contained special education to regular class settings. *Psychology in the Schools, 21,* 375–380.

Schumaker, J., & Deshler, D. (1995). Secondary classes can be inclusive, too. *Educational Leadership, 52*(4), 50–51.

Schumaker, J., & Deshler, D. (1992). Validation of learning strategies intervention for students with learning disabilities: Results of programmatic research effort. In B. Wong (Ed.), *Contemporary intervention research in learning disabilities: An international perspective* (pp. 22–46). New York: Springer-Verlag.

Schumaker, J., Deshler, D., & McKnight, P. (1991). Teaching routines for content areas at the secondary level. In G. Stover, M. Shinn, & H. Walker (Eds.), *Interventions for achievement and behavior problems* (pp. 473–494), Washington, DC: National Association of School Psychologists.

Sheinker, J., & Sheinker, A. (1989). *Metacognitive approach to social skills training: A program for grades 4 through 12.* Rockville, MD: Aspen Publishers.

Silver, E. (1981). Recall of mathematical problem information: Solving related problems. *Journal for Research in Mathematics Education, 12,* 54–64.

Slavin, R. (1989). Research on cooperative learning: Consensus and controversy. *Educational Leadership, 47*(4), 52–56.

Smith, M., & Schloss, P. (1988). Teaching to transition. In P. Schloss, C. Hughes, & M. Smith (Eds.), *Community integration for persons with mental retardation* (pp. 1–16). Austin, TX: Pro•Ed.

U. S. Department of Education. (1990). *Twelfth annual report to Congress on the implementaion of the Education of All Handicapped Children Act.* Washington, DC: U.S. Government Printing Office. (ERIC Document Reproduction Service No. 321–513).

Weinstein, C., Ridley, D., Dahl, T., & Weber, E. (1989). Helping students develop strategies for effective learning. *Educational Leadership,* January, 126–128.

Wood, E., Woloshyn, V., & Willoughby, T. (Eds.) (1995). *Cognitive strategy instruction for middle and high schools.* Cambridge, MA: Brookline Books.

Chapter 11

Strategy Instruction

STEPHANIE L. CARPENTER & MARGARET E. KING-SEARS

◆ ADVANCE ORGANIZER ◆

Traditional methods of instruction used by special educators—such as tutoring students on content that meets only day-to-day classroom demands, or breaking down each task into steps and teaching each step in isolation—have not been successful at promoting students' independent accomplishment of tasks across a variety of settings. This chapter describes strategy instruction as a viable means of teaching students with a range of disabilities to approach academic, social, and work-related tasks in a more planful manner. Strategy instruction is related to students' achievement of self-determination and independence, and key student and teacher behaviors are described. Examples of strategy steps for a variety of areas are described. Two models of strategy instruction are presented from which educators can compare their current approach to teaching students *and* develop their own strategy systems that are responsive to their students' characteristics and corresponding setting demands. Additionally, a framework (SPEED) outlines the strategic behaviors used by students to solve problems and respond to situational demands.

Steven, a seventh grader, came home from school anxious to share his school day experiences with his mother. He was particularly excited because he had used a strategy he had been learning, but in a new way. The paraphrasing strategy he had learned had already given him more confidence in his seventh grade reading class. He had been very worried when his reading teacher introduced "speed reading" because not only was he a slow reader, he had difficulty remembering and understanding what he read. Using the RAP strategy had helped him focus on and remember the important information he read in paragraphs by following a few steps: (1) Read a paragraph. (2) Ask yourself the main idea and details. (3) Put the main idea and details in your own words. Now the same RAP strategy had helped him overcome confusion in his science class. He and his "strategies" teacher had discussed adapting the RAP strategy for situations other than reading paragraphs, when he might want to understand something better. And today in science it had worked! "Boy, Mom! When I got to science today I felt lost! Mrs. Freeman began explaining the systems of a frog's body. I had no idea what she was talking about. At first I was so confused. Then I decided, hey just use RAP, but for listening. It worked! I began to understand what the teacher was talking about and was able to complete my assignment, too!"

Student independence and self-determination are critical indicators of the effectiveness of instructional programs and, indeed, the success of the educational system as a whole. Educators play a major role in equipping students who have a variety of disabilities with the strategies to acquire skills and competencies that lead to independence and self-determination. Persons who are self-determining do the following:

- Define goals, set goals, and try to achieve goals (Deci & Ryan, 1985)
- Evaluate their progress toward meeting their goals and adjust their performance (Field & Hoffman, 1994)
- Create unique approaches to solve problems (Martin, Marshall, & Maxson, 1993)
- Use information to make choices (Schloss, Alper, & Jayne, 1993)
- Self-regulate their actions (Wehmeyer, 1994)

Independence ultimately consists of self-direction.

Turnbull & Turnbull, 1985

Many students with disabilities exhibit learning and performance characteristics that are not indicative of self-determination and are not conducive to achieving independence. (Refer to Figure 11-1 for a description of typical student characteristics versus the necessary student characteristics for self-determination.) However, these students can learn how to solve problems and enhance their decision-making performance in spite of their learning characteristics that place them at risk for difficulties in attaining independence and self-determination. Students who are taught how to approach tasks using a strategy have increased their previous performance in a variety of academic, vocational, self-help, and social areas (Deshler, Ellis, & Lenz, 1996; Hughes, 1992; Sawyer, Graham, & Harris, 1992; Wehmeyer & Kelchner, 1994; Welch, 1992).

Instructional opportunities abound during the school years to prepare students to be independent and make choices. At times, however, educators may find themselves constrained by more traditional methods of instruction that historically place the majority of control over choices and decision making in the hands of teachers instead of teaching students how to make those choices and decisions. For example, Realon, Favell, and Lowerre (1990) found that individuals with severe disabilities who were given choices spent more

What We Have

Product-oriented to accomplish tasks versus process-oriented to learn how to learn
Fragmented learning on many tasks versus cohesive learning on sets of tasks
Unfocused on what is important versus focused on critical features of tasks
Dependent on others to learn versus independent learning
Passive involvement versus active and proactive behaviors

What We Want

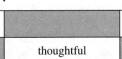

	effective		efficient
independent		thoughtful	
	goal-oriented		proactive
self-evaluative		confident	
	planful		successful

Strategic Learners

FIGURE 11-1   Student learning characteristics.

time engaging in leisure activities than when no choice was given. How often do educators tell students what to do instead of giving choices *and* teaching students how to make choices? Similarly, Hughes and Schumaker (1991) found that students with learning disabilities who were taught a test-taking strategy increased their test and report card grades. How often do educators help students keep up with the day-to-day classroom demands instead of teaching students how they can keep up with those demands themselves?

> *Community instruction for individuals with severe disabilities rarely incorporates programming for independence.*
>
> Hughes & Agran, 1993

For students to be successful in inclusive classrooms and in community settings, it is imperative that they are taught to use strategies that help them to successfully accomplish task demands within those environments. In some instances, intensive instruction in using strategies is necessary so that students learn "how to learn." Furthermore, the settings for this instruction may not be the general education classroom. Where strategy instruction occurs is not nearly as important as that it occurs—sometimes it needs to occur in community settings, sometimes in work areas, and sometimes in a classroom separate from content instruction. This is not to say that strategy instruction occurs in isolation. Strategy instruction is most meaningful when students see the connection between the strategy they are learning and the tasks they are (or will be) required to perform in the general education classroom. Students make the greatest and most lasting gains in learning and using strategies when they have opportunities to apply strategies in authentic situations as they are engaged in the "learning" of the strategy. However, Deshler and Schumaker (1993) note that the amount of practice and feedback necessary to teach some students with learning problems how to use strategies independently may preclude the general educator from being the primary strategy instructor *when extensive and intensive instruction in strategies is needed.* Nevertheless, all educators are promoting students' use of strategies, and there *are* situations in which general educators and parents and students are the strategy teachers. In fact, when students—with or without disabilities—are able to sufficiently learn strategies (e.g., visualize the situation, make a prediction, try different ways to get the answer) by being exposed to solid strategic instruction from teachers, then there is not a need for educators to explore more intensive instruction on strategies.

One of the more recent emphases within general education has been on teaching students not only what the "right" answer is, but *how* to get answers, *how* to solve problems, and *how* to gather and use information. General educators and special educators increasingly have been moving toward more of a strategic orientation in their teaching (see Chapter 10 for more information on general educators' use of strategy-based instruction) with a focus that extends beyond providing content knowledge but also on providing process knowledge (i.e., strategic knowledge). When students can acquire those strategies (e.g., "Draw a picture to help you get that answer." or "Look back over the text for the answer.") from typical instruction in general education classrooms (provided the teacher is emphasizing strategic knowledge and processes during instruction) then there is a good match between student characteristics and teacher instruction. Some students with disabilities (and some of their peers who have not been labeled with a disability), however, may need more intensive and ongoing instruction in learning what the strategies really mean (e.g., "I know I need to draw a picture, but I don't know what to put in the picture." or "I am looking back over the text for the answer, but I don't know when I see it unless it's worded the exact same way as the question.") as well as intensive practice in using the strategies before they can independently apply them.

Consequently, the issue of where intensive strategy instruction occurs depends on several factors. First, if the majority of students in a classroom need intensive instruction then the general education class may be the appropriate group to target for intensive instruction. Second, the person delivering the instruction (whether this person is the general educator, special educator, or the two working as a team) must be knowledgeable about and competent with teaching strategies. Finally, sufficient practice time such that each student reaches a mastery level at several places during strategy instruction must be allotted. Most students in general education classrooms will be able to use new strategies fairly quickly after teacher instruction.

Some students, however, will need more time. The fact that some students need more time does not negate the fact that *all* students need to be taught strategies (see Pressley, Brown, El-Dinary, & Afflerbach, 1995, for a synthesis of reading comprehension strategies).

The focus of this chapter is on those students who require more intensive instruction in order to sufficiently learn how to use strategies. Who are those students?—Students at-risk for school failure who have not been labeled, or may not qualify, for special education services. Students with learning disabilities who do not "catch on" to strategic processes when most students do. Students with emotional or behavioral disorders who realize that others are "getting it" but that they are not. Students with hearing impairments who may be missing critical cues for active learning. Students with moderate cognitive disabilities who are capable of learning strategies but who need more explicit instruction in the fine elements of learning and using the strategies. Yet it is not only students with mild to moderate disabilities (e.g., learning disabilities, mild to moderate mental retardation, emotional or behavioral disorders) who need a more strategy-oriented approach to instruction; evidence is emerging that students with severe cognitive disabilities (e.g., severe to profound mental retardation, autism) also benefit from similar instruction (Hughes & Agran, 1993; Lagomarcino & Rusch, 1989).

Traditional techniques and approaches, although effective "for the moment," are typically limited in terms of promoting learner independence across tasks or situations. For example, a teacher who responds to a student request for help with finding a word in the dictionary by finding the word for the student *does* help the student meet the immediate setting demand of finding the word in the dictionary, but this does not provide the student with information so that the student can do it on his or her own the next time. Traditional techniques also may not explicitly incorporate the need to promote the learners' belief of their competence and capability to accomplish learning. Students who have learned that asking for help means somebody else will help them may be learning that they cannot help themselves. Moreover, traditional techniques may promote student dependence on others instead of self-reliance.

For example, three eighth-grade students who have significant learning disabilities in organizing and remembering information are receiving instruction in a general education social studies class. These students are responsible for memorizing several lists of information for portions of their tests. Currently the students use inefficient memorizing strategies such as repeating the information to themselves until they know it. Sometimes they are able to study with other students who have already "chunked" the information, developed study cards with the important items, or devised a mnemonic to help them remember the information. When these joint study sessions occur, the students generally make better test grades. Sometimes their special education teacher is able to make study cards for them. However, although each of these situations can result in higher test grades, neither situation empowers them to make their own study cards, decide what is the important information to put on the study cards, and develop their own mnemonics for remembering the items. If their special education teacher were teaching the students the FIRST-Letter Mnemonic Strategy (Nagel, Schumaker, & Deshler, 1986), then they would be in a better position to successfully *and* independently accomplish these tasks.

The FIRST-Letter Mnemonic Strategy teaches students how to select the critical information to place on study cards, how to develop a mnemonic to remember the information, and how to study the information until they remember it. Because daily instruction for at least a month is needed for some students to master the strategy, the special education teacher feels she must justify how taking this long to teach the strategy fits in with inclusion: Strategy instruction complements inclusive practices because it provides students with disabilities the necessary tools to independently *and* successfully accomplish tasks in general education classrooms. Yet strategy instruction does not exist in a vacuum in a special education room—general educators play key roles because they identify the classroom demands (i.e., what do students need to be able to do to be successful in their classrooms?), prompt and encourage students to use the strategy, and reinforce and extend applications of the strategy.

A traditional educational approach has been to tutor students to study content for a test versus teaching students *test-taking strategies,* or telling students what to do to organize information instead of teaching students *how they can learn to organize information,* or directing students about what to do to complete a task instead of teaching students *how to complete the task.* Unquestionably, the instructional programs for students with disabilities must become more strategic in nature before students can be expected to be more strategic learners. Ellis (1994) states that a teaching fallacy is believing that all students who are deficient in strategy use can simply interact with students who are proficient in strategy use, and that the former students will automatically master these strategies in an effective and efficient manner. Strategy instruction by osmosis does not work for some students. Preparing students to meet the demands of academic and nonacademic settings by providing direct instruction and guidance in the acquisition and generalization of learning strategies is one way that educators can support students' progress toward becoming self-determining and independent learners (Deshler et al., 1996; Wehmeyer, 1992).

> *Give a man a fish and feed him for today. Teach a man to fish and feed him for a lifetime.*
>
> Chinese Proverb

Definitions of Strategy

Swanson (1993) quite simply defines *a strategy as a set of responses organized to solve a problem.* Another definition is that *a strategy is an individual's planful approach to a task.* Putnam, Deshler, and Schumaker (1993) suggest that a strategy be viewed

> *as a "tool" that can be used by learners to facilitate their analysis of the demands of a given problem or setting, to help them make decisions regarding the best way(s) to address the problem, and to guide their completion of the task while carefully monitoring the effectiveness of the process along the way. (p. 327, 328)*

Throughout the literature on strategy instruction, three concepts are found repeatedly: cognition, metacognition, and problem solving. In general, *cognition* refers to a student's ability to know what to do in order to complete a task. Tasks can be paraphrasing, writing sentences or paragraphs, identifying unknown words, completing vocational duties, or responding appropriately in varied social situations. Students' cognition involves knowing what to do to complete a task.

Metacognition refers to students' ability to monitor their performance while completing a task, such as checking to make sure they're paraphrasing accurately, regulating their writing to ensure the words convey the meaning they intended, or making decisions about correct word pronunciations. Metacognitive abilities extend beyond cognitive abilities in that metacognition involves "thinking about one's thinking." Students' metacognition involves not only knowing what to do, but having the ability to flexibly change plans when the task is not being successfully completed, to make decisions about when the plan needs to be changed, and to know which plan to use, when to use it, and why to use it. According to Palincsar and Brown (1987), using a metacognitive approach to instruction accomplishes each of the following:

- increases the learner's awareness of the task demands
- teaches the student how to use appropriate strategies to facilitate task completion
- teaches the student to monitor the application of these strategies

Omission of any of these elements reduces long-term effectiveness and the student's independent use of the strategy.

A strategy is an individual's approach to a task; it includes how the person thinks and acts when planning, executing, and evaluating performance on a task and its outcomes.

Deshler & Schumaker, 1986

Problem solving consists of a variety of processes such as planning, reasoning, selecting relevant information, and monitoring one's performance (Meltzer, Solomon, Fenton, & Levine, 1989). Problem-solving processes can be quite abstract and complex processes, especially for students with disabilities. Ellis (1994) suggests that concrete representations serve as beginning points for understanding a problem-solving process. For students with moderate to severe disabilities, pictures or objects are used to represent a sequence of steps in a problem-solving process. For students with mild disabilities, concrete representations are initially communicated in writing and are typically accompanied by a mnemonic to aid in the memory of the process (refer to Table 11-1 for several examples of mnemonic devices). As students' understanding of and ability to self-regulate the strategic process become more proficient, the pictures or cues that are used initially to help students remem-

TABLE 11-1 Mnemonics used to help students remember steps in a strategy.

DRAW to Solve Math Computations

Discover the sign.
Read the problem.
Answer, or draw and check.
Write the answer.

Source: Mercer, C. D., & Miller, S. P. (1992). Teaching students with learning problems in math to acquire, understand, and apply basic math facts. *Remedial and Special Education, 13*(3), 19–35.

RAP to Comprehend Reading Passages

Read a paragraph.
Ask yourself: What's the main idea and two details.
Put it in your own words.

Source: Schumaker, J. B., Denton, P. H., & Deshler, D. D. (1984). *The paraphrasing strategy.* Lawrence, KS: University of Kansas.

PLEASE Write Good Paragraphs

Pick a topic.
List your ideas about the topic.
Evaluate your list.
Activate the paragraph with a topic sentence.
Supply supporting sentences.
End with a concluding sentence and evaluate your work.

Source: Welch, M. (1992). The PLEASE strategy: A metacognitive learning strategy for improving the paragraph writing of students with mild learning disabilities. *Learning Disability Quarterly, 15,* 119–128.

IMAGES for Problem Solving

Inventory your abilities.
Make a list of skill requirements.
Ask yourself if there are differences (between performance and task requirements).
Gather ideas for performing the task.
Evaluate your performance.
Set goals.

Source: Carpenter, S. L. F. (1990). *Adolescents with physical impairments: Metacognitive procedures for the acquisition and generalization of nonverbal communication behaviors.* Doctoral dissertation, University of Florida, Gainesville. (University Microfilms No. DAO 64793)

I PLAN for Self-Advocacy

Inventory your strengths and weaknesses.
Provide inventory information at a meeting.
Listen to others.
Ask questions during the meeting.
Name your goals.

Source: Van Reusen, A. K., & Bos, C. S., Schumaker, J. B., & Deshler, D. D. (1987). *The educational planning strategy.* Lawrence, KS: Edge Enterprises.

ber the steps in the strategy are faded as students become less dependent on overt prompts and more independent with remembering the cues. Concurrent with this proficiency in the strategy process, students also develop more personalized and adaptive perspectives on the process, making the strategy more useful to them in a variety of situations *and* helping them to be more planful in developing their own strategies.

Harris and Pressley (1991) note that strategy instruction has sometimes been misinterpreted to mean "telling children what to do and expecting them to memorize and reproduce the steps of a strategy procedure exactly" (p. 393). Some teachers may confuse the use of a mnemonic as identical to the use of a strategy. The mnemonic itself lists steps in a strategy, but the mnemonic alone is not the strategy as the term "strategy" is discussed in this chapter. Simply knowing mnemonic steps is not considered equivalent to knowing how to use those steps proficiently and strategically. Swanson (1984) studied teacher behaviors related to strategy instruction and found that teachers tend to mistake strategy instruction for occasions when they asked students questions or provided directive statements during academic instruction. On the contrary, effective strategy instruction involves teaching students *how to* identify procedures that empower them to accomplish important academic, functional, social, and vocational tasks. Swanson also found that although teachers strongly agreed that strategy instruction was important, their instruction did not consistently nor frequently include such instruction.

Similar observations were reported by Paris and Oka (1986) who noted that because strategies are not taught explicitly in many classrooms, they remain ambiguous and unused by students who would greatly benefit from them—students who have learning problems. Perhaps teachers find themselves in a similar situation to that of some of their students in that they know they need to teach strategies, but they may not be well-versed in how to teach them. The following section identifies common teacher behaviors among strategic instruction models and describes in more depth two models of instruction with a focus on how a strategy is presented and taught.

Teacher Behaviors and Models of Strategy Instruction

Explicit instruction is necessary in not only what the strategy is, but in how and when to use the strategy, and methods for students to monitor their use of the strategy and its effectiveness. Ellis (1994) notes that explicit instruction is necessary, especially for students with learning disabilities, because they are poor discoverers of new skills and may continue ineffective applications of skills if direct teaching is not used. Strategy instruction is intensive (e.g., daily) and extensive (e.g., a minimum of four weeks to teach one strategy), and requires substantial practice and feedback for students to achieve mastery. A wide variety of traditional methods of instruction frequently seen in schools are not designed to include a student's strategic performance. Consequently, teachers will need to plan to incorporate critical strategic components into their instruction. Instructional elements consistently found in research and incorporated into successful strategy models that strongly favor strategic instruction include the following (Palincsar & Brown, 1987):

- Students were provided with information on the usefulness of the strategy.
- Students were provided with corrective feedback on their success in performing the strategy.
- Mastery or criterion performance was required during instruction before moving on to the next phase or stage of instruction.
- Students' mastery of information about the strategy at previous stages was directly related to the students' ability to use independently the strategy in the future.
- Students were taught to self-correct by both recording and analyzing their errors.
- Students first practiced strategy use on some type of controlled material (such as reading passages at their ability level or correcting errors on specifically developed materials instead of their own).

The more that students understand and take ownership of the strategy, the more likely they are to retain and spontaneously employ the strategy.

[Strategy] instruction is not complete until [students'] independent application of the strategies is ascertained.

                                                                    Palincsar & Brown, 1987

There are several teacher and student behaviors that permeate all models of strategy instruction. Among the key features are the following:

- Active student involvement in the learning process through ongoing dialogues about how they're doing, why they're doing well, and what they need to do to improve their performance.
- Explicit movement from teacher-directed feedback to student self-evaluation.
- Ongoing focus that the strategy being taught/learned has meaning and applicability within multiple contexts in students' responses to real-life demands both in and outside of school.
- Constant and persistent instruction that requires students to stretch, challenge, and extend their learning to reach levels that both students and the teacher would not have thought possible under typical and traditional instructional circumstances.

The types of tasks that students are required to do in general education classrooms, work settings, home situations, and community environments are examined to determine the skills that require a strategic approach for proficient performance. Examples of skills such as students acquiring composition skills (Sawyer et al., 1992), learning vocabulary definitions (King-Sears, Mercer, & Sindelar, 1992), or taking tests (Hughes & Schumaker, 1991) are based on the need for students' strategic performance of these skills across settings. Note that targeted strategies are not based on narrowly defined setting demands. Students are expected to write compositions, learn new vocabulary definitions, and take tests in a number of school settings. Consequently, they are more motivated to learn a strategy that can be used in a number of settings. Special educators' specialized instruction is based on (1) examining the demands students with disabilities are expected to successfully complete, (2) determining what strategies students need to learn so that they can more independently respond to a variety of setting demands, (3) developing strategies to meet those demands, and (4) teaching students how to use strategies.

The Strategy Intervention Model

An **eight-stage instructional sequence** is featured next to illustrate one model of how to teach students strategies (Ellis, Deshler, Lenz, Schumaker, & Clark, 1991). This sequence was developed and validated by researchers at the University of Kansas Center for Research on Learning (see Deshler et al. 1996, for more detail on the Strategy Intervention Model and the Learning Strategies Curriculum), and it is the most comprehensive model to date for teaching students strategies. Other instructional sequences are identified in Table 11-2. Ellis (1992) compares each stage of instruction to how players and their coach engage in learning and using basketball plays. This analogy can also be used with students to help them understand the purpose of each stage (refer to Table 11-3).

TABLE 11-2   Instructional sequences featured in models of strategy instruction.

Strategy Intervention Model	Scaffolding	Strategy Instruction with Self-Regulation	Direct Explanation
Pretest and obtain commitment from the student to learn the strategy	Present cognitive strategy	Preskill development	Introduce focus of lesson and provide declarative and conditional knowledge about strategy
Describe the strategy	Regulate difficulty during guided practice	Conference with student	Model use of the strategy
Model the strategy	Provide varying contexts for student practice	Discussion of the strategy	Guided practice
Verbal practice	Provide feedback	Modeling and goal-setting	Independent practice
Controlled practice and feedback	Increase student responsibility	Mastery of the strategy steps and self-statements	Opportunities to apply the strategy
Advanced practice & feedback	Provide independent practice	Collaborative practice with goal-setting	
Posttest and obtain commitment to generalize		Independent practice with goal-setting	
Generalization		Generalization and maintenance	

Source: Deshler & Schumaker, 1986; Rosenshine & Meister, 1992 synthesis; Sawyer, Graham, & Harris, 1992.

TABLE 11-3   How learning a strategy is like learning a new basketball play.

Learning a Basketball Play	Shared Characteristics	Learning a Strategy
Coach draws the play on chalkboard and tells players what is supposed to happen and the advantages of using the play.	**Describe Stage** An expert explains what to do.	Teacher provides students with a copy of the strategy steps and tells what happens in each step and the advantages of using them.
Coach demonstrates key parts of the play.	**Model Stage** Modeling by an expert.	Teacher demonstrates what to do for each step.
Players discuss the play and then memorize what they are supposed to do.	**Verbal Practice Stage** Understand and memorize.	Students explain the strategy steps to each other and then memorize them.
On the practice court, players walk through the play in slow motion; coach helps players do it correctly.	**Controlled Practice Stage** Learning how it feels to do it in simple situations.	Students practice performing the strategy on easy words; teacher helps them to do it correctly.
Players practice on the court against other team members to see what it will be like in a real game; coach watches and gives feedback.	**Advanced Practice Stage** Learning how to do it in situations similar to the real thing.	Students perform the strategy on real vocabulary words from school and take practice quizzes; teacher gives feedback.
Players run the play in real games.	**Generalization Stage** Using on the real thing.	Students use the strategy to study for real tests.
Players watch films of the play after the game; change the play or practice more if necessary; create new plays by changing play in various ways.	**Generalization Stage** Evaluating and adapting.	Students check to see how well the strategy helped; change it or practice it more if necessary; create new strategies based on this one.

Source: Ellis, E. S. (1992). *The LINCS strategy.* Lawrence, KS: Edge Enterprises. Cue Card # 12. Reprinted by permission of the publisher.

Stage One: Pretest

Pretest students on the categories of skills that the strategy covers. For example, students who may be learning a Word Identification strategy that focuses on their ability to decode multisyllable words (Lenz, Deshler, Schumaker, & Beals, 1984) are pretested to determine how many words they can read correctly from a brief passage in their social studies textbook. Students who are learning a Sentence Writing strategy (Schumaker & Sheldon, 1985) may be pretested by writing a brief story and analyzing the variety of sentence types used. When scores are determined, they are graphed on a progress chart to provide students with a visual representation of their performance.

Explain to students the results of the pretest and discuss why it is important that students are able to do the items assessed on the pretest. Involve students by eliciting from them additional reasons to learn the strategy. Students must value those reasons, so it is important that the teacher is able to relate the task demands to both in-school and out-of-school situations so there is meaningful application of the strategy evident to the student.

Ms. Jenna, a special educator, has students with learning disabilities in eighth grade who have significant difficulty understanding what they read. She has recently received training in the Paraphrasing strategy (Schumaker, Deshler, & Denton, 1984) and targets this strategy for her students. During Pretest, she has each student read a brief passage (400 words or so) with comprehension questions. The passages are written on an eighth grade reading level. Results of the pretest confirm that the students are not understanding the information. Pretest results are discussed individually with each student, and the importance of being able to comprehend accurately is discussed. Ms. Jenna informs students that she knows a strategy that can help them comprehend more information that they read, and elicits their commitment to learn the strategy. As a group, they discuss situations in which they can use the strategy, how learning the strategy can benefit them, and why learning the strategy is important to them.

Stage Two: Describe

Once students understand their pretest results and are motivated to learn the strategy, the teacher describes the strategy. At this point, many teachers have a tendency to teach the students how to use the strategy. However, simply giving an overview of the strategy will suffice during the Describe stage. Exposure includes the teacher describing the instructional steps the student will be using with the strategy.

For example, in the Word Identification strategy, the teacher describes the steps of the strategy by reading a paragraph with multisyllable words and using the mnemonic DISSECT (**D**iscover the context, **I**solate the prefix, **S**eparate the suffix, **E**xamine the stem, **C**heck with someone, **T**ry the dictionary) to assist with decoding the words (Lenz et al., 1984). Although some new information is exposed to students through the use of DISSECT, the teacher does not worry at this point about having students learn all of the new information. During Describe, the emphasis is on exposing students to the steps of the strategy and how those steps are used by a person who is proficient in using that strategy.

The steps in the Paraphrasing strategy are: (1) **R:** *Read a paragraph, (2)* **A:** *Ask yourself what the main idea and two details are, and (3)* **P:** *Put the main idea and details in your own words. Ms. Jenna uses a grade level passage to demonstrate each of the steps of the Paraphrase strategy. During the Describe stage, she is telling students what the strategy is and showing how RAP is used when reading.*

Stage Three: Model

Teacher behaviors required in the Model stage are critical because they expose the student to the inner thought processes that strategic learners use. Although teachers may feel awkward initially talking aloud about what they are thinking, failure to model by talking aloud clearly and frequently can deny students of the opportunities to view a strategic thinker's way of thinking. During the Model stage, the teacher is teaching the student how to use self-instruction by repeating the steps in the strategy along with verbalizing what the teacher is thinking when using each step.

Some of the initial research conducted with students on "talking to themselves" to help them control their impulsive behaviors was conducted by Meichenbaum and Goodman (1971). Of the significant information in this study was the transformation of previously covert "private speech" to overt "talk out loud" speech in order to both ensure students were using the correct steps to self-instruct and to remind the students of the steps they needed to use. Meichenbaum and Goodman (1971) report that students were taught to use their private speech to orient, organize, regulate, and self-reward so that the end result was more self-control. The instructional sequence that was most effective in bringing about self-control consisted of *both* modeling and self-instruction. During the Model stage of instruction, students observe the teacher modeling a set of verbalizations and behaviors that characterize the strategy. The teacher includes in this modeling errors and self-corrections, as well as positive self-talk related to each student's performance.

Ms. Jenna uses another reading passage to model the use of the Paraphrasing strategy. During the Model stage, her concentration is repeating what she did using RAP in the Describe stage but adding to that description her thought processes while she is using RAP. Modeling RAP sounds something like this:

> *"OK. First I need to read the paragraph to myself. I'll do that. . . . I did the first step in RAP, now I need to do the next step which is asking myself what the main idea and two details are in the paragraph I just read. Hmmm, this is harder for me to do, but I know I can do it when I use several tips. One tip is to see if the main idea is in the first sentence. Another tip is to look for repeated phrases or words in the paragraph. There are other tips, but I'm going to try these first. Is the main idea in the first sentence? Yes, it is. Now for the details. Let me see, there are also tips for finding details. One tip for details is to find more information that's related to the main idea. I need to go back through the paragraph and. . . .OK. I have my main idea and two details. Now for my last step—putting the main idea and details into my own words. I know this is the hardest part for me because I usually just repeat exactly what the paragraph says, and that doesn't count as a paraphrase. Where are my guidelines for paraphrasing? Here they are. . . . All right—through with that paragraph. Looks good to me. Now for the next paragraph . . ."*

Stage Four: Verbal Practice

By the time students are at the Verbal Practice stage, their teacher has already described the strategy (usually a set of mnemonic steps accompany the strategy, or for younger or students with more cognitive disabilities the steps may be accompanied by pictures) by telling them what it is and how to use it (remember, no mastery was required here) and modeled the strategy by again demonstrating the strategy but adding the thinking aloud to their demonstration. During the Verbal Practice stage, students are required to memorize the steps in the strategy so that they will be able to instruct themselves later when using the steps. Mastery of the strategy steps (e.g., the mnemonic steps of the strategy) is required here. If students do not memorize the steps at this point, then they will not be able to focus on *using* the steps during later instruction and practice. Expect to spend as much time here as is necessary for students to memorize the steps of the strategy. However, the responsibility for students mastering the strategy steps does not rest solely with the teacher. Students are involved by setting goals for themselves, helping each other study the steps, and assisting the teacher with the development of activities that help them reach mastery. Students know what they need to do and are involved in helping themselves do it.

Ms. Jenna's Instructor's Manual for the Paraphrasing strategy lists several requirements for students to master before exiting the Verbal Practice stage. Among those requirements are that students verbally identify the following information during one quiz session: (1) describe what the Paraphrasing strategy is used for; (2) identify the steps in the Paraphrasing strategy; (3) identify several requirements for accurate paraphrases; and (4) tell one situation in which paraphrasing can be used. Ms. Jenna keeps quiz scores on worksheets for the students to note what they know and what they need to practice until they know it. Most students can quickly repeat the steps in the strategy but have more difficulty telling some requirements for paraphrasing. Each student must identify all of the required information during one session in order to move on to the next stage. At this point in the strategy, Ms. Jenna begins to have students working at different stages, depending on how quickly they master each stage. What has been group instruction so far now becomes more individualized as students begin to use the strategy themselves—on materials that are written on their reading level, not on their grade level.

Stage Five: Controlled Practice and Feedback

During the Controlled Practice stage, students practice using the strategy at their current performance level. For example, seventh grade students with learning disabilities in reading who are learning a reading comprehension strategy and read at third grade level will practice using the strategy at their current performance level of third grade. Students who are learning a test-taking strategy will practice using the strategy on "practice tests" in which they already know much of the information so that they can concentrate on applying the strategy to "easier" tests and become proficient with using the strategy at that level. Mastery is required for this stage. If students do not master using the strategy on information that is relatively "easy" for them then they do not learn more detailed features about how to use the strategy (remember that good strategy users automatically "get" this information and do not need this much practice to understand features of the strategy) nor do they attain a high level of proficiency (and confidence) from which they can build future strategies. During the Controlled Practice stage, students are instructing themselves to use the steps of the strategy while using materials that are relatively easy for them to use—"controlled" levels.

Essential at this stage, as students initially struggle with applying the strategy, is the way that teachers give feedback to students. Feedback progresses from more direct feedback given by the teacher (teacher-mediated feedback) to the teacher prompting the student to be more actively involved in the feedback process so that the student learns to self-evaluate his or her performance using the strategy (student-mediated feedback). Although this

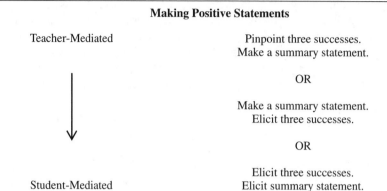

Making Positive Statements

Teacher-Mediated

Pinpoint three successes.
Make a summary statement.

OR

Make a summary statement.
Elicit three successes.

OR

Elicit three successes.
Student-Mediated   Elicit summary statement.

Using an Error Routine

Teacher-Mediated   →   Student-Mediated

			Teacher-Mediated	Student-Mediated
→	→	Step 1	Specify one error category.	Elicit one error category.
↑		Step 2	Review rule or concept.	Elicit rule or concept.
↑	→ →	Step 3	Model application.	Prompt application.
↑ ← ↑ ←		Step 4	Prompt application.	Model application.

FIGURE 11-2   Moving from teacher-mediated to student-mediated feedback by making positive statements and using an error routine.

Source: University of Kansas Institute for Research on Learning Disabilities. (1989). *Learning Strategies Instruction Training Materials,* Feedback pages 9 & 10. Reprinted by permission of the publisher.

feedback process is more time intensive initially, if teachers do not take students through this process so that the students end up being able to monitor their performance then students do not learn how to independently self-evaluate their future performance. In actuality teachers more quickly get the student to independent use of the strategy when they take the time to give feedback that requires the student to self-evaluate (see Figure 11-2 for an example of how feedback flows from teacher-mediated to student-mediated).

One of Ms. Jenna's students, Alex, mastered the Verbal Practice information after four sessions. He begins Controlled Practice by reading passages written at the fourth grade level, and then answering questions about each passage. When reading the passage, here's what Alex does: He reads the first paragraph and then asks himself what the main idea and two details were. Then he puts that information into his own words, and reads that information into a tape recorder so that his teacher can score it later. He reads the next paragraph using RAP, and records his next paraphrase into the tape recorder. He continues with this process until he's through with the whole passage (usually a 400-word passage is sufficiently long). Then he answers questions about the passage. This completes one session of Controlled Practice for what he needs to do, except responding to feedback. Alex gives Ms. Jenna his tape, passage, and answers to questions so she can score them

Ms. Jenna listens to each paragraph's paraphrase on the tape recorder and fills out a score sheet to help her provide detailed feedback to Alex. Most paragraphs have been paraphrased accurately, but there are problems with two of them. The mastery criteria for students passing Controlled Practice is 90 percent of paraphrases are accurate and 80 percent of the questions are answered correctly. Alex's score on his first Controlled Practice reading is 60 percent accurate paraphrases and 70 percent correct answers; he needs to complete another Controlled Practice reading passage using RAP, but not before Ms. Jenna provides feedback on this one.

Ms. Jenna and Alex conference on the scores (which have been graphed to provide more visual and concrete information for Alex) he received on his first passage, and they spend time discussing what types of errors he made as well as how he can avoid making those errors in the future. During the first conference, Ms. Jenna is more direct in telling him where he made errors and how to correct them. However, her feedback is explicit enough so that Alex is learning how to look at incorrect information and figure out why he made errors, tell the rule or guideline that should help him get items correct the next time, and tell what the correct answer should be. Alex is learning how to self-evaluate his work by studying his mistakes, noting the rule he knows that applies to the mistakes, and correcting the mistakes.

These feedback sessions are time-consuming and individualized according to the types of errors students make. Ms. Jenna realizes, however, that if she doesn't take the time now to be explicit with students and to require them to begin self-evaluating, then they will not be able to independently paraphrase more difficult information.

Stage Six: Advanced Practice and Feedback

After students have mastered using the strategy at their current performance level, then they begin practicing on more advanced materials or information. Depending on the strategy, students may be advancing to grade-level materials or information, or they may be advancing to a more difficult level of application. Teacher feedback and support during this stage is also necessary here, as it was in the previous stage. As students begin using the strategy on more difficult information then the teacher feedback may be more specific and guiding initially, while it is still the teacher's intent to move toward feedback that prompts the student to self-evaluate. Mastery is required at the Advanced Practice stage. Materials used should either be, or resemble, materials from the general education setting in which students are expected to learn or find information. For example, students who are learning the Paraphrasing Strategy (Schumaker et al., 1984) can use their content textbooks during the Advanced Practice stage. Students self-instruct during Advanced Practice by remembering the steps in the strategy (which they memorized during Verbal Practice), and now they are applying those steps at an even more advanced level by using more complicated or difficult material.

> *Alex passed Controlled Practice when five reading passages were completed. Boy, did he feel good seeing those scores rise on his progress chart! He spent over two weeks on Controlled Practice, and he spent a lot of time with Ms. Jenna during feedback conferences. He's on a roll, and now he's ready to use RAP on grade level information. He completes his first passage using the same procedures as in Controlled Practice: stopping after reading each paragraph, asking himself what the main idea and details are, and putting that information in his own words by dictating into a tape recorder. Then he answers questions about the passage and turns all the information in to Ms. Jenna to score.*
>
> *Feedback time: His scores are down from his last Controlled Practice session, and Alex finds that disappointing at first. However, Ms. Jenna points out to him that he should expect his performance to decline for his first passage in Advanced Practice because now he is working with more complex reading material. Ms. Jenna also emphasizes that (1) his progress chart shows similar scores when he first began Controlled Practice passages, but those scores improved when he used RAP, and (2) all of his scores are above his Pretest scores, which shows in general that he has become a more proficient paraphraser since he began strategy instruction almost a month ago. Alex is learning that hard work does pay off and that his performance does improve when he consistently and accurately uses RAP. Now his goal is to reach mastery levels on paraphrases and comprehension questions on grade level materials (Advanced Practice materials) within three weeks.*
>
> *Alex and Ms. Jenna are still holding feedback conferences after she scores each passage. Again, these conferences are initially guided by Ms. Jenna identifying errors, telling him the rule that applies to the errors, and showing him how to use the rule to correct the errors. Eventually, though, the sessions are more directed by Alex using self-evaluation to figure out the rules that apply to errors and how to correct them on his own.*

Stage Seven: Posttest

The posttest content and format is similar to that used for the pretest. In this way, students are able to compare the before and after effects of using the strategy (refer to Figure 11-3 for an example of one student's pre- and posttest writing sample). The comparison of results can be a powerful motivator in and of itself to students that the effort they put forth throughout the strategy instruction is resulting in improved performance. With this information in mind, the teacher discusses with students how they can continue to use the strategy to help them perform in general education classroom situations. The teacher and students leave the Posttest stage with a renewed commitment to using the strategy and with an agreement that they will continue to have periodic checks on how well students are using the strategy elsewhere. They leave the Posttest stage with a plan for generalization.

Pretest ▶

fee, 4, 1991

> ¹a Big Mhoshen in frlte of
> ²it garoad way, urlet. pink
> ³fouewa urlet. green soneenane
> ⁴green tree and green grass
> ⁵urhea a uhit fall wall look
> ⁶clike a pool urth is soke
> ⁷aver neay, it is a sun
> ⁸day in Maryland.

Name:

SIMPLE SENTENCE LESSON ④A 4B 4C 4D   4-10-91
(Circle one)

Instructions:

1. In the space below, write at least six sentences about the topic listed
    on your Assignment Sheet. Include in this group of sentences at least one
    of each of the four kinds of simple sentences. Use your Formula Card
    for reference as needed.

Posttest ▶

2. Use the Subject-Verb Identification Procedure and a <u>Simple Sentence</u>
    <u>Checklist</u> to check the kinds and number of simple sentences you have written.
3. Attach your completed <u>Simple Sentence Checklist</u> to this sheet when you
    are done.

Topic: **Learning Stategies**

> 1   The learning stategies are
> 2 hard to pass. Last year I learned
> 3 a strategy call DISSEct. It was
> 4 hard and wasa big strategy.
> 5 Me and my friends are working
> 6 on the pavaphrasing stratcgy
> 7 and yoa have to read a lot. Pens
> 8 is harder than all thei stratcgies
> 9 that I have learned, Me and
> 10 my friends are working on the Pens
> 11 Stratcgy.

What a difference a strategy makes!

**FIGURE 11-3   Before and after writing samples from a student who learned the "Simple
Sentence Writing Strategy."**

Source: From Schumaker, J. B., & Sheldon, J. (1985). *The sentence writing strategy.* Lawrence, KS: University of Kansas.

Alex can't believe how much he's improved his scores since the pretest he took two months ago. His pretest score for paraphrases was 33 percent; his posttest score is 90 percent. His pretest score for comprehension was 40 percent; his posttest score is 100 percent. What a difference understanding what he reads makes! Now he needs to commit to using RAP in other places. Actually, he's already been using it in other classes, and even when reading magazines at home. But now Ms. Jenna wants him to formally record when he's used RAP, where he's used RAP, and how using RAP has benefited him on at least three occasions each week. He uses a self-recording checklist that he and Ms. Jenna developed to document his use of RAP during the week.

Stage Eight: Generalization

Generalization consists of students' continued use of the strategy in situations other than their training sessions, students' adaptation of the strategy to fit slightly different situations, and students' ability to continue using the strategy without having been prompted to do so. For example, students who learn the Word Identification strategy should be using the strategy regularly whenever they encounter a multisyllable word they do not know (Lenz et al. 1984). New situations may occur while reading in content classes, while reading a movie advertisement in the shopping mall, while looking through a magazine, or while studying the manual for their driver's license test. Although the formal last stage of instruction is called Generalization, in reality the teacher and students have been talking all along (actually, ever since the Pretest) about what the strategy can be used for, when it can be used, how it can help the student in other situations, and why it is important to use.

Ms. Jenna is pleased with Alex's progress using the Paraphrasing strategy, and she asks his teachers to remind him to use RAP whenever they assign class reading material. Instead of Ms. Jenna describing the strategy for each teacher (she's already discussed it with them briefly and provided reading material on it), she delegates that responsibility to Alex. Some teachers have the RAP steps listed on a bulletin board in their classroom to remind Alex to use it, but he also uses a bookmark that has the steps listed on it as a reminder. One teacher really likes the strategy and wants her other students to learn it. Ms. Jenna has an idea: How could Alex be a co-teacher for his peers learning RAP?!

The Generalized Skills Model: Self-Instruction with Multiple Examples

Self-instruction is a method that requires students to talk themselves through steps while completing a task. The benefits of using self-instruction as a way to help students mediate their strategic performance abound (see Table 11-4 for a summary of benefits). Students with all types of disabilities can use self-instruction, but the types of tasks that students with severe disabilities use for self-instruction are quite different from the strategies learned by students with mild disabilities. Students with severe disabilities may be learning categories of strategies related to self-help skills, self-care skills, vocational tasks, or leisure activities. Hughes and Agran (1993) note that using self-instruction as a strategy for students with

TABLE 11-4   Benefits of self-instruction for students with mild, moderate, and severe disabilities.

Benefits of Self-Instruction for Students

- Encourages active monitoring of thought processes
- Reduces learner passivity
- Facilitates the maintenance and generalization of strategy use
- Increases students' attentiveness while performing academic work
- Promotes more proficient problem solvers
- Improves students' ability to verbalize appropriate problem-solving strategies
- Improves performance on academic tasks
- Assists students' focus on relevant verbal cues and use of these cues
- Helps students to regulate their behaviors
- Increases students' attention, memory, and motivation
- Helps students control their impulsive behaviors

Source: Compiled from information in the following literature: Miller, 1985; Palincsar & Brown, 1984; Whitman, 1987.

severe disabilities involves teaching students how to verbalize statements that prompt them in how to accomplish tasks. Despite learner characteristics that seem to indicate that students with language and problem-solving difficulties would not be good candidates to use self-instruction, Whitman (1987) describes those characteristics as the very reasons why self-instruction helps them to mediate their deficit areas (see Table 11-5).

TABLE 11-5   Reasons to use self-instruction with students who have language and problem-solving difficulties.

Student Characteristics	Why Self-Instruction Is Beneficial
Receptive and expressive language deficits	Assists students with linguistic deficits to process strategic information presented in an external fashion and to translate the stored information into appropriate action patterns.
Do not spontaneously use private speech	Overtly teaches private speech.
Poor general knowledge information	Verbal cues enable students to integrate new information into existing knowledge base structures.
Lack problem-solving skills	Provides a problem-solving vehicle (self-verbalization) for actively processing information and by providing specific and general information needed in problem-solving situations.

Source: Information from Whitman, T. L. (1987). Self-instruction, individual differences, and mental retardation. *American Journal of Mental Deficiency, 92,* 213–223.

Hughes (1994) recommends that teachers construct strategies for students with severe disabilities using a Generalized Skills Model that focuses on self-instruction and multiple examples of the same tasks. Her framework for teacher construction of strategies follows:

1. Select an array of examples (responses).
2. Classify responses into teaching sets.
3. Divide members of sets into instructed responses and generalization probes.
4. Teach instructed responses using self-instruction.
5. Evaluate the effects of teaching.
6. Withdraw teaching and evaluate the effects of teaching withdrawal.

The instructional sequence when teaching students from the Generalized Skills Model includes modeling, guided performance (from easy to more difficult tasks), corrective feedback (from teacher-mediated to student self-evaluation), and reinforcement. Each of these instructional methods is also evident in the Strategy Intervention Model of instruction, providing educators with common strategic behaviors useful for teaching students with mild, moderate, and severe disabilities. However, the focus of the methods changes somewhat to accommodate the unique characteristics of students who have more severe cognitive disabilities (e.g., severe to profound mental retardation).

The nature of the tasks targeted for students with severe disabilities is derived from a functional life skills curriculum rather than from a traditional academic curriculum. Teachers of students with severe disabilities are accustomed to breaking down each task into discrete steps and teaching each step of the task. However, Hughes (1992) notes that the use of self-instruction for students with severe mental retardation more effectively achieves generalization when *multiple examples of tasks are taught instead of a single task.* Instead of teaching students with severe disabilities each solution for each problem using only a task analysis approach, she targeted categories of problems and taught the solutions as a set. She instructed adults with mental retardation in three general problem-solving activities in which the solutions involved "finding" (the dust spray and dusting, the soap and washing hands, and the toothbrush and brushing teeth), "moving" (the hamper out of the corner and putting the chair in the corner, the cord out of the way and vacuuming floor), or "plugging in" objects (the radio and turning it on, the lamp and turning it on). All three solutions were taught concurrently (versus a more traditional approach by teaching one at a time) to a set of items.

Pretest

Students can be pretested by noting their response to verbal directions or by asking them to respond to a specific situation. A pretest can consist of simply noting whether students are able to complete tasks or follow directions. Then students are told why they need to be able to complete the tasks and how it will benefit them (i.e., they are provided a rationale for training the problem-solving situations). If students are working for a specific reinforcer or item, then displaying the reinforcer and reminding the students what they are working for can also be used to elicit student motivation.

For example, Elaine is an eighth-grade student with severe cognitive disabilities who does not bring the correct items she needs to class. Her teacher pretests by noting the items missing: books, pencil, and paper. Because all of these items belong to a category of "things Elaine should be getting from her locker," her teacher has identified this set to use for self-instruction. An even broader category could be targeted: "things Elaine needs to bring to each class." Discussion with Elaine also occurs around the following issues: why it's important to bring items to class each day; how being prepared for class helps her to get her "job" done during classtime; what being prepared for class looks like, feels like, and means for her; how often during the day she needs to arrive prepared to work; which situations have found her unprepared in the past and what the results have been; and how to make decisions about what to bring to class. The teacher and Elaine leave this part of instruction with concrete reasons why Elaine needs to learn a strategy, how it can help her in a variety of situations, and how Elaine's motivation and determination to learn the strategy can influence future outcomes. At this point, Elaine should be ready to listen to what the strategy is and watch her teacher using the strategy; the rationale has already been established.

Describe and Model

The teacher models the appropriate task response by describing verbally what he or she is doing. The verbalizations used should approximate the language skills of the students. Hughes and Agran (1993) suggest that teachers consider whether students talk aloud, the words they consistently use, and the use of signing as a means of self-instructing students with hearing impairments, limited language, or autistic behaviors. However, they caution against educators making language usage the sole consideration for the steps in the strategy of self-instruction. Students may be able to understand and use more self-instructions than they can verbalize or vocalize.

Next, students perform the same response while the teacher instructs the students aloud. Then, students perform the response again while self-instructing aloud. Hughes (1992) suggests using a five-step framework for developing the strategy steps:

1. State the problem: "What am I supposed to do?"
2. State a generic response to the problem: "_____ is what I'm supposed to do."
3. State a specific response to the problem and do it: "OK. I need to _____. That's what I'll do right now."
4. Self-evaluate the response you did to solve the problem: "Did _____ work?"
5. Self-reinforce if you did it correctly: "Good, I did _____ right."

Active Practice and Feedback

Teacher behaviors during active practice and feedback include prompting students about the steps of the strategy they should be using, modeling (and remodeling) the steps of the strategy and how to do it, practicing each step so that the sequence is both remembered and performed by the student, providing corrective feedback that lets students know where they made a mistake and how they need to correct it, and giving verbal praise for correctly completing the sequence of steps.

Elaine, her teacher, and a peer buddy are practicing each morning the five-steps she needs to say out loud and do while she is at her locker:

1. State the problem: "What am I supposed to do?"
2. State a generic response to the problem: "I'm supposed to get things I need for class."
3. State a specific response to the problem and do it: "OK. I need to get my paper, books, and pencil. I'll get those right now."
4. Self-evaluate the response you did to solve the problem: "Did I get everything?"
5. Self-reinforce if you did it correctly: "Good, I have everything I need for class."

Note that this same self-instruction can be used for a variety of tasks that Elaine is expected to do throughout the day. What is critical is that she remembers each step; otherwise, the tasks cannot be completed. Sometimes the tendency is to teach students through Step 3 and not teach the whole sequence. If Elaine cannot remember to perform the whole sequence then she is not able to independently and correctly complete the task herself.

Initially, self-reinforcement may be prompted by the teacher and accompanied by external reinforcement systems. Token reinforcements and verbal praise from the teacher that are used when students are beginning to learn self-reinforcement can often be faded to intermittent schedules of reinforcement once students have acquired the new behavior (e.g., self-reinforcement).

Generalization

Students with severe disabilities are more likely to use their newly acquired behaviors in different situations and with different behaviors when they are (1) told during instruction to respond as if they were in a new setting, (2) reminded to self-instruct when working independently, and (3) taught using multiple examples of the same task (Hughes, 1992). These ways of preparing students to independently use new skills in new settings and with different behaviors were actually targeted for use *during* instruction, not at the end of instruction.

Critical to students' ability to successfully and independently perform tasks is that *all* of the instructional steps are used. That is, if students are only stating the problem, then they are likely to be unsuccessful in independently completing the task. Similarly, students who are able to state the problem and the solution are also not as successful as those who self-evaluated the effects of their efforts *and* self-reinforced themselves for being successful. Reminders to use self-instruction are also necessary initially but can be faded from frequent reminders after students are using self-instruction independently. As with the Strategy Intervention Model's Generalization stage, other teachers, paraprofessionals, peers, and parents are involved from start to finish with the Generalized Skill Model in that they play a key role in: (1) reminding students to use the strategies they are learning; (2) reinforcing students' use of new strategies; (3) providing opportunities for strategy practice; (4) determining what types of strategies are necessary for students to learn, based on the demands within their settings; and (5) extending the application of strategy learning beyond the strategy training sessions.

What has been described so far in this chapter are ways that teachers can teach strategies to students with mild, moderate, and severe disabilities. Additionally, it has been acknowledged that *all students benefit from a strategic orientation* during instruction, but that *some students need more intensive instruction* in how to become more strategic in their approach to tasks. At the beginning of the chapter, a case was made for teaching strategies to students because strategies can enable students to become more independent and self-determining youngsters. However, if the focus of instruction only deals with teacher behaviors then the end result will not be independence and self-determination. Student behaviors must also be explicitly addressed. To that end, students can learn a framework from which they can problem solve in a variety of situations.

The next sections of this chapter address two areas related to teaching students strategic behaviors. First, student behaviors that both underlie and transcend strategic performance are identified and described. Second, a framework (SPEED) for students to use when developing and performing a strategy for specific purposes is presented.

Students' Strategic Behaviors

Students can be actively engaged in the learning process by setting goals, regulating their own learning and performance, and generalizing their use of strategies, wherein:

1. Setting goals for learning and performance includes choosing which strategies are most meaningful based on present capabilities and preferences as related to present/future setting demands and making a commitment to learn and perform.
2. Regulating the use of strategies includes using self-talk as a guide to learning and remembering the strategy, self-monitoring as a guide to performing the strategy, self-evaluation as a means of determining performance proficiency or mastery, and self-feedback as a guide to improving performance.
3. Generalizing the use of strategies includes using the strategy within natural contexts, adapting the strategy for novel situations, and creating new strategies to approach new situations.

Teachers' understanding of the components of the goal setting process and its importance to student performance is critical to effective strategy instruction. An in-depth presentation of the thought and decision processes that comprise goal setting is presented here because these processes are foundational to students' independent functioning but are often overlooked when teaching students with disabilities. Although students' self-regulation of strategy implementation and generalization of strategy use (and teachers' roles in instruction for these behaviors) are also important, these behaviors are presented elsewhere in this text: self-instruction and generalization are discussed earlier in this chapter; self-management behaviors (self-monitoring, self-evaluation, and self-reinforcement) are presented in Chapter 12.

Goal Setting

Goal setting is a pivotal behavior in students' development of strategic behaviors for learning and performing. The criteria for learning and performing begin with goals (whether personally or externally set) and continue to be redefined based on the accomplishment of goals. Goal setting leads to the development of strategies, or ways, to achieve the goal (Locke, Shaw, Saari, & Latham, 1981). Similarly, it is the development and use of strategies that lead to goal accomplishment. Thus, goal setting and strategies have a synergistic relationship that leads to achievement and independence.

Goal setting encompasses a composite of behaviors that include:

- Knowing oneself
- Making choices
- Identifying desired outcomes (e.g., product or performance goals)
- Planning to accomplish the outcomes (e.g., process goals)

One behavior is not necessarily a prerequisite of another in the sense that the behaviors must be mastered in sequence. However, all behaviors will be present to some degree in order for goal-setting, and ultimately strategic behaviors, to develop within a framework that promotes independence.

Knowing Oneself

Self-knowledge is inherent to acting in one's self-interest and establishing goals (Field & Hoffman, 1994). Knowing oneself can be defined as students' understanding of their strengths, weaknesses, needs, and preferences within the context of present and/or future personal desires, setting demands, or life events. Ellis, Lenz, and Sabornie (1987b) link students' self-knowledge to their motivation to learn and generalize strategies. If students identify their strengths and weaknesses in relation to setting demands and personal preferences, they are more likely to see the need for or the benefits of developing a strategy (Ellis, Lenz, & Sabornie, 1987a). They are also more likely to see a connection between their performance, the strategy used, and goal accomplishment.

Viewing their capabilities and preferences in relation to performance opportunities (e.g., setting demands) sets the stage for students to view their present levels of performance in relation to "where they what to be" or "what they want to do." Knowing oneself requires that students: (1) be aware of the breadth of opportunities for participating within home, school, and community settings; (2) identify their preferences for participating; and (3) identify areas of strengths and weakness by assessing their performance relative to opportunities and preferences (Field & Hoffman, 1994). As students become more aware of opportunities and a desire to participate, identifying strengths and weaknesses provides them information about what they will need to do in order to be successful in what they attempt.

Students may obtain information about opportunities for participation and their current performance levels through both informal and formal means. Students may become aware of participation opportunities and requirements through observation of their same age peers or by referring to inventories or menus (Day & Elksnin, 1994). Bigge (1982) outlines "Tools for Life Management" for individuals with physical disabilities that can be completed in an inventory or interview format and includes fundamental skills and adaptive behaviors across seven areas: interpersonal effectiveness, self-care and personal needs, minimum academic knowledge, work habits, self-reliance in transportation and mobility, selection of work, and adaptation of work environments.

An informal indicator of students' strengths and weaknesses is their degree of success when participating in activities. Pretests for specific skills or problem-solving behaviors provide a more formal source of information about students' present level of performance in relation to present or future setting demands. When teachers communicate pretest results to students, students become aware not only of their performance strengths and weaknesses but of the effectiveness of their current approaches to learning and performing (Harris & Pressley, 1991). Students' knowledge of pretest results leads to their understanding of how successful they currently are at meeting certain situational demands and provides a rationale for acquiring strategies to enable them to meet present and future demands more effectively and efficiently (Lenz, 1992). Just as teachers use pretest information to set goals for instruction for particular (or groups of) students, students' knowledge of pretest results provides them the information needed to become goal setters based on the relationship among their present performance, what they want to do, and ways available to resolve the discrepancy.

Van Reusen and Bos (1990; 1994) developed a strategy that uses students' self-knowledge as the basis for developing long-range learning and performance goals. Using the strategy, students identify their capabilities and communicate their learning preferences during their individualized education program conferences. As part of the strategy students with learning disabilities were taught to:

1. "Inventory" their perceived learning strengths across academic, social, and career/vocational areas by answering a series of questions for each category.
2. Determine what areas needed improving by listing skills needed in their classes and comparing skills needed for success to their identified strengths.
3. Identify their interests, career goals, and academic goals by reflecting on personal preferences.
4. List their preferences for learning such as size of learning group, instructional activities, and type of test by considering past experiences with classroom learning and studying.

Students' knowledge of their capabilities (strengths and weaknesses) and preferences in relation to present and future setting demands leads to making more informed choices and setting goals that are relevant to preferred outcomes.

Making Choices

Once students have identified their capabilities and preferences related to desired outcomes, in order to have input in decisions that affect their lives they must make choices (Kozleski & Sands, 1992; Wehmeyer, 1992). Choice can be defined as the opportunity to make selections from two or more alternative events, consequences, or responses for which the individual has the responsibility for deciding which option will be selected (Brigham, 1979; Steiner, 1979). "Choice and decision making entail learning to identify alternatives, recognize consequences and locate resources necessary to act upon one's decisions" (Wehmeyer, 1992, p. 309). Within the goal-setting process, making choices uses students' self-knowledge as the basis for identifying and prioritizing desired outcomes and determining the means to achieve them.

Individuals are more likely to initiate, continue, persist, and complete tasks when they have choices in what they will do, how they will do it, how long they will do it, and how well they will do it. Students who are given choices, including those with severe disabilities, evidence faster and higher task completion rates (Brigham, 1979), more time on task (Realon et al., 1990), and higher achievement (Brigham, 1979). Despite the benefits in learning and performing associated with making choices, individuals with disabilities may be inexperienced with making choices either because of the lack of opportunities for choice (Sands, Kozleski, & Goodwin, 1992) or the absence of decision-making skills needed to make choices that lead to desired outcomes (Schloss, Alper, & Jayne, 1993; Wehmeyer, 1992).

Teachers can promote increased student involvement, persistence, and achievement in learning activities by building in opportunities for choice and/or providing systematic instruction in choice-making skills. Schloss, Alper, and Jayne (1993) developed a framework for expanding the choice repertoire of persons with disabilities in which the degree of control exercised by the individual is viewed along a continuum. Two dimensions of choice within this model include the amount of input the individual has in making a particular decision (ranging from complete responsibility to no input) and the degree to which the input of others must be accepted by the individual with disabilities (ranging from nonbinding input to total control). Schloss and colleagues recommend a prompt management method to guide students in developing choice-making skills. Teachers provide only the level of input necessary to elicit an appropriate choice response from the student: (1) the student has total independence in making a choice; (2) teacher guidance is given but does not restrict the actual response of the student; (3) teacher guidance partially restricts the actions of the student; (4) teacher guidance more fully restricts the actions of the student; or (5) the teacher fully restricts or acts on behalf of the student.

The amount of input individuals have in decisions that affect their lives is related to independence (Kozleski & Sands, 1992). Given a variety of learning, social, motivational, and executive strategies, students who are aware of their strengths, weaknesses, and preferences can choose strategies that help them to accomplish tasks that they recognize as important or are the means to desired outcomes (Harris & Pressley, 1991). Students' participation in choosing the strategies that will help them to achieve desired outcomes provides a decision-making opportunity that can lead to greater commitment to learn and use strategies (Deshler & Schumaker, 1993), increased rates of acquisition of strategies, higher achievement levels, and ultimately more independence.

Identifying Desired Outcomes (Product or Performance Goals)

Outcome:	*"something that follows as a result or consequence"*
Goal:	*"the end toward which effort is directed"*
	"what one purposes to accomplish or attain"

Merriam-Webster, 1973

Once an outcome has been identified as desirable, it in effect becomes a goal. By definition establishing goals includes a degree of commitment to work to achieve the goal. The relationship between goals and effort is supported through research as well as by definition. The goal-setting–performance relationship is strengthened when goals are specific (e.g., particular actions or levels of performance are identified), proximal (e.g., short term), individualized (e.g., based on the student's current skill level), difficult (e.g., challenging), and

---

Goals

- are based on a student's present level of performance
- represent more challenging skills or behaviors or strategies
- are more attainable when prerequisite skills or behaviors or strategies are present
- lead toward more effective and efficient use of instructional time and learning
- elicit higher achievement from students

+   +   added value   +   +

+ can be more difficult goals
+ result in improved outcomes
+ result in greater student satisfaction when goals are perceived as difficult
+ result in more skillful independent goal-setting

What adds the value?
Students are actively involved and learn to
make choices.

FIGURE 11-4   Characteristics of goals.

attainable (e.g., the prerequisite skills are present) (see Figure 11-4). As students learn to make choices for their learning and performance based on their capabilities and preferences, identifying desired outcomes or goals in terms of the quality of the performance or the end product is a natural next step. The nature or definition of the goal itself depends on several factors including the students' skill levels in relation to the setting demand, whether the behavior already exists in the students' repertoire, and the level of mastery required for skillful performance (Schunk & Gaa, 1981).

Setting goals for task performance or desired outcomes is associated with more time and effort devoted to accomplishing tasks, better grades (Morgan, 1985; 1987), and higher achievement (Fuchs, Fuchs, & Deno, 1985; Locke, Shaw, Saari, & Latham, 1981). Although achievement gains are evident even when goals are set by someone else, some researchers report that students' involvement in goal-setting results in: more difficult goals (Fuchs, Fuchs, & Deno, 1985), improved outcomes (Maher, 1981; Lochman, Burch, Curry, & Lampron, 1984), greater satisfaction when goals are perceived as difficult (Barbrack & Maher, 1984), and more skillful independent goal-setting (Schunk & Gaa, 1981).

Planning to Accomplish Desired Outcomes (Process Goals)

Schunk and Gaa (1981) differentiate between product or performance goals and process goals. Product or performance goals refer to the outcome of efforts or behaviors such as the shoe that has been tied, the notebook that has been organized, the test that has been passed, the book that has been read, or the term paper that has been written. *Process goals* refer to the means of accomplishing *product goals* such as the subtasks (process) involved in passing a science test (the product goal). The students may plan to attend class daily, take notes from lectures and readings, make note cards using mnemonics when possible, study the note cards nightly, and take the test within the allotted time. Process goals are usually short term and, once mastered, often can be used across situations to accomplish different product goals.

Students' knowledge of the operations, subtasks, or steps needed for skillful performance affects the planning process for goal attainment. For many students this planning process merely involves articulating what they will do, how, when, where, and for how long. However, students with disabilities may know only that they need or want to master a situational demand or "problem." They may not know how to go about achieving their goal in a way that is likely to lead to the desired outcome. In the example above, strategic learners only need to know what topics will be covered and the date that the test will be given (situational demand). Given this information, strategic learners will devise a plan that includes all or part of these steps because they know what needs to be done as part of an effective study routine. Plan variations for individual students only may vary in terms of their timeline for studying. Students who are not already proficient at using study routines to prepare for tests may benefit from guidance about steps to include in a plan to pass the test or about what to do during the study stages.

SPEED as Framework for Students' Problem Solving

Students' acquisition and generalization of strategic behaviors are directly related to the qualities embodied in self-determination and independence. The framework presented next focuses on student behaviors necessary for strategic performance (see Figure 11-5). The framework was developed from a synthesis of research on goal-setting, problem solving, self-regulation, choice making, metacognition, independence, and self-determination. SPEED is used as a mnemonic to assist students in remembering the steps involved in problem solving as a strategic process.

Strategic behaviors for solving problems or responding to situational demands include:

- **S**etting goals
- **P**lanning to accomplish goals
- **E**xecuting the plan
- **E**valuating the execution of the plan and the final product or performance
- **D**eciding what to do next (whether to retain or redefine the goal and whether to retain or revise the plan)

The emphasis in strategic problem solving is on enabling students to independently approach new, different, or novel situations and respond proficiently across a variety of situational demands. "Problem" here refers to any situation or task demand that students encounter to which they must respond in order to accomplish an outcome. SPEED provides students a planful approach for responding to problems. Skillful performance is an ongoing process in which demands are encountered, desired outcomes are identified, plans are devised to accomplish the outcomes, and the plans are executed. *However, the process does not end with task completion.* The implementation of the plan is evaluated, *and* the actual outcome is evaluated in relation to the desired outcome so that decisions can be made about future performances. The evaluation and decision steps enable students to learn from prior experiences and to use that information to make adjustments to future goals and plans. Thus, the framework of SPEED is not a linear approach to solving prob-

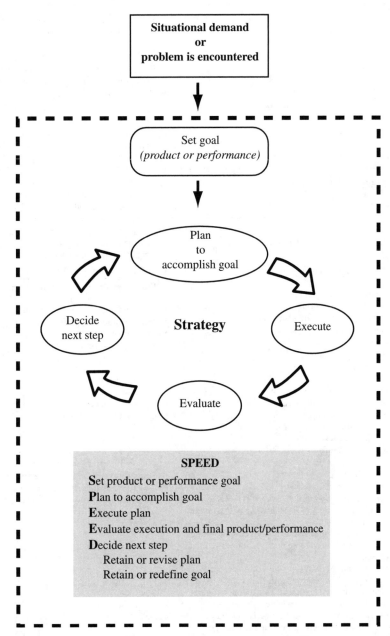

FIGURE 11-5   Strategic behaviors for problem solving.

lems but is recursive in nature. Often the completion of a task or activity is presented as the end point of a strategy yet in this model the "end point" serves as the beginning for the next performance. Table 11-6 contains key behaviors in which students engage during strategic problem solving. Table 11-6 also contains key teacher behaviors that can be used

TABLE 11-6   The development and use of strategic behaviors: Student and teacher roles.

Student Behaviors	Teacher Behaviors
Preparation • Know self. • Identify preferences, needs, strengths, and weaknesses.	• Query students about thoughts and desires. • Assess students' strengths, weaknesses, preferences, and needs. • Communicate results to student.
• Make informed choices.	• Present potential benefits of participation. • Present continuum of choices or options. • Provide least intrusive prompts.
• Identify situational demand or problem.	• Assign tasks; alert students to "problem."
Set goals • Commit to accomplish the task. • Identify product or performance goal.	• Commit to support student learning. • Request students' commitment. • Suggest product or performance goal.
Plan to accomplish the task/goal • Identify subtasks/steps that lead to goal. • Identify when, how, where to use steps.	• Analyze task and arrange into subtasks. • Describe possible strategy or steps. • Guide planning and elicit students' input.
Execute the plan • Recall steps of plan using self-talk.	• Demonstrate self-talk and application. • Provide memory device. • Require verbal mastery of steps.
• Rehearse plan verbally and/or physically	• Provide rehearsal opportunities.

• Perform steps of plan.
  - Look for specific opportunities to use.
  - Perform all steps in the manner planned.
  - Follow timeline.
  - Use self-talk.
  - Use self-monitoring.
	• Provide practice opportunities in simulated and actual conditions as needed.
	• Prompt students' use of steps/strategy.
	• Monitor students' performance.
	• Encourage self-talk.
	• Encourage self-monitoring.

Evaluate • Assess execution of the plan in relation to following the steps with accuracy and fluency. • Compare final product or performance to initial goal. • Use self-evaluation. • Generate self-feedback. • Respond to teacher/supervisor feedback.	• Assess students' execution of the plan. • Evaluate product or performance compared to initial goal. • Provide feedback. • Elicit students' self-feedback.

Decide what to do next
• Retain or redefine goal
  - *Keep same goal* if appropriate (e.g., if it needs to be done, is highly desired, or is achievable with same or revised plan).
  - *Set new goal* if original goal is no longer appropriate (e.g., if it does not need to be done, is not desired, was too difficult).
• Retain or revise plan:
  - *Keep same plan* if it worked and will continue to work for same or redefined goal; if it wasn't done properly the first time but seems reasonable to try again.
  - *Revise plan* if it was executed properly but didn't work or is no longer appropriate for a revised goal.
• Adapt the plan for novel situations.
	• Suggest revised product or performance goal.
	• Describe possible strategy or steps.
	• Guide planning and elicit students' input.

Encounter another situation or problem
• Same or similar situation or problem
  - Refer back to prior decisions and set goals
• New or different situation or problem
  - Create new strategies to approach novel tasks or situations and set goals.
	• Commit to support students' learning.
	• Request students' commitment.
	• Suggest product or performance goal.

to facilitate students' development of a strategic approach to problem solving within the SPEED framework.

Strategic problem solving is initiated by encountering a situational demand or problem. Students need (or want) to write a poem, complete their homework, clean the cafeteria tables, ride a bike, or go grocery shopping. In order to respond to the situational demand or "problem", students must have an adequate understanding of the event itself. Students' prior knowledge base, fund of general experience, and previous performance on a variety of tasks contribute to their understanding of the situational demand.

Once the situational demand or problem has been encountered, in order for problem solving to be set in motion, students must acknowledge that something needs to be done. This sounds fairly obvious, but some students do not seem to realize that action is required of them when certain events or situations present themselves. For example, an announcement that there will be a test on Friday should prompt a response from students, *"There's a test on Friday. This is a good time to use the FIRST-Letter Mnemonic strategy to prepare for the test."* Similarly, a flower pot with a wilting plant might prompt a different type of response, *"The leaves are drooping. This flower needs water. I should water this plant today."*

Upon recognizing that there is a situational demand or task that requires an action, students must decide to respond or not to respond to the demand. Hopefully this *choice* will be based on students' knowledge of their own preferences and capabilities as well as other criteria such as school or job requirements (in certain situations to choose not to begin a task leads to undesirable consequences!). Students who make informed choices are usually more motivated to perform at their "best."

> *Amanda works at a restaurant where her job responsibilities include folding napkins around silverware, setting tables, and refilling customers' water glasses. Getting the silverware ready is not difficult for her to remember because it is the first task she does when she arrives at work and her shift supervisor usually has all the supplies ready. Setting tables is not difficult either because the busboy tells her when to prepare a new table. Refilling water glasses is the hardest because when the restaurant is busy it is hard to see the empty glasses. Amanda's supervisor helped her use the SPEED strategy to fulfill her job responsibility of refilling water glasses. The situational demand is the need to refill water glasses in a timely manner.*

Set Product or Performance Goals

There are two distinct behaviors associated with setting product or performance goals: making a commitment and identifying the desired outcome. First, making a commitment to perform is a type of goal in and of itself (Lenz, 1992). A commitment may consist of a simple statement, *"I will study for the test on Friday."* Second, identifying the desired outcome either describes what the end product will look like or targets a particular level for performance. This is the heart of the goal because it establishes a criterion against which the final product or performance can be compared. *"I want to earn a B or better,"* indicates the desired quality of the test grade (product). Sometimes one statement provides the commitment and the end product. For example, the outcome is evident from the statement, *"I will wash and dry the tablecloths."* It is evident that the end "product" will be tablecloths that are clean and dry.

Amanda needs to visit each table at least once every 20 minutes to refill the water glasses. Customers should not make a complaint about their water.

Plan to Accomplish Goals

After goals have been set, students plan to accomplish goals by identifying what will be done to achieve the desired outcome or to display the desired level of performance. Within the "plan" is what needs to be done (steps or subtasks), where it needs to occur, when it will be done, how it will be done, and so forth. For example, a student who is writing a research report may set a product goal to earn an "A." In order to earn an "A" the student must include all required components and demonstrate proficient application of the appropriate writing skills. The student's plans for accomplishing this include the following:

Week 1: Spend two days at the library for research, obtain at least ten references, read materials for at least six hours, and make notecards.

Week 2: Make an outline and write the introduction to the paper.

Week 3: Write remaining sections of the paper including the conclusion.

Week 4: Make revisions, ask classmate to read, and make additional revisions.

Week 5: Turn in finished paper.

In order to devise a plan, students need to consider all necessary details but select only those ideas that are relevant to "getting the job done." The plan should be detailed enough that students know exactly what to do when they are executing the plan. Sequencing steps in the plan helps students remember what to do later. When possible, using mnemonics or other cues to remember the steps in the plan may also help students execute the plan.

The first part of Amanda's plan includes the order in which she will go to tables. The second part of the plan includes refilling any water glass that is less than approximately two-thirds full unless the customer asks her not to refill the glass. Amanda will go to each table along the window side of the room first and then to each table along the center wall of the room next. The following steps outline what she will do.

Step 1: Go to corner table by the window.

Step 2: Look at each water glass.

Step 3: Decide whether water is low.

Step 4: If water is not almost full, pour more water in the glass.

Step 5: Go to next table.

Repeat steps 2 through 5 until all tables have been visited. Start with Step 1 again.

Execute Plan

Rehearsing the plan in advance by reciting the steps of the plan orally will assist students in remembering the subtasks of the plan and increase the likelihood that students will be able to execute the plan with the least amount of support or monitoring by the teacher or, in a work-related setting, a supervisor. Physically rehearsing some plans may be appropriate. Again, just as students needed to recognize situational demands initially, recognizing opportunities to execute the plan is imperative. The plan will not result in desired outcomes if it is not used at appropriate times.

When executing the plan, students use self-talk to guide them so they will remember to perform all the steps in the manner planned. Self-monitoring is also useful because it provides students a mechanism for staying with the plan once they have begun. See Chapter 12 for a more in depth description of students' use of self-monitoring.

> *Customers have arrived, and it is time for Amanda to begin her duties of refilling the water glasses. As she goes through her duties she repeats the steps of her plan to herself. "Go to table. Look at one glass. Is the water low? Yes. Pour water. Look at another glass. Is the water low? No. Do not pour water. No more glasses. Go to the next table." This process continues throughout the afternoon.*

Evaluate Execution and Final Product/Performance

Once the plan has been executed, students evaluate two aspects of their performance: the execution of the plan and the final product or skill level. During the evaluation stage students provide feedback to themselves. Feedback often comes from outside sources as well (e.g., the teacher or supervisor), but students' ability to recognize similarities and differences between (a) what was planned and what was done, and (b) the target goal and the actual result prepares them to learn and perform in unsupervised situations, a major indicator of independence.

> *Amanda's shift is over. It is time to think about whether she accomplished her goal. Amanda filled each glass before it was completely empty and no customers complained. She asks herself the following questions while determining whether she did what she wanted to do. She asks her supervisor, "Did I pour water once every 20 minutes?" The supervisor responds that she did. Then Amanda asks herself, "Did I follow my plan? Yes. I went to each table, looked at each glass, and poured water in glasses that were low."*

Decide Next Step

After students have evaluated whether they completed the steps for goal accomplishment according to their plan and whether they accomplished the goal at the level intended, they decide what to do next: (1) retain or redefine the goal or (2) retain or revise the plan (see Table 11-6). Students make adjustments to their product/performance goal and plan by using their self-evaluation to decide what to do next time. Martin and colleagues (1993) describe the decision process as follows: "Students may change goals, tasks, self-management strategies, starting or ending times, or task outcomes. . . . Adjustments connect future action with past performance. Students reflect on their interests, plans, preferences, feedback, and outcomes. For example, before beginning another assignment, students review feedback . . . and select goals, plans, and performance objectives accordingly. (p. 59)

After talking to her supervisor and finding out that she filled the water glasses on time and after thinking about what she did and finding out that she followed all parts of her plan, Amanda is ready to decide what to do the next afternoon when it is time for her to fill water glasses. "I followed my plan and I filled the water glasses on time. I will use the same plan tomorrow when it is time to pour water." If Amanda had not filled the glasses in a timely manner, at this point she could make a new plan for circulating to the tables and filling the glasses (e.g., change her plan) or she could talk to her supervisor about reducing the number of tables she served (e.g., change her "product" goal).

Conclusions

Students with disabilities frequently lack strategies that are both effective and efficient for learning and performing. Although all students may benefit from instruction in how to approach task and learning demands in a strategic manner, in order to become proficient users of strategies, students with disabilities usually require strategy instruction that is both extensive and intensive. The roles of both teachers and students are key to students' acquisition and generalization of strategies. For teachers, an instructional sequence provides a guide for key teaching behaviors when introducing students to new strategies to meet task and setting demands. For students, a problem-solving framework provides a guide for key student behaviors when encountering a task or setting demand. The ultimate goal of strategy instruction is for students to become independent learners and performers by generating their own strategies. Teaching students to use strategies for learning and performing is one way that educators can promote student independence in school and community settings.

References

Barbrack, C. R., & Maher, C. A. (1984). Effects of involving conduct problem adolescents in the setting of counseling goals. *Child and Family Behavior Therapy, 6*(2), 33–43.

Bigge, J. L. (1982). *Teaching individuals with physical and multiple disabilities* (2nd ed.). Columbus, OH: Charles E. Merrill.

Brigham, T. A. (1979). Some effects of choice on academic performance. In L. C. Perlmuter & R. A. Monty (Eds.), *Choice and perceived control* (pp. 127–154). Hillsdale, NJ: Lawrence Erlbaum Associates.

Carpenter, S. L. F. (1990). *Adolescents with physical impairments: Metacognitive procedures for the acquisition and generalization of nonverbal communication behaviors.* Doctoral dissertation, University of Florida, Gainesville. (University Microfilms No. DAO 64793)

Day, V. P., & Elksnin, L. K. (1994). Promoting strategic learning. *Intervention in School and Clinic, 29,* 262–270.

Deci, E. L., & Ryan, R. M. (1985). *Intrinsic motivation and self-determination in human behavior.* New York: Plenum.

Deshler, D. D., Ellis, E. S., & Lenz, B. K. (1996). *Teaching adolescents with learning disabilities.* Denver: Love Publishing.

Deshler, D. D., & Schumaker, J. B. (1986). Learning strategies: An instructional alternative for low-achieving adolescents. *Exceptional Children, 52,* 583–590.

Deshler, D. D., & Schumaker, J. B. (1993). Strategy mastery by at-risk students: Not a simple matter. *The Elementary School Journal, 94,* 153–167.

Ellis, E. S. (1992). *The LINCS strategy.* Lawrence, KS: Edge Enterprises.

Ellis, E. S. (1994). An instructional model for integrating content-area instruction with cognitive strategy instruction. *Reading & Writing Quarterly, 10,* 63–90.

Ellis, E. S., Deshler, D. D., Lenz, B. K., Schumaker, J. B., & Clark, F. L. (1991). An instructional model for teaching learning strategies. *Focus on Exceptional Children, 23*(6), 1–23.

Ellis, E. S., Lenz, B. K., & Sabornie, E. J. (1987a). Generalization and adaptation of learning strategies to natural environments: Part 1: Critical agents. *Remedial and Special Education, 8*(1), 6–20.

Ellis, E. S., Lenz, B. K., & Sabornie, E. J. (1987b). Generalization and adaptation of learning strategies to natural environments: Part 2: Research into practice. *Remedial and Special Education, 8*(2), 6–23.

Field, S., & Hoffman, A. (1994). Development of a model for self-determination. *Career Development for Exceptional Individuals, 17,* 159–169.

Fuchs, L. S., Fuchs, D., & Deno, S. L. (1985). Importance of goal ambitiousness and goal mastery to student achievement. *Exceptional Children, 52,* 63–71.

Harris, K. R., & Pressley, M. (1991). The nature of cognitive strategy instruction: Interactive strategy construction. *Exceptional Children, 57,* 392–404.

Hughes, C. (1992). Teaching self-instruction utilizing multiple exemplars to produce generalized problem-solving among individuals with severe mental retardation. *American Journal of Mental Retardation, 97,* 302–314.

Hughes, C. (1994). Teaching generalized skills to persons with disabilities. In R. Gardner, D. M. Sainato, J. O. Cooper, T. E. Heron, W. L. Heward, J. Eshleman, & T. A. Grossi (Eds.), *Behavior analysis in education: Focus on measurably superior instruction* (pp. 335–348). Belmont, CA: Brooks/Cole.

Hughes, C., & Agran, M. (1993). Teaching persons with severe disabilities to use self-instruction in community settings: An analysis of applications. *Journal of the Association for Persons with Severe Handicaps, 18,* 261–274.

Hughes, C. A., & Schumaker, J. B. (1991). Test-taking strategy instruction for adolescents with learning disabilities. *Exceptionality, 2,* 205–221.

King-Sears, M. E., Mercer, C. D., & Sindelar, P. T. (1992). Toward independence with keyword mnemonics: A strategy for science vocabulary instruction. *Remedial and Special Education, 13* (5), 22–33.

Kozleski, E. B., & Sands, D. J. (1992). The yardstick of social validity: Evaluating quality of life as perceived by adults without disabilities. *Education and Training in Mental Retardation, 27,* 119–131.

Lagomarcino, T. R., & Rusch, F. R. (1989). Utilizing self-management procedures to teach independent performance. *Education and Training in Mental Retardation, 24,* 297–305.

Lenz, B. K. (1992). Self-managed learning strategy systems for children and youth. *School Psychology Review, 21,* 211–228.

Lenz, B. K., Deshler, D. D., Schumaker, J. B., & Beals, V. L. (1984). *The word identification strategy.* Lawrence: University of Kansas.

Lochman, J. E., Burch, P. R., Curry, J. F., & Lampron, L. B. (1984). Treatment and generalization effects of cognitive and goal-setting interventions with aggressive boys. *Journal of Consulting and Clinical Psychology, 52,* 915–916.

Locke, E. A., Shaw, K. N., Sarri, L. M., & Latham, G. P. (1981). Goal setting and task performance: 1969–1980. *Psychological Bulletin, 90,* 125–152.

Maher, C. A. (1981). Effects of involving conduct problem adolescents on goal setting: An exploratory investigation. *Psychology in the Schools, 18,* 471–474.

Martin, J. E., Marshall, L. H., & Maxson, L. L. (1993). Transition policy: Infusing self-determination and self-advocacy into transition programs. *Career Development for Exceptional Individuals, 16,* 53–61.

Meichenbaum, D. H., & Goodman, J. (1971). Training impulsive children to talk to themselves: A means of developing self-control. *Journal of Abnormal Psychology, 77,* 115–126.

Meltzer, L. J., Solomon, B., Fenton, T., & Levine, M. D. (1989). A developmental study of problem-solving strategies in children with and without learning difficulties. *Journal of Applied Developmental Psychology, 10,* 171–193.

Mercer, C. D., & Miller, S. P. (1992). Teaching students with learning problems in math to acquire, understand, and apply basic math facts. *Remedial and Special Education, 13*(3), 19–35.

Miller, G. E. (1985). The effects of general and specific self-instruction training on children's comprehension monitoring performances during reading. *Reading Research Quarterly, 20,* 616–828.

Morgan, M. (1985). Self-monitoring of attained subgoals in private study. *Journal of Educational Psychology, 77,* 623–630.

Morgan, M. (1987). Self-monitoring and goal setting in private study. *Contemporary Educational Psychology, 12,* 1–6.

Nagel, D. R., Schumaker, J. B., & Deshler, D. D. (1986). *The FIRST-letter mnemonic strategy.* Lawrence, Kans: Edge Enterprises.

Palinscar, A. S., & Brown, A. L., (1984). Reciprocal teaching of comprehension-fostering and comprehension-monitoring activities. *Cognition and Instruction, 1,* 117–175.

Palincsar, A. S., & Brown, D. A. (1987). Enhancing instructional time through attention to metacognition. *Journal of Learning Disabilities, 20*(2), 66–75.

Paris, S. G., & Oka, E. R. (1986). Self-regulated learning among exceptional children. *Exceptional Children, 52,* 103–108.

Pressley, M., Brown, R., El-Dinary, P. B., & Afflerbach, P. (1995). The comprehension instruction that students need: Instruction fostering constructively responsive reading. *Learning Disabilities Research & Practice, 10,* 215–224.

Putnam, M. L., Deshler, D. D., & Schumaker, J. B. (1993). The investigation of setting demands: A missing link in learning strategy instruction. In L. J. Meltzer (Ed.), *Strategy assessment and instruction for students with learning disabilities* (pp. 325–354). Austin, TX: Pro-Ed.

Realon, R. E., Favell, J. E., & Lowerre, A. (1990). The effects of making choices on engagement levels with persons who are profoundly multiply handicapped. *Education and Training in Mental Retardation, 25,* 299–305.

Rosenshine, B., & Meister, C. (1992). The use of scaffolds for teaching higher-level cognitive strategies. *Educational Leadership, 49*(7), 26–33.

Sands, D., Kozleski, E. B., & Goodwin, L. D. (1992). Quality of life for workers with developmental disabilities: Fact or fiction? *Career Development for Exceptional Individuals, 15,* 157–177.

Sawyer, R. J., Graham, S., & Harris, K. R. (1992). Direct teaching, strategy instruction, and strategy instruction with explicit self-regulation: Effects on the composition skills and self-efficacy of students with learning disabilities. *Journal of Educational Research, 84,* 340–352.

Schunk, D. H., & Gaa, J. P. (1983). Goal-setting influence on learning and self-evaluation. *Journal of Classroom Interaction, 16* (2), 38–44.

Schloss, P. J., Alper, S., & Jayne, D. (1993). Self-determination for persons with disabilities: Choice, risk, and dignity. *Exceptional Children, 60,* 215–225.

Schumaker, J. B., Denton, P. H., & Deshler, D. D. (1984). *The paraphrasing strategy.* Lawrence: KS: University of Kansas.

Schumaker, J. B., Deshler, D. D., & Denton, P. (1984). *The learning strategies curriculum: The paraphrasing strategy.* Lawrence: University of Kansas.

Schumaker, J. B., & Sheldon, J. (1985). *The sentence writing strategy.* Lawrence: University of Kansas.

Steiner, I. D. (1979). Three kinds of reported choice. In L. C. Perlmuter & R. A. Monty (Eds.), *Choice and perceived control* (pp. 17–28). Hillsdale, NJ: Lawrence Erlbaum Associates.

Swanson, H. L. (1984). Does theory guide teaching practice? *Remedial and Special Education, 5* (5), 7–16.

Swanson, H. L. (1993). Principles and procedures in strategy use. In L. J. Meltzer (Ed.), *Strategy assessment and instruction for students with learning disabilities* (pp. 61–92). Austin, TX: Pro-Ed.

Turnbull, A. P., & Turnbull, H. R. (1985). Developing independence. *Journal of Adolescent Health, 6,* 108–119.

Van Reusen, A. K., & Bos, C. S. (1990). I PLAN: Helping students communicate in planning conferences. *Teaching Exceptional Children, 22,* (4), 30–33.

Van Reusen, A. K., & Bos, C. S. (1994). Facilitating student participation in individualized education programs through motivation strategy instruction. *Exceptional Children, 60,* 466–475.

Van Reusen, A. K., & Bos, C. S., Schumaker, J. B., & Deshler, D. D. (1987). *The educational planning strategy.* Lawrence, KS: Edge Enterprises.

Wehmeyer, M. L. (1992). Self-determination and the education of students with mental retardation. *Education and Training in Mental Retardation, 27,* 302–314.

Wehmeyer, M. L. (1994). Employment status and perceptions of control of adults with cognitive and developmental disabilities. *Research in Developmental Disabilities, 15,* 119–131.

Wehmeyer, M. L., & Kelchner, K. (1994). Interpersonal cognitive problem-solving skills of individuals with mental retardation. *Education and Training in Mental Retardation and Developmental Disabilities, 29,* 265–278.

Welch, M. (1992). The PLEASE strategy: A metacognitive learning strategy for improving the paragraph writing skills of students with mild learning disabilities. *Learning Disability Quarterly, 15,* 119–134.

Whitman, T. L. (1987). Self-instruction, individual differences, and mental retardation. *American Journal of Mental Deficiency, 92,* 213–223.

Chapter *12*

Behavior Management Methods

STEPHANIE L. CARPENTER, TERI L. MUSY,
& MARGARET E. KING-SEARS

◆ ADVANCE ORGANIZER ◆

Effective management of student behavior is a primary area of concern for educators in today's schools. Educators' concerns are compounded when they consider the inclusion of students with disabilities who have a wide range of challenging behaviors in general education classrooms. In inclusive schools, student behavior is acknowledged to be a product of the interaction between the unique characteristics of the individual and the demands or events in the learning environment. In this chapter we present interventions that focus on different variables within schools that impact student behavior: school variables, classroom variables, and student variables. In doing so we compel educators to thoroughly examine their view of student behavior, their current methods of responding to challenging behaviors, and their potential to promote more appropriate student behaviors through the use of respectful and systematic application of behavior management techniques.

I'll never forget my first day of teaching first grade students in an urban elementary school that had just begun "including" students with a range of abilities and disabilities in the same classes. I felt prepared to teach the students based on their unique learning characteristics. What I didn't anticipate was that my students' background experiences might have a greater impact on my lesson plans than their learning differences. Discussing our classroom rules was one of the first morning's activities. I had an idea of what the class-room rules should be, and I had purchased cute decorations with pictures to remind students to share, raise their hands, work quietly, and put their things away.

When I asked the class about the importance of rules, I was slightly surprised to hear, "Rules are made so we know what not to do." Our discussion led to suggestions for our classroom rules. A little boy at my feet yelled, "No smoking!" Not sure what to do, I wrote, "No smoking" on a chart. Another child hollered, "No drinking beer!" From there we had, "No sitting in the trash can", and "No bringing guns or drugs to school." Finally a little girl said, "No saying _ _ _ _! " The children were taking this very seriously, but none of the rules matched my cute decorations. The year promised to be a long one... That night I stored my decorations for classroom rules in a box on the top shelf and went back to the "drawing board."

Linda Marchineck, first grade teacher, Baltimore County Schools

In the past, students who were described as having "chronic behavior problems" were often placed in self-contained special education classrooms for instruction. As more students with disabilities are educated in general education classrooms (Cheney & Harvey, 1994), the resulting academic and behavioral diversity places more demands on teachers. Consequently, behavior management systems that used to be provided primarily by special education teachers in special education classrooms are now critical for general educators to know and use. Moreover, as illustrated in this chapter's opening scenario, many children enter their school years with very different background experiences than those expected by most educators.

In this chapter a model for behavior management is presented that addresses not only the characteristics and experiences that students bring to school, but also addresses an approach to behavior management that focuses on the school as a learning community. In schools where all children are welcome, the administration, teachers, support staff, and students all have a responsibility to develop productive behaviors within the students there. The chapter is based on a systemic model for behavior management within schools. A rationale and fundamental principles of a systemic model for behavior management are described. Interventions for behavior management are presented that address different levels of influence on student behavior: school variables, teacher variables, and student variables. The guidelines and procedures described in this chapter can promote the success of students with disabilities who are included into general education schools and classrooms, but more importantly, the approach described herein promotes the inclusion and success of all students.

A Systemic Model for Behavior Management

School discipline or classroom management programs are often arranged into models that characterize the focus of the methods used to manage students' behaviors in school settings. Educators in inclusive classrooms have a variety of models of behavior management from which to choose. Curwin and Mendler (1988) present a **three-dimensional approach** in which the focus is on the purpose of the interventions in relation to students' misbehavior: prevention, action, and resolution. Similarly, Charles (1992) describes behavior management methods as preventive, supportive, and corrective. **Prevention** procedures are used to establish the conditions for appropriate student behaviors to occur. Rules and routines, sometimes presented as a class-wide social contract, fall within the category of preventive techniques. **Action or support** procedures are used to address misbehavior once it occurs. The intent is to "take action" so that misbehavior does not escalate or worsen and to "support" the student in developing appropriate behaviors. In one application of action or support procedures, the teacher acts upon misbehavior by following through with previously established consequences. **Resolution or correction** procedures are used in response to chronic offenders or "out-of-control" students whose behaviors continue to be inappropriate despite preventive or supportive discipline techniques. Correction or resolution behavior management techniques are tailored to the individual needs of the student using creativity in planning and systematic manipulation of events in the school environment. Correction or resolution procedures may take the form of individualized behavior contracts and consequences, behavior rating cards, reinforcement protocols, family intervention, specific interactional techniques, positive confrontational strategies, or other specialized methods.

Bender and Mathes (1995) describe a **hierarchical approach** to behavior management for students with attention deficit hyperactive disorder in which the focus is on the nature of the methods in relation to the amount of structure needed by students with attention deficits or hyperactivity to work successfully in general education settings: (1) unstructured interventions, such as effective teaching behaviors during instructional delivery; (2) moderately structured interventions, such as specific descriptive, data collection, and reinforcement techniques; and (3) structured interventions, such as interventions that are coordinated across all of a student's teachers. A critical aspect of effective behavior management in inclusive settings is the involvement of all school personnel. Positive consequences are used to increase appropriate behaviors. Negative consequences are applied consistently in response to inappropriate behaviors. As students' need for structure increases, the types of behavior management methods used become more individualized and require more resources in terms of preparation, time during instruction, and additional personnel.

In each of the of the aforementioned models the focus of the intervention(s) is on students' behaviors. Effective behavior management is the goal of the models, and certainly students may be viewed as the ultimate benefactors of effective behavior management programs. However, the model in which methods are presented may carry an implicit message about the source of behavior problems in schools: *Students are the "problem" and interventions should be designed to target only student behaviors alone.*

An alternative view is that multiple variables within schools are determinants of students' conduct and that interventions should be designed to target these multiple variables systemically. In a systemic model, behavior management is viewed as a comprehensive and coordinated effort among faculty, staff, and students to promote interpersonal interactions in school that will allow maximal learning and participation for all students. In a **systemic approach** the focus is on the levels at which interventions within behavior management programs occur. Gottfredson, Gottfredson, and Hybl (1993) propose that student behavior is correlated with variables that occur at three levels within schools:

- Schoolwide—the behavior management approach applied by faculty and staff within the school as a whole, across the school day
- Classroom—the behavior management approach used by individual teachers within their separate classrooms
- Individual—the personal characteristics of each student

The interventions at each of these levels target different individuals. At the schoolwide level, the interventions address the role of all school staff in implementing the behavior management programs. At the classroom level, interventions address the behavior management practices of individual teachers. At the individual level, interventions address students' individual characteristics.

A systemic approach is used in this chapter in which three levels within schools serve as the focus of interventions for developing the "social" behaviors of students: schoolwide programs, teacher practices, and individual student characteristics. At each level a basic framework provides an outline of behavior management strategies, but the quality and integrity of interpersonal interactions are the "glue" that maintain the soundness and effectiveness of the interventions. Part of what dictates the quality and integrity of interpersonal interactions is a belief that effective behavior management programs are based on some fundamental principles.

Fundamental Principles

Within inclusive schools effective behavior management programs must be responsive to individual and group behaviors for interactions and participation within classrooms and the school as a whole. Effective behavior management is analogous to effective teaching. Just as certain instructional practices are associated with high levels of achievement for students with a range of abilities (or disabilities), certain fundamental principles of behavior management programs are associated with productive school behaviors for students with a range of behavioral characteristics. When the principles are applied throughout all aspects of behavior management within a school (e.g., applied systemically), a wide range of student behaviors and needs are addressed. The overarching premise is that *effective behavior management programs are proactive.* Four elements comprise proactive behavior management programs: instructional orientation, positive climate, dynamic and responsive interventions, and collegial interactions (see Table 12-1).

Instructional Orientation

An instructional orientation toward students' behaviors is at the center of a proactive behavior management program. Instead of relying on punitive measures or negative consequences such as reprimands, loss of privileges, detention, and suspension to change behavior in the desired direction, educators approach students' participation and interaction behaviors in the same manner as academic skills (Reitz, 1994). Students are provided structured opportunities to learn and practice desirable behaviors. Using an instructional orientation educators (Colvin, Kameenui, & Sugai, 1993) identify teaching objectives, explain

TABLE 12-1   Fundamental principles: Proactive behavior management programs.

Proactive Elements	Teacher Behaviors
Instructional orientation	• Communicate behavioral expectations to students. • Provide meaningful and concrete examples of expected behaviors. • Structure opportunities to practice expected behaviors. • Use supportive, corrective, and positive feedback.
Positive learning climate	• Seek multiple opportunities to recognize desired behaviors. • Promote congenial atmosphere that minimizes criticism and maximizes students' progress.
Responsive and dynamic interventions	• Elicit student input. • Establish challenging but attainable expectations. • Match students' individual characteristics to performance expectations. • Recognize when plans aren't working. • Adjust instructional method or performance expectation to ensure students' success.
Collegial interactions	• Problem-solve together. • Meet periodically to share ideas and discuss concerns. • Be receptive to new ideas. • Listen to different perspectives. • Seek the expertise of others (e.g., teachers, community agencies, paraprofessionals). • Provide support for others. • Celebrate successes.

procedures, design practice activities, prompt and reinforce performance accuracy, give feedback, and monitor ongoing performance for "social" behaviors.

> *The lessons students learn about behavior, communication, and getting along with others make a . . . lasting impression.*
>
> Curwin & Mendler, 1988

Positive Learning Climate

The second element of a proactive behavior management program is a positive learning climate. The climate of the learning environment may influence students' desire to attend school and to persist in their learning efforts, particularly when faced with concurrent academic difficulties. Interactions that display a negative regard for students compound the academic difficulties that at-risk students may experience. For example, Bauwens and Hourcade (1992) found that teachers' interpersonal interactions with students, such as teasing, screaming, and favoritism and their use of negative management procedures, contributed to the school-based stress experienced by at-risk elementary and secondary students. Conversely, Mayer and colleagues (1993) found that when teachers increased their approval responses, decreased their disapproval responses, and provided positive consequences for desirable behaviors, a climate was created that made the class a pleasant place for high school students who were at-risk for dropping out of school. Subsequently, students' on-task behaviors increased and suspensions decreased. Educators in effective inclusive settings are well aware of the quality of their responses to students' behaviors and consciously focus primarily on a positive range.

Responsive and Dynamic Interventions

The third element of a proactive behavior management program is responsive and dynamic interventions. When interventions are responsive, the unique needs and characteristics of an individual student are addressed. When interventions are dynamic, educators "adjust interventions in response to students' changing behaviors" (Carpenter & McKee-Higgins, 1996, p. 7). Responsive and dynamic programming may be particularly useful with students who typically have had difficulty fitting into the mold of traditional discipline programs within general education settings. For example, Crowley (1993) found that anger was a pervading theme in the perceptions of mainstreamed adolescents with behavioral disorders. The six students who were interviewed viewed teachers' rigidity and use of punitive discipline as unhelpful. However, these same students perceived teachers as helpful when they communicated with the students and implemented academic and behavioral programs in a flexible manner. Helpful communication included establishing a personal rapport, seeking students' opinions, answering their questions, and stating clear academic and behavioral expectations. Flexible academic and behavioral programming included permitting student choice, use of rewards, and opportunities for the students to make amends for errors or transgressions. The use of "helpful communication" and flexible academic and behavioral programming demonstrates responsiveness to the unique needs of these students. Beginning the expectations at a point where the students experience success and over time raising expectations demonstrates dynamic programming. By using responsive and dynamic programming educators in inclusive settings take students from "where they are" and move them in a direction of more acceptable, appropriate, and rewarding performance.

Collegial Interactions

The fourth element of a proactive behavior management program is collegial interactions among educators. Collegial interactions provide support for changes in teacher behaviors and consistency in programming. In inclusive schools, collegial interactions can make or break educators' efforts toward effective inclusion. Teachers' consistent implementation of behavioral programs is related to their proficiency in using the interventions as indicated by improved student outcomes (Reimers, Wacker, & Koeppl, 1987). Through collegial interactions with other educators, administrators, support personnel, families, mental health agencies, or university faculty, teachers may enhance their application of behavioral interventions as they are able to discuss and receive feedback about the decisions they are making while they implement a program (Cheney & Harvey, 1994; Dettmer, Thurston, & Dyck, 1993; Idol, Nevin, & Paolucci-Whitcomb, 1994). Collegial interactions also result in increased communication about students and their responses to the behavior management programs that are in use. The resulting consistency in support and predictability across the school environment is critical for both students who are at-risk for school failure and students who are already identified with disabilities and caught in the cycle of what they perceive as self-failure (Colvin et al., 1993). *By engaging in collegial interactions teachers within inclusive schools can make changes in their own behavior that will result in improved behaviors for students throughout the school.*

A proactive behavior management program not only provides a plan for responding to inappropriate student behaviors, but provides a plan for developing the social behaviors and work habits that will promote students' active participation as contributing members to the school as a learning community. To be responsive, the proactive behavior management program must include enough structure to serve as a framework as well as enough flexibility to respond to unique individual characteristics. Instead of a crack through which students slip, such a framework has a safety net that releases in response to students' needs that are not met by the main structure. A positive climate for learning in which teachers engage in collegial interactions is characteristic of a proactive behavior management program. Within inclusive schools all behavior management methods are developed, implemented, and evaluated based on the premise that *effective programs are proactive.*

School-Focused Interventions

School-focused interventions address the policies and procedures that are implemented throughout a school as evidenced by the interactions between staff and students. The basic framework for school-focused interventions is an effective school-wide discipline policy. An effective school-wide discipline policy (Colvin et al., 1993):

- Is implemented by everyone in the school.
- Produces cooperation among students and school staff that promotes learning.
- Results in increases in desirable behaviors and decreases in undesirable behaviors.
- Meets the needs of all students including those with disabilities.

If an effective schoolwide discipline policy is not already in place, teachers and administrators—with input from students, parents, and community members—should work together to assess the current practices, make revisions to the policy, and implement new practices. Several features are found in school discipline policies that result in staff and students working together as part of a learning community (see Table 12-2). As students with disabilities are included in general education schools, behavior management should first be examined within the larger context of behavior management for all students in schools and classrooms.

TABLE 12-2   **Features of an effective schoolwide discipline policy.**

Features of an Effective Schoolwide Discipline Policy

1. A proactive approach to managing behavior is consistent across the school.
2. School rules are clear and consistently followed by staff and students.
3. Communication with families is frequent and includes positive information.
4. Support of individual teachers and students is promoted through collegial teams.
5. A safe, secure school environment is ensured through training and involvement.

Approach

The first feature of an effective schoolwide discipline policy is an approach to managing behavior that is proactive and consistent (Colvin et al., 1993). Although school discipline policies typically consist of rules and consequences, schools with a proactive approach use an instructional orientation to behavior management. The school discipline policy is viewed as a means of student success, not as a means of control. Proactive schools do not ask, "What rules do students need?" and "How do we get students to stop misbehaving?" Instead, schools with a proactive approach ask, "What success behaviors do students need to know in order to participate and learn?" and "What is the best way for students to learn and practice success behaviors?" In answering these questions, the most effective schools demonstrate respect for all students by ensuring that "policies, procedures, and curricula enhance [students'] feelings of self-control, self-preservation, and self-esteem" (Gorski & Pilotto, 1993, p. 51). To promote consistency, all building personnel, from administrators to teachers to cafeteria workers, play a role in behavior management. Learning and achievement characterize schools in which students' sense of dignity is actively supported by all (Curwin & Mendler, 1988).

School Rules

The second feature of an effective schoolwide discipline policy is school rules that are clear and consistently enforced (Gottfredson, Gottfredson, & Hybl, 1993). Students and staff understand expectations for student behaviors and consequences for misbehavior. When misbehavior occurs, consequences are applied consistently according to the previously communicated rules. A well-publicized program of reinforcement is used in response to students' desirable behaviors. Reward systems may take the form of student of the month recognition, positive referrals, good deed certificates with eligibility for prize drawings, or bulletin boards with pictures of successful students. However, a system of positive reinforcement is not enough to produce positive student outcomes. Fewer episodes of misconduct and rebellious behavior are associated with a reduction in the use of punitive techniques.

Family Communication

The third feature of an effective schoolwide discipline policy is family communication that is frequent and positive (Topper, Williams, Leo, Hamilton, & Fox, 1994). Frequent communication with families creates the opportunity for consistency and follow through at home for student behaviors. Informing parents of instances of desirable or improved student behaviors reduces the apprehension that parents may feel about communicating with school personnel about their child, particularly a child who has a history of challenging behavior or poor school performance. Parents are valuable sources of information, sometimes offering a broader perspective about students' strengths and needs in nonschool settings, strategies for dealing with behavioral challenges, key persons who may serve as resources, or ongoing stressors that may affect students' performance at school. Students whose parents participate on school-level discipline and behavior review committees demonstrate improved behaviors (Morrison, Olivos, Dominguez, Gomez, & Lena, 1993). A variety of methods are available for increasing positive communication with students' families including letters, phone calls, student recognition ceremonies, informal home visits, home visits by home-school liaison specialists, school visits by family members, and parent participation in school activities.

Collegial Teams

The fourth feature of an effective school-wide discipline policy is collegial teams that are collaborative and supportive (Colvin et al., 1993). Teachers and administrators participating on School Improvement Teams foster successful implementation of proactive methods schoolwide by providing training, monitoring, suggestions, and ongoing technical assistance for their colleagues. Specialized support teams that include school personnel, parents, students, or persons from the community provide a forum for identifying techniques to develop behaviors needed by students who are at high risk for behavior difficulties (Reitz, 1994).

> *Our experience is that the process for problem solving situations, developing supports, and building positive relationships is the same for any student, with or without labels, and whether or not they present intensive behavior challenges.*
>
> Topper, Williams, Leo, Hamilton, & Fox, 1994

School Environment

The final feature of an effective school-wide discipline policy is a school environment that is safe and secure (Gorski & Pilotto, 1993). First, a safe environment means an environment that is safe for learning and risk taking. The majority of students, with and without disabilities, want boundaries to be consistently set in a structured and respectful environment (Fuhr, 1993). Setting and enforcing limits gives students a sense of security and, rather than inhibiting or stifling students, such an environment promotes freedom as it increases students' options and ability to make choices (Fuhr, 1993; Alberto & Troutman, 1990). Both general and special educators have an obligation to provide a safe learning environment that reflects the individual needs of their students. Second, the premise is that all students have a right to an environment that is secure or safe from physical harm. Rising incidents of interpersonal violence and delinquency among youth are an increasing concern for urban and rural schools and communities alike (Lerner, 1995). Plans to address aggressive behaviors at school encompass a combination of proactive and reactive strategies. Students and staff should receive training that addresses prevention, recognition, and responses for situations that have a potential for danger. Possible topics include solving conflict, reporting crimes, dealing with strangers, anger management, suicide, death, and handling fear. Peer groups may be used to shape norms for nonviolent behavior and health practices. Schools' cooperative relationships with law enforcement authorities may encourage youths' understanding and appreciation for the legal consequences of criminal acts.

A comprehensive presentation of crisis intervention for violent and aggressive behaviors is beyond the scope of this chapter. When school faculty and staff must intervene in crisis situations, specific procedural and ethical guidelines must be followed to resolve the crisis situation, protect those involved from physical harm, maintain the dignity and emotional well-being of those involved, and provide follow-up. For a comprehensive presentation of techniques to address delinquent, violent, and aggressive behaviors, educators may refer to the following sources: school and district guidelines; Chapter 10 of this text for conflict resolution techniques; *Techniques for Managing Verbally and Physically Aggressive Students* (Johns & Carr, 1995); and *Reducing School Violence Through Conflict Resolution* (Johnson & Johnson, 1995). Reactive techniques should be viewed as temporary measures for isolated incidents of crisis. Schools that achieve the greatest reduction in antisocial behaviors with corresponding decreases in suspensions and expulsions are those with a consistent, pervasive positive approach to students' misbehavior (Gorski & Pilotto, 1993; Gottfredson et al., 1993; Mayer et al., 1993). Thus, the focus of methods within this chapter maintains an instructional orientation toward the development of students' productive school behaviors.

The schoolwide discipline policy provides a framework for school-focused interventions. However, it is through the interactions among school staff and students that the interventions are operationalized to provide a school climate that supports students in their development and practice of social behaviors related to participating in school settings. Both the plan (or policy) and the responsive daily interactions among staff and students are required for effective school discipline.

Teacher-Focused Interventions

Teachers often associate administrative support with their ability to effectively manage students' behaviors and educate students with a range of abilities and/or disabilities in inclusive classrooms (Cheney & Harvey, 1994). However, classroom level behavior management variables are greater determinants of positive student outcomes, in terms of both behavioral and academic performance (Gottfredson et al., 1993; Wang, Haertel, & Walberg, 1990).

Teachers who focus solely on academic instruction without simultaneously using behavior management techniques "lose" those students whose behaviors interfere with learning.

Mrs. M. walked into the room to pick up her class from music. Several students were under the table, one was swinging on the curtains, others were playing a form of musical chairs, while two students were sitting with the teacher, books open on their laps. In response to Mrs. M.'s startled expression, the music teacher said, "I only teach students who want to learn."

On the other hand, teachers who focus only on behavior management sacrifice academic instruction and often find their hands full with unruly classes. *Effective instruction requires that classroom management and academic instruction go hand-in-hand.* Reitz (1994) points out that the most well-developed behavior management system, even if implemented appropriately, will not be effective if students do not have meaningful and productive work to do.

The literature is replete with effective instruction and behavior management techniques that reflect common criteria for appropriate teacher behaviors (Algozzine, Ysseldyke, & Campbell, 1994; Anderson, Evertson, & Brophy, 1979; Christenson, Ysseldyke, & Thurlow, 1989; Fuhr, 1993), including:

- Preparation
- Consistency
- Setting high expectations
- Ongoing monitoring
- Modeling
- Feedback
- Establishment of rules and routines

Yet there is not a textbook, research study, or journal article with a definitive behavior management system that will work for every teacher, with every student all of the time. However, certain behavior management strategies and principles have proven to be effective for students with disabilities and enhance the experiences for students without disabilities as well.

Ysseldyke, Christenson, and Kovaleski (1994) state that academic performance, or learning, is "a function of an interaction between the students and the learning environment" (p. 37). By structuring the instructional setting and their instructional interactions with students, teachers can inhibit inappropriate behaviors from occurring before they start (Charles, 1992; Conroy & Fox, 1994; Kennedy & Itkonen, 1993). The teacher-focused interventions presented in the following sections include variables within the instructional setting and teachers' instructional interactions with students that facilitate desired student behavior. The possible effects of these variables on the performance of students with disabilities are highlighted. Then specific suggestions are given for some areas in which teachers may need to make changes in what they typically do in order for students with disabilities to participate fully and to gain the greatest benefit from instruction.

Instructional Setting

Although teacher influence or control over events that occur outside of the school day is often minimal, creating a classroom environment that is orderly with consistent expectations provides students an environment that is conducive for learning and performing as part of a classroom community (see Chapter 13 for more information on establishing a classroom community). Setting events under the teachers' control include rules, routines, physical environment, and scheduling.

Rules

Students need to know what is expected of them. Rules are statements that provide "students with . . . guidelines for the types of behaviors that are required and the types of behaviors that are prohibited" for classroom conduct (Cangelosi, 1993, p. 309). Rules and their consequences should be clearly delineated *and* explicitly taught to students at the start of the school year using practice sessions to ensure understanding (Christenson et al., 1989; Shores, Gunter, Denny, & Jack, 1993). Guidelines for establishing rules include (Christenson et al., 1989; Reitz, 1994; Sabatino, 1987):

1. Actively involve students in developing class rules.
2. State rules in behavioral and observable terms.
3. Ensure that rules are enforceable.
4. Use as few rules as possible.
5. Clearly delineate consequences for both desirable and undesirable behavior.
6. Provide students opportunities to practice rules and desirable behaviors.

By communicating and enforcing rules from the first day, while remembering to give explicit feedback and praise for appropriate behavior displayed in the classroom, teachers set the stage for student behavior that contributes to a positive climate in the classroom (Gartland, 1990; Sabatino, 1987). The more that students are involved in the classroom organization and structure, the more they will want to preserve a cooperative working relationship with the teacher and other students.

Routines

Classroom routines are the procedures "by which students move through transition periods and learning activities" (Cangelosi, 1993, p. 308). Routines should be established for such things as starting and ending the class period, turning in assignments, requesting assistance, what to do when assigned work is completed, and use of class materials (Charles, 1992). Routines in the classroom are important to establish from the beginning of the school year or on the first day of class in a new semester. Not only do they provide students with a sense of security, they assist in establishing and maintaining order. Englert (1984) reports that fewer behavior problems are manifested in classrooms where established routines are followed.

The use of a silent reading period immediately following recess is a routine that many elementary school classrooms follow. Students asking for water and bathroom breaks often turn this routine into a chaotic time period. A first grade teacher solved this problem by teaching her students the following routine. All students came into the room, picked a book, and sat at their desks. The first student in the front row quietly left to use the bathroom and get a drink. When that student returned, he tapped the next student (who quietly left the room) and then went to his desk. Upon returning to the class, the second student tapped the next student and so the routine went on until all the students had a turn . . . no student had to say a word or approach the teacher.

Although routines serve to minimize confusion, disruptions, and down time for all students, for students with disabilities routines become a mechanism for organization. The structure imposed by routines can facilitate time and material management by students who are typically disorganized. As students learn the routines, they are better able to anticipate what is required of them and perform accordingly.

Physical Environment

The physical arrangement of the classroom contributes to the efficient day-to-day operation of instructional activities. The type of instructional activities that occur across the school day and throughout the year influence the arrangement of the available work space. The physical arrangement of the classroom must (1) support instructional activities that take place and (2) allow the teacher to be constantly aware of student activities. Desks should be arranged in a way that allows students to see and participate in activities. The amount of desired student-to-student interaction will influence decisions about arranging work spaces. Greater levels of interaction are facilitated when students are facing each other or seated side-by-side; students' on-task behaviors are enhanced when desks are placed in rows with space between each (Shores et al., 1993).

When designing the layout of the classroom, high traffic areas deserve special attention (Gartland, 1990). Students need to have easy access to materials (e.g., paper, glue), equipment (e.g., pencil sharpener), and resources (e.g., dictionaries) without disrupting small group instruction and other learning activities. Placing materials in close proximity to the corresponding activity minimizes disruptions and down time when these items are needed.

Planning preferential seating for students with special physical, attentional, learning, or behavioral needs facilitates their successful performance academically and behaviorally in inclusive settings. Students may benefit from visual prompts (e.g., bulletin boards), close proximity to the teacher, or easy access to materials. Other students have visual or auditory processing deficits or are highly distracted by visual or auditory stimuli. Preferential seating for students with attentional difficulties may include sitting in the front of the room, near a teacher's desk, at a separate study carrel, or away from high traffic areas such as computer stations, windows, or the door to the classroom. Conversely, students who are withdrawn may benefit from increased opportunities for interaction that occur in high traffic areas and cooperative seating arrangements.

Scheduling

Effective scheduling functions as a setting event that enhances students' understanding of expected daily events (Salend, 1994). When students with disabilities have a variety of service providers (i.e., speech/language pathologist, occupational therapist, special education teacher), the likelihood increases for fragmentation of the students' daily schedule. Programming for these students should address the need for multiple services while maintaining a stable routine. Stable routines provide structure for students who are habitually disorganized and provide a sense of security for students who do not respond well to change. A well-designed schedule allots adequate time for meeting the students' IEP goals and objectives as well as the school district's curriculum when appropriate.

In the elementary grades, schedules are determined by the classroom teacher in collaboration with teammates, art, music, and physical education teachers, as well as special educators. At middle and high schools the guidance counselor, parents, teachers, and students also have input into individual schedules.

Instructional Interactions

Instructional interactions encompass a range of teacher behaviors that are used as teachers interact with students within the instructional setting. The interactions that occur throughout the day set the tone for expectations for learning and performance behaviors for each student. Table 12-3 contains a composite list of teacher behaviors that support desired student behaviors. Teacher behaviors that affect interactions in the classroom include belief systems and attitudes, modeling, surface management techniques, and consistency.

TABLE 12-3   Quick reference for teacher behaviors.

Technique	Description
Planned ignoring	No response to behaviors that have a low spread potential.
Signal interference	Use nonverbal techniques to express disapproval and control.
Proximity control	Move closer to student who is behaving inappropriately.
Interest boosting	Present novel activity to increase attention.
Tension decontamination	Use humor to reduce anxiety producing atmosphere.
Hurdle lessons	Provide assistance before student reaches frustration level.
Restructure lessons	Use instructional methods that are meaningful to students to create an atmosphere conducive to academic achievement.
Follow routines	Follow established routines to maintain a predictable classroom structure and procedures.
Remove seductive objects	Remove materials or objects that are distracting students' attention.
Antiseptic bouncing	Temporarily remove student from situation that is likely to result in inappropriate behavior.
Private reprimands	Talk to student in a quiet voice and in close proximity.
Model appropriate behaviors	Demonstrate desired interpersonal and classroom behaviors. Give attention to students who are behaving appropriately.
Avoid power struggles	Firmly and calmly state expectations for behavior; do not engage in an "argument" during class time.

Source: Compiled from information in (1) Charles, C. M. (1992). *Building classroom discipline* (4th ed.). New York: Longman. (2) Long, N.J., Morse, W. G., & Newman, R. G. (Eds.) (1971). *Conflict in the classroom* (2nd ed.). Belmont, CA: Wadsworth.

Teacher Belief Systems and Attitudes

Teacher belief systems and attitudes have a significant impact on what has been characterized as teacher effectiveness (Agne, Greenwood, & Miller, 1994; Fuhr, 1993), particularly in terms of classroom management. Educators are responsible for motivating students, teaching students responsibility, and teaching academic content (Mendler, 1993). Educators who do this and are consistent and fair are also generally liked or, more importantly, respected by their students.

Effective teachers believe they have the ability and skill to affect student achievement; they believe that their own behavior directly affects or determines outcomes and events (Agne et al., 1994). "Teachers with a high sense of efficacy [are] more likely . . . to define low-achieving students as reachable, teachable, and worthy of teacher attention and effort" (Ashton & Webb, 1986, p. 72). Similarly, teachers' attitudes toward students' disabilities, ethnic backgrounds, and economic backgrounds may ultimately affect their students' performance. Students often live up to what they perceive teachers' expectations to be. Proactive and effective classroom management is preceded by the belief that:

- Behavior management is part of the job of teaching.
- The teacher can make a difference in students' behavior in their classrooms.

Teachers are one of the most significant models in students' lives. Teachers have the opportunity to present students with examples of appropriate social interactions, responses to a variety of situations, and enriched language. Mendler (1993) recommends that teachers demonstrate to students respectful, nonviolent, and verbally nonaggressive solutions to conflicts. He encourages teachers to apologize to students when in error and to promote friendliness and courtesy by smiling and speaking to students in the way teachers would like students to speak to them.

Students are aware of how teachers respond to situations that induce anger, anxiety, or uncertainty, as well as amusement and approval. Teacher responses act as both consequences (may increase or decrease student behavior) and antecedents (may serve as a cue or prompt for student response). *Teachers need to be conscious of the message their behavior communicates so that the message they intend to send is the message received by students.* More importantly, students' prior experiences will influence their reactions to teachers' words and behaviors. Students who have language disabilities or limited English proficiency may be self-conscious about their language differences. Students with disabilities may be sensitive to the stigma of special education labels. Understanding the cultural and familial influences, as well as other background experiences, of students in their classes will enhance teachers' ability to communicate effectively and respectfully with all students.

Surface Management Techniques

Surface management techniques are those techniques that address behavior before it becomes problematic (Long, Morse, & Newman, 1971). These techniques include "withitness" and body language. Teachers who display "withitness" are those who give the impression that they are aware of *everything* that is going on in the room throughout the school day (Kounin, 1970). The old adage "actions speak louder than words" is relevant to this trait. Withitness is communicated to students when the teacher intervenes with the correct

TABLE 12-4   Guidelines for teachers to promote consistency.

Do	Don't
1. Enforce rules and apply consequences for appropriate and inappropriate behaviors.	1. Make a rule that you cannot or will not enforce.
2. Reinforce the desired behavior immediately when teaching or promoting a new behavior.	2. Respond only to inappropriate behaviors.
3. Apply a technique for at least three to five days before deciding that it doesn't work.	3. Use a technique indefinitely that is not producing desirable results.

student (the instigator), and the intervention takes place before the behavior is given time to spread or to intensify (Cangelosi, l993).

Teachers' *body language* is a subtle yet powerful behavior management technique (Jones & Jones, 1986). Effective body language includes physical proximity, eye contact, body carriage, facial expressions, and gestures. Most inappropriate behavior occurs some distance away from the teacher. However, teachers' close *physical proximity* discourages students' misbehavior.

Establishing *eye contact* communicates to students that the teacher is aware of what is happening and allows the teacher to redirect students without the use of verbal reprimands. Eye contact may be encouraged by moving closer to the student or briefly stopping instruction (silence can be very disconcerting). Once eye contact is made, students may attend to *facial expressions* and/or *gestures* such as nodding, pointing, or a palm up to indicate "stop." The use of meaningful, nonverbal, signals allows the teacher to monitor students working independently, while teaching another group (Christenson et al., 1989). A characteristic commonly found in students with various disabilities is their difficulty with reading or interpreting social cues correctly. Students with disabilities in an inclusive environment may need explicit instruction in the correct interpretation of social cues.

Teachers often complain that behavior management strategies don't work. They may have tried praise, time-out, a token economy, contracts, candy! Yet, students are still "out of control." The importance of *consistency* cannot be overemphasized. Mendler (l993) points out that it takes time to discipline. Behavior management strategies or discipline must be applied consistently over time to be effective (see Table 12-4).

Adapting Classroom Interventions

Even when teachers establish an instructional environment and patterns of interpersonal interactions that result in the desired behaviors for most students, some students will benefit from additional adjustments that can be made at the classroom level. Many such adjustments can be easily incorporated into teachers' current practices and may prevent the need for more intensive student-focused interventions. Thus for students who have not responded to the general classroom behavior management system, teachers may fine tune methods they are already using to meet students' individual needs. Suggestions include the following:

Make changes in the scheduling, seating arrangements or the overall physical arrangement of the classroom

Schedule nonpreferred activities before preferred activities. If Dale, Elizabeth, and Lynn talk constantly throughout science, separate them. It may be that Holly is overly stimulated by noises out in the hall and needs to be seated in another part of the room, or Cidney can't see the board unless she is in the first row. Teachers may find that during small group instruction, they can't see the group of students at the centers...and the students take full advantage of this. Rearrange the room so the teacher can monitor all of it at all times.

Modify materials to accommodate individual student needs

Materials should not be so difficult that they induce frustration or too easy that they induce boredom. A student may be required to complete fifteen math problems instead of thirty, or may use a worksheet rather than have to copy from a book. Be clear about the purpose for assignments. When teaching note-taking skills teachers might provide outlines for assistance but require students to take their own notes as well. Students may record or have a peer assist in taking notes during lecture periods. Some students are able to better demonstrate comprehension of material through nonverbal means (pointing, writing) while others perform better orally (see Chapter 9 for more on modifying assignments).

Make changes in instructional delivery

Some inappropriate behavior serves as a way for students to escape or avoid nonpreferred activities (Gunter, Shores, Jack, Denny, & DePaepe, 1994). Teachers' style of instruction may affect students' willingness to participate in group or individual learning experiences. The means of instruction may be aversive to some students if students feel incapable of performing or participating correctly. Preparation for and delivery of instruction must ensure that the curriculum is appropriate for the individual student's level of functioning (Conroy & Fox, 1994) and that instruction is delivered in such a way as to reduce incorrect responding.

Modify teacher behaviors

Scan the room frequently and use proximity control to suppress disruptive behavior as it begins. Collect and check work on a regular basis. Give verbal reminders and redirect students' attention, checking on the students' progress soon thereafter (Emmer, Evertson, Sanford, Clements, & Murray, 1989). Provide an incentive system wherein students may participate in a preferred activity after they have completed an assigned task and behaved appropriately. Intervene when problem behaviors begin to be manifested by providing "hurdle help" (provide direct assistance to get student past a difficult point), removing the student from the situation, or by removing a distracting object (Charles, 1992). Minimize down time by providing efficient help.

Teach socially acceptable behaviors

Many students with disabilities need instruction in conversation skills, interpreting social cues, and expressing likes and dislikes in a socially appropriate manner (Lalli, Browder, Mace, & Brown 1993; Hunt, Alwell, & Goetz, 1988) (see Chapter 13 for more on developing appropriate social skills).

*Identify aversive conditions in the classroom and take steps
to eliminate or reduce them*

Increase positive interactions with the students. Make frequent statements that express approval and decrease the number of comments that express disapproval (Mayer et al., 1993). Reinforce students who are exhibiting appropriate behavior. This reinforcement serves to increase or maintain that student's behavior, and it provides models for students exhibiting inappropriate behavior. Teachers' use of social reinforcement is effective in both increasing appropriate behavior and in decreasing the frequency of inappropriate behavior (Reitz, 1994). Use tangible reinforcers when social reinforcers have proven to be inadequate. Tangible reinforcers often consists of a point or token system (Reitz, 1994) and may include primary reinforcers, such as edibles. Schedule the delivery of reinforcement at a rate that is responsive to the immediacy and frequency needed by the individual to maintain desired behaviors (Shores et al., 1993). Identify appropriate consequences for inappropriate behavior, such as having students make restitution when objects are damaged or destroyed, prompting compliance to classroom demands, removing student from the situation, or removing problem objects (i.e., toys, scissors).

While much behavior can be addressed using teacher-focused interventions, the behavior of some students may require more intensive intervention to develop and use behaviors that allow them to participate fully and productively in inclusive settings. What is important for teachers to realize is that their behavior management is not ineffective, but that their current methods are not responsive to a particular student. Prepare to examine the students' needs. Seek out collegial support and collaboration!

Student-Focused Interventions

The next section of this chapter identifies and describes a continuum of behavior change methods that begin with the most positive *and* the least intrusive and end with more punishing and intrusive techniques. Educators in inclusive settings are well-informed about the range of techniques to choose from as well as how to use each technique—and combinations of techniques—systematically and effectively.

The underlying assumption of behavior management is that most behavior is learned (Alberto & Troutman, 1990; 1995; Colvin, Sugai, & Patching, 1993). Consequently much behavior can be predicted and effective behavior management programs can be developed and implemented to change behavior (Rooney, 1993). Many of the techniques within student-focused interventions are based on the behavioral principles of reinforcers and punishers. Reinforcers are consequences, for example, events or items, following a behavior that *increase* the likelihood that the behavior will occur again. Punishers are consequences following a behavior that *decrease* the likelihood that the behavior will occur again.

Thus, whether a particular consequence is a reinforcer or punisher for a particular individual is determined by its effect on the behavior it follows. It is possible that the same consequence may be reinforcing for some students and punishing for others based on their previous experiences. It is also possible that consequences that are considered rewarding or punishing by teachers are interpreted differently by students. For example, whereas some students seek out and value teacher praise, other students may find teacher attention uncomfortable or embarrassing. Some students may not "hear" the praise and must be taught to appreciate praise. Similarly, although removal from the classroom (e.g., being sent to the principal's office, in-school suspension, or time-out) is an aversive experience for some students, others will welcome the opportunity to escape the academic or social demands of the classroom.

When students have had limited success in school settings in the past, their responses to traditional behavior management systems may differ from many of their same age peers. Herein lies the crux of the effectiveness of many behavior management techniques. Given that students' individual responses to specific consequences will vary, the effectiveness of behavior management methods must be evaluated in relation to their effect on each student's behaviors. Student-focused behavior management methods provide a mechanism by which teachers may fine tune behavior management systems to meet the needs of individual students.

It is beyond the scope of this text to sufficiently describe each behavior management technique available to use with students. However, what is described herein is a range of options from least intrusive and most positive (as well as most natural) to more punishing and intrusive techniques (see Table 12-5 for a continuum of traditional behavior management techniques).

TABLE 12-5   **A continuum of behavior management techniques from least intrusive to most intrusive.**

1. Natural reinforcement	Least intrusive
2. Social reinforcement	and
3. Modeling from peers	More positive
4. Behavioral contracts	
5. Activity reinforcement	
6. Token reinforcement	
7. Tangible reinforcement	
8. Edible reinforcement	↓
9. Tactile, sensory reinforcement	
10. Manipulation of antecedent events	↓
11. Differential reinforcement	
12. Extinction	
13. Verbal aversives	
14. Response cost	
15. Timeout	More punishing
16. Overcorrection	and
17. Physical aversives	Most intrusive

Source: Compiled from information in (1) Alberto, P. A., & Troutman, A. C. (1995). *Applied behavior analysis for teachers* (4th ed.). Englewood Cliffs, NJ: Merrill/Prentice Hall. (2) Nelson, C. M., & Rutherford, R. B. (1989). Behavioral interventions with behaviorally disordered students. In M. C. Wang, M. C. Reynolds, & H. J. Walberg (Eds.), *The handbook of special education: Research and practice.* (Vol. 2). Oxford, England: Pergamon. (3) Smith, D. D., & Rivera, D. P. (1995). Discipline in special education and general education settings. *Focus on Exceptional Children, 27* (5), 1–14.

Traditional Behavior Management Methods

Perhaps the most compelling and natural use of positive consequences is that of *social praise*. Teachers who "catch students being good" and comment on appropriate behaviors provide students with two things. First, the student who is exhibiting appropriate behavior is recognized as having done so. Teachers who take good behavior for granted may be missing opportunities to reinforce students within the natural context of daily interactions. Second, the teacher comment that includes specifically what the behavior is and why it is appropriate has the potential to inform other students about the particular behavior the teacher desires and why it is important. Simply commenting and using verbal praise will not teach *all* students to use appropriate behavior—however, ignoring appropriate behaviors deprives students and teachers of one of the most natural and cost-effective management techniques available.

Providing students with *choices* is another positive and nonintrusive technique that both increases desired behaviors and allows students to be involved more directly in a behavior management system. Munk and Repp (1994) reviewed a number of studies in which teachers' use of certain instructional behaviors was successful at reducing problem behaviors of students with severe disabilities, autism, and mental retardation. Instructional methods teachers used that resulted in decreased problem behaviors included allowing students to choose the task they wanted to work on first; varying tasks so that students could work on some tasks that they had already mastered and some tasks that were new; and interspersing high-probability tasks (those that students were more likely to want to do) with low-probability tasks.

Developing a *behavioral contract* with an individual student is a technique that can be used to individualize a behavior management system. In a behavioral contract, the teacher and student write an agreement that includes a description of the desired behavior and what the student will receive when the desired behavior is performed at the level agreed upon (see Table 12-6 for a checklist of components for a behavioral contract). For students with disabilities, discussion with their teacher about the behavior contract provides a more concrete explanation of the desired behavior. Moreover, teachers may encourage students to determine their reinforcer (e.g., what the student will receive) to increase students' motivation and involvement in their behavior program.

Activity reinforcement is the pairing of a high-interest activity that the student is willing to work toward with an activity or task that the student considers less interesting or motivating. Sometimes referred to as the Premack Principle, activity reinforcement involves an "if you do _____, then you will be allowed to _____" scenario. For example, Christopher (who has been labeled seriously emotionally disturbed) enjoys using the computer to play games. His teacher would like to see him increase his use of appropriate language when interacting with his peers during class. Christopher's teacher talks with him about some words and phrases to replace the inappropriate language, some anger management techniques, and how he can earn computer time by completing three class periods without any instances of inappropriate language. Note that his teacher is not simply saying, "don't use inappropriate language," but that there are instructional dimensions used with the student to teach him what words to use and how to control his anger. Concurrently, Christopher is working with his special education teacher and school counselor for more instruction and discussion that surround his emotional difficulties.

TABLE 12-6 **Checklist of necessary components of a complete behavioral contract.**

_____ 1. A clear statement of the target behavior.

      _____ defined in operational terms

      _____ stated positively

      _____ stated in behavioral objective form

_____ 2. Designation of all persons directly involved.

_____ 3. Description of a data-collection method.

      _____ described in reliable and replicable terms

      _____ summarized in chart or graph terms

_____ 4. Clear identification of all reinforcers to be used.

      _____ specified schedule of delivery

      _____ designation of who will deliver

      _____ indication of how much will be delivered

_____ 5. Specification of behaviors, responsibilities, and/or conditions for earning or securing behaviors.

_____ 6. Specification of consequences for failure to meet expectations and responsibilities or emission of inappropriate behaviors.

      _____ procedures for renegotiation

_____ 7. Specification of a bonus clause for exceptional performance.

_____ 8. Designation of specific timelines.

      _____ beginning or start date

      _____ deadline for ending contract

      _____ review dates for assessing progress

_____ 9. Signatures of all involved and dates of agreement.

Source: From M. Wolery, D. B. Bailey, & G. M. Sugai, *Principles and procedures of applied behavior analysis with exceptional students.* Copyright © (1988) by Allyn and Bacon. Reprinted/adapted by permission.

Some students increase their use of appropriate behaviors when they have opportunities to earn points or tokens that can later be exchanged for reinforcers. *Token reinforcement* typically requires students to accrue a certain quantity of tokens that will be exchanged later for a desired reinforcer. When teachers deliver the tokens soon after the desired behavior occurs, students understand which appropriate behaviors have been reinforced. Table 12-7 provides guidelines for establishing and implementing a token economy with students.

A combination of ignoring inappropriate behaviors and reinforcing appropriate behaviors is *differential reinforcement.* Differential reinforcement of incompatible behaviors requires the teacher to provide reinforcement when a student is exhibiting a behavior that cannot occur concurrently with the inappropriate behavior. For example, a student who is completing a science project by working quietly at her desk cannot simultaneously run

TABLE 12-7   Guidelines for establishing and operating a token economy.

Characteristics of Useful Tokens

1. Portable, i.e., easily transported
2. Can be given immediately
3. Teacher controlled
4. Compatible with educational or treatment program
5. Resistant to satiation
6. Practical to setting
7. Easily dispensed

Planning and Implementation Steps

1. Select and define target behaviors.
2. Identify possible backup reinforcers.
3. Select possible object or symbol for token.
4. Build token as conditioned reinforcer.
5. Establish exchange system and relative value of backup reinforcers.
6. Inform students of rules for token economy.
7. Develop plan for fading use of token system.
8. Establish clear record-keeping system.

Basic Operation Guidelines

1. Deliver tokens and backup reinforcers consistently.
2. Control for token inflation.
3. Focus on increasing desirable behaviors and skills.
4. Specify rules and procedures in specific and observable terms.
5. Obtain as many free, inexpensive, and student-selected backups as possible.
6. Engage in marketing and merchandising.
7. Incorporate instructional opportunities into token economy, e.g., banking.
8. Pair token and backup reinforcers with praise and other natural reinforcers.
9. Obtain approval and informed consent from administrators and parents.
10. Establish clear procedures for student noncompliance and teacher misuse.

Fading a Token Economy

1. Move from artificial to natural token and backup reinforcers.
2. Delay the presentation of reinforcement.
3. Move from continuous and predictable to more intermittent and unpredictable schedules of reinforcement.
4. Transfer stimulus control from artificial to more natural setting stimuli.
5. Teach students to self-manage the token economy.

Source: From M. Wolery, D. B. Bailey, & G. M. Sugai, *Principles and procedures of applied behavior analysis with exceptional students.* Copyright © (1988) by Allyn and Bacon. Reprinted/adapted by permission.

around the room or have a tantrum, the incompatible behaviors. Repp and Karsh (1994) found that two students with severe mental retardation who exhibited tantrums were actually positively reinforced by the teacher attention they gained after tantrums. When their teachers began differentially reinforcing their appropriate behaviors and ignoring the tantrums, then the tantrums decreased because they were no longer serving their function of gaining attention. In actuality, the attention getting function of the tantrums was replaced by teacher attention gained through exhibiting appropriate behaviors.

> *Some students learn to communicate needs such as "Leave me alone," "Pay attention to me," "I don't want to do this," "I don't understand this—I need help" by engaging in disruptive and sometimes even dangerous behaviors.*
>
> Hitzing, 1992

Although the behavioral methods described here may be incorporated into teachers' ongoing repertoire of responses to students' appropriate and inappropriate behaviors, some students benefit from a more systematic application of behavioral techniques, targeting specific behaviors for change. When teachers follow a structured process for the development of behavioral programs that are responsive to particular students' needs, the likelihood increases that the desired results will be achieved.

Developing Interventions

Designing and implementing student-focused behavior change programs requires an investment of time and possibly resources. The investment is worthwhile given the positive and lasting student outcomes that can be achieved. Interventions that are dynamic and responsive to specific student behaviors range from simple to more complex behavioral procedures and systems. Most can be integrated successfully into class routines within general education settings if accompanied by careful planning and, when needed, technical assistance. The Collaborative Support Team mentioned earlier in this chapter may be "called into action" when student behaviors fall outside teachers' realm of expertise or resources. Often as teachers' understanding, experience, and success with behavioral programming increase, their comfort level for trying new practices also increases (Reimers et al., 1987). However, even for the "experts," meeting with others to get a wide lens perspective enhances their ability to provide valid and comprehensive behavior management programs (e.g., experienced educators benefit from collegiality as much as novice educators do!).

A six-step behavioral process model that corresponds to an instructional process model (Cangelosi, 1993) can be effectively applied to developing interventions to correct inappropriate behavior and to support appropriate behavior in the classroom. The behavioral process model incorporates the following steps:

1. Conduct a functional assessment.
2. Determine behavioral goals/objectives.
3. Design the intervention.
4. Prepare for the intervention.
5. Apply the intervention.
6. Conduct ongoing assessment.

Conduct a Functional Assessment

Increasingly educators are recognizing that application of behavior management techniques cannot occur in isolation of examining the function of a student's inappropriate behavior (Cooper & Harding, 1993; Hitzing, 1992). Students who exhibit challenging and troubling behaviors do so for a variety of reasons. Many inappropriate behaviors are communicative in nature in that they serve to fulfill students' needs (Demchak, 1993; Hunt, Alwell, & Goetz, 1988). Topper and colleagues (1994) propose six categories of needs: (1) to gain attention; (2) to avoid an unpleasant event; (3) to control events; (4) to seek revenge (e.g., punish others); (5) to have fun (e.g., play); and (6) to self-regulate areas such as feelings, energy levels, or work demands (e.g., coping response). In an alternative view of the purposes for students' behaviors, O'Neill, Horner, Albin, Storey, and Sprague, (1990) identify two primary functions for behavior: to obtain internal or external stimulation and to escape/avoid internal or external stimulation. Internal stimulation refers to sensory pleasure or discomfort. External stimulation refers to attention (e.g., smiles, praise, frowns, scolding) and objects, activities, tasks, or events (e.g., food, money, "fun" activity, difficult tasks, change in routine, stopping "fun"). Regardless of the paradigm for viewing the function of behavior, traditional behavior management techniques will be more effective when implemented within the context of a functional assessment of the communicative purpose of the behavior of concern and environmental variables that affect the behavior.

Functional assessment is a process of identifying "relationships between environmental events and the occurrence or nonoccurrence of a target behavior" (Dunlap et al., 1993, p. 275) in order to first determine the purpose (e.g., function) of a behavior and then determine intervention options that are likely to increase desired behaviors and decrease undesired behaviors. Two premises underlie the functional assessment of behavior:

1. If the purpose of an inappropriate behavior is understood, a more desirable behavior may be developed to replace the "function" of the inappropriate behavior.
2. If the relationship between environmental variables and the inappropriate behavior is understood, the environmental conditions can be altered to promote a replacement (e.g., desirable) behavior to serve the same purpose, while inhibiting the inappropriate behavior.

Analysis of gathered information should assist the teacher in predicting the circumstances under which the inappropriate behavior will and will not occur (O'Neill et al., 1990). This allows the teacher to systematically manipulate the antecedent events and consequent events surrounding the behavior in order to decrease or eliminate it, while providing the student with alternative behaviors that serve to meet the student's needs. Antecedents are the events that occur preceding the behavior of interest. Consequences are the events that occur following the behavior.

The first step in functional assessment is to gather information about the behavior of concern and the students across settings and people (DeLuke & Knoblock, 1987), focusing on the context in which the inappropriate behaviors occur (Colvin, Sugai, & Patching, 1993). Sources of information include school records, people who are directly involved with the students, the students themselves, and direct observations of the students. O'Neill and colleagues (1990) recommend gathering background information pertaining to the follow-ing: diet, medical concerns (including medications), sleep cycles, daily schedule, and the degree of control the student has over the events in his/her day-to-day life. Pertinent infor-mation related to specific behavioral issues includes the time of day (e.g., in the morning, during transitions) and physical setting in which the behavior occurs, activities or setting events and people present or absent when the behavior occurs, specific antecedents to the behavior, and the outcome or consequences of the behavior.

A vital source of information is direct observations of students. There are times at which it is difficult to pinpoint exactly what is wrong. Alberto and Troutman (1990; 1995) suggest keeping anecdotal records of students' behaviors across the school day, and then structuring these notes to pinpoint, or identify, the target behavior. A visual organizer can be used to structure the antecedents, behavior, and consequences (ABC organizer) that occur throughout the day (see Table 12-8). Once the behavior has been identified in observ-able terms, direct observations can be conducted that target specific behaviors in order to

TABLE 12-8   Sample antecedent/behavior/consequence visual organizer.

Date/Time	Antecedent	Behavior	Consequence
9/25 9:00	Teacher asks Jim to read sight word list during small group reading instruction.	Jim screamed, "I can't read those *!&# words." He threw his pencil, sat with his head down and cried.	Teacher praised Jim for staying in his seat, then asked another student to read the flashcards.
10:00	Jim was part of a small group playing "Junior Boggle." Jim had been playing for 15 minutes and it was now Lisa's turn.	Jim cried, "I hate this game." He threw the pieces of the game, knocked over his chair, and climbed under the table.	The other students picked up the game. The teacher came over and said, "You need to go to time-out until you can calm down."
11:00	Teacher gave instruction to line up for art.	Jim refused to line up. He threw his papers and chairs.	The teacher sent Jim to the office.
12:30	Whole class handwriting instruction. Everyone has just copied the first line of a poem from the board. Students were told to write the second line of the poem.	Jim shouted, "I finished this @#!&#! poem." Then he tore up the paper and threw his pencil.	The teacher praised Jim for writing the first line. Jim picked up his pencil and paper and sat at his desk for the rest of handwriting.
1:30	Jim completed half of the math worksheet.	Jim started to cry. He started to use profanity and to throw objects.	The teacher took Jim's paper and told him to go to time-out.

Behavior: Tantrum
Throws objects (pencils, chairs, etc.), cries, screams, uses profanity, rips up papers

Student: Jim

Comments:

identify relationships between the behavior and events that precede and follow the behavior. Teachers may then look for patterns among environmental occurrences and behaviors. What usually occurs immediately before the behavior occurs? In other words, what is the antecedent? What usually happens immediately after the behavior occurs, for example, what is the consequence? Is there consistency? What seems to be prompting or maintaining the inappropriate behavior? What function is the behavior serving for the student?

For example, upon examining the ABC organizer in Table 12-8, the teacher finds that work activities or stopping something he enjoyed preceded Jim's tantrums. The consequences to the tantrum varied from being sent out of the room to being praised for an appropriate behavior he had displayed prior to the outburst. When Jim was praised for something he had done "well," he appeared to settle down and sit quietly for the remainder of the activity. One interpretation of the ABC data is that Jim tantrums to escape or avoid doing something unpleasant. Another is that he is seeking attention. He appears to respond well to teacher praise, at least when no further task demands are made. What other variables should be considered? The behavior sample in this description may not give enough information to definitively identify the function of the behavior, the variables maintaining the behavior, or to design an intervention. However, it does give enough information to guide the focus of additional direct observations of the behavior, and some initial patterns seem to be emerging.

Determine Behavioral Goals/Objectives

Just as specific goals and/or objectives are identified for academic outcomes, specific goals and objectives are necessary for behavioral outcomes. Teachers must decide under what conditions they want behavior to be eliminated and with what behavior the inappropriate behavior will be replaced (Colvin, Sugai, & Patching, 1993). Consideration needs to be given to (1) a description of the behavior in observable terms (Colvin, Kameenui, & Sugai, 1993; Alberto & Troutman, 1990; 1995), (2) the conditions under which the behavior should or should not occur, and (3) the criteria for acceptable performance.

Once the teacher has evaluated the learning environment, noting the antecedents and consequences that may be affecting the students' behaviors, the next step is to prioritize behaviors for intervention (Demchak, 1993). In a class of twenty-five to thirty students, teachers may have difficulty addressing a number of behaviors at once. One guideline for prioritizing behaviors for intervention is to address the most serious behaviors first. Is the behavior dangerous to the student or others? Then it must be dealt with immediately. Which behavior has the most potential for spreading to other students? Address that behavior before addressing those behaviors that cause less disruption. Which behaviors interfere with students' learning and interactions within the class or important nonclass settings? Intervene on those behaviors that have social or functional relevance for students versus behaviors that are simply different.

Specify or pinpoint the behavior targeted for change. Refer to the functional assessment and give consideration to what makes the behavior inappropriate. Is the behavior too intense, not intense enough, not appropriate to a given situation? What form does it take? What purpose does the behavior serve for the student? Is there an appropriate behavior that can be reinforced that will serve as a functional replacement?

Use verbs or precise terms to describe the behavior so that the behavior is observable and measurable. What exactly do you want the student to do or not do? This ensures consistency across observations and observers, and it reduces subjectivity when dealing with students and problem behavior. What does it mean when a student is disruptive, doesn't pay attention, is always talking? Table 12-9 gives examples of "school survival skills" described in observable and measurable terms.

Decide under what conditions the behavior is to occur (or not occur). It may be that it is acceptable for Meghan to talk without permission during a cooperative learning project, but it is not acceptable for her to talk without permission during a whole class lecture period. It is acceptable to run outside at recess but not in the halls. It is acceptable for Emily to get up to sharpen a pencil but not to get up to visit with Kristin during independent work periods.

Identify the minimally acceptable performance criteria of the behavior (Alberto & Troutman, 1990; 1995). Although teachers should have high expectations, criteria should also be realistic. Criteria should be established based on a student's current level of performance and past rate of progress, behavioral expectations for the rest of the class and school

TABLE 12-9   Description and measurement of school survival skills.

School Survival Skill	Behavior	Assessment
Complete homework assignments	Complete and turn in homework assignments	**Number of completed assignments** turned in on time
Using school work time efficiently	Beginning and completing assigned work during the school day	**Number of minutes** it takes a student to begin work after teacher directions; **Work turned in** by the end of the period
Organizing materials	Uses folders, notebooks, or other organizers to place work in and then find it quickly	**Checklist** used to periodically assess organization throughout the school day
Following directions	Begins to follow directions within one minute	**Amount of time** it takes for student to begin following directions
Raising hand to participate in class discussions	Participates in class discussions only after raising hand and being called on by the teacher	**Number of times** student calls out without permission from the teacher
On-task	Completes assignments with a specified amount of accuracy	**Percentage of work** completed within allotted time and with a predetermined accuracy rate

Source: King-Sears, M. (1994). *Curriculum-based assessment in special education* (p. 157). San Diego: Singular. Reprinted by permission of the publisher

standards, and behavioral characteristics directly related to a disability that may affect progress. If a student routinely gets out of her seat an average of fifteen times per class period, staying in her seat 100 percent of the time may not be a realistic objective with which to start. While students' profanity is never appropriate during the school day, if a student uses curse words an average of ninety-five times a day, it is not reasonable to expect zero incidents per day within one week. Although high school students may listen to a forty-five-minute lesson presentation, expecting first grade children to sit for forty-five minutes for a teacher-directed lesson is unrealistic.

Criteria may be stated in terms of frequency (e.g., zero times across a school day; five of six opportunities to participate), accuracy (e.g., put all English assignments in correct notebook section), duration (e.g., for twenty minutes), latency (e.g., within thirty seconds), or force (e.g., whisper; close the door without slamming it). The criteria should reflect the teacher's expectations for socially acceptable (and relevant) behavior and students' characteristics related to disability, age, and grade.

Design the Intervention
Interventions may fall into two categories: (1) interventions that target one individual or group of students with similar needs and (2) interventions that can be used for the whole class with adjustments for particular students (see group-oriented behavior management systems later in this chapter). The functional assessment serves as an ongoing tool for designing appropriate interventions and assessing progress (Demchak, 1993). Systematically review gathered information, and develop interventions that are based on the function that the inappropriate behavior serves (Lalli et al., 1993) and the relationship between environmental events and the target behaviors (Dunlap et al., 1993). Although a comprehensive presentation of behavioral principles and techniques is beyond the scope of this chapter, several guidelines that are related to information gained during the functional assessment will be useful as interventions are planned.

Antecedent events that have been shown to elicit both appropriate and inappropriate behavior should be directly addressed. Antecedents may include instructional content and presentation. Instruction should match the student's level of development and learning style. The classroom arrangement should accommodate students' disabilities. Alberto and Troutman (1990; 1995) identify six categories of antecedent stimuli:

- Verbal requests or instructions (i.e., given the instruction to "come to reading group" or "raise your hand when you want to speak")
- Written instructions or format (i.e., given directions written on the board or worksheets)
- Demonstration (i.e., given a model)
- Materials to be used (i.e., given shapes and a sorting box; given a communication board; given a math worksheet with twenty basic addition facts)
- Environmental setting or timing (i.e., given a reading period; given a half-hour recess period; during whole group instruction; during independent work periods)
- Manner of assistance (i.e., independently; with spelling aids)

In addition to addressing the antecedents to students' behaviors to design effective interventions, educators should consider the *consequences* that have been shown to increase or maintain both appropriate and inappropriate behavior. Students may need teachers to teach or reinforce replacement behaviors. Principles of reinforcement and "punishment" should be applied within the parameters of information obtained during the functional assessment. Consequences that have been reinforcing unacceptable behavior should be discontinued. Consequences that have been identified as reinforcers for the desired behavior should be implemented, more frequently at first and then on a schedule that is natural for the behavior and setting.

Prepare for the Intervention

Classrooms with few discipline problems are those in which adequate advance planning and preparation has been done by the teacher (Fuhr, 1993). Lack of planning often results in too much unstructured time as well as indecision and inconsistency on the part of the teacher. Educators in inclusive settings:

- Coordinate plans with others who will play a role in the intervention, including the student.
- Ensure that all persons involved understand what they will do and what will happen.
- Communicate with students about the rationale for the intervention and targeted objectives.
- Give students explicit instructions about the behavior expected of them and provide training on the expected or appropriate behavior before students must perform in the targeted context (i.e., the classroom situation in which the inappropriate behavior typically occurs) (Colvin, Sugai, & Patching, 1993).
- Provide consistent follow-up to reduce the inferences students have to make about classroom demands (Howard-Rose & Rose, 1994).
- Gather all necessary materials in advance, including materials to collect and maintain accurate data on the behavior and effects of the intervention (i.e., data sheets, stop watch, counter, tape recorder).

Adequate preparation enables teachers in inclusive settings to be more consistent in maintaining reasonable expectations and in implementing effective interventions.

Apply the Intervention

Implement the intervention as planned. Whether or not an intervention is used should not depend on the teacher's mood but on established expectations. Consistency is the key issue. Refer to the guidelines for promoting consistency in Table 12-4.

The intervention should be applied in a way that is considerate of the students' self-esteem. In other words, make every effort to treat students with dignity (Mendler, 1993). This can be done by accepting and acknowledging students' feelings while providing correction in a firm, yet nonsarcastic manner (Ginott, 1971).

Conduct Ongoing Assessment

Student participation and learning is enhanced when teachers actively and frequently monitor student performance (Christenson et al., 1989). This can be done informally by collecting and checking work on a regular basis, visually scanning the classroom, and keeping written records of individual student behavior. However, formal data collection techniques are particularly useful for documenting changes in the occurrence of behaviors. Several data collection techniques are described in Table 12-10. Data should be gathered for times

TABLE 12-10 Data collection techniques and examples.

Term	Description	Example
Duration recording	Length of time between beginning and end of specific target behavior.	Add each amount of time to get the **total number of minutes** student engages in inappropriate behavior; use when length of time behavior lasts is of concern.
Event recording	Each time a specific behavior occurs.	**Total number of times** that student talks out in class without permission; use when behavior occurs frequently.
Interval recording	Divide length of time into blocks and note if behavior occurred at any time during each time block.	Student stops doing his or her work for part of a one-minute time block then off-task behavior is recorded for the whole time block, yielding a **percentage of time** student is off-task; use when any occurrence of the behavior during a time period is of concern; sometimes used when teacher cannot record every instance of behavior but can note if behavior occurs once during time span.
Time sample recording	Divide length of time into blocks and note if behavior occurred at the end of each time block.	Student is observed only at the end of the time period for target behavior; usually the **percentage of time** is noted on graph for behaviors; teacher cannot record every occurrence of behavior but time span is short and manageable enough to yield a reliable result.
Latency recording	Note amount of time that elapses between teacher request and student compliance.	Graph the **amount of time** it takes for a student to begin initiating a response.
Continuous recording	Behaviors of target student and others in environment written down.	Useful when conducting a **functional analysis** and attempting to determine antecedent events (possible causes, provocations, preceding events), description of target behavior, and consequences following target behavior; typically not for daily use on an ongoing basis, but extremely useful when determining where to start with CBA.

Source: King-Sears, M. (1994). *Curriculum-based assessment in special education* (p. 154). San Diego: Singular. Reprinted by permission of the publisher.

of particular interest during the day. The more frequently and consistently data are collected, the more accurate the picture of the behavior occurrence will be. However, in most classrooms teachers will need to balance the desire for accurate documentation of behavior change with the practicality of collecting data in the midst of ongoing instruction. Data collected using the techniques identified can be graphed to provide an ongoing visual indicator of performance levels.

Teachers should continue with the planned intervention until the desired behavior is achieved or a new intervention is warranted because the anticipated outcomes have not been achieved. If desired results are not forthcoming, problem solve. Reconvene the Collaborative Support Team to meet formally, or meet informally, with colleagues to assess the situation. If the student's behavior is not improving, is the intervention being implemented correctly and consistently by all persons involved? Have other environmental variables (class, school, home, friends, or other) changed or are they impacting the intervention in an unpredicted way?

While there are many models of discipline and myriad options for changing and managing behavior, it is critical to know and remain mindful of the function the behavior serves for the student. The bottom line is, when educators know what is maintaining the behavior, they can do something about it.

Teaching Students Self-Management Systems

The previous sections of this chapter have focused primarily on teacher behaviors that can positively influence student behavior in inclusive settings. Preparing independent and self-controlled students, however, requires that the students themselves assume responsibility for managing their behaviors. Students of all ages from varied disability categories have effectively managed their behaviors using self-management techniques, making it a robust procedure that transcends disability severity and grade levels.

Definitions of Self-Management

Self-management is defined as the application of behavior change processes to modify or maintain one's own behavior (Hughes, Korinek, & Gorman, 1991). Varied terms are used in the literature to depict self-management, such as self-control and self-regulation, and some authors refer to these terms interchangeably. For purposes of this chapter, self-management is the term used to describe the procedures comprising self-monitoring (or self-recording), self-evaluation (or self-assessment), and self-reinforcement (or self-reward). Furthermore, Cole and Bambara (1992) distinguish forms of self-management on two dimensions: contingency-based approaches (focusing on consequences of behavior) and cognitive-based procedures (focusing on antecedents of behavior). In this text, cognitive procedures, including self-instruction, are described in Chapter 11 as a strategy procedure. This chapter will focus on the contingency-based approaches, which include students' use of self-monitoring, self-evaluation, and self-reinforcement of their behaviors.

> *Self-management interventions involve the gradual loosening of teacher control or authority, the transfer of control from teachers to students, and the ultimate goal of empowering students.*
>
> Cole & Bambara, 1992

Feedback from teachers and students who have used self-management techniques confirms the social validity of these systems. Hughes and colleagues (1991) report that students in some research studies have independently requested self-monitoring forms for their use in other classrooms. Furthermore, students noticed that they were completing more work, earning better grades, and receiving fewer negative remarks from their teachers. Teachers noted that fewer disruptive behaviors occurred, more time on-task resulted, and students' academic competence increased.

Given the variety of behaviors with which educators must contend in inclusive settings, the extent to which teachers can involve the students themselves via self-management techniques is not only a timesaver because it is one less system for the teacher to manage, but it is also important for promoting student independence. Self-management techniques are an essential set of methods for teachers to have in their repertoire. King-Sears and Cummings (1996) provide several guidelines to help educators make decisions about student behaviors that can be targeted for self-management. Several instructional principles apply when teaching and using any of the self-management systems described here (see Table 12-11 for a summary of these guidelines and principles).

TABLE 12-11 Selecting student behaviors and using instructional principles for self-management.

Guidelines for Selecting Behaviors for Self-Management

1. Select a behavior that is already in the student's repertoire.
2. Choose a mild behavior problem initially.
3. Target a manageable behavior.
4. Select behaviors that can be defined, counted, and evaluated.
5. Use external systems initially for more severe behaviors.

Instructional Principles When Using Self-Management

1. Reinforce the student's appropriate use of self-management.
2. Alter self-management techniques when necessary.
3. Use combinations of self-management techniques.
4. Make decisions about the effectiveness of self-management.
5. Supervise the use of self-management.
6. Involve the student in the development of self-management systems.

Source: From King-Sears, M. E., & Cummings, C. S. (1996). General educators' inclusive practices. *Remedial and Special Education, 17,* 217–225. Copyright © by Pro•Ed, Inc. Reprinted by permission.

Self-management techniques typically consist of self-monitoring, self-evaluation, and self-reinforcement. Each of these techniques is described in the following sections, which provide instructional sequences (see Table 12-12 for a listing of the sequences) and examples of varied forms and formats that can be used within inclusive settings.

Self-Monitoring

Self-monitoring requires students to note the occurrence of a specific behavior they are exhibiting by making some sort of notation on a checklist, index card, or other type of tally sheet. Self-monitoring has been especially effective for students with disabilities because it makes them more aware of their behavior and compels them to focus their attention on a specific dimension of a behavior. Teacher directions and expectations in inclusive settings may be obvious to most students, but are not necessarily obvious for some students with disabilities.

Self-monitoring involves (1) self-observation (e.g., "I can see that I just waited until I received permission to talk out . . .") and (2) self-recording ("so I'll mark another tally for myself"). In-seat, on-task, appropriate noise levels, classwork completion, and desirable

TABLE 12-12   Instructional sequence for teaching self-management.

Self-Monitoring	Self-Evaluation	Self-Reinforcement
Select and define the target behavior.	Select target behavior's evaluation standard.	Select target behavior and reinforcement system.
Develop the data collection system.	Develop the data collection system and scale.	Develop the data collection system, scale, and signal for reinforcement.
Determine the time interval for when to self-monitor.	Determine the time interval for self-evaluation.	Determine the time interval for reinforcement.
Teach the student how to use self-monitoring (7-step process).	Teach the student how to use self-evaluation (7-step process).	Teach the student how to use self-reinforcement (7-step process).
Measure how well the student performs the target behavior.	Measure how well the student performs the target behavior.	Measure how well the student performs the target behavior.

7-Step Training Process

1. Identify and demonstrate examples and nonexamples of the target behavior.
2. Practice the target behavior and discuss its effects.
3. Describe the self-management system and its benefits.
4. Model (think-aloud) using the self-management system while performing the target behavior.
5. Discuss the specific situation in which self-management will be used.
6. Provide guided practice through role-play of target behavior while using the self-management system.
7. Assess student's mastery of the self-management system.

class participation—each of these behaviors has been achieved when students used self-monitoring techniques. A "reactivity" effect frequently occurs when self-monitoring is used in that a behavior may *improve* when students count or tally the occurrence of the behavior even if no other intervention is used.

Self-Evaluation

Self-evaluation, or self-assessment, requires students to compare their behavior to either a self- or externally-determined standard. Often, self-evaluation procedures are taught after students have first learned to self-monitor. However, some students may be able to use self-evaluation as their initial self-management technique if they are already aware of their behaviors. During self-evaluation, students make a judgment about some qualitative aspect of their behavior, not the occurrence or nonoccurrence per se. These judgments may be based on how well, how intense, how much, or how long the target behavior occurs. Typically students use some type of standard, or scale, to help them make a decision about the quality of their performance.

Self-Reinforcement

Self-reinforcement, or self-reward, requires students to decide whether they have achieved ratings that entitle them to access a predetermined reinforcement. Teachers may select the reinforcement in advance, although student involvement is strongly encouraged to increase motivation and responsibility.

Five phases may be used as an instructional sequence when implementing any of the self-management systems (refer to Table 12-12 for the instructional sequence). Teacher planning and organization occur during phases one through three. Phase four delineates a seven-step process for teaching students how to use self-management. Phase five is primarily an assessment phase, reminding teachers to measure the target behavior to ensure that the self-management system is resulting in desired student performance. The following sections describe in more detail phases one through four for each of the three self-management techniques. Note that in some examples students are involved in the planning phases with the teacher.

Phase One: Select the Behavior

Self-monitoring.   Select the student behavior to change, and then clearly define the target behavior so students understand what actions comprise the behavior. Without a clear definition of what the target behavior looks like and feels like, students may be uncertain about precisely what behavior the teacher wants them to exhibit. For example, some observable behaviors that depict "appropriate class participation" are (1) raising hand and waiting to be called on before talking out in class, (2) not talking when others are talking, or (3) contributing to class discussions.

Self-evaluation.   In addition to the teacher's selection and identification of the target behavior, the teacher identifies the criteria that will be used during self-evaluation for determining the behavior's quality. Again, student involvement may be elicited so that the "quality indicators" are determined with input from the student. It is important to clearly define both the behavior *and* how the quality of that behavior will be judged so that these aspects can be explained to the student in a concrete manner. The teacher devises an evaluation system that the student can use to determine the behavior's rating. For young children or students with more severe cognitive disabilities, rating scales using "0 to 2" or pictures (smiley faces are popular) may be appropriate. For older students, more complex systems can be used that include a wider range of ratings (e.g., 1 to 7, rubrics).

Self-reinforcement. Students must first understand the meaning underlying the self-monitoring and self-evaluation systems before using self-reinforcement. Select reinforcers by seeking students' input and considering students' interests. Keep in mind that a reinforcer is defined by its effect on behavior. Choose reinforcers that are meaningful to students.

During self-reinforcement, students note the occurrence of a behavior, the quality of that behavior, *and* a point in time at which they will reward themselves for a quality performance of that behavior. Teachers will need to communicate clearly to students the amount and quality of work that is required prior to students' earning a reinforcer for themselves. However, students who set goals for themselves that teachers may believe are too high may make greater gains than when the teacher sets the goals (Fuchs, Fuchs, & Deno, 1985).

Phase Two: Develop the Data Collection System

Self-monitoring. Students may use data collection systems such as tally sheets, checklists, wrist counters, or index cards to record the occurrence (or nonoccurrence) of their target behavior. Data collection systems for younger students or students with severe disabilities may have pictures, words, or symbols that relate to the target behavior. In order to be inconspicuous, data collection systems for students in middle and high school may be small and devoid of picturesque qualities.

Examples of systems used with individuals with developmental disabilities include marking a form or photo, pressing a counter, putting a ring on a dowel rod, moving beads on a bracelet, or taking a token, coin, or sticker (Harchik, Sherman, & Sheldon, 1992). Consider having students develop their own data collection system, perhaps after being provided with a sample format from the teacher. See Figure 12-1 for a sample self-monitoring form.

Self-evaluation. Evaluation forms include criteria or indicators with which students rate their performance of the target behavior. Written directions or prompts may be helpful when students are first learning to evaluate their behavior, but often can be faded after the student understands how to use the form for self-evaluation.

Self-reinforcement. Self-reinforcement systems include an indicator for the criteria and timing for students to obtain the previously identified reinforcer. Forms used to prompt and record self-reinforcement may be similar to the data collection systems used for self-monitoring or self-evaluation. Students may use a highlighter or other symbol to indicate when the reinforcement should be delivered.

Ask yourself: **"Did I successfully complete each of these behaviors?"**

	Mon.		Tues.		Wed.		Thurs.		Fri.	
	yes	no	yes	no	yes	no	yes	no	yes	no
1. In seat before bell rang.										
2. Began work within 30 seconds.										
3. Worked without interrupting anyone.										
4. Completed work.										
5. Turned in work.										
6. Began next assignment.										

$$\frac{\text{Total YES for the week:}}{\text{Total possible YES for the week: 30}} \times 100 = \quad \%$$

FIGURE 12-1   Sample self-monitoring form.

***Phase Three: Select the time interval for administering
the self-management technique.***

Self-monitoring.   Select the time interval and signal for recording the behavior. After selecting the data collection system, the teacher determines when a student will record the occurrence of a behavior. Event recording may be used if a student notes every occurrence of a behavior ("I just interrupted the teacher. That's another tally for not waiting to receive permission to talk."). Time sampling may be used if some type of signal is given (e.g., a tape recording or kitchen timer with periodic "beeps" to provide an audible signal) that prompts the student to think about what they're doing right then, and then the occurrence or nonoccurrence of the target behavior ("There's the signal. What was I just doing?") is recorded. Interval recording may use a signaling system that prompts the student to think about the previous time lapse and to note whether the target behavior occurred, or not, at any time during the specific time period ("I just heard the signal. Now, have I been participating appropriately during the time since the last time I heard the signal?"). Permanent product recording can be used when students are keeping track of their test scores, assignment grades, and other formative evaluations. Signals to prompt self-monitoring include pocket timers, bells, verbal prompts, and timers that automatically reset at the end of preset intervals.

The time period that is selected will be influenced by what is practical to use in a classroom setting and whether the time interval gives an adequate representation of the target behavior's occurrence so that a difference is likely to be noticed. If the time period (e.g., the frequency of "beeps") selected is not capturing enough of a sample of the target behavior to indicate a difference, a more frequent recording schedule or another data collection procedure may provide a more accurate account of the behavior's occurrence.

Self-evaluation.   Determine how often students will self-evaluate their performance. The time interval for how frequently, or at what point, the teacher wants students to rate their behavior is both determined and practiced before the entire self-evaluation system is implemented. Signals such as audible prompts at the end of the page or at the end of the class period can be used.

Self-reinforcement.   Determine a signal for reinforcement. Some students may need reinforcement immediately upon meeting the preestablished criteria for performance. During the initial stages of self-reinforcement techniques, immediate reinforcement may motivate students and ensure that they recognize the relationship between the quantity and quality of their behavior and reinforcement. Eventually, the amount of time between the behavior and the reinforcement should increase so that students can put off rewards until more convenient or appropriate times.

Phase Four: Teach students how to use the system
The seven-step process depicted in Table 12-12 is used with each self-management system. Students who exit training sessions (typically a total of two hours is necessary, preferably spread over several days) with a clear understanding of the desired behaviors and how to use the self-management system are more likely to independently and correctly use the system. If time is not taken in the beginning to teach the behaviors and system adequately, self-management procedures may not produce the desired results because students do not understand what to do and when to do it. Below is the seven-step process for teaching students to use self-management systems:

   1. **Identify and demonstrate examples and nonexamples of the target behavior.** Students with disabilities need to have a clear understanding of what on-task looks like and feels like, of what appropriate class participation is and is not, or the example/nonexample of whatever behavior the teacher has targeted.
   2. **Practice the target behavior and discuss its effects.** Teachers incorporate rationales into this step when they discuss with the student the benefits of doing, or not doing, the target behavior.
   3. **Describe the self-management system and its benefits.** Once students understand examples and nonexamples of the target behavior, as well as the anticipated benefits of exhibiting more (or less) of the target behavior, teachers introduce the data collection system to students. The introduction of the data collection system provides students a description and sample of the format they will use to monitor their performance of the behavior that has been previously discussed and practiced.
   4. **Model (think aloud) using the self-management system while performing the target behavior.** Students need to hear the teacher, who is a proficient thinker and performer of the target behavior, express his or her thoughts while using the self-management system to perform the target behavior. By talking aloud, the teacher provides students with a model of what their thoughts should be when using the self-management system.

5. Discuss the specific situation in which self-management will be used. Teachers and students identify a specific time during the day in which students will use the self-management system initially.

6. Provide guided practice through role-play of the target behavior while using the self-management system. This step requires students to pull all parts of the system together and practice both exhibiting the target behavior (or not) and using the self-management system. Examples and nonexamples, modeling, and teacher feedback are important in this step.

7. Assess student's mastery of the self-management system. Students are not required to use the self-management system independently until they have demonstrated proficiency when they are under teacher guidance (i.e., during the training sessions). A recommended mastery criteria for this step is 100 percent accuracy in the practice situation. During practice students show examples and nonexamples of the target behavior while using the self-management system, identify when to use the system during the school day, and tell how they expect the self-management system to help them to improve their school performance.

Each step from the seven-step process is individualized for the type of self-management system used, the type of behavior(s) selected, the age of students, and any other relevant classroom, teacher, assignment, or student characteristics that influence the development and implementation of self-management systems.

Phase Five: Measure how well the student performs the target behavior

As with any intervention, whether academic or social, whether used for an individual or used for a group, if the intervention is not having the desired effect the teacher needs to reconsider, restructure, or revise the system so that the intended outcome occurs. Teachers will not be able to make those decisions, however, unless they are *revisiting* the target behavior. Measure, monitor, assess, evaluate—one of these must be occurring to determine how well the self-management system is impacting on the target behavior.

The next section of this chapter describes ways that groups of students, including whole classes, can be involved in management systems that relieve the teacher of full responsibility for maintaining control in classrooms.

Group-Oriented Behavior Management Systems

In inclusive classrooms, teachers may find it difficult to solitarily implement a wide variety of time-intensive behavior management techniques with many different students. Although some students benefit from more specialized techniques, the logistical constraints on teachers must be considered when designing such interventions. One method of allowing students with disabilities to become a more natural part of the general education environment is the use of group-oriented behavior management systems. In this way, teachers may use the same system for all students and also be able to individualize the behaviors targeted for particular students.

Alberto and Troutman (1995) suggest using the following principles when applying group-oriented behavior management systems: (1) be certain that each member of the group is capable of performing the target behavior; (2) be sure some member does not find it reinforcing to sabotage the group's efforts; and (3) structure the group-oriented behavior management system to minimize the possibility that some members of the group perform the target behavior for others. The following research illustrates several effective applications of group-oriented management systems.

Salend, Whittaker, and Reeder (1993) implemented a group management system in secondary classrooms with students who had learning disabilities and emotional or behavioral disorders. The targeted behavior for students' use of a self-evaluation system was "talkouts during class time" because the teachers noted that students' inappropriate verbalizations interfered the most during academic instruction. Students were divided into two teams, and team members rated themselves as a team on how well their team's rating matched teachers' ratings of the number of talkouts. In this way, the students were not really competing against each other; they were competing to accurately have their ratings match teachers' ratings. Teams earned points that were then exchanged for tokens. The tokens could be used to acquire a variety of reinforcers, such as homework passes, posters, school supplies, and computer time. Inappropriate verbalizations prior to the group-management technique averaged approximately 140, and after the group technique was used the average decreased to less than 10. Particularly appealing for inclusive classrooms is the concept of students' controlling and monitoring their behaviors that interfere with academic instruction.

Group-oriented management techniques can be used with academic content. Pigott, Fantuzzo, Heggie, and Clement (1984) taught students in a fifth grade general education class how to implement a student-administered group-oriented system that resulted in increased arithmetic performance. Student teams were made up of four students, and each student performed a role during small group activities:

> ***Coach:*** *Informed the group of their daily goal for their academic task and reminded peers of methods they knew to do the work.*
>
> ***Scorekeeper:*** *Counted the number of math problems completed correctly by each team member and wrote the number on each student's math sheet.*
>
> ***Referee:*** *Also counted the number of math problems to provide an internal check for the scorekeeper.*
>
> ***Manager:*** *Added up the team's score and compared it with the daily goal.*

After four days of meeting the team's goal, the team was eligible to receive their predetermined reinforcement. Before using this method, the students learned to perform the roles during several training sessions totalling two hours. Roles were rotated daily to provide each student with experience in each role. This type of group-oriented behavior system can be especially useful in inclusive classrooms when (1) students' academic work is individualized yet still earns points for their team, (2) students assume more responsibility for setting goals, monitoring their performance, and determining when they have met their goals, and (3) teacher involvement after training the students focuses on reinforcing students who are working well (in both academic and social areas) and assisting students when necessary.

By concurrently targeting increased academic performance and decreased disruptive behaviors, teachers can combine the accomplishment of two targeted (one desirable, the other undesirable) behaviors within one management technique used for a class of students. Kern, Dunlap, Childs, and Clarke (1994) found that students with emotional or behavioral disorders who were taught a classwide self-management program increased on-task behaviors and decreased disruptive behaviors. Teachers in inclusive settings who use group-oriented management techniques may be increasing their instructional opportunities through decreasing the amount of time they need to spend dealing with off-task, disruptive, or other types of behaviors that deflect from instruction.

Conclusions

Effective behavior management is an issue faced by all schools. However, as the diversity of students' characteristics within a school increases, educators must be prepared with a comprehensive behavior management approach that is structured enough for teaching and learning to occur, but flexible enough to provide opportunities for all students to acquire behaviors that allow them to participate meaningfully. A proactive instructional orientation to behavior management is a mechanism for developing productive school behaviors for all students.

A systemic model targets three levels within schools for intervention: the school as a whole, individual teachers and their classrooms, and individual students. First, school-focused interventions set the stage for consistency and teamwork across the school while recognizing the value of family and community participation. Second, teacher-focused interventions address teachers' roles in promoting desirable student behaviors. By tailoring the instructional setting and instructional interactions within their classrooms to facilitate the successful participation of all students, teachers may prevent misbehavior and support students' display of appropriate classroom behaviors. Third, student-focused interventions include both externally managed and self-managed behavioral techniques that are focused on the specific behavioral characteristics of individual students who display challenging behaviors that are detrimental to their performance and participation in schools. A hallmark of an effective inclusive classroom is the teacher's ability to successfully identify the function of a student's inappropriate behaviors *and* implement positive and instructive techniques that promote more desirable and socially acceptable behaviors. Additionally, students who learn self-management techniques are better prepared to participate with appropriate behaviors across a variety of school and community settings. Ultimately it is the students themselves who must take responsibility for and control of their behavior.

References

Agne, K. J., Greenwood, G. E., & Miller, L. D. (1994). Relationships between teacher belief systems and teacher effectiveness. *The Journal of Research and Development in Education, 27* (3), 141–152.

Alberto, P. A., & Troutman, A. C. (1990). *Applied behavior analysis for teachers* (3rd ed.). New York: Merrill/Macmillan.

Alberto, P. A., & Troutman, A. C. (1995). *Applied behavior analysis for teachers* (4th ed.). Englewood Cliffs, NJ: Merrill/Prentice Hall.

Algozzine, B., Ysseldyke, J. E., & Campbell, P. (1994). Strategies and tactics for effective instruction. *Teaching Exceptional Children, 26* (3), 34–36.

Anderson, L. M., Evertson, C. M., & Brophy, J. E. (1979). An experimental study of effective teaching in first-grade reading groups. *The Elementary School Journal, 79* (4), 193–223.

Ashton, P., & Webb, R. (1986). *Making a difference: Teachers' sense of efficacy and student achievement* (Research on Teaching Monograph series). New York: Longman.

Bauwens, J., & Hourcade, J. J. (1992). School-based sources of stress among elementary and secondary at-risk students. *The School Counselor, 40,* 97–102.

Bender, W. N., & Mathes, M. Y. (1995). Students with ADHD in the inclusive classroom: A hierarchical approach to strategy selection. *Intervention in School and Clinic, 30,* 226–234.

Cangelosi, J. S. (1993). *Classroom management strategies* (2nd ed.). New York: Longman.

Canter, L., & Canter, M. (1986). *Assertive discipline: Phase two in-service media package.* Santa Monica, CA: Lee Canter and Associates.

Carpenter, S. L., & McKee-Higgins, E. M. (1996). Behavior management in inclusive classrooms. *Remedial and Special Education, 17,* 195–203.

Charles, C. M. (1992). *Building classroom discipline* (4th ed.). New York: Longman.

Cheney, D., & Harvey, V. S. (1994). From segregation to inclusion: One district's program changes for students with emotional/behavioral disorders. *Education and Treatment of Children, 17,* 332–346.

Christenson, S. L., Ysseldyke, J. E., & Thurlow, M. L. (1989). Critical instructional factors for students with mild handicaps: An integrative review. *Remedial and Special Education, 10* (5), 21–31.

Cole, C. L., & Bambara, L. M. (1992). Issues surrounding the use of self-management interventions in the schools. *School Psychology Review, 21,* 193–201.

Colvin, G., Kameenui, E. J., & Sugai, G. (1993). Reconceptualizing behavior management and school-wide discipline in general education. *Education and Treatment of Children, 16,* 361–381.

Colvin, G., Sugai, G., & Patching, B. (1993). Precorrection: An instructional approach for managing predictable problem behaviors. *Intervention in School and Clinic, 28,* 143–150.

Conroy, M. A., & Fox, J. J. (1994). Setting events and challenging behaviors in the classroom. *Preventing School Failure, 38* (3), 29–34.

Cooper, L. J., & Harding, J. (1993). Extending functional analysis procedures to outpatient and classroom settings for children with mild disabilities. In J. Reichle & D. P. Wacker, *Communicative alternatives to challenging behavior* (pp. 41–62). Baltimore: Brookes.

Crowley, E. P. (1993). A qualitative analysis of mainstreamed behaviorally disordered aggressive adolescents' perceptions of helpful and unhelpful teacher attitudes and behaviors. *Exceptionality, 4,* 131–151.

Curwin, R. L., & Mendler, A. N. (1988). *Discipline with dignity.* Alexandria, VA: Association for Supervision and Curriculum Development.

DeLuke, S. V., & Knoblock, P. (1987). Teacher behavior as preventive discipline. *Teaching Exceptional Children, 19* (4), 18–24.

Demchak, M. (1993). Functional assessment of problem behaviors in applied settings. *Intervention in School and Clinic, 29* (2), 89–95.

Dettmer, P., Thurston, L. P., & Dyck, N. (1993). *Consultation, collaboration, and teamwork for students with special needs.* Boston: Allyn & Bacon.

Dunlap, L. K., Dunlap, G., Koegel, L. K., & Koegel, R. L. (1991). Using self-monitoring to increase independence. *Teaching Exceptional Children, 23* (3), 17–22.

Dunlap, G., Kern, L., dePerczel, M., Clarke, S., Wilson, D., Childs, K. E., White, R., & Falk, G. D. (1993). Functional analysis of classroom variables for students with emotional behavioral disorders. *Behavioral Disorders, 18,* 275–291.

Emmer, E. T., Evertson, C. M., Sanford, J., Clements, B. S., & Murray, M. E. (1989). *Classroom management for secondary teachers.* Englewood Cliffs, NJ: Prentice Hall.

Englert, C. S. (1984). Measuring teacher effectiveness from the teacher's point of view. *Focus on Exceptional Children, 17* (2), 1–14.

Fuchs, L. S., Fuchs, D., & Deno, S. L. (1985). Importance of goal ambitiousness and goal mastery to student achievement. *Exceptional Children, 52,* 63–71.

Fuhr, D. (1993). Effective classroom discipline: Advice for educators. *NASSP Bulletin, 77* (549), 82–86.

Gartland, D. (1990). Classroom management: Preventive discipline. *LD Forum, 15* (3), 24–25.

Gartland, D. (1992). Classroom management: Corrective discipline. *LD Forum, 17* (2), 26–28.

Gearheart, B. R., Weishahn, M. W., & Gearheart, C. J. (1992). *The exceptional student in the regular classroom* (5th ed.). New York: Merrill/Macmillan.

Ginott, H. G. (1971). *Teacher and child.* New York: The MacMillan Company.

Gottfredson, D. C., Gottfredson, G. D., & Hybl, L. G. (1993). Managing adolescent behavior: A multi-year study. *American Educational Research Journal, 30,* 179–215.

Gorski, J. D., & Pilotto, L. (1993). Interpersonal violence among youth: A challenge for school personnel. *Educational Psychology Review, 5* (1), 35–61.

Graham, S., Harris, K. R., & Reid, R. (1992). Developing self-regulated learners. *Focus on Exceptional Children, 24* (6), 1–24.

Gunter, P. L., Shores, R. E., Jack, S. L., Denny, R. K., & DePaepe, P. A. (1994). A case study of the effects of altering instructional interactions on the disruptive behavior of a child identified with severe behavior disorders. *Education and Treatment of Children, 17,* 435–444.

Harchik, A. E., Sherman, J. A., & Sheldon, J. B. (1992). The use of self-management procedures by people with developmental disabilities: A brief review. *Research in Developmental Disabilities, 13,* 211–227.

Hitzing, W. (1992). Support and positive teaching strategies. In S. Stainback & W. Stainback (Eds.), *Curriculum considerations in inclusive classrooms* (pp. 143–158). Baltimore: Paul H. Brookes Publishing Co.

Howard-Rose, D., & Rose, C. (1994). Students' adaptation to task environments in resource room and regular class settings. *The Journal of Special Education, 28* (1), 3–26.

Hughes, C. A., & Boyle, J. R. (1991). Effects of self-monitoring for on-task behavior and task productivity on elementary students with moderate mental retardation. *Education and Treatment of Children, 14,* 96–111.

Hughes, C. A., Korinek, L., & Gorman, J. (1991). Self-management for students with mental retardation in public school settings: A research review. *Education and Training in Mental Retardation, 26,* 271–291.

Hunt, P., Alwell, M., & Goetz, L. (1988). Acquisition of conversation skills and the reduction of inappropriate social interaction behaviors. *Journal of the Association for the Severely Handicapped, 13,* 20–27.

Idol, L., Nevin, A., & Paolucci-Whitcomb, P. (1994). *Collaborative consultation* (2nd ed.). Austin, TX: Pro•Ed.

Johns, B. H., & Carr, V. G. (1995). *Techniques for managing verbally and physically aggressive students.* Denver, Colo: Love Publishing.

Johnson, D. W., & Johnson, R. T. (1995). *Reducing school violence through conflict resolution.* Alexandria, VA: Association for Supervision and Curriculum Development.

Jones V. F., & L. F. (1986). *Comprehensive classroom management: Creating positive learning environments.* Boston: Allyn & Bacon.

Kennedy, C. H., & Itkonen, T. (1993). Effects of setting events on the problem behavior of students with severe disabilities. *Journal of Applied Behavior Analysis, 26,* 321–327.

Kern, L., Dunlap, G., Childs, K. E., & Clarke, S. (1994). Use of a classwide self-management program to improve the behavior of students with emotional and behavioral disorders. *Education and Treatment of Children, 17,* 445–458.

Kern, L., Dunlap, G., Clarke, S., & Childs, K. E. (1994). Student assisted functional assessment interview. *Diagnostique, 19* (2–3), 29–39.

King-Sears, M. (1994). *Curriculum-based assessment in special education.* San Diego: Singular.

King-Sears, M. E., & Cummings, C. S. (1996). General educators' inclusive practices. *Remedial and Special Education, 17,* 217–225.

Kounin, J. S. (1970). *Discipline and group management in classrooms.* New York: Holt, Rinehart, & Winston.

Lalli, J. S., Browder, D. M., Mace, F. C., & Brown, D. K. (1993). Teacher use of descriptive analysis data to implement interventions to decrease students' problem behaviors. *Journal of Applied Behavior Analysis, 26,* 227–238.

Lalli, E. P., & Shapiro, E. S. (1990). The effects of self-monitoring and contingent reward on sight word acquisition. *Education and Treatment of Children, 13,* 129–141.

Lerner, R. M. (1995). *America's youth in crisis: Challenges and options for programs and policies.* Thousand Oaks: Sage.

Long, N. J., Morse, W. G., & Newman, R. G. (Eds.) (1971). *Conflict in the classroom* (2nd ed.). Belmont, CA: Wadsworth.

Mayer, G. R., Mitchell, L. K., Clementi, T., Clement-Robertson, E., Myatt, R., & Bullara, D. T. (1993).

A dropout prevention program for at-risk high school students: Emphasizing consulting to promote positive classroom climates. *Education and Treatment of Children, 16,* 135–146.

Mendler, A. N. (1993). Discipline with dignity in the classroom: Seven principles. *Education Digest, 58* (7), 4–9.

Minner, S. (1990). Use of a self-recording procedure to decrease the time taken by behaviorally disordered students to walk to special classes. *Behavioral Disorders, 15,* 210–216.

Morrison, J. A., Olivos, K., Dominguez, G., Gomez, D., & Lena, D. (1993). The application of family systems approaches to school behavior problems on a school-level discipline board: An outcome study. *Elementary School Guidance & Counseling, 27,* 258–272.

Munk, D. D., & Repp, A. C. (1994). The relationship between instructional variables and problem behavior: A review. *Exceptional Children, 60,* 390–401.

Nelson, C. M., & Rutherford, R. B. (1989). Behavioral interventions with behaviorally disordered students. In M. C. Wang, M. C. Reynolds, & H. J. Walberg (Eds.), *The handbook of special education: Research and practice* (Vol. 2). Oxford, England: Pergamon.

O'Neill, R. E., Horner, R. H., Albin, R. W., Storey, K., & Sprague, J. R. (1990). *Functional analysis of problem behavior.* Pacific Grove, CA: Brooks/Cole.

Pigott, H. E., Fantuzzo, J. W., Heggie, D. L., & Clement, P. W. (1984). A student administered group-oriented contingency intervention: Its efficacy in a regular classroom. *Child & Family Behavior Therapy, 6* (4), 41–55.

Reimers, T. M., Wacker, D. P., & Koeppl, G. (1987). Acceptability of behavioral interventions: A review of the literature. *School Psychology Review, 16,* 212–227.

Reitz, A. L. (1994). Implementing comprehensive classroom-based programs for students with emotional and behavioral problems. *Education and Treatment of Children, 17,* 312–331.

Repp, A. C., & Karsh, K. G. (1994). Hypothesis-based interventions for tantrum behaviors of persons with developmental disabilities in school settings. *Journal of Applied Behavior Analysis, 27,* 21–31.

Rooney, K. J. (1993). Classroom interventions for students with attention deficit disorders. *Focus on Exceptional Children, 26* (4), 1–15.

Sabatino, D. A. (1987). Preventive discipline as a practice in special education. *Teaching Exceptional Children, 19* (4), 8–11.

Salend, S. J. (1994). *Effective mainstreaming creating inclusive classrooms* (2nd ed.). New York: Macmillan.

Salend, S. J., Whittaker, C. R., & Reeder, E. (1993). Group evaluation: A collaborative, peer-mediated behavior management system. *Exceptional Children, 59,* 203–209.

Shapiro, E. S., & Klein, R. D. (1980). Self-management of classroom behavior with retarded/disturbed children. *Behavior Modification, 4,* 83–97.

Shores, R. E., Gunter, P. L., Denny, R. K., & Jack, S. L. (1993). Classroom influence on aggressive and disruptive behaviors of students with emotional and behavioral disorders. *Focus on Exceptional Children, 26* (2), 2–10.

Smith, D. D., & Rivera, D. P. (1995). Discipline in special education and general education settings. *Focus on Exceptional Children, 27* (5), 1–14.

Topper, K., Williams, W., Leo, K., Hamilton, R., Fox, T. (1994). *A positive approach to understanding and addressing challenging behaviors: Supporting educators and families to include students with emotional and behavioral difficulties in regular education.* Burlington: University of Vermont, Center for Developmental Disabilities.

Wang, M. C., Haertal, G. D., & Walberg, H. J. (1990). What influences learning? A content analysis of review literature. *Journal of Educational Research, 84* (1), 30–43.

Wolery, M., Bailey, D. B., & Sugai, G. M. (1989). *Principles and procedures of applied behavior analysis with exceptional students.* Boston: Allyn & Bacon.

Ysseldyke, J. E., Christenson, S., & Kovaleski, J. F. (1994). Identifying students' instructional needs in the context of classroom and home environments. *Teaching Exceptional Children, 26* (3), 37–41.

Chapter 13

Establishing the Classroom as a Community

DONNA K. GRAVES AND DIANNE F. BRADLEY

◆ ADVANCE ORGANIZER ◆

As changing demographics and increasing diversity impact our schools, educators need to ensure that each student is an integral part of the learning process. Students need ways to interact with diverse groups of peers and to solve problems together. One way to address these needs is to establish a classroom atmosphere that promotes a sense of community.

This chapter describes cooperative learning as a means to build classroom community. First, competitiveness, individualism, and cooperation are examined in light of the school culture. Outcomes for special and general education populations are then examined. Next, a variety of cooperative learning structures are explained. Finally, research-based benefits and essential elements of cooperative learning are explored.

As I sat in the workshop on cooperative learning, I was skeptical. Although I was intrigued with the concept of peer support—after all, kindergartners require a lot of assistance—my kids just seemed too young to be able to work successfully in cohesive groups. Besides, there were so many behavior problems in my class this year, even when I was up in front of them. No telling what they would do on their own in groups!

After the workshop I voiced my skepticism to the workshop leader. As I shared my frustrations about my class, she began to paint a picture of cooperative learning that was geared to small children. I decided with her help to give it a try.

I started with small groups of three. I removed individual materials from the tables and instituted a policy of sharing materials. Each member of the group would have a job assignment (get materials, pass out papers, etc.) and an academic assignment. Their first project was to make a group picture of a Thanksgiving feast. One student drew the turkey, one the vegetables, and one the dessert. They were to work on the social skills of taking turns and using quiet voices. Much to my surprise, they did a pretty good job! It still seemed like a lot for kindergartners to handle, but I took it slowly and did a lot of reinforcement and modeling.

As the year continued and the students cultivated their ability to work together, share, and be friendly to one another, I discovered some advantages for myself as well. I found I enjoyed being a facilitator. I learned more about my students as I went from group to group interacting with them than I did standing up in front of them feeling like I had to entertain them. I found they were all involved when working in small groups, and I didn't have to reprimand those who would tune out and fidget around during a large group activity. I saw that the students had greater opportunities to interact, process, and use social skills. The best thing that happened was that their behavior in the classroom changed dramatically. Classroom management went from me trying to manage them to them managing themselves. I still find it amazing that kindergartners can handle cooperative learning and that they benefit so much from this technique.

When individuals work together toward a common goal, their mutual dependency often motivates them to work harder to help the group, and thereby themselves, to succeed. In addition, they often must help specific members of the group do well and they often come to like and value the members of the group.

Murray, 1994

In conjunction with the inclusion of students with mild, moderate, and severe disabilities in general education classrooms, dramatic changes in the demographics of the United States have significantly altered the nature of schools as most educators experienced them when they were students. Now, as we come face to face with a new millennium, our task is to prepare young people to live and learn in a world that is markedly distinctive from the one we experienced for most of the twentieth century.

Ever increasing diversity, the globalization of business and industry, the rapid growth of technology, and the information-related nature of many jobs demand expertise in interpersonal skills. Significant changes in the world of work have intensified the interdependent nature of successful enterprise, requiring that schools operate in fundamentally different ways.

In 1991, the Secretary of Labor and the Secretary's Commission on Achieving Necessary Skills (SCANS) examined the demands of the workplace and the implications for schools in preparing young people for the world of work. In their report, the ability to develop and maintain effective interpersonal relationships is identified as one of the five essential competencies for effective job performance. This competency specifies the ability to do the following:

- Participate as a member of a team contributing to the group effort
- Teach others new skills
- Negotiate and resolve divergent interests
- Work with people from diverse backgrounds

These skills were identified as paramount to productivity. The three-part foundation of competencies fundamental for workplace success pinpoints not only basic skills and thinking skills as critical to work success, but also personal qualities that enhance the ability to communicate with and learn from others. Not only are high performance work environments fueled by collaboration and teamwork, but Kagan (1994) reports that the most frequent reason for people to be fired from their first job is **lack** of interpersonal skills.

In the last ten to twenty years, research in cognitive psychology has contributed dramatically to our understanding of the learning process. We now know that many mental functions and accomplishments are grounded in social relations, and that often the best solutions to problems originate through interactions with others—discussions, negotiations, debates, and compromises (Murray, 1994). Kagan (1994) tells us that "teachers who wish to maximize what the child can accomplish will minimize the time the child works alone on school tasks" (p. 9). Marzano (1988) identified an instructional framework for cognitive development that promotes student thinking and learning in five types or dimensions of learning (see Table 13-1).

Threaded through Dimension 2, *acquiring and integrating knowledge,* Dimension 3, *extending and refining knowledge,* and Dimension 4, *using knowledge meaningfully,* are strategies and techniques whereby students work directly with a partner or as a member of a team to forward their thinking and mastery of the content. The basis of Dimension 1, *developing positive attitudes and perceptions about learning,* and Dimension 5, *developing productive habits of mind,* are grounded in the social nature of learning that permits and promotes an atmosphere of academic trust, risk taking, and the development of habitual behaviors that lie at the heart of successful functioning in school, at work, and in personal relationships.

TABLE 13-1 Dimensions of learning.

1. Developing positive attitudes and perceptions about learning
2. Acquiring and integrating knowledge
3. Extending and refining knowledge
4. Using knowledge meaningfully
5. Developing productive habits of mind

Additionally, the workplace is especially important to people with disabilities as an arena in which to establish friendships and other meaningful relationships with adults in the general population (Rosen & Burchard, 1990). Moreover, businesses are beginning to realize that supportive employment to people with disabilities creates a culture that can increase a company's products and services and acts as a support to other employees as well (PACE-SETTER, 1995). However, as the employer of a person with mental retardation new skills may be required. Working alongside a person with a severe disability in a supported employment situation may change the dynamics of the workplace. Building productive working/learning relationships to solve problems and make decisions is essential.

The case for establishing classrooms as communities is evident, not just in terms of individual cognitive, social, emotional, and physical development, but for our very existence as a democratic society. The new paradigm of teaching and learning emphasizes the preparation of students for their future roles in society.

Competition and Individualism versus Cooperation

> *When individuals take action there are three ways what they do may be related to the actions of others. One's actions may promote the success of others, obstruct the success of others, or not have any effect at all on the success or failure of others.*
>
> Johnson & Johnson, 1975

Individualism and Competition

The cooperative, competitive, and individualistic goal structures described by Johnson and Johnson (1975) operate in all aspects of life and have profound implications for educators. Traditionally, schools have embodied the individualistic and competitive goal structures that typify the American culture. Weaver (1994) offers compelling evidence of the high value placed on individual achievement, action, self-reliance, independence, and individualism in the American "to do" culture. These values have been exemplified throughout our history by such heroes as the American cowboy who has been revered for the self-reliance and independence that enabled him to endure despite the overwhelming hardships of a harsh and relentless landscape. The pervasive American culture, which reinforces individual and competitive goal structures, has been that if you work hard, you will progress along the social and economic ladder. As Americans, we have traditionally placed a high value on individual achievement that overcomes all obstacles and results in personal success.

In schools, competition has been the mainstay for success. The smartest, quickest, and best prevail in academics, athletics, and extracurricular activities. Witness the hierarchies that develop and the ensuing academic and social status that emerges among students. Students perceived with high academic and social status are likely to dominate the classroom and those with perceived low status for competence too often flounder in an atmosphere of low teacher, peer, and self-expectations that lead to poor academic and social performance. Clear academic and social winners and losers emerge (Cohen, 1986). This atmosphere is especially detrimental to the inclusion of students with disabilities. More often than not, because of difficulty with traditional school work, a slower pace of learning, or behavior that distracts from traditional learning, they end up on the bottom of this hierarchy. Consequently, these students as well as others who do not excel in these areas, have the potential to contribute to school, society, and business life but are not provided with the chance to fully develop their skills.

Further cause for concern lies in the lack of skills that students display in their repertoire of problem-solving abilities. As early as 1971, studies showed that once students got into the competitive structure of school, they usually did not even consider cooperative solutions to problems (Kagan & Madsen, 1971). However, through participation in cooperative classroom structures more students are inclined to recognize and select cooperative strategies to solve problems (Kagan et al., 1985).

Cooperation

Cooperation results in classrooms where students perceive mutual responsibility for meeting common goals. The success of the individual hinges on the contribution of each individual team member as they strive toward a shared goal. What's more, development and maintenance of the group becomes equally important to the accomplishment of the learning task. Individual uniqueness, regardless of its origin—racial, ethnic, cultural, gender, cognitive, physical, or social—is respected and valued. Putnam (1993) contends that "the weakest group that one could assemble would be one whose members were all alike, with the same perspectives, strengths, and limitations" (p. xii). Diversity *enriches* not distracts from the learning process. Working in cooperative group structures allows students to develop and nurture caring and supportive relationships with their peers that result in personal satisfaction and social competence (Johnson & Johnson, 1993).

> *Reggie is a student with severe physical disabilities who is included in a regular fifth grade class. Among his challenges are that he uses a wheelchair to get from place to place, he has only a ten word vocabulary, and he cannot feed himself. His class functions as a community where students take the responsibility for seeing that everyone is included in as many classroom, playground, and social activities as possible. Reggie provides the class with specific challenges such as his participation in the class play, moving from one area of the school to another, and going on field trips. The teacher offers these challenges as opportunities for the students to brainstorm and problem solve as they create, test out, evaluate, and alter their ideas in order to reach the mutual class goal of including Reggie in all their activities. Some of their solutions have included a class job of reminding the person who sets up field trips to make sure the bus has a lift, devising a schedule so that each student in the class has the responsibility to push him from one place to another, and creating a stationary nonverbal part in their play (e.g., holding up signs to indicate scene changes).*

Developing Interpersonal Skills

Given the pervasive and deeply embedded individualistic and competitive nature of the American culture, many young people have limited opportunities to learn and internalize the cooperative and collaborative skills required for successful personal, social, and workplace success in a pluralistic society. Kagan (1994) refers to the "socialization void" that many students display due to the breakdown of family structure, exposure to violence, and their lack of social skills and attachments. This results in students who "do not know how to get along well with each other, care for each other, or care for themselves" (p. 2:3). Changing the structure of schools from a focus on competitive and individualistic to an emphasis on cooperation and the acquisition of social skills can help to fill this social void.

Over the years, teachers have employed a variety of strategies to reinforce cooperative group behaviors. Most obvious is the rewarding of students who display the interpersonal skills that forward learning and group cohesiveness. These rewards vary from a pat on the back, private and public verbal recognition, and concrete rewards such as stickers and stars, to the granting of special privileges, such as being first in line, extra computer time, or no homework passes. Though initially these tokens of success are often effective, especially for students who are motivated by teacher-imposed rewards, the transfer to an intrinsic value for cooperation is not always evident. Teacher modeling of cooperative behavior is another common strategy for boosting cooperation, however, casual modeling is often too subtle and erratic for some students to recognize and imitate, especially those who are unable to identify and display appropriate social skills. Teachers also establish classroom norms that value cooperative behavior in an effort to reinforce desirable group behaviors. However, most often classroom rules define individual student behaviors advantageous for maintaining order in traditional classrooms: Raise *your* hand to speak, keep *your* hands to yourself. The message, both explicit and implicit, has been, "Worry about yourself and don't be concerned with other students." Although these behaviors are appropriate for many classroom tasks, classroom rules that emphasize cooperative skills such as, "Show respect for other students" and "Listen while others are speaking" give a different, more collaborative message.

Likewise, competition has been built into classroom management systems. The quietest person is rewarded by being appointed line leader. The quickest person to get their work done has first choice of free-time activities or class time to complete homework. The perfect papers are pinned to the bulletin board. Although rewarding appropriate behavior, casual teacher modeling, and usual classroom rules serve as positive re-enforcers of appropriate social interactions, they are not sufficient for many children to learn the cooperative skills needed for successful living.

First, for students to acquire and internalize new cooperative skills, classroom norms must define the new set of behaviors that encourage students to be mutually supportive. Rules like, "Use your twelve-inch voice" (adjusting the volume of the voice so as to only be heard by someone twelve inches away) to give assistance to a classmate, and "Three before me," meaning students are expected to consult with three classmates to have directions clarified before going to the teacher, deliver a message that interdependence and cooperation with others are positive behaviors. These rules establish a climate for cooperation and define the behaviors valued by society for collaborative endeavors.

Teachers can also assist students to adopt a "we" instead of an "I" approach to classroom life by explicitly introducing cooperative social skills and assisting students to recognize the value of adopting them (Johnson & Johnson, 1993). The specific component skills of cooperation such as taking turns, listening, asking for help, checking for understanding, and praising should be introduced one at a time and practiced until a certain degree of mastery is achieved before a new one is introduced (see Chapters 10 and 14 for a more detailed explanation of teaching social skills). Teachers must devote the same time and attention to direct instruction in these skills that is given to math calculation, scientific investigation, and reading comprehension. With that investment, at least initially, students will have adequate time to practice and internalize cooperative skills that can then be used in conjunction with academic activities. When teachers observe outcomes such as students putting forth greater efforts to achieve in their academic subjects, more positive relations among all students, and an increase in self-esteem, social competence, and positive adjustment, they are assured that this time is well spent (Johnson & Johnson, 1995).

Devoting time to the teaching of new social skills communicates the high value placed on the skill by the teacher. The expectation for appropriate behavior is defined and students know exactly what behaviors they should be practicing. Moreover, once this pattern of behavior is established in the classroom, it is more likely to spill over onto the playground, the bus, and situations outside of school.

Cooperative Learning and the Student with Disabilities

Cooperative learning, a technique that facilitates instruction in heterogeneous groups, is a reflection of a learning-centered classroom (Collopy & Green, 1995). Studies have shown that cooperative learning activities increase not only the social acceptance, but also the academic achievement of students with disabilities (Hunt, Staub, Alwell, & Goetz, 1994; Johnson & Johnson, 1994; Slavin, 1990). For instance, Slavin, Madden, and Leavy (1984) compared math instruction in three different settings—cooperative learning, individual instruction, and traditional teacher-directed instruction. Their findings show that for mainstreamed students with mild disabilities who were instructed through cooperative learning, there was an increase in the following areas:

- Social acceptance
- Development of friends
- Positive attitudes toward math
- Teacher behavior ratings

There was no significant different in math achievement among the three groups.

Students with moderate and severe disabilities who participated in cooperative learning activities in general education and recreational settings (Eichinger, 1990; Johnson, Johnson, DeWeerdt, Lyons, & Zaidman, 1983; Rynders, Johnson, Johnson, & Schmidt, 1980; Wilcox, Sbardellati, & Nevin, 1987) showed increases in the following areas:

- Social interaction
- Verbal interaction
- Personal interaction
- Academic achievement

Cooperative learning structures contain a variety of approaches and strategies to address the needs of various students and learning situations. They are based on heterogeneous groups working toward a common purpose. Because they facilitate the participation of students with disabilities with the general education population, cooperative learning activities provide access to a core curriculum that benefits all students.

When students with mild, moderate, and/or severe disabilities participate in the cooperative learning activities described in this chapter, various accommodations can be made without a great deal of effort. Students who are nonreaders/writers can be read to, draw the answers, or receive help from another team member. They can participate as part of a duo or triad if necessary. In classrooms where students are encouraged to function as a community that cares about the success of *all* its members, students become very creative in the use of methods to assist each other in reaching their goals.

> *Mr. Strand, a second grade teacher, structured his literature lesson so that his two students with mild learning disabilities, his student with moderate speech/ language disabilities, and his student with moderate mental retardation could participate. Goals for all the students included comprehension and vocabulary development. Students were assigned a short story to read—they had a choice of reading with someone in their heterogeneous cooperative group, listening to someone in their group read, or reading alone. When everyone in the group had read the story, each student was assigned one or two questions tailored to their specific level. After each student had answered their questions on a card (some were required to answer in complete sentences, some in phrases, and some dictated their answers), they shared their answers with their group members as a way of checking and getting feedback from the group. It was then the group's collective responsibility to sequence the answers so they retold the story. As groups hung their sequenced answers on a bulletin board, the teacher conducted a lesson in comparing the vocabulary words that were used in each group's answers to locate synonyms and phrases with similar meanings.*

Cooperative Learning and the Student in General Education

Not only are there positive outcomes for students with disabilities when cooperative group structures are used in the classroom, Kagan's studies (1994) show the following:

1. The achievement of *all* students increases when students work cooperatively to solve problems.
2. Students feel better about themselves and tend to adjust better psychologically when they are part of a cooperative group.
3. Students who work cooperatively in groups more readily accept differences.

In addition, studies by Johnson and Johnson (1989), Kagan, Zahn, Widaman, Schwarzwald, and Tyrell (1985), and Slavin (1983) highlight important areas of gain, including:

- Academic achievement, especially for minority students and students who tend to be low achievers
- Improved race-relations in integrated classes
- Improved social development among all students
- Improved classroom climate
- Improved self-esteem among all students
- Improved time on-task, attendance, and acceptance of students with disabilities

Cooperative Learning Structures

Sharing Responsibility

One cooperative learning structure that lends itself to taking turns and sharing responsibilities is called "Numbered Heads." In this activity, each student is assigned a specific role in the group such as *go-for* (the person who gets the materials for the group), *reader* (the person who reads the directions for the task), the *recorder* (the person who records the group's observations/data), and the *facilitator*, who keeps everyone on task. Roles are flexible and can change periodically. Ultimately, each member of the team is responsible for knowing their assigned material.

> *In Ms. Sanchez's second grade class there are four or five students working in each cooperative math group on measurement. A student with a developmental disability is paired with the "go-for" to get writing paper and rulers for each group member. This student counts the number of rulers and pieces of paper for each student in the group to address her goal of one-to-one correspondence. She then works with her partner on the measuring skills.*

Classbuilding

One highly effective and pleasurable way to build students' willingness to engage in cooperative behavior is through classbuilding (Johnson, Johnson, & Maruyama, 1983; Kagan, 1992). Classbuilding provides structured opportunities for students to become acquainted with peers they would not normally seek out on their own. Most of us can no doubt think back to our own school days and remember at least one classmate that we avoided all together. Perhaps that person had a different skin color, dress, behavior, or speech. Children, like adults, don't easily know people whose culture, race, religion, language, socioeconomic status, or whose presence of a disability makes them seem different from others they know. As teachers, we have an obligation to help children recognize that discomfort with differences often stems from a personal, unexpressed fear that can be relieved by acknowledging differences. We can provide opportunities for students to interact so they can see differences as a point for uncovering similarities. The number of ways that teachers can help students develop caring, supportive relationships with their peers through classbuilding is limitless. Several specific suggestions follow.

Vanity Plates

Provide each student with a sheet of oak tag cut to the dimensions of an automobile license plate. Explain that they may use letters, numbers, symbols, and pictures to create their own personal vanity plate that gives important information about themselves. It is usually preferable for the teacher to model a personal vanity plate to help students get started. For example, in the plate shown in Figure 13-1, the student has communicated a great deal of personal information about herself—her favorite leisure activity is reading mystery stories, she has a pet dog and a baby brother, her favorite subject is math, and her favorite food is pizza. After students have completed a vanity plate, they share the information with their classmates. This is an activity in which most students, regardless of disability can participate, with or without peer support. It works well in conjunction with art and oral speaking activities. Students who experience difficulty speaking in front of their peers have the visual prop from which to organize an oral presentation. After students have presented their plates, tape them around the room for everyone to enjoy.

Line Ups

Typically, the teacher asks the class for form a line based on their response to a shared trait. For instance, a teacher might ask students to line up based on the month and day of their birthday; the student born closest to January 1st would be the first person in line and the person born closest to December 31st would be at the other end, with all other students in chronological order in between. Next, one half of the line steps forward and turns toward the other half of the line, moving forward so that two parallel lines of face-to-face students

FIGURE 13-1   Sample vanity plate.

are formed. Pairs then have a specified amount of time, dependent on their age and maturity, usually one to two minutes, to share with their partner their thinking on some specific topic related to the line up. At the elementary level, pairs could discuss their favorite birthday party, the best gift they ever received, or their "dream" birthday party. Older students may be asked to line up based on their agreement with a statement such as "Honesty is always the best policy." After folding the line, partners might discuss an instance when that statement was true or not true for them.

Successful line ups are highly structured by the teacher so that students are clear about what they are to discuss with their partner. Curriculum-related material can also be used for discussion such as an opinion about a character in a novel or play, the meanings of multi-definition words, or sentiments about a controversial political figure. Young students new to this structure will find it easier to line up based on some concrete criteria such as the number of buttons they have on that day or the number of aunts and uncles they have in their family. Students can also line up on a scale of 1 to 5 or 1 to 10 based on content-related criteria such as how well they think a particular author expressed his or her point of view or by the rank they would assign to the importance of some historical event.

Corners

This popular structure allows students to make a personal choice given four alternatives designated by the teacher. For instance, the teacher might ask students to select their favorite season of the year and move to the corner of the room designated for that season. Once in their chosen corner, pairs or triads form to exchange the reasons for their choices. Corner choices may be related to the curriculum by having students select their favorite from among four authors whose short stories were read in class or by choosing the invention from the Industrial Revolution they consider to have had the most profound impact on their own life. As they get to know others in their class with similar preferences/opinions, they also practice providing supportive details and defending their answers.

Classbuilding is not just a first day of school activity. It is an essential, ongoing process that helps establish the classroom as a caring, problem-solving community that incorporates each member's needs and contributions. They need these opportunities throughout the school year to discover their commonalities and to begin to develop respect and appreciation for their differences. It is usually advisable to schedule more frequent classbuilding interactions at the start of the school year and gradually lessen them as the class demonstrates positive and productive interactions. The social and academic dynamic in the classroom will determine the frequency and type of classbuilding to be done.

Team Building

Whole class get-acquainted activities help set the stage for more intensive friendship-building and work-oriented activities that can be structured between smaller groups of students who work together cooperatively for a more extended period of time on a particular task. In this case, students must establish and maintain relationships of trust and mutual support that will facilitate the completion of the task and help them to value and appreciate each team member's contributions to the group process. Several cooperative structures lend themselves well to team building.

Round Robin

This all-purpose structure provides a quick and easy way to organize informal opportunities for students to get to know their teammates. In a clockwise fashion, students take turns sharing information about themselves based on a specific question posed by the teacher. Initially, the teacher might give the students two minutes to talk about their favorite television program, book, weekend leisure activity, fast food restaurant, or movie. All students must share within the given time. It may be necessary for the teacher to indicate when each team member should complete sharing and pass to the next person. As teams begin to "gel" they will become more adept at equalizing the distribution of individual talk time. As students begin to recognize their superficial commonalities, the team building can be structured to promote deeper personal relationships by asking them to share career interests, the significance of their names, personal heroes and heroines, and individual interests and strengths. The written variation is generally known as "Round Table." This activity can be extended to academic areas.

> *Mr. Marcus, a high school government teacher, has his students record words that express their ideas, thoughts, and feelings on statements made by the potential presidential candidates. Each student writes and discusses one thought, then passes the paper so the next person can continue the activity.*

Three-Way Interview

Another highly effective structure for team building is know as the three-way interview. Teams of four or six are subdivided into pairs who interview each other and then share the information they learned from their partner within the whole team. Students learn to listen carefully since they will report on their partner's answers, not their own. As with Round Robin and Round Table, the success of this structure hinges on giving students a specific topic and a specified amount of time to complete the activity. The amount of time given will depend on the students' age, maturity, familiarity with the structure, and the topic for sharing.

The teacher's reasons for spending instructional time engaging students in classbuilding and team building activities should be made clear to students from the start. Students must have explicit knowledge of the advantages for developing supportive and caring relationships with individuals of varying backgrounds and experiences. Teachers can share the cognitive, social, and emotional advantages of developing positive interpersonal relationships given at the start of this chapter with students, as appropriate.

Cooperative Communication Structures

The ability to effectively communicate ideas, thoughts, feelings, and information is critical to successful functioning in all aspects of life. Volumes have been written documenting the complex nature of verbal and nonverbal communication in academic and social pursuits. Kagan (1994) offers a wide range of cooperative structures that promote students' ability to communicate effectively. The following discussion overviews some of the more prominent and widely used classroom applications for developing communication skills.

"Think-Pair-Share" is a technique that can be used during class discussions to help students organize and express their thoughts. The teacher introduces a topic for discussion. Students take about thirty seconds to formulate their thoughts on the subject, then turn to their nearest neighbor to share them. The teacher then solicits sharing on the topic from the students. In this way, each student gets a chance to respond to the topic, and having been on task and discussing their thoughts, reluctant students are more likely to share with the whole class. This structure also gives students with language and processing disabilities an opportunity to organize their thoughts before expressing them to a large group.

> *In seventh grade literature class, the students were assigned to read a short story on their own. One student tape recorded the story for a student with a reading disability whose reading goal was to identify the main characters. The students got into groups of two or three to describe the traits of the main characters named by the student with the disability. Members of the group then shared the ideas they discussed with the whole group. The student with a reading disability was able to participate in all facets of the assignment.*

"Talking chips" is a strategy for promoting equal participation in small group discussions. Each group member is given an equal number, usually two to five, small token-like chips or other similar objects. Each time group members contribute a point to the discussion, they place one of their chips in the center of the table. As the discussion continues, members continue to give up chips as they forward ideas to the group. When an individual's chips are used up, that person may not speak again until all the other members of the group have used up their chips. At that point, all chips are redistributed and the discussion can continue. This structure ensures that no group member dominates the discussion and that each member has equal opportunities to put forth ideas. Group members may use their chips to comment on the ideas contributed by other members rather than making new points. The concreteness of this structure is particularly effective for young students learning the fine points of discussion, for students with social or behavioral problems, and for students who have a tendency to dominate or let others take over the group.

"Spend-A-Buck" is another highly effective structure for helping students come to a decision among several alternatives. Each student is given ten "dimes" or tokens representing ten cents. Once the pros and cons of each alternative are discussed, each group member spends their dimes on the alternatives of their choice. The unique feature of spend-a-buck is that students are required to divide their dollar among a stipulated number of alternatives. For example, if four to six options are discussed, students must spend a portion of their dollar on at least three of the alternatives. Unlike voting, this structure forces students to weigh the merits of a variety of possible solutions and to recognize the relative advantages of many possible solutions.

Cooperative Structures for Sharing Ideas

There are several cooperative structures during which students share their ideas to solve a problem. *"Team Word Webbing"* is a structure that helps students provide supporting details and to discover relationships among ideas. Each group is given one large sheet of paper, and each student is given a different color marker or pen. A main idea such as "Causes of the Civil War" is written in the middle of the paper. On lines radiating from the main topic, each team member can then add subtopics and supporting details as well as draw lines that connect ideas. The teacher can immediately identify individual student contributions based on color.

"Send-A-Problem" and *"Carousel"* are two ways in which students can work with others to engage in team brainstorming and then share those ideas with others. In send-a-problem, three groups work together to solve three problems. Each group receives one problem and brainstorms solutions to it. Each problem is then passed to the next group who adds to the solutions. Finally the problem is passed to the third group, which synthesizes and reports the information. Carousel is similar except that the problems are on charts around the room and anyone can go to any chart and add a solution or idea. Students with moderate or severe disabilities can work with a partner on these activities.

"Jigsaw" is a way for a group to work together to compile information on a specific topic (expert group). The group prepares a presentation that will be given by each member. Then each group member becomes a member of a new group to report their findings (sharing group) (see Figure 13-2). This technique works especially well as an alternative to individual or group reporting to the whole class.

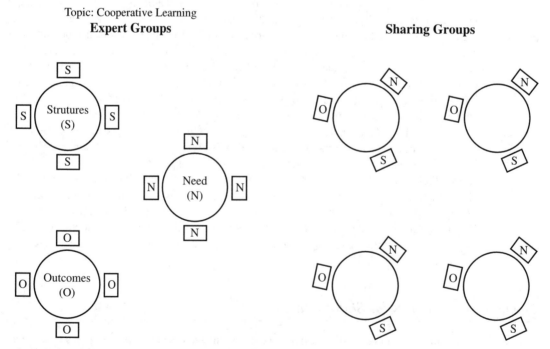

Topic: Cooperative Learning
Expert Groups   **Sharing Groups**

FIGURE 13-2   Cooperative learning jigsaw.

Advantages of Cooperative Structures

The academic and cognitive benefits of cooperative learning have been substantiated in the literature for well over thirty years, though documentation of the advantages of collaborative enterprise can be traced back centuries to early Greek teachers and philosophers. The renewed interest in the implementation of cooperative learning over the past two decades is due to the recognition that cooperation plays an integral part in fostering student thinking and learning. Johnson and Johnson (1995) have completed a comprehensive review of existing research on the effects of cooperative learning. They found that students involved in cooperative learning experiences demonstrate the following:

- An elevated use of higher order critical thinking and reasoning skills
- A greater ability to explore the perspectives of others
- An increased retention of the materials being studied
- More time on-task
- An increased ability to transfer skills and knowledge learned in one situation to other situations

Teachers who implemented cooperative learning structures as a way to incorporate students with mild and moderate disabilities in general education classes during their practicums at Johns Hopkins University offered the following comments pertaining to academic achievement:

- Students scored higher marks on independent work in the areas where cooperative learning was used.
- My students enjoy spelling more now that they help each other learn the words and they do better on their tests as well.
- Student products were of a higher quality following the implementation of a cooperative learning program.
- Their writing expanded in length and detail. In addition, their attitudes improved in science.

As can be seen in Figure 13-3, students selected at random from a third grade class increased their class participation when cooperative learning was instituted. Teachers also noticed improvements in the use of the skills in social situations:

- The students began to request to work in teams or with a partner in other areas of study.
- The students' willingness to help each other when taught the skills is most beneficial.
- When walking into my room there is an atmosphere of sharing and cooperating which I feel will benefit my students for the rest of their lives.
- I saw encouraging behavior and camaraderie that you don't see during competitive activities.

Students who have been given opportunities to work in cooperative groups offered the following comments:

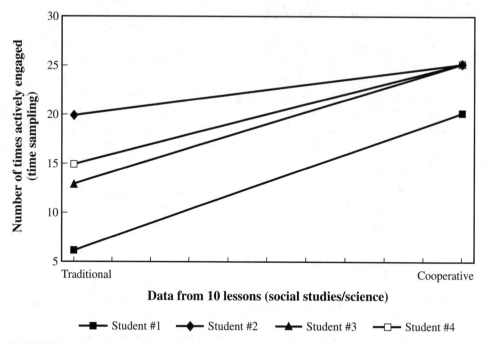

Data from 10 lessons (social studies/science)

─■─ Student #1   ─◆─ Student #2   ─▲─ Student #3   ─□─ Student #4

FIGURE 13-3   Increase in student participation during cooperative learning.

- I never feel like I'm alone.
- This is a fun way to learn.
- With more people you have a better finished product.

A student new to the country in a high school English class offered the following comment:

- Cooperative learning helped me get to know people better—both in the subject matter and socially. It made me feel part of a community.

Elements of Cooperative Learning

The reasons for these substantial benefits in both academics and attitudes can be attributed to the basic elements common in all cooperative learning situations, regardless of students' grade level, age, ability, or the specific content of the lesson. These features differentiate cooperative learning from traditional group work and require a significant change in teacher preparation and implementation of instruction. First, *positive interdependence* establishes the group norm for working together in such a way that every member perceives that the attainment of their individual learning goal is contingent upon the success of other group members. Individuals take responsibility for their own learning as well as for making sure all the other group members master the material or accomplish their individual objectives.

Typically, this is accomplished by assigning complementary roles to group members, dividing the information and/or materials students need to complete the task, and structuring group rewards that are dependent on the individual success of group members.

The second element of cooperative learning is *face-to-face interaction,* which requires students to give and receive explanations, to trade ideas and examine opinions and knowledge of others, and to process information in a way that produces synergetic and serendipitous results. This continuous, dynamic exchange among members broadens and deepens understanding and leads to new insights often stifled in competitive and individualistic learning. In addition, it provides more opportunities for all students to use verbal language skills.

Individual accountability, the third common feature of cooperative groups, ensures that no group members take a "free ride." In other words, though each student is responsible for the learning of their teammates, group members must individually demonstrate their mastery of the material. Unlike traditional small group work, where one of the students may take over, carrying along the rest of the group on his/her coattail, each member is assessed on individual learning and must meet an established (sometimes individualized) criteria for acceptable performance. Individual objectives can be set up for students at various achievement levels. Additionally, the total group performance must measure up to a standard set forth for each student by the teacher. This group accountability intensifies the value that students place on the group process.

In order for students to achieve their learning goals in a cooperative manner, they must possess and value the use of the specific collaborative skills required for successful group functioning. Too often teachers assume that students know how to ask for and give help, encourage equal participation of group members, question the validity of a conclusion, check for understanding, and compliment others for actions that facilitate the group process. Cooperative learning requires a broad range of collaborative skills that have not been systematically and explicitly taught to students in competitive and individualistic learning situations. Thus, the fourth element, the *acquisition of interpersonal and social skills,* is inextricably linked to academic achievement and cognitive development. Teachers must identify, define, teach, and provide students with multiple opportunities to practice new skills and receive feedback on their performance (see Chapters 10 and 14 for further information on this topic).

Group processing is the final element present in learning situations that are cooperatively structured. Students need ongoing opportunities to reflect on the effectiveness of group functioning and to make collective decisions about what they might do to improve learning and enhance the group process.

> *Authentic cooperative learning activities encourage students to demonstrate learning outcomes that have relevance and enable a child to succeed in his or her current and future environments. The greater the input of students themselves in the selection of topics and themes for cooperative learning, the more motivated and empowered they will be to become self-directed learners. (Putnam, 1993)*

Diligent attention to these five elements is a challenge. Most teachers did not experience cooperative learning as students and many are without the collegial supports that facilitate implementation. Including students with mild, moderate, and severe disabilities in cooperative learning activities can intensify these challenges. Resolving the "glitches" that inevitably develop during implementation takes time and a willingness to reflect. However, a plethora of outstanding print resources are available to guide teachers committed to providing their students with cooperative learning experiences.

Conclusions

Educators are pivotal in helping students develop skills and attitudes that facilitate their interactions with diverse groups of people, including those with various disabilities. Establishing a classroom that functions as a community which values the contributions and challenges of all its members requires time, effort, and commitment to the creation of schools as places where individuals can learn, grow, and reach their maximum potential. The results can enhance the future worlds of work and community. Cooperative learning is a vehicle for realizing that vision.

References

Cohen, E. G. (1986). *Designing groupwork: Strategies for the heterogeneous classroom.* New York: Teachers College Press.

Collopy, R. B., & Green, T. (1995). Using motivational theory with at-risk children. *Educational Leadership, 53*(1), 37–40.

Eichinger, J. (1990). Effects of goal structures on social interaction between elementary level nondisabled students and students with severe disabilities. *Exceptional Children, 56,* 408–417.

Hunt, P., Staub, D., Alwell, M., & Goetz, L. (1994). Achievement by all students within the context of cooperative learning groups. *JASH, 19,* 290–301.

Johnson, D. W., & Johnson, R. T. (1975). *Learning together and alone: Cooperation, competition, and individualization.* Englewood Cliffs, NJ: Prentice-Hall.

Johnson, D. W., & Johnson, R. T. (1989). *Cooperation and competition: Theory and research.* Edina, MN: Interaction Book Company.

Johnson, D. W., & Johnson, R. T. (1993). *Circles of learning* (4th ed.). Edina, MN: Interaction Book Company.

Johnson, D. W., & Johnson, R. T. (1994). *Joining Together: Group theory and group skills* (5th ed.). Englewood Cliffs, NJ: Prentice Hall.

Johnson, D. W., & Johnson, R. T. (1995). *Reducing school violence through conflict resolution.* Alexandria, VA: ASCD.

Johnson, D. W., Johnson, R. T., DeWeerdt, N., Lyons, V., & Zaidman, B. (1983). Integrating severely handicapped seventh-grade students into constructive relationships with nonhandicapped peers in science class. *American Journal of Mental Deficiency, 87,* 611–619.

Johnson, D. W., Johnson, R. T., & Maruyama, G. (1983). Interdependence and interpersonal attraction among heterogeneous individuals: A theoretical formulation and a meta-analysis of the research. *Review of Educational Research, 53,* 5–54.

Kagan, S. (1994). *Cooperative learning.* San Juan Capistrano, CA: Kagan Cooperative Learning.

Kagan, S. (1992). *Cooperative Learning.* San Juan Capistrano, CA: Kagan Cooperative Learning.

Kagan, S., & Madsen, M. C. (1975). Cooperation and competition of Mexican, Mexican-American, and Anglo-American children of two ages under four instructional sets. *Developmental Psychology, 5,* 32–39.

Kagan, S., Zahn, G. L., Widaman, K., Schwarzwald, J., & Tyrrell, G. (1985). Classroom structural bias: Impact of cooperative and competitive classroom structures on cooperative and competitive individuals and groups. In R. Slavin, S. Sharan, S. Kagan, R. Hertz-Lazarowitz, C. Webb, & R. Schmuck (Eds.), *Learning to cooperate, cooperating to learn.* New York: Plenum.

Marzano, R. J. (1988). *Different kind of classroom: Teaching with Dimensions of Learning.* Alexandria, VA: Association for Supervision and Curriculum Development.

Murray, F. B. (1994). Why understanding the theoretical basis of cooperative learning enhances teaching success. In J. S. Thousand, R. A. Villa, & A. I. Nevin (Eds.), *Creativity and collaborative learning* (pp. 3–11). Baltimore: Paul H. Brookes Publishing Co.

PACESETTER. (1995, February). Worksite supports: Cultivating the natural, 16–17.

Putnam, J. W. (1993). *Cooperative learning and strategies for inclusion.* Baltimore: Paul H. Brookes Publishing Co.

Rosen, J. W., & Burchard, S. N. (1990, June). Community activities and social support networks: A social comparison of adults with and adults without mental retardation. *Education and Training in Mental Retardation,* 193–204.

Rynders, J., Johnson, R., Johnson, D. W., & Schmidt, B. (1980). Producing positive interaction among Down's Syndrome and nonhandicapped teenagers through cooperative goal structuring. *American Journal of Mental Deficiency, 85,* 550–558.

Secretary's Commission on Achieving Necessary Skills (SCANS). (1991). U.S. Department of Labor. Washington, DC.

Slavin, R. (1983). When does cooperative learning increase student achievement? *Psychological Bulletin, 94,* 429–445.

Slavin, R. E. (1990). *Cooperative learning: Theory, research and practice.* Englewood Cliffs, NJ: Prentice Hall.

Slavin, R. E., Madden, N. A., & Leavy, M. (1984). Effects of team assisted individualization on the mathematics achievement of academically handicapped students and nonhandicapped students. *Journal of Educational Psychology, 76,* 813–819.

Weaver, R. (1994, July). Cross cultural communication in the classroom. Presentation given at the Maryland State Department of Education meeting on Education that is multi-cultural. Salisbury, MD.

Wilcox, J., Sbardellati, E., & Nevin, A. (1987). Cooperative learning groups aid integration. *Teaching Exceptional Children, 20*(1), 61–63.

Student Support Networks

DIANNE F. BRADLEY AND DONNA K. GRAVES

◆ ADVANCE ORGANIZER ◆

The formation of relationships with other people is essential in everyone's life. For people with disabilities, the importance of social support to mental and physical well-being is well documented. Students with disabilities who have traditionally been isolated for their education often have few occasions to interact with students other than those with a similar disability. However, as these students are increasingly included in general education classrooms, they have more opportunities to develop a wider circle of collegial relationships.

This chapter describes ways in which educators can facilitate acceptance and support among students with and without disabilities. The development of social skills, student support networks, peer advocacy approaches, and peer tutoring programs are discussed as ways to encourage and promote positive interactions between all students.

My senior year of high school had finally arrived, and I could not wait to graduate. All I had to do was complete my remaining credits, and my high school years would all be over. When I realized that I had to fill one more period I went straight to my guidance counselor and told him I wanted to be a teacher's aide. That is when he offered me the opportunity to work with Cecelia. I knew who Cecelia was, but I had never met her. I did not know if I wanted to take on the responsibility that would accompany working with a teenager with Downs syndrome. To this day I am not sure why I decided to become one of Cecelia's helpers, but I realize what a wise decision it was. Not only has this program been a benefit to Cecelia, but it also taught me a valuable lesson in the satisfaction of accomplishment and the importance of friendship.

I was very apprehensive about meeting Cecelia. I slowly walked into her second period English class. Cecelia's teacher was very welcoming. She explained exactly what was expected of me and the curriculum that Cecelia and I were to follow. Our first task was to study William Shakespeare's Romeo and Juliet. *Although Cecelia was assigned a child's version of the book, it still enabled her to participate in the same activities that the other students engaged in.*

Then, Cecelia and I were formally introduced. From the moment she met me, Cecelia was enthused about being my friend. She sat down and acted as if she had known me for years. In fact, I was welcomed with a great big hug. I almost wish everyone could be as unconditionally welcoming as Cecelia was.

Due to the fact that the first couple of days were still only an orientation for both Cecelia and me, we really did not do much work. We basically just talked and colored in pictures. After about a week, the real work began. Cecelia was eager to learn, but also very stubborn. She definitely liked to do things her own way. Sometimes everything would run very smoothly. While the class read their version of Romeo and Juliet *Cecelia and I read ours. The teacher made sure that Cecelia had her chance to participate in class, and she loved that. In my opinion, Cecelia's favorite thing was to have an audience. Cecelia also had to take quizzes on what she read. For the most part, with a little bit of help, she could answer most of the questions correctly. This illustrated how well Cecelia really was comprehending the story. After a few weeks, Cecelia and I completed the play and were ready to move on.*

The second book we read was a simplified version of The Odyssey. *Cecelia began by coloring pictures of the different characters. Then we began to read. Once again, Cecelia had to read and then take a quiz to illustrate her comprehension. For the most part, she did very well. She even got to give a presentation in class, and nothing could have made her happier. When we completed our studies of* The Odyssey, *it was time to move on to grammar. Grammar was probably Cecelia's least favorite part of the English. Actually, I think she hated it. On most days it was a struggle to get Cecelia to do her work. In the beginning, the concepts of verbs, nouns, and adjectives were very foreign to her. I think her lack of concentration may have been a result of frustration. As time went on, Cecelia gradually began to recognize the different components that contribute to a sentence. She began to understand that a noun was a person, place, or thing and that a verb was an action. It was gratifying to both Cecelia and me every time she would answer a question correctly. I think we both felt a special sense of accomplishment and pride.*

As the semester slowly came to an end, I began to look back on the days that we had spent together learning and talking. Although at times she was very difficult, we had formed a special bond. Cecelia and her family would even come and eat at the restaurant where I worked. I loved seeing her there. I don't think I have ever experienced the type of joy which accompanied each obstacle Cecelia was able to overcome. With hard work and a will to learn, Cecelia grew so much in just the short amount of time I worked with her. I am so pleased this program has been implemented, and I hope it continues to benefit others as much as it benefited both Cecelia and me.

Kim Goodman, Indiana University student, Bloomington, Indiana

> *There is an undeniable link between healthy interpersonal relationships and physical wellness.*
>
> Chopra, 1993

It is commonplace to learn from television and radio or from reading a newspaper or popular magazine that people who develop and maintain nurturing social and personal relationships live longer and healthier lives. According to Adlerian psychology, a healthy and satisfying life springs from the ability to work together, maintain friendships and social relationships, and establish strong emotional relationships that exist through love (Driekurs, 1950).

Establishing and Maintaining Friendships

Friendship is a fundamental feature of the human experience. The critical impact of friendship on personal and social development is universally recognized (Grenot-Scheyer, 1994). Through friends we know ourselves more fully, give and receive support and comfort, experience a sense of belonging and acceptance, and establish values, attitudes, and skills essential for a satisfying life. School is usually the first place people learn to relate to those outside their families, and so it is where most of these essential relationships are initially formed. Friends are a critical ingredient in the learning process. Forest (1990) believes that the establishment of positive relationships and friendships are preconditions for learning in schools. Resnick (1990) contends that learning itself is a social act that is more closely related to socialization than to instruction.

Within almost any classroom, some students, due to physical, social, intellectual, behavioral, and/or cultural characteristics are perceived by their peers as being of low status. Cohen (1986) suggests that hierarchies develop whereby some group members are perceived as being more active and influential and thus, dominate peer interactions. Children who are isolated, for whatever reason, have limited opportunities to form meaningful reciprocal relationships with their peers. Merely placing students in close physical proximity to each other does not ensure the development of caring and supportive peer relationships. Without programming tailored to the social needs of students with and without disabilities, the formation of friendships among all students does not happen. Educators must structure opportunities where social success is possible for all students.

Facilitating the Development of Social Skills

Specific instruction in social skills is one way in which educators can facilitate the development of friendships among diverse groups of students. Where there is careful implementation and follow-up of social skills, students are able to actively participate in peer relationships with a variety of students. Skillstreaming, one model for teaching students to interact appropriately in social situations, enumerates a variety of prosocial skills which can be addressed in the classroom setting (see Figure 14-1) (Goldstein, Sprafkin, Gershaw, & Klein, 1987; McGinnis, Goldstein, Sprafkin, & Gershaw, 1984). Skillstreaming materials are available for elementary students as well as adolescents (see Chapter 10 for additional social skills curricula).

Group I. Classroom Survival Skills

1. Listening
2. Asking for help
3. Saying thank you
4. Bringing materials to class
5. Following instructions
6. Completing assignments
7. Contributing to discussions
8. Offering help to an adult
9. Asking a question
10. Ignoring distractions
11. Making corrections
12. Deciding on something to do
13. Setting a goal

Group II. Friendship-Making Skills

14. Introducing yourself
15. Beginning a conversation
16. Ending a conversation
17. Joining in
18. Playing a game
19. Asking a favor
20. Offering help to a classmate
21. Giving a compliment
22. Accepting a compliment
23. Suggesting an activity
24. Sharing
25. Apologizing

Group III. Skills for Dealing with Feelings

26. Knowing your feelings
27. Expressing your feelings
28. Recognizing another's feelings
29. Showing understanding of another's feelings
30. Expressing concern for another

31. Dealing with your anger
32. Dealing with another's anger
33. Expressing affection
34. Dealing with fear
35. Rewarding yourself

Group IV. Skill Alternatives to Aggression

36. Using self-control
37. Asking permission
38. Responding to teasing
39. Avoiding trouble
40. Staying out of fights
41. Problem solving
42. Accepting consequences
43. Dealing with an accusation
44. Negotiating

Group V. Skills for Dealing with Stress

45. Dealing with boredom
46. Deciding what caused a problem
47. Making a complaint
48. Answering a complaint
49. Dealing with losing
50. Showing sportsmanship
51. Dealing with being left out
52. Dealing with embarrassment
53. Reacting to failure
54. Reacting to failure
55. Saying no
56. Relaxing
57. Dealing with group pressure
58. Dealing with wanting something that isn't mine
59. Making a decision
60. Being honest

FIGURE 14-1   Skillstreaming: Prosocial skills.

Source: McGinnis, E., & Goldstein, A. P. (1984). *Skillstreaming the Elementary School Child: A Guide for Teaching Prosocial Skills* (pp. 43–44). Champaign, IL: Research Press. Copyright 1984 by the authors. Reprinted by permission.

Skills teaching can take place in either the real life or simulated settings in which students actually apply the skill. Thus, in addition to the classroom, groups may be conducted on the playground, in the gymnasium, or in the lunchroom.

Skillstreaming follows a specific set of procedures for each skill. The first step in teaching any social skill is to identify a specific skill on which students will focus; for example, listening. After identifying the particular social skill, define the skill and lead a discussion of real life experiences in which use of the skill resulted in a positive consequence, or where the absence of the skill had a negative result. This a particularly important initial step since students must understand how acquisition of the skill is relevant and self-enhancing. For instance, students could share circumstances that resulted in misunderstandings because people did not listen to each other. Or they could discuss how it feels when they believe someone has really listened to them. Discuss the advantages of practicing the skill and possible consequences of not practicing the skill in specific situations. Include classroom, school, home, and community situations so that students realize the broad life value of the skill.

After helping students identify particular situations when the skill could be useful, the teacher guides the students in identifying the specific behaviors associated with the skills being taught. Ideally these are modeled by teachers and other adult leaders before the students practice the skill in role-playing exercises while the teachers take on a coaching role. Role-playing is an excellent way to help students understand what a skill looks like and sounds like in action.

Following each role-play situation, take the time to process the students' feelings and reactions to the demonstration of the skill. Encourage them to think of other verbal and nonverbal behaviors that could be used to demonstrate the skill in similar situations. Keep a classroom log or a chart of specific verbal and nonverbal behaviors such as eye contact, not interrupting, and head nodding, that evidence the skill posted in the classroom as a referent for students as they practice the skill of listening. Encourage students to add to the log or chart as they discover new ways of demonstrating the skill.

> *Mr. Graham was having difficulty getting his sixth graders to listen to him as well their classmates. He decided to teach the* skill *of listening to his class. He started with a demonstration of listening by inviting a class member to talk for one minute on her favorite movie while the other students were to observe what he did and said. During the talk, Mr. Graham made eye contact, nodded his head several times, and asked a relevant question. The students then described what they saw him do as he listed the behaviors on a chart. A discussion followed about what it is like when people do and don't listen to each other. The students had a visual model from which to remember and practice the skills of listening.*

Ask students to be alert to instances of appropriate peer use of the social skills. One way in which to do this is to keep a "Smile Box" in which students deposit a brief description of an instance when they observed one of their classmates doing an outstanding job of using a particular skill. On a regular basis in class, review the cards and publicly acknowledge students' exemplary behavior.

Discussion, observation, and practice are often not enough to help students "own" social skills. Students need constructive feedback from their teachers and peers as well as ample time to reflect on their personal use of the skill. Ongoing discussions about how well particular skills work in a wide array of situations and time to assess the skills of the group are imperative if students are to internalize the skills. Skillstreaming exercises include a series of highly structured homework assignments that reinforce and maximize demonstration of the new skill and assist students in generalizing and internalizing the skills they are learning.

> *Ms. McDonald's history class is working in cooperative groups to research causes of the Civil War. In order to encourage students to work together in a supportive way, she teaches them how to give compliments. Students are first encouraged to discuss reasons to compliment, how it feels to receive a compliment, and what constitutes a compliment. As the discussion continues, it encompasses the ideas of sincerity, appropriateness, and accompanying body language. Students are given the chance to contribute suggestions of their own as well as to model and role-play giving compliments as their peers give feedback. Students then practice the skills in their discussion and research about causes of the Civil War. As each group devises a poster with the causes divided into categories, students might be heard saying to each other, "Great idea!" "I know you read the chapter," and "I'll write that answer in the economic category." Laughter, head nodding, and high fives might also be observed. In a large group, students can share the ways in which they gave and received compliments and how it felt to do each. They can be further encouraged to examine situations in which they could practice giving compliments such as at home, to their other friends, or at their jobs.*

Structuring Supportive Relationships

> *My buddies are students who spend a study period in my classes helping me do my work. My math buddy is Erin. She is also my best friend. She visited me at home after my back operation and we go out to lunch on Saturdays quite often. I also have a buddy in English class. She's helping me read* Romeo and Juliet. *Last year I read* MacBeth, Oedipus the King, Catcher in the Rye, *and* A Man for All Seasons. *This year I have read* Huckleberry Finn *and* The Crucible. *I also wrote term papers for two of my classes. I go to many school events. I was at the homecoming dance with my friend, Bruce. In school I am in the clay club and the school chorus. I sing in school concerts. Last June I went to Disney World with the chorus to sing. On weekends I go to football, soccer, or basketball games. Some of my buddies are cheerleaders and I lead cheers with them during the games. I have a lot activities after school. In the summer I am on the swim team. At church I am an altar server. I also sing in the church choir.*

> *Cecelia Pauley, high school student, Potomac, Maryland*

Students can be a great social and academic support to one another. Students with disabilities need both formal and informal relationships with their peers who do not have disabilities. Proximity to other students is a necessary ingredient to facilitate friendships and become involved in extracurricular activities. In addition, social opportunities are critical to the remediation of social skills deficits. There are several ways to facilitate these relationships.

Special Friends Clubs

One model for elevating the perceived low status of students with disabilities involves the establishment of a Special Friends Club. In this model, high status students (athletes, scholars, student government members, class officers) and other interested students are recruited to join students with disabilities in social settings on a regular basis. Once a month or so, students participate in organized activities like pizza parties, games, or service projects such as walk-a-thons to raise money for charities. The specific activities can be determined by the entire group.

Initially the high status students receive direct instruction on disabilities. As they participate in disability simulations and discussions with a teacher sponsor, students' awareness and appreciation of differences is enhanced to facilitate the development of friendships. These friendships result in positive outcomes for both groups (Helmstetter, Peck, & Giangreco, 1994). Students with disabilities benefit from their positive interactions with the high status students, and their general status is enhanced throughout the school.

A large high school in Maryland started a Special Friends Club when they opened the school with a special education program which included forty students with mental retardation. The club was advertised in the Extracurricular Activities Bulletin as "a social club to integrate special education students into school life." Activities included attending plays and talent shows, sponsoring a holiday breakfast, putting together food gifts for needy families, and participating in volleyball and basketball games. They also joined with other clubs to do service projects such as a canned food drive.

Membership in this Special Friends Club has resulted in a number of positive outcomes:

- *At awards night when several members of the club (with and without disabilities) received awards, the parents of a student with disabilities became aware of the number of scholarships received by seniors. They decided to sponsor a yearly college scholarship for a senior who had been an outstanding member of the Special Friends Club.*
- *One student from the general education population who seemed directionless and anxious about peer opinions at the beginning of his senior year, came to a meeting as a favor to a friend. He became interested in the students and started asking the sponsor about particular students' disabilities. As he continued to attend meetings, participate in the activities, and interact with the students, he extended his friendship to the students with disabilities in other areas of the school such as in the halls and at lunch. By the end of his senior year he knew that he wanted to major in special education in college!*
- *One student with Downs syndrome had such a good time in the club and in her school experience that she made the following statement regarding her label, "I don't know why they call it 'Downs'; I wish they would call it 'Ups'".*

Penny Torrence, club sponsor, Gaithersburg, Maryland

Circle of Friends

A Circle of Friends (e.g., a network of peer support) is something that most of us take for granted. However, a new student in a school or classroom, especially one who has a significant needs, does not have this built-in circle. Sometimes a circle of friends develops naturally. However, often, students with disabilities do not independently initiate and form relationships with their peers. Students who are just "put in" to general education classes often experience rejection, isolation, little peer support, and few friends (Stainback & Stainback, 1990). For a student who is not socially connected or has "low status," a Circle of Friends process can serve as a way to build relationships among students with and without disabilities.

A Circle of Friends is a network of peers on whom a student can depend for social activities and connections (Forest & Lusthaus, 1989). It is a flexible and informal network set up to encourage relationships between students with and without disabilities. They meet on a regular basis and are facilitated by an adult such as a teacher or counselor.

The first step in the process of setting up a circle is to work with the class before the student with disabilities arrives. Each student is asked to draw four concentric circles. In the middle they write their own name. In the first circle, they list the people to whom they are the closest and who they really love. This will include family members and maybe a best friend. In the second circle, they put in people who are good friends. In the third circle, they list organizations, teams, social, and work networks—people they do things with. And in the fourth circle are the people who are paid to provide services such as teachers, doctors, baby sitters, etc. Each student then has a powerful graphic representation of support systems within their lives (see Figure 14-2).

After students have filled in their circles and talked about the importance of each circle in their lives, the facilitator gives some information about the new student who is coming. Often when a student is new to a school or classroom and has previously been isolated for their schooling, their first circle and fourth circles have people in them, but the second and third circles do not. The facilitator can draw the circle on the board of a person who has developed few relationships. Ask students to compare this circle with their own. How would they feel? What would they do?

After this discussion, tell the students a little about the new student and solicit volunteers to help fill up the circles. Discuss the types of activities they might want to do with this student if they decide to be in the circle, such as eat lunch together, play at recess, ask the person over, or invite them to be in a club or scouts. Emphasize that not all the students have to be in the Circle of Friends, but they all are expected to be friendly.

As an inclusion facilitator, I was asked to introduce a new student who had autism to his sixth grade class through a Circle of Friends activity. After the students drew their circles and examined the relationships in their lives, I drew the circles of the new student, which consisted only of family and people who were paid to interact with this student. When I asked, "How would you feel if your circles looked like this?" the students gave words like depressed, lonely, left-out, suicidal, out-of-it, and rejected. When asked how they would behave if they felt that way, they described a variety of acting out and "acting in" behaviors and concluded that behavior is often the result of feelings.

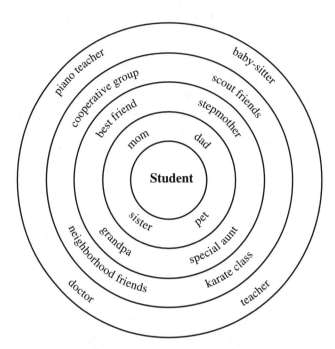

FIGURE 14-2   Circle of Friends.

When the new student's behaviors were described to the other students, they did not see the disability as the problem; they saw the fact that he had no friends as the problem. Because the students knew the social milieu of the school, they felt empowered to manipulate the social environment so he could be included in all aspects of the school day, including having a job and changing classes. If the students believe that the behavior is based on the disability, then they feel powerless. These students believed that the behaviors were due to feelings about not having friends. As a result, the students felt they had the power to control the environment and to change the circles for this student with autism.

Bonni Rubin-Sugarman, inclusion facilitator, Mt. Laurel, New Jersey

Noncompetitive Games

Nonacademic situations can provide a means for helping students make personal connections with peers with whom they might not normally interact. The playground and school gymnasium, usually the scenes of exclusively competitive sports and games, are ideal places to help children build caring and supportive relationships through *cooperative* play. Although competition has its place, we do not want school sports arenas to turn into battle grounds and our playgrounds to become devoid of play because of a motivation to make a person or team the loser. We need to balance our focus on competition with cooperative play options (Kagan, 1994).

In cooperative games and sports, students play without the stress of being judged negatively or rejected because they can't compete with stronger, taller, or faster peers. Students play together to overcome a challenge, not each other. This shared challenge and the positive interdependence that are the hallmark of cooperative play permit each individual to contribute to a mutual "win." Unlike competitive play, where the fun often deteriorates or is completely eliminated for some of the players, cooperative play frees all the participants to enjoy being engaged in an exuberant activity simply for the fun of it. Students develop positive social interaction skills, feel included and valued for their contributions, and gain experience resolving a common dilemma.

One way to organize cooperative play is to transform popular competitive games so that the spirit of cooperation and fun remains intact. This may be accomplished by eliminating hard and fast rules, officials who regulate the game, and extrinsic rewards, and instead, institute collective scoring. For instance, traditional volleyball could be played by two teams, each with a blanket that is used to pass the ball back and forth over the net. Scoring becomes a group function of the total number of times the ball is caught and tossed by both sides. "Winning" is dependent on the total group effort to improve the group score by keeping the ball in play, not individual side scores. There is no official to control the game or keep each side's score. The reward comes from improving the total number of times the ball is in play before hitting the ground.

Traditional relay races can be refashioned into marathon races in which the goal becomes the total time required to complete the total distance by the relay teams. In this way, each team contributes to the overall score. Each relay team is supported by the other teams who cheer and encourage their improvement in time, regardless of the time it takes.

Students can also be engaged in new nontraditional, cooperative games to encourage whole group collaboration. Younger children may enjoy *Caterpillar Over the Mountain* (Orlick, 1978), in which a group of students team to move and turn over some large objects such as a bench or small canoe to construct a "mountain." Students have the option of building a "mountain" from scratch with oversized blocks, crates, or other appropriate objects of their choice. Once the mountain is in place, students work together to drape a large gym mat over the mountain. Students then create a caterpillar by using their hands to link to the ankles of the student in front. The linked caterpillar crawls around and then over the mountain without breaking apart. Preschool can use the same concept to form a snake that wiggles across the floor from one end to the other.

Older elementary students will enjoy a variation of freeze tag in which pairs of "freezers," holding hands, tag pairs of runners, who are also holding hands (Orlick, 1978). To unfreeze tagged pairs, each member of other running pairs shake hands with each person in the frozen pair. To emphasize the importance of cooperation, at the conclusion of the game, the teacher processes the activity by asking how many frozen pairs were unfrozen by running pairs. The students share the strategies they used to unfreeze as many of their classmates as they could together.

Students of all ages will enjoy playing *Co-op Can Throw* (Orlick, 1982), a game derived from the Australian Outback. A line is formed by the participants, each of whom clutches an empty soda can or like object. As a ball or hoop is rolled on the ground, each person attempts to hit the ball or throw their can through the hoop. The game can be modified by adjusting the size and/or speed of the target, increasing the distance between the players and the target, or by throwing the target in their air. A collective score is given based on the number of cans that hit the ball or are tossed through the hoop. The shared goals, collective scoring, and ease of modifying the game to the appropriate challenge, makes this versatile cooperative game fun for students with widely divergent skills and abilities.

Once students begin to understand the features of competitive play that lend themselves to cooperative restructuring, they can be encouraged to extend their new knowledge to problem solve. They can develop ideas for adjusting the rules and scoring of their favorite sports and games to include all their classmates. Encourage them to use their rich imaginations to devise new games and to modify existing games so that every classmate can participate, regardless of their individual skills and physical abilities. The spirit of fun and sense of belonging inherent in cooperative play fosters the accepting and caring atmosphere that nourishes friendships.

Student-to-Student Tutoring

Another way to promote the collaborative ethic among students and to address academic issues is through cross-age and peer tutoring arrangements. These can take the form of reciprocal tutoring such as classwide peer tutoring, where students in the same class take turns tutoring each other; cross-age tutoring, whereby older students help younger ones; or students of any age working with those who need assistance in a particular subject. As students participate in assisting others in the learning process, not only do social and academic benefits accrue (Maheady & Harper, 1987; Rekrut, 1994; Scruggs, Mastropieri, & Richter, 1985), but "active learning, listening, and a spirit of cooperation flourish" (Gartner & Reissman, 1994, p. 58). Additionally, peer tutoring reflects a "learning-focused" class (Collopy & Green, 1995).

Studies have shown that the tutor often benefits academically and socially as much as the tutee (Gartner & Reissman, 1994; Rekrut, 1994). Students serving in the role of tutor often gain numerous benefits from the tutoring relationship, such as an increase in problem-solving skills, an opportunity to develop higher order thinking skills, an increase in self-esteem, and the development of empathy for others (Pino, 1990; Villa & Thousand, 1992; Yogev & Ronen, 1982). Thus, the benefits are not only in the areas of content, skills, and strategies, but also in self-confidence and friendship building.

Classwide Peer Tutoring

Classwide peer tutoring is an instructional arrangement that allows all students to be both a tutor and a tutee as they interact with a variety of students within their own classroom (Greenwood et al., 1987; King-Sears & Bradley, 1995; Mathes, Fuchs, Fuchs, Henley, & Sanders, 1994). It can serve as a way to reinforce and practice skills in a variety of areas. There are several steps involved in setting up a classwide peer tutoring program (see Table 14-1). It is important that students understand and practice these steps before the program is implemented.

TABLE 14-1 Steps for implementing classwide peer tutoring.

1. Prepare materials
    Make posters that describe the CWPT process.
    Make a bulletin board with pockets that have students' names on them
    with cards with their partners' names on them in the pockets.
2. Decide how long each session should be and at what time of day the session
    will take place.
3. Train students how to be "good sports" by teaching encouraging statements.
4. Prepare lists for study sessions (i.e., spelling, vocabulary words, math facts, history facts).
5. Pair students. Consider academic and social levels of students.
6. Practice transitioning into and out of CWPT.

Source: Compiled from information in Homon, C. M., Jardeleza, E. M., McKee E. E., & Towers, R. B. (1994). *Classwide Peer Tutoring: An introduction and steps for implementation.* Rockville, MD: Johns Hopkins University.

Classwide peer tutoring provides a method for individualizing instruction. This strategy not only benefits students who are having difficulties in a particular subject area, but as can be seen in Figure 14-3, progress occurs for high and average achieving students as well. Maheady, Sacca, and Harper (1988) found that high school students who participated in a classwide peer tutoring program attained average or better grades in the subjects in which this strategy was implemented.

Franca, Kerr, Reitz, and Lambert (1990) conducted a study in which the academic and social benefits to students tutoring each other in math were measured. They found improvement occurred in the following areas:

• Tutors' math performance
• Tutees' math performance
• Tutees' attitudes toward math
• Social interaction within the class
• Positive verbal interaction

In addition, King-Sears and Bradley (1995) shared statements from students expressing their opinions of classwide peer tutoring:

• I like CWPT because it helps me to understand my reading work.
• It made me learn how to spell better and faster.
• CWPT helped me to be a better reader, and I remember what I read.
• When you get a wrong answer, people don't laugh at you. They say, "I'm sorry, that's incorrect."
• I can learn how to cooperate better.

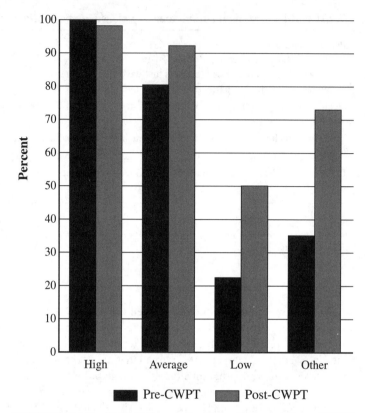

FIGURE 14-3 HALO Scores Spelling: Pre- and Post-CWPT (Spelling word difficulty increased two grade levels for high achievers during CWPT).

Source: Homon, C., Jardeleza, E., Mckee, E., & Towers, R. (1994). *Classwide Peer Tutoring: An introduction and steps for implementation* (p. 16). Rockville, MD, Johns Hopkins University. Reprinted with permission of publisher.

The benefits of classwide peer tutoring are numerous and include (King-Sears & Bradley, 1995):

- More time on-task for all students
- Immediate feedback on progress
- Practice in learning from and teaching peers
- A supportive classroom atmosphere
- Academic gains for all students
- An improvement in attitude toward subject matter
- An increase in enjoyment of working with each other
- An increase in self-competency

Cross-Age Tutoring

Social and academic benefits occur for students who are engaged in cross-age peer tutoring as well (Barbetta, Miller, Peters, Heron, & Cochran, 1991; Scruggs & Osguthorpe, 1986). Berliner and Casanova (1986) suggest that students who have difficulty reading be selected as tutors for younger students with difficulties in this area. "Not only can they benefit from what they learn about proper reading behavior, but the responsibility of helping others to learn can also help them to feel more competent" (p. 14). Often the students will study and remember the material that they are teaching to others, providing them with strategies they can use in their own work. One group of students who benefit by being in the role of *tutor* are students with disabilities. Junior high school students with learning disabilities who had a history of truancy and tardiness served as tutors for elementary students with learning disabilities. In only six weeks, the *tutors* had demonstrated significant decreases in truancy and tardiness and had also improved their self-control and self-concepts (Lazerson, Foster, Brown, & Hummel, 1988).

Gartner and Reissman (1994) cite some benefits from their work with cross-age tutoring programs:

> *A second grader who tutors a kindergartner confides, "I can teach him because it's fun. My tutee makes me happy." A fifth grade special education student has gained confidence. "Whenever my tutee needs help, she comes to me and I feel great, like a teacher." And, explains a sixth grade bilingual student, "It's not only that Benny is learning from me, but that I'm also learning from him." (p. 58)*

High school students who were emotionally disturbed served as tutors for students with mental retardation in an elementary school. The following resulted (Maher, 1984):

- Tutors completed more of their own assignments.
- Tutors improved their academic performance.
- There were less disciplinary referrals for tutors.
- Tutees completed more class assignments.
- Tutees improved their performance on tests and quizzes.

Not only were the academic skills of *both* groups enhanced by peer tutoring efforts, but students who were classified as emotionally disturbed showed improvement in their behavior and school adjustment.

Setting up Peer Tutoring Programs

Often peer tutoring programs can be set up within a single school building. *Classwide peer tutoring* occurs within one classroom. Students can work with a partner who is on the same level in such subjects as reading or spelling to memorize words, practice vocabulary, answer comprehension questions, use words in sentences, or read stories. In subjects such as social studies and science, students can tutor each other in reading the material, answering questions, memorizing sequences, and learning related vocabulary. While learning math facts, students who are at varying levels can tutor each other. Thus a student who is learning addition facts to five can tutor a student who is learning subtraction or division facts because the tutor is supplied with the answers to the problems.

Within the classroom, a student who is functioning at a higher level can tutor a student who is having difficulty or who is at a lower level academically in a particular subject. For instance, a student who is adept at a particular subject can tutor a student who has difficulty with the concepts or who was absent. At another time, the tutee might help that student with drawing or a sport activity.

One method for *cross-age tutoring* to occur within a school is for two classes, one primary and one intermediate, to team up, with the older students serving as tutors for the younger ones. This works especially well in the areas of writing, computer skills, and math. Each person in the class can be assigned a buddy with whom to work on these skills. Skills increase for the younger students, and self-esteem and confidence are raised for the older ones. In addition, "the preparation for effective teaching requires the use of higher level thinking skills (e.g., synthesis, task or concept analysis) and promotes more in-depth understanding of the curricular content being taught" (Villa & Thousand, 1992, p. 122).

Often high school students are required to perform community service for credit in order to graduate. Many students choose to do this by working as mentors and tutors for younger children. Often this can be arranged during the student day. Students in middle school who are housed close to elementary schools can serve as tutors as well. As indicated previously, when given the responsibility to participate in someone else's learning, individuals who are experiencing some sort of difficulty in their own school situation (such as learning or behavior problems) often benefit. Moreover, this type of "service learning" enhances community spirit and often provides opportunities for cross-age friendship and role modeling to occur. The possibilities for student-to-student tutoring are endless and incorporate one of the most abundant, economical, and motivated resources we have in the school system—our students.

Student Advocacy

Once students become comfortable in friendship and tutoring roles with students with disabilities, they often gravitate toward becoming true advocates for these students. Villa and Thousand (1992) refer to "Peer Power" as students participating as (1) members of instructional teams to help establish techniques for supportive learning in general education classes; (2) peer advocates who attend IEP and planning meetings; and (3) classroom and school decision makers serving in the role of peer mediators and members of decision-making committees in the school.

One way in which to include general education students as advocates is to invite them to the IEP or planning meeting where goals, objectives, and strategies are discussed. A popular process for addressing these needs is the McGill Action Planning System (MAPS) (Forest & Lusthaus, 1989; Vandercook, York, & Forest, 1989). Maps provide us with directions and help us get where we want to go. Similarly, the MAPS process is a way to provide direction to students' educational programs so that long-term goals can be achieved. Family members, educators, and peers collaborate as a team to design an integrated school program that addresses the question below. Each questions can be put on a piece of chart paper and the answers recorded at the meeting.

1. **What is the student's history?**
   Parents can be asked to prepare a five-minute summary of the student's history that might include major milestones, school history, and other information they consider relevant.
2. **What are our dreams for the student?**
   First, ask the parents their goals for their child. Think about long-term (independence, employment), as well as short-term (inclusion in middle school and high school programs).
3. **What is our nightmare for the student?**
   This is an opportunity for parents and other team members share their fears. Reassure them that the discussion is taking place so these fears can be avoided.
4. **What are the characteristics of this student?**
   Have each person write a characteristic or two on a post-it. As each person shares, the post-it is placed on the chart.
5. **What are this student's gifts, talents, and strengths?**
   This is an area in which the student participants can add dimensions that adults may not consider.
6. **What are this student's need areas?**
   If there are a lot of responses to this question, it might be helpful to have each member prioritize their contributions. These ideas are especially helpful in developing IEP goals.
7. **What would an ideal day look like for this student?**
   The group describes a typical school day, reviews the student's strength and need areas, and devises ways in which the student can participate in the general education classroom. As accommodations and necessary supports are discussed, student participants often generate creative ideas and identify natural supports that they can implement.

This type of meeting allows student advocates to contribute their knowledge, hopes, and ideas for including the student in a broad range of school activities. Members of a student's Circle of Friends make appropriate members on a MAPS team. "Students often understand the necessary ingredients of such a plan far better than adults, and unless some young people are present, it is impossible to get the same results" (Forest & Lusthaus, 1989, p. 52).

Giving and Receiving Assistance

A distinguishing feature of inclusive classrooms is the students' demonstrated ability to help each other achieve academic and social goals. However, the concept of helping is commonly misunderstood by students. Many interpret helping as simply telling others the correct answer to a teacher-posed question or problem, telling others what to do, or performing a task for someone. Students with disabilities, who often find themselves on the receiving end of help, have not had enough experience in giving help to effectively intercede in problematic situations. Knowing *when* and *how* to offer assistance requires explicit instruction.

One model for teaching students the skill of giving help is proposed by Johnson, Johnson, and Holubeck (1988). A distinguishing feature of this model is the construction of a T-chart in which the teacher guides students in identifying what a particular skill "looks like" and "sounds like." To do this, the teacher engages the students in a discussion in which the students' ideas about nonverbal behaviors and specific words, phrases, or sentences that model effective use of the skill are recorded. An example of a T chart for the skills of giving help can be found in Figure 14-4.

If it is necessary, the teacher can role play inappropriate helping to guide students in identifying the opposite, desirable behaviors. It is a good idea to use large chart paper to construct T-charts so that they can be posted as handy referents for students. Use them to cue students before beginning a cooperative task or anytime that the particular behavior is desirable. As with many social skills instruction models, students should be given time to reflect on their own implementation of the charted behaviors in a wide variety of situations. T-charts can be used to teach specific behaviors and can be adapted for use in particular situations, such as the inclusion of a new student with problematic behavior.

Heightening awareness of individual learning styles is another way to teach students helping behaviors. Most students have little conscious knowledge of the conditions that maximize their own learning. Many believe there is only one way to learn, which the "smartest" students have mastered. Others think successful learning is a matter of luck. To dispel these erroneous notions, involve students in discussions that focus on a variety of ways that people go about learning a specific skill or piece of information. Ask students to be aware of what they do to facilitate their own learning. Have them experiment with a number of different ways to learn their vocabulary words, to solve word problems, or to practice new skills introduced in class. Teach them Gardner's theory of multiple intelligences (See also Chapter 6 for ways to assess students using Multiple Intelligences) (Gardner, 1993) and have them identify their strongest intelligence for learning. Encourage students to share what they did to learn successfully with each other so that they broaden their personal strategies for studying and learning. As students become increasingly aware of the many ways people learn, they develop a viable repertoire of helping strategies that facilitate peer teaching and learning.

It is important to note that helping does not always mean giving assistance. Students also need to learn how to ask for help. Because many students perceive the need for help as an indictment of incompetence, they must be taught to understand that everyone, even the

Looks Like	Sounds Like
Seeing one person think aloud the steps they used to solve a problem.	"Do you want some help with that problem?"
Two people with their heads together.	"How can I help?"
	"I did the problem this way."
	"Do you want to talk about . . . ?"

FIGURE 14-4   Giving help.

smartest students, sometimes need help doing something. Try establishing a bulletin board with the song title, "With a Little Help From My Friends" on which students share in words, pictures, and writing the ways they have been helped by another person. An excellent way to encourage students to ask for help without feeling incapable or unworthy is to teach them to say, "I can do this, but right now I need a little help. Can you help me?" Peer tutoring programs and buddy systems with flexible and interchangeable roles that allow everyone to be helped and to be the helper go a long way in establishing cohesive classrooms.

To bolster students' comfort in asking for help, the teacher can be a powerful model. By sharing personal situations and the positive consequences of asking for help, either as a student or as an adult, the teacher establishes the realistic expectation that everyone needs help sometime. Sharing stories about famous men and women who, with help, overcame formidable obstacles to achieve greatness, is another way to help students understand positive interdependence. History is replete with such examples.

Conclusions

> *True inclusive education occurs when students with disabilities are included physically, instructionally, and socially.*
>
> Nicoll, 1993

If people with disabilities are expected to participate in community life, they need a network of friends, acquaintances, and local resources. Friendships between students with and without disabilities can be the foundation for these life-long support systems. Peer relationships have been found to impact social and cognitive development in powerful ways. Johnson, Johnson, and Holubeck (1988) found that peer relationships provide:

- Models for prosocial behavior
- Perspectives other than one's own, which aids problem solving
- Frames of reference for perceiving oneself
- Greater productivity and achievement in collaborative environments
- Positive influence on educational aspirations

Conversely, "students in our public schools learn very powerful lessons when students with special needs are separated from them. Since they do not get to know these students well, they often come to believe that these children and young adults are different and scary, and *should* be separated from them" (Davern & Schnorr, 1991). Thus, it is critically important that educators structure opportunities for students to establish and nurture positive peer relationships and develop meaningful friendships. "Typical students who get to know peers with disabilities are often motivated to become their friends, good neighbors, and even future employers" (Putnam, 1993, p. 9).

References

Barbetta, P. M., Miller, A. D., Peters, M. T., Heron, T. E., & Cochran, L. L. (1991). Tugmate: A cross-age tutoring program to teach sight vocabulary. *Education and Treatment of Children 14,* 19–37.

Berliner, D., & Casanova, U. (1986). How to make cross-age tutoring work. *Instructor, 95*(9), 14–15.

Chopra, D. (1993). *Ageless body, timeless mind: The quantum alternative to growing old.* New York: Harmony Books.

Cohen, E. G. (1986). *Designing groupwork: Strategies for the heterogeneous classroom.* New York: Teachers College Press.

Collopy, R. B., & Green, T. (1995). Using motivational theory with at-risk children. *Educational Leadership, 53*(1), 37–40.

Davern, L., & Schnorr, R. (1991). Public schools welcome students with disabilities as full members. *Children Today, 20*(2), 37–41.

Driekurs, R. R. (1950). *Fundamentals of Adlerian psychology.* Chicago: Alfred Adler Institute.

Forest, M. (1990, February). *MAPS and Circles.* Presentation at PEAK Parent Center Workshop, Colorado Springs, CO.

Forest, M., and Lusthaus, E. (1989). Promoting educational equality for all students: Circles and Maps. In S. Stainback, W. Stainback, & M. Forest (Eds.), *Educating all students in the mainstream of regular education* (pp. 43–58). Baltimore: Paul H. Brookes Publishing.

Franca, V. M., Kerr, M. M., Reitz, A. L., & Lambert, D. (1990). Peer tutoring among behaviorally disordered students: Academic and social benefits to tutor and tutee. *Education and Treatment of Children, 13*(2), 109–128.

Gardner, H. (1993). *Multiple intelligences: The theory in practice.* New York: Basic Books.

Gartner, A. J., & Reissman, F. (1994). Tutoring helps those who give, those who receive. *Educational Leadership, 52*(3), 58–61.

Goldstein, A. P., Sprafkin, R. P., Gershaw, J. & Klein, P. (1987). *Skillstreaming the adolescent: A structured learning approach to teaching prosocial skills.* Champaign, IL: Research Press.

Greenwood, C. R., Dinwiddie, G., Bailey, V. I., Carta, J. J., Dorsey, D., Kohler, F. W., Nelson, C., Rotholz, D., & Schulte, D. (1987). Field replica-tion of classwide peer tutoring. *Journal of Applied Behavior Analysis, 20,* 151–160.

Grenot-Scheyer, M. (1994). The nature of interactions between students with severe disabilities and their friends and acquaintances without disabilities. *JASH, 19,* 253–262.

Helmstetter, E., Peck, C. A., & Giangreco, M. F. (1994). Outcomes of interactions with peers with moderate or severe disabilities: A statewide survey of high school students. *The Journal of the Association for Persons with Severe Handicaps, 19,* 263–276.

Homon, C. M., Jardeleza, E. M., McKee, E. E., & Towers, R. B. (1994). *Classwide peer tutoring: An introduction and steps for implementation.* Rockville, MD: Johns Hopkins University.

Johnson, D. W., & Johnson, R. T. (1989). *Cooperation and competition: Theory and research.* Edina, MN: Interaction Book Company.

Johnson, D. W., Johnson, R. T., & Holubeck, E. J. (1988). *Cooperation in the classroom.* Edina, MN: Interaction Book Company.

Kagan, S. (1994). *Cooperative learning.* San Juan Capistrano, CA: Kagan Cooperative Learning.

King-Sears, M. E., & Bradley, D. F. (1995). Classwide peer tutoring: Heterogeneous instruction in general education classrooms. *Preventing School Failure.*

Lazerson, D. B., Foster, H. S., Brown S. I., & Hummel, J. (1988). The effectiveness of cross-age tutoring with truant, junior high school students with learning disabilities. *Journal of Learning Disabilities, 21*(4), 253–255.

Maheady, L., & Harper, G. F. (1987). A class-wide peer tutoring program to improve the spelling test performance of low-income, third- and fourth-grade students. *Education and Treatment of Children, 10,* 120–133.

Maheady, L., Sacca, M. K., & Harper, G. F. (1988). Classwide peer tutoring with mildly handicapped high school students. *Exceptional Children, 55,* 52–59.

Maher, C. A. (1984). Handicapped adolescents as cross-age tutors: Program description and evaluation. *Exceptional Children, 51,* 56–63.

McGinnis, E., Goldstein, A. P., Sprafkin, R. P., & Gershaw, N.J. (1984). *Skillstreaming the elementary school child: A guide for teaching prosocial skills.* Champaign, IL: Research Press Company.

Mathes, P. G., Fuchs, D., Fuchs, L. S., Henley, A. M., & Sanders, A. (1994). Increasing strategic reading practice with Peabody classwide peer tutoring. *Learning Disabilities Research & Practice, 9,* 44–48.

Nicoll, J. M. (1993). *Tools for facilitating relationships between students with disabilities and their non-disabled peers.* Unpublished manuscript.

Orlick, T. (1978). *The cooperative sports and games book: Challenge without competition.* New York: Pantheon Books.

Orlick, T. (1982). *The second cooperative sports and games book.* New York: Pantheon Books.

Pino, C. (1990). Turned on by tutoring. *American Educator, 14*(4), 35–36.

Putnam, J. W. (1993). The movement toward teaching and learning in inclusive classrooms. In J. Putnam (Ed.), *Cooperative learning and strategies for inclusion* (pp. 1–14). Baltimore: Paul H. Brookes Publishing Co.

Rekrut, M. D. (1994). Peer and cross-age tutoring: The lessons of research. *Journal of Reading, 37,* 356–362.

Resnick, L. (1990). Literacy in school and out. *Dedalus, 119,* 169–185.

Scruggs, T. E., & Osguthorpe, R. T. (1986). Tutoring interventions within special education settings: A comparison of cross-age and peer tutoring. *Psychology in the Schools, 23,* 187–193.

Scruggs, T. E., Mastropieri, M. A., & Richter, L. (1985). Peer tutoring with behaviorally disordered students: Social and academic benefits. *Behavior Disorders, 10,* 283–294

Stainback, W., & Stainback, S. (1990). *Support networks for inclusive schooling: Interdependent integrated education.* Baltimore: Paul H. Brookes Publishing Co.

Vandercook, T., York, J., & Forest, M. (1989). MAPS: A strategy for building the vision. In J. York, T. Vandercook, C. Macdonald, & S. Wolff (Eds.), *Strategies for full inclusion* (pp. 45–64). Minneapolis: Institute on Community Integration.

Villa, R. A., & Thousand, J. S. (1992). Student collaboration: An essential for curriculum delivery in the 21st century. In S. Stainback & W. Stainback (Eds.), *Curriculum considerations in inclusive classrooms* (pp. 117–142). Baltimore: Paul H. Brookes Publishing Co.

Yogev, A., & Ronen, R. (1982). Cross-age tutoring: Effects on tutors' attributes. *Journal of Educational Research, 75,* 261–268.

Index